BEATRICE WEBB
A LIFE

BEATRICE WEBB

A LIFE

Carole Seymour-Jones

IVAN R. DEE
Chicago

BEATRICE WEBB: A LIFE. Copyright ©1992 by Carole Seymour-Jones. All rights
reserved, including the right to reproduce this book or portions thereof in any form. For
information, address: Ivan R. Dee, Inc., 1332 North Halsted Street, Chicago 60622.
First American edition. Manufactured in the United States of America
and printed on acid-free paper.

Carole Seymour-Jones hereby asserts her moral right to be identified as
Author of the Work.

Library of Congress Cataloging-in-Publication Data:
Seymour-Jones, Carole.
Beatrice Webb : a life / Carole Seymour-Jones.
        p.   cm.
Includes bibliographical references and index.
ISBN 1-56663-001-0
1. Webb, Beatrice Potter, 1858–1943. 2. Women socialists—Great Britain—Biography.
3. Socialism—Great Britain—History. 4. Fabian Society (Great Britain)—History.
I. Title.
HX244.7.W42S49   1992
335'.14'092—dc20
[B]   92-16656

Remembering
Sophie Victoria 1969–73
and
for my children,
Emma, Edward and Lucy,
whom I thank for their support and love.

CONTENTS

PREFACE

Beatrice Webb is well known as one half of the famous partnership of Sidney and Beatrice Webb, the industrious worker bees who toiled in the cause of Fabian Socialism, who founded the London School of Economics and the *New Statesman*, and who wrote a string of books on trade unionism, local government and Soviet Russia: in Beatrice's own words, 'gradgrinds'. But this worthy reputation masks a more complex truth, which dual biographies of the firm of Webb have ignored. Mary Agnes Hamilton's 1933 biography of the couple is reverential, as is Margaret Cole's of Beatrice in 1945. Kitty Muggeridge's 1967 biography of her 'aunt Bo' is a useful corrective to this point of view, for if Beatrice was much loved, she was also much hated, as any reader of H. G. Wells's cruel satire of the couple in *The New Machiavelli* cannot fail to realise. She had, Wells said, a bony soul and 'at the base of her was a vanity gaunt and greedy'. Censorious, didactic, ascetic, humourless, were all adjectives applied to Beatrice. Lloyd George's passionate desire to 'dish the Webbs' by bringing in the National Insurance Act of 1911, which destroyed her chances of seeing her Minority Report on the Poor Law pass on to the statute books, reveals the depth of emotion Beatrice inspired.

In reality Beatrice's story is a very modern one, which deserves to be told in the context of the movement for women's emancipation which was stirring in England from the 1850s. It is a story of choices: between sexual desire for charismatic politician Joseph Chamberlain, and a position of wealth and privilege, or a career as a sociologist and reformer in partnership with her husband Sidney, a man she found physically repulsive; between maternal fulfilment or life as a 'brain-worker'; between mystical love of God or the secular religion of Fabian Socialism. In short, Beatrice's story is one of sexual repression, renunciation and sacrifice as, painfully, she reworked the Victorian feminine ideal of the 'angel in the house' to follow her own original path as a social investigator.

She set up these choices because they appealed to the two sides of her dual personality, for the brittle and controlled façade Beatrice showed to the world hid an inner life of unrelenting conflict between the ego and the id, conscience and feeling, positive and negative. Leonard Woolf witnessed her 'neurotic turmoil of doubt and discontent, suppressed or controlled, an ego tortured in the old-fashioned way . . .' Although Beatrice's fierce will demanded that she followed her own inner vision of an 'epic life', she paid a heavy price. The pleasure principle always beckoned, and the stress of denying her instincts led to mental breakdown, anorexia nervosa, and the ultimate hardening of her personality into a mould which many people found unattractive. It seems to me too, that it was because she had invested so much in the Socialist chimera that she allowed herself to be blinded into accepting Stalinist Russia as the 'land of milk and honey' for which she yearned.

I was first drawn to the personality of Beatrice Webb through her MS diaries and her letters, many of which are published here for the first time. Beatrice's diary was 'the Other Self', a projection of her own personality, to whom she talked compulsively. It operated as a survival mechanism allowing her to maintain a precarious mental equilibrium in the face of the family 'Weltschmerz'. Significantly, she could not write it when Sidney was present, nor was he allowed to see it. Reading the diaries was like stepping through the Janus door into another world, the battlefield of Beatrice's emotions, and the experience left me with a profound admiration for a great, essentially Victorian woman in whose life a tangled thread of paradox runs continually, as triumph and tragedy intertwine.

ACKNOWLEDGEMENTS

I owe a debt of gratitude to the descendants of Richard and Lawrencina Potter (the R.P.s) who have kindly agreed to talk to me, and have generously loaned family papers and photographs. Firstly I should like to thank Kitty Muggeridge for her time and hospitality; Nicholas Meinertzhagen, for his continual encouragement, and the genealogical research he has done on the ancestry of the Potter family; Seddon and Ann Cripps for kindly loaning Theresa Cripps's photograph album; Jonathan King for allowing me to read and quote from Lawrencina Potter's journal; Lord Parmoor for permission to reproduce photographs; Lord Methuen for permission to make use of the family tree he compiled of the R.P. descendants; Lady Rothschild for talking to me; Belinda Norman-Butler for her time, and permission to quote from her book, *Victorian Aspirations*; Lady Davie for permission to reproduce photographs. I should also like to thank Valerie Hardwick of Passfield Corner and other owners of houses where Beatrice Potter lived or visited, who have allowed me to 'footstep' around them.

My task would have been immeasurably harder without the patient and knowledgeable help of Dr Angela Raspin and Sue Donnelly and the staff at the British Library of Political and Economic Science; I am particularly indebted to Dr Raspin for directing me to the Lloyd and Citrine Papers. I should also like to thank the staff of Sussex University Library, the London Library, the Fawcett Library, Nuffield College, Oxford, the Public Record Office, and the British Library for their assistance. I am indebted to Eileen Yeo and Alun Howkins at Sussex University, for their encouragement and criticism, and to scholars such as Norman MacKenzie and A. M. McBriar who have done so much work on the Webbs previously.

I wish to thank the following for permission to quote: the London School of Economics and Political Science, who hold the copyright of the Diary of Beatrice Webb and the Passfield Papers and the Courtney

Collection, and Virago Press for permission to print extracts from the Diary; the Fabian Society for permission to quote from Fabian pamphlets and to reproduce the Fabian window; the Society of Authors for quotations from George Bernard Shaw; the estate of H. G. Wells for quotations; Virago Press for the loan of negatives from the Webbs' photograph album; the Hulton Picture Co. for photographs of Joseph Chamberlain.

Lastly, but most importantly, I wish to thank Moira Williams for her unfailing support, encouragement and sense of humour, and for finding me my agent, Rachel Calder, to whom I am deeply grateful for her faith in this book from its earliest beginnings. I owe a debt to Peter Day, editorial director, and the staff at Allison & Busby, and to my inspired and diligent editor Jenny Parrott. Evelyn Morgan made illuminating comments on the proofs, and Allan Husband contributed to the index. I should also like to thank Olivia Bennett with whom I discussed the book at every stage, Michael Holford-Walker for help with the photographs, and Deirdre Lay for her constant support and secretarial help. I remember with respect and affection Kay Stedmond who taught me history at St Mary's, Calne. In addition I wish to thank very much my parents and my children for encouraging me when I faltered, especially Emma for doing the cooking and Lucy for making the coffee.

BEATRICE WEBB
A LIFE

CHAPTER

I

THE SEEDS OF CONFLICT

*'The sadness and suffering of my early life brought out the
nether being in me.'*
Beatrice Webb, *My Apprenticeship*

DAWN STREAKED THE SKY as the snow-speckled hills of Gloucestershire
emerged from the darkness; in the other rooms of Standish House the
household held its breath, but in the master bedroom Lawrencina
Potter tossed restlessly on the bed. She was, she knew, about to enter
the second stage of labour. She was, after all, already the mother of
seven girls, and had come to accept with grim resignation the continual
childbearing which dominated her life. The intellectual companionship
she had anticipated when she married Richard Potter had proved to
be but a dream; the reality was conception, pregnancy, birth, and
lying-in, until the painful but inescapable process started again. Right
now Lawrencina did not mind the pain, for it might presage the event
she longed for – the birth of a son.

She was not alone, she was glad of that. Lawrencina's lips curved
into a smile as she looked into the eyes of Martha, her housekeeper.
Now the pain knotted and unknotted within her rhythmically, and
her knuckles stood out whitely as she clenched a balled handkerchief.
She did not fight the pain, but let it flow through her whole body
while she panted, trying not to cry out.

If it were a boy – and it had to be a boy – she would call him
Richard after her husband. She would take care not to spoil him,
despite having seven sisters. Images of her own childhood floated
through her mind, of tomboy games and shared lessons with her
adored brothers. This world of frocks and dolls, of burgeoning
womanhood, necessitated by such an unnatural number of daughters,
was anathema to her.

She gave a sudden cry, and there was a flurry of activity. The
doctor sprinkled chloroform on a cotton mask and held it over her
face. The midwife was listening to her baby's heartbeat; she leaned
over Lawrencina, her ear pressed to the trumpet she held against
her patient's swollen abdomen. Lawrencina clutched Martha's hand

fiercely, as the doctor guided first the baby's head, then its tiny body into the world. There was a cry as he held the infant up by its legs. Painfully Lawrencina raised herself from the pillow.

'You have a healthy daughter, Mrs Potter,' said the doctor, but Lawrencina had already seen the baby's sex. She fell back in despair.

The arrival of Beatrice Potter on 22 January 1858 was neither welcome nor auspicious. She was the eighth daughter born to railway magnate Richard Potter and his wife Lawrencina: the eldest, Lawrencina or Lallie, was followed by Kate, Mary, Georgina, Blanche, Theresa and Margaret. The 'sisterhood', or 'monstrous regiment of women' as their husbands were to call them later, was a source of pride rather than grief to their father, who accepted with equanimity the arrival of another female. Richard Potter was, as Beatrice remarked, unusual in his high opinion of women. 'He worshipped his wife, he admired and loved his daughters; he was the only man I ever knew who genuinely believed that women were superior to men, and acted as if he did.'[1]

For Lawrencina, however, the birth of Bobo or Bee, as she was usually called, was nothing less than a tragedy, to be recorded with weary stoicism in her journal: 'My strength much impaired by having little Beatrice, my eighth daughter, and now I am again enceinte . . .'[2] Lawrencina had been brought up with men and disliked women. Her mother had died young of consumption and her father had reared his young family alone. Lawrence Heyworth idolised the daughter who bore his name, and from an early age treated her as exceptional. Taught to worship at the bright fire of the masculine intellect, to believe that she was as a paragon of virtue and learning, educated beside her brothers as a 'scholar and a gentlewoman',[3] Lawrencina was handicapped by having a high opinion of her own abilities.

Her father, Lawrence Heyworth MP, came from a family of hand-loom weavers, but left the cotton town of Bacup north of Manchester and made his fortune trading with South America. Later he became Radical MP for Derby, and set up home at Yew Tree House, West Derby, near Liverpool. He was a friend of Richard Potter, Beatrice's other grandfather, and both men knew Cobden and Bright, and believed in free trade and parliamentary reform. Heyworth was a God-fearing man, a JP and strict teetotaller, and had married the strikingly beautiful Betsy Aked, his second cousin and servant. Betsy was noted for her melancholy nature; both her brother and sister committed suicide, and she left to her descendants the tendency to manic-depression.[4]

When the young Lawrencina met Richard Potter in Rome on the Grand Tour they fell instantly in love. They were the same age – both born in 1821 – and their backgrounds were remarkably similar; their fathers belonged to the manufacturing classes and were Radical Nonconformists who had made good. Richard's grandfather, John Potter, kept a draper's shop in Tadcaster which prospered so well that he was able to buy a farm. Beatrice's grandfather Richard proved an astute businessman who ran a cotton warehousing business and became MP for Wigan and nothing gave the family greater pride than the visit of 'Radical Dick' to Court in 1832. He helped to found the *Manchester Guardian*, and protested against Peterloo and the Corn Laws, but at heart he was a true representative of the factory-owning classes who firmly banned working-class representatives from the Reform Committee he founded in 1826 to fight for the vote.[5]

In 1815 Radical Dick married a good-looking, gypsy-like girl called Mary Seddon, who was said to be of Jewish blood. Within a year her first son died, and four more children followed in quick succession. Richard Potter, Beatrice's father, was born a month early in 1817. As his father remarked, 'the poor little fellow ... got rather awkwardly used on being born, so they wrapped him in my nightshirt, the consequence is he become chill and breathes badly, we hope it will please the Almighty to preserve him.'[6] In July 1823 Mary gave birth to her last daughter, Catherine, and by 29 August was showing signs of acute post-natal depression. Paranoid delusions that the other people in the house wished to kill her and visions calling her to lead the Jews back to Jerusalem inspired her to run away to Paris, where her horrified husband caught up with her. Suffering suicidal tendencies, she was confined to Spring Vale, a lunatic asylum, where the proprietor forbade her any visitors or contact with her family. Her son Richard released her from the asylum after his father's death, and Mary settled near Standish. The blood legacy of both maternal and paternal grandmothers to the Potter 'sisterhood' included the persistent depressive gene Beatrice later labelled as a tendency to 'Weltschmerz'.

As a gentleman of means, Richard Potter did not anticipate the need to work. Educated at Clifton and, as a Unitarian, at University College London, he was called to the Bar without intending to practise, but the financial crisis of 1847 to 1848 swept away his modest fortune. He turned to his father-in-law for help, and Lawrence Heyworth offered him a directorship of the Great Western Railway. At the same time an old school friend, W. E. Price, suggested a partnership in his timber business near Gloucester. Richard accepted both offers and, at the age of thirty, began a new life.

Lawrencina Potter's learning was no mere veneer, and was far removed from the pretty accomplishments of piano playing, purse-netting and needlework, which passed for an education amongst the majority of upper- and middle-class women. In her youth she had written pamphlets supporting the Anti-Corn Law and was a keen student of political economy. Languages were her especial forte, as the French economist Michel Chevalier discovered on his first visit to the Potters where he was amazed to find 'that the mistress of the house knew much more Greek than himself, apologised, and retired from the field; then, out of pleasantry, she wrote down his English sentence in Greek'. Nor was it merely Lawrencina's facility in the classics that impressed him, 'Note that this female Hellenist is a woman of the world, and even stylish. Moreover, she has nine daughters, two nurses, two governesses, servants in proportion, a large well-equipped house, frequent and numerous visitors; throughout all this perfect order; never noise or fuss; the machine appears to move of its own accord.'[7] Lawrencina was to translate Chevalier's work into English.

Early married life had brought Lawrencina a circle of distinguished friends and admirers, and she was remembered by the Liberal MP John Bright (whom Beatrice met in 1884) as, 'One of the two or three women a man remembers to the end of his life as beautiful in expression and form.'[8] But domesticity closed around her at Standish House, a mansion nine miles from Richard's timber-yard at Gloucester.

While Lawrencina's spirits drained away in pregnancy and child-birth, Richard Potter quickly discovered himself to be a born entre-preneur. Determined, restless, physically strong, a man with an eye to the main chance, yet impetuous enough to resign in a fit of pique, by 1863 he was chairman of the board of the Great Western. His luckiest strike was making £60,000 from supplying wooden huts to both the British and French armies in the Crimean War. When the French government refused to pay its debts he followed the advice of his colleague, Tom Brassey: 'Go to the Bank of France and cash a cheque for £1000; give the porter at the ministry twenty francs and pay your way handsomely until you get to the minister; then put down £500 and you will get your money all right.'[9] Bribery had the desired result, and the lesson was not lost on Potter.

Although his daughter Beatrice liked to think that her father 'struggled against this adverse moral environment'[10] in fact he enjoyed it. In the opinion of his successor as chairman of the Great Western,

Potter was both crafty, and dishonest,[11] and his brother-in-law Charles Macaulay, brother to the historian Thomas Babington Macaulay, considered that he could also be cruel; he was known to whip his dog until he bled, for disobeying a command. He was a man who put his own, his family's and his friends' interests before those of the company, and although he became president of the Grand Trunk Railway of Canada in 1869, many of his grandiose schemes failed. Yet Potter's sanguine temperament led him to take his losses in his stride, so that poor speculative investment in the Welsh coal mines was soon overcome by shrewd investment in the Barry Docks. Handsome, genial and extrovert, he had, wrote Beatrice, 'A winning personality, a pleasant voice, a strong will, and a clearly conceived aim . . . Moreover, he believed in the Jewish maxim – a maxim he often cited – that a bargain is not a good bargain unless it pays both sides.'[12]

He adored his clever, autocratic and unhappy wife, but he took the precaution of taking a daughter or two with him on his foreign travels to prevent his eye straying. Potter had a simple and literal faith, attending church regularly and even as a grown man repeating the child's prayer, 'Gentle Jesus, meek and mild'. Unlike Lawrencina he was untroubled by spiritual or political doubts, having abandoned the radicalism of his father to become a staunch Conservative. Beatrice remembered her father, despite his frequent absences, as 'the central figure of the family life – the light and warmth of the house'.[13] He was the much-loved paterfamilias for the clatter of whose carriage wheels on the drive the girls would wait impatiently, who would swing them into his arms as he ran to greet them. He was never too busy to provide tender concern, as one of his early letters to Beatrice shows. He was writing from their rented London house in July 1874, while Beatrice remained at Standish:

My dearest Beatrice,
Those thoughtless daughters who were in Princes Gardens last Thursday opened a letter from you to me and I have never seen it or read it for when I came home it could not be found. But I am told it was a very nice affectionate letter and it would have given me great pleasure. I was very angry and still am when I think of it . . . God bless you, dearest little Bee.

Your affectionate Father,
Richard Potter[14]

Beatrice's love for her father never wavered, and she found it easier to identify with him than with Lawrencina, who appeared increasingly to reject her: when Beatrice was four Lawrencina's overwhelming desire for a male child was fulfilled, and a little boy, Richard, was born. She called him Dicky, and ecstatically recorded his birth in her journal. 'A son has been given to us, now eight days ago, of most promising appearance, exceedingly healthy, strong, full sized and like his papa, placid beyond all my former infants.'[15]

Beatrice had never been her mother's favourite, but now she was relegated completely to the background. A nurse was engaged solely to care for the new male heir, and she did not regard the care of Beatrice as any part of her duties. Beatrice's earliest memory was of being shut outside the nursery naked, her clothes flung after her by the nurse who was too busy to help a four-year-old girl with her buttons and bows. Lawrencina had a particularly low opinion of her youngest daughter. 'Beatrice,' she wrote, 'is the only one of my children who is below the average in intelligence.' Lawrencina did not recognise until the end of her life that Beatrice and she shared the same iconoclastic intellect which had passed by the rest of the sisterhood.

Coldly indifferent to her youngest daughter, Lawrencina shut herself away and showered Dicky with the kisses and caresses that Beatrice was denied. The little boy was allowed to play on Lawrencina's bed in the morning, and went out for drives with her alone while the sulky and difficult Beatrice was left staring after them from the nursery window. Beatrice's memory of her mother was, 'A remote personage discussing business with my father or poring over books in her boudoir; a source of arbitrary authority whose rare interventions in my life I silently resented. I regarded her as an obstacle to be turned, as a person from whom one withheld facts and whose temper one watched and humoured so that she should not interfere with one's own little plans.'[16]

As a consequence of her upbringing Beatrice found physical relationships problematical in adulthood. Her obsessional puritanism and habitual repression of her feelings owed much to her early experiences. Fortunately there were at least the servants for Beatrice to talk to, and the affection she received from her mother's companion, Martha Jackson, in some way compensated for Lawrencina's neglect.

Martha was a poor relation from Lawrencina's mother's family, and she had accompanied her mistress to Rome when she had met her future husband. Martha soon became the indispensable nurse and surrogate mother to the growing family of girls, who gave her the nickname of 'Dada'. 'Dada was a saint, the only saint I ever knew,' recalled Beatrice, 'she mothered all the members of the large household, whether children or servants, whether good or naughty; she nursed them when they were ill, comforted them when they were in trouble, and spoke for them when they were in disgrace.'[17]

Despite Dada's kindness, Beatrice could not help being woefully jealous of Dicky, and desperate for her mother's attention. She tried hard to please, writing her mother anxious, careful letters in a painstaking copperplate hand. Left alone at Standish while her sisters accompanied her mother to London, she wote at the age of five:

> Dear Mama,
> I am quite well and very good. I shall be glad when sisters come home. I love dear little Dicky very much . . . With best love to Papa, Lallie and you, I am dear Mama,
> Beatrice.[18]

She did not take the same care writing to her sister Kate, and allowed her natural exuberance to show.

> Dear Katie,
> Papa had bought or is going to buy Blanche and Theresa a pony which is coming tomorrow for him to see it is not nearly as tall as Robin was it has been accustomed to hunt . . . the old hen has laid eight eggs which Papa is going to give to sisters for their collection Mamma has bought me a nice new book Do you know that Dicky has got six teeth . . . My dear Kate I must really finish as I have written a nice little letter so with best love I remain your *very* affectionate sister Beatrice.[19]

Lawrencina was happiest during Dicky's lifetime, and it is conceivable that, at last secure in the knowledge that she had borne a son, she might have developed a closer relationship with Beatrice. But a few days before Christmas 1864 Dicky became ill. 'I went at once to the little fellow and found him pale, breathing with difficulty and looking as though he would have a fit,' recorded Lawrencina. She at once called in the doctor, who gave the child a purgative of rhubarb and jalop. The 'eruption' which followed wore out the two-year-old patient. A second doctor was called in, who shook his head at hearing that a purge had been administered, and mixed some chlorate of potash in orangeade and ordered Lawrencina to make Dicky eat. Fearfully Lawrencina obeyed her instructions, although 'poor little Dicky' was feverish, and had no appetite; 'But whatever I wished him to do he did with beautiful obedience.' Hot and restless, he cried for 'water out of the bottle' but the doctor told her 'not to give it to him too freely for fear of diminishing the tone of his stomach'. Plied with beef tea, arrowroot, barley water and even grilled chicken, Dicky could only sip a saucer of Lawrencina's tea. 'Do you love me?' he asked his mother earnestly, and when she promised she did he said, 'I will never be a naughty boy again.' At 11.30 p.m. on Christmas Day 1864, Dicky died of scarlet fever.

'Sorrow such as we have never known overwhelms our hearts: for our dear lovely good little son, our darling Dicky has been removed from us, after seven days great suffering . . .' wrote his anguished mother. She felt it ironic that the son she loved so much should die while her daughters were spared. The litany of daughters had become a lament. In her journal she railed at the fate which took Dicky and left Beatrice, but within two hours of Dicky's death Richard Potter made her join him in a solemn act of submission to the will of God, and together they vowed to dedicate themselves to the care of the remaining children.[20]

It was a vow Lawrencina found impossible to keep. She had always considered Dicky a remarkably gifted child, both in intelligence and character, and compared Beatrice adversely to him. Beatrice could never compete with the idealised memory of Dicky, and after his death Lawrencina could hardly bear to look at her. Lawrencina blamed herself for Dicky's death and, overwhelmed by guilt, she made a shrine to Dicky in her boudoir, and his baby clothes, slippers and toys were kept in a glass cabinet.

In July 1865 a ninth and last daughter was born, Rosalind Heyworth Potter. 'We were very much disappointed that she was not a son,' recorded Lawrencina, but the baby was large, placid and healthy, and Lawrencina smothered her with love. Rosy was very attached to her mother, 'whose charming, dignified manners and exquisite personal daintiness surrounded her with a kind of mysterious halo'. Rosy knew she was one of Lawrencina's favourites: 'Moreover she was extremely fond of me and lavished on me much of the tender affection which lay concealed beneath the more domineering aspects of her character and which would have nearly all been given to my little brother had he lived . . . When I arrived at first, being another girl, I was but a very poor compensation, but later her thwarted love centred to some extent around her latest born, possibly to the detriment of others, especially to that of my next sister who was only four years older than my brother, and $7^{1}/_{2}$ years my senior.'[21] Lawrencina had an exaggerated opinion of Rosy's intelligence, just as she had a poor one of Beatrice's. She gave Rosy individual lessons in Latin and English composition, and on Sunday evenings read the Bible to her in her boudoir.

Beatrice was abandoned to the care of the servants, whose kindly toleration gave her a lasting affinity with the working class. 'I spent my childhood in quite a special way among domestic servants, to whom as a class I have an undying gratitude. I was neither ill-treated nor oppressed: I was merely ignored.'[22] 'Creeping up in the shadow of my baby brother's birth and death,' Beatrice became a changeling child, left to roam at will through the backstairs world of Standish House, the square institutional mansion among the Cotswold hills which was their main home.

The front rooms at Standish looked over the vale of Severn and were furnished in a fashion typical of mid-nineteenth-century Victorian taste. Ornament was not a luxury but an absolute necessity,[23] and successful capitalists such as Richard Potter were anxious to show off their new riches in sumptuous and richly-carpeted rooms, and Lawrencina's luxurious boudoir was crammed with elaborate furniture. The large and sunny dining room was used by all the family for luncheon, but the library and study were reserved for Beatrice's elder sisters, the billiard and smoking room for her father and his guests. Beatrice's province was backstairs, where the stone-flagged passages connected the 'housekeeper's room for the upper servants with the larger servants' hall for the underlings',[24] and led across a stone-paved yard to the kitchen, scullery, laundry and stables; upstairs long corridors joined one identical bedroom to the next. There were the day and night nurseries, the gaunt schoolroom, the governesses' bedrooms and a single bathroom.

This world became Beatrice's refuge; on Mondays the hot and steaming laundry was out of bounds to her, but on Tuesdays she was allowed to chatter to the head laundry maid and her assistants. The hayloft was also a favourite hiding place where she would curl up among the bales with a large tabby cat for company; in the woods and shrubberies she created secret grottos. There she hid from the outside world, isolated from her older sisters who were fast making their way from the schoolroom to the altar by way of the London Season, and from her mother, cosseted with her little sister or absorbed in her books.

Beatrice learnt to read without any assistance from the governess of the time, and her earliest remembered occupation was reading alone.

She browsed unheeded through the books in the library and study, choosing between the latest periodicals or the new arrivals from the bookshop. Her father did not censor her reading, being of the opinion that 'a nice-minded girl can read anything'. Since he talked to his daughters as his equals about religion, politics and sex, Beatrice had none of the prurient curiosity of those from whom the facts of life are hidden. 'I recollect no curiosity about sex; my knowledge of the facts always outrunning my interest in the subject.'[25]

The schoolroom, where a train of ill-qualified governesses taught tedious lessons to the young Potter sisters, was a room to be avoided. Whenever lessons threatened Beatrice developed a psychosomatic illness which prevented her from studying; 'bouts of neuralgia, of indigestion, of inflammation of all sorts and kinds, from inflamed eyes to congested lungs' shielded her from the unpleasant prospect of 'disagreeable tussles with arithmetic or grammar'.[26] The family doctor proved an agreeable ally, prescribing fresh air and exercise, and once the elder Potter sisters had all 'come out' and a nursery governess was required for Rosy, any pretence at formal education for Beatrice was abandoned.

Beatrice may have found an easier camaraderie with the servants but she was aware of her place in the social hierarchy; she grew up knowing that she belonged to the 'class of persons who habitually gave orders, but who seldom, if ever, executed the orders of other people'. Her mother 'sat in her boudoir and gave orders – orders that brooked neither delay nor evasion'.[27] Her father spent his whole life telling people what to do, and Beatrice watched in fascination as with a wave of his hand he fixed the direction of a new railway line or decided where a new coalfield should be exploited. The movement of capital and labour was ceaselessly discussed and the manipulation of shares was a constant topic of conversation.

The easy assumption of authority came naturally to Beatrice, so that she was soon writing to her nurse Fanny:

My dear Fanny,
Have you spoken to Copnor about my chickens. Tell him to keep them up at the farm till I come back, tell him also please to send down my hen without a tail. I am afraid you will be getting tired of messages, but I have a heap more to tell you. Will you tell Walters to mind and write down all the eggs he sends to the house ... Miss Theresa is wrather [sic] weaker today I am sorry to say.[28]

This upper-class confidence was so deeply ingrained in Beatrice that even when later she disguised herself as a trouser-hand in a sweatshop in the East End, and was quickly criticised for her bungled buttonholes, the wife of the sub-contractor instantly decided that she had the 'voice and the manner' to be put in charge of the outworkers. It was a voice and manner that was later to disconcert Sidney Webb as he struggled with dropped aitches and an inferiority complex.

Although Beatrice's clearest childhood memories were of Standish, it was only one of several rented homes; the Argoed, a Jacobean farmhouse in Monmouth which was useful for holidays with the younger children, was the only house Richard Potter bought. Lonely Rusland Hall in Westmorland, which was close to his timber yards in Barrow in Furness, was also leased. A town house was necessary for the London Season, particularly with so many daughters to present in society, so in the spring the family went first to Prince's Gate and later to Kensington Palace Gardens. Beatrice was often homesick for Standish.

The nomadic life of the Potters meant that they were not integrated into any particular society, nor did any political party or church claim their loyalty. Perhaps the greatest sufferer was Lawrencina, left alone while her husband travelled the world, for, as Beatrice acknowledged, 'My mother lived where it suited him to live, and he came and went as he chose.'[29]

Dicky's death had exaggerated Lawrencina's tendency to depression and introspection, and from 1865 she scarcely left her room, overseeing the household by remote control and speaking only to her maid. Every daughter had to take her turn in actually running the household in the most economical way so that Lawrencina could be free to devote herself to religion and her studies. She prayed regularly and read the Greek New Testament and the Imitation of Christ, although this attempt to find a mystical union with God brought her little comfort; she yearned for the consolation of religion but her questioning mind continually challenged the doctrines. Beatrice considered that her mother's divided personality was reflected in her face, which in profile appeared harsh and forbidding, but in full face was soft and graceful.[30]

Lawrencina turned later to the obsessive study of foreign grammars, making an idiosyncratic collection of 'a Greek grammar in French, a Latin grammar in Italian, a Hebrew grammar in German, and a Spanish grammar in some Scandinavian language'.[31] This occupation brought her a measure of peace, in that the rules of grammar appeared to impose an apparent pattern and order, although her intellectual aspirations brought her nothing but ridicule and criticism from her daughters. Mary, one of the more prosaic of the brood, expressed her opinion to Beatrice the year after their mother died. Who, she asked, would consider the pursuit of knowledge 'an adequate exchange for an ordinarily happily married life with children of one's own? . . . What happiness did poor Mother's studies bring her? It is the melancholy tendency of such studies to separate people from their friends and neighbours and fellow creatures, in whom alone lies one's happiness.'[32]

Lawrencina might have been less dissatisfied if the novel she wrote, *Laura Gay*, had met with critical success, but the reviews were uniformly bad and she put away her pen, after confiding to her journal: 'I did not feel sure of being an author and doubted the continuance of my profession.'[33] Beatrice also had a strong desire to write fiction, and towards the end of her life, Lawrencina encouraged her. After Lawrencina's death Beatrice felt closer to her mother than ever she had in her lifetime: 'So Mother seems to stand by my side, to be watching me, anxious to reach out to me a helping hand; at any rate to bless me . . .'[34]

'Beneath the surface of our daily life . . . there runs a continuous controversy between an Ego that affirms and an Ego that denies. On the course of this controversy depends the attainment of inner harmony.'[35] In these terms Beatrice sought to express the paradoxical nature of her own character, the two-sided or 'duplex personality' which troubled her all her life, leading her to the heights of ecstasy and the deep abyss of despair, to anorexia and neurasthenic breakdown.

Undeniably the gloomily religious, melancholic streak inherent within her, and her tirelessly questioning intellect, were inherited from her mother. The divided personality Beatrice saw in her mother was passed on to her, and was intensified by the peculiar circumstances of her home life, the contrast between her ebullient and outgoing father and the morbid religiosity of her mother. The positive Ego, in Beatrice's eyes, was masculine, achieving, believing; the negative Ego feminine, sceptical, denying. The struggle between the Egos was to arise in two particular conflicts in Beatrice's life: firstly, between the mystical need to believe in some form of religion and the rational need to find a scientific explanation for the problems of human existence. This conflict appeared to be resolved in her autobiography, *My Appren-*

ticeship, with the discovery of socialism as a creed by which to live. The second conflict lay between the desire for intellectual independence and Beatrice's natural urge for sexual and maternal fulfilment in marriage; this too was a source of great pain to her. Her soul hungered for God, her body for the satisfaction of physical needs, but her mind could not allow these needs to be easily met. Beatrice could not escape the sad legacy of her earliest years, and was driven by her own personal Harpies to seek a new creed and forge a new future for her sex.

II

EARLY INFLUENCES

*'Man is more courageous, pugnacious and energetic than
woman, and has a more inventive genius.'*
Charles Darwin, *The Descent of Man* 1871[1]

IF THE DOMESTIC WORLD OF the nursery was not the refuge Beatrice might
have wished, her free-thinking, nouveau-riche family provided a sharp
contrast to the complacency of mid-Victorian middle-class society. The
sisterhood read avidly if indiscriminately from the pages of St Augus-
tine or Rousseau, Auguste Comte or Zola. No topic was taboo and
everything was discussed, from the origin of the species to sexual
perversion or the exchange rates. According to Beatrice, part of
Lawrencina's disillusionment with her daughters was that they refused
to be educated; instead, as Georgina's son remarked, 'they mixed with
intellectual people to a degree which was extraordinary',[2] and this
intellectual aristocracy helped form Beatrice's ideas.

In homes like hers the 'woman question' was a major topic of
discussion, for Beatrice was born the year after Florence Nightingale's
return from the Crimea. All England was agog with Florence's exploits,
which challenged preconceived notions of women's inferiority, passiv-
ity, and unfitness for mental and physical challenge. Florence, born in
1820, belonged to the first generation of women pioneers such as
Caroline Norton, Harriet Martineau, Elizabeth Fry and Barbara
Bodichon. These women had sprung from unlikely soil, for the
Industrial Revolution had resulted in an increasing demarcation of
male and female roles. In pre-capitalist society women had frequently
worked in partnership with men, whether in small workshops, in
cottage industry, or as employers in their own right. But by the 1830s
and 1840s women's work choices were shrinking as, no longer
employers, women had become marginalised into the servicing sector.
Increasingly lacking the skills and expertise to enter many businesses
the world of the middle-class woman had narrowed into a purely
domestic and social role.

In the words of Virginia Woolf, 'The history of the professions is
predominantly and pervasively a history of gentlemen, with all the

differing and accumulative meanings that the history of the term has, and the nineteenth-century history of the professions is largely about safeguarding careers for gentlemen, and defining and redefining structures of work in relation to male power.'[3]

The idealised woman, excluded from the masculine world of action, was considered a 'lover, a virgin, an angel, a young and beautiful woman . . . a being who scarce touches the earth with the tips of her wings';[4] women who failed at least to want to meet these exacting criteria were deemed sinful misfits. The polarisation of the 'ideal' and the 'material' was most complete in the poets and writers who portrayed the perfect woman as having no contact with material life, and this representation of the ideal had no bearing on what could be realised. 'Femininity as impossibility'[5] was the deadening image presented to women, of a sex inconceivably spiritual, moral, ethereal, self-sacrificing. It was an ideal which bore painfully upon Lawrencina Potter, who suffered deeply, and with ill grace, from the constraints and contradictions of her role as a married woman at a time when the polarisation of roles was at its most extreme. The example of married life she held before Beatrice was one not of happiness and fulfilment but of subordination and bitter frustration.

The contradictions inherent in this dual vision of women as either saints or sinners, and the impossibility of realising an ideal which did not accord with the reality for the many women whom economic necessity drove into the marketplace, led to the stirrings of revolt. By the 1860s the 'woman question' was frequently discussed in the periodicals of the time. A small group of women formed an embryonic women's movement under the leadership of Barbara Leigh Smith, and spearheaded the revolt against the notion of woman's inferiority so deeply branded in Victorian psyches.

Female dependence in every area of life upon men was based on the unchallenged assumption of masculine mental superiority. Women might be allowed moral superiority, but the brain of a woman was claimed by the growing medical profession to have a smaller cubic capacity than a man's, and to work in opposition to the uterus. In the mid-century women were believed to have no sexual feelings until they had experienced intercourse, and even after marriage a woman was seen as innately asexual. 'A modest woman seldom desires any sexual gratification for herself. She submits to her husband's embraces, but principally to gratify him; and were it not for the desire of maternity, would far rather be relieved from his attentions . . . the married woman has no wish to be placed on the footing of a mistress.'[6] Her reproductive system was seen increasingly as disqualifying her from serious thought, and the onset of menstruation was believed to make the education of girls a risky enterprise.

Florence Nightingale wrote bitterly of a childhood in which 'the morning is spent sitting round a table in the drawing room, looking at prints, doing a little worsted work, and reading little books'.[7] No serious study was permitted; as Harriet Martineau said: 'When I was young it was not thought proper for young ladies to study very conspicuously; and especially with pen in hand. Young ladies (at least in provincial towns) were expected to sit down in the parlour to sew, – during which reading aloud was permitted, – or to practise their music; but so as to receive callers, without any sign of blue stockingism which could be reported aloud.'[8] In consequence, Florence Nightingale, Harriet Martineau, and even Beatrice in the 1880s, were forced to rise early and study at dawn, the only time available to them.

For Florence Nightingale the result was anger turned inward. 'The accumulation of nervous energy, which has nothing to do during the day, makes them feel every night when they go to bed as if they were going mad; they are obliged to lie long in bed in the morning to let it evaporate and keep it down . . . some are only deterred from suicide because it is in the most distinct manner to say to God, "I will not do as thou wouldst have me do".'[9] Aimlessness and frustration, and the prohibition on ambition, led to psychosomatic illnesses. As a child Beatrice spent much time suffering from illness which can be partly attributed to her own unhappiness within the family, but also to the restrictions and contradictions of the female role, which provided no real outlet for her talents, but instead forced her energies into the narrow mould of 'accomplishments' such as music and drawing, for which she had no aptitude and which made her feel inferior to her more artistic sisters. Had she had a brother who attended one of the new public schools, she would have been exposed to a more disciplined programme of learning than that provided by the haphazard series of governesses who attempted to teach the Potter sisterhood. Many upper- and middle-class girls came into contact with Latin and Greek, and learnt their mathematics from their brothers; but it was commonplace in the upper and middle classes to educate daughters at home, where 'femininity' could best be learnt. Very few early feminists attended school, although Frances Power Cobbe was sent to boarding school in Brighton, and Harriet Martineau was always grateful for the period she spent at a boys' grammar school.

Beatrice was educated at home to begin with, but had the benefit of a far better-stocked library than most of her contemporaries and, like so many notable women, was exposed to radical and philosophical arguments from an early age. She could not have failed to hear discussions on the 'strong minded women' of the 1860s who were formulating the demand for women's rights and, although Beatrice, like Florence Nightingale, did not sympathise with the feminists till late in life, these women were bringing about radical changes in women's lives which would affect her.

It was the contempt in which men held women that Barbara Leigh Smith[10] wanted to change into respect, and she realised that this could only be achieved through changing women's standing in law, and opening new avenues of employment to them. Barbara's radicalism owed much to her background; she was the illegitimate cousin of Florence Nightingale, who knew her as one of 'the tabooed family', since her father, Benjamin Leigh Smith, MP for Norwich, had never married her mother, who was a milliner's apprentice. By the age of twenty-two Barbara was writing, 'I hope there are some who will brave ridicule for the sake of common justice to half the people in the world.'[11]

The trumpet-blast with which she began the 'petticoat rebellion', as it was called, was the pamphlet, *A Brief Summary in Plain Language of the Most Important Laws concerning Women*, which exposed the iniquitous position of women in English law. A married woman had no legal existence; she was considered as 'feme covert', so that the dictum 'My wife and I are one and I am he' expressed women's lack of rights over property, liberty, conscience and children. There was no divorce before 1857 except by Act of Parliament, and until 1891 a man still had the right to imprison his wife at home, and to beat her with a stick, provided it was no thicker than his thumb.

Barbara's 1857 Married Women's Property Bill failed in the Commons, despite twenty-six thousand signatures on the petition, including those of Elizabeth Barratt Browning, Harriet Martineau, Mrs Gaskell, and Marian Evans, but the 'woman question' had been brought into the public arena, and later that session the government passed the 1857 Divorce Act which gave limited property rights to deserted wives.

An organ for feminist opinions was founded in the *English-woman's Journal*, a ladies' paper bought by Barbara and her friends. Their offices at 19 Langham Place became the hub of the embryonic women's movement, although they were by no means a united sisterhood. The Langham Place Group founded the Society for Promoting the Employment of Women, and Emily Faithfull set up the Victoria Press to print the *Journal*. Unemployed governesses and underemployed young ladies crowded into the Langham Place offices to offer their services, and soon the *Journal* was demanding why there were no women hairdressers, no hotel managers, no women in the Royal Academy. Why were the Marylebone Swimming Baths closed to women? Why could not Elizabeth Garrett be admitted to medical school? At the National Association for the Promotion of Social Science, the centre of the humanitarian movement, women were admitted to membership from the beginning. Papers on 'the woman question' were read at meetings, and Louisa Twining reported on the progress of her Workhouse Visiting Society, Mary Carpenter agitated for her Ragged Schools, and the Ladies' National Association for the Diffusion of Sanitary Knowledge distributed tracts against tight lacing and inadequate perambulators. Philanthropy revealed to middle-class women their powerlessness to alleviate poverty and ignorance, and led inexorably to the demand for women's rights.

The *Saturday Review*, which was the strongest opponent of the campaign, attacked Barbara Leigh Smith and other spinsters for their demands for employment when they should be preparing themselves for marriage. There was concern at the number of 'surplus' women revealed by the 1851 and 1861 censuses, estimated at seven hundred and fifty thousand. 'Married life is a woman's profession,' insisted the *Saturday Review*, 'and to this life her training – that of dependence – is modelled. Of course, by not getting a husband, or losing him, she may find that she is without resources. All that can be said of her is, she has failed in business and no social reform can prevent such failures.'[12] Men were reluctant to marry, so it was said, because young women were 'too fast'. Mrs Lynn Linton, the first woman reporter, who made her début on the *Morning Chronicle*, but by the 1860s was a fervent anti-feminist, fired a broadside at the modern girl with her article 'The Girl of the Period'. Instead of the 'fair young English girl of the past' a woman was now no longer her husband's friend but his rival – not that she found it easy to find a husband: 'Men are afraid of her, and with reason. They may amuse themselves with her for an evening, but they do not readily take her for life . . . the girl of the period is a creature who dyes her hair, and paints her face, as the first articles of her personal religion; whose sole idea of life is plenty of fun and luxury . . . Nothing is too extraordinary and too exaggerated for her vitiated taste.' Instead of keeping her hair in a plain style, 'clean and healthily crisp, she dries and frizzes and sticks hers out on end like certain savages in Africa . . . and thinks herself the more beautiful the nearer she approaches in look to a maniac or a negress.'[13]

Queen Victoria was a dogmatic opponent of women's rights. In 1870, when Beatrice was twelve, Lady Amberley, mother of Bertrand Russell, demanded more opportunities for women. Outraged, Victoria denounced, 'This mad, wicked folly of "Women's Rights" with all its attendant horrors, on which her poor feeble sex is bent, forgetting every sense of womanly feeling and propriety. Lady Amberley ought to get a good whipping.'[14]

Subconsciously Beatrice assimilated the feminine ideal of the period, but she was also becoming aware that a choice existed: whether to conform to the ideal, or whether instead to seek a more adventurous, stimulating and intellectually satisfying path, for which she would have to pay a price but which her own nature demanded of her. For her sisters, however, no flicker of discontent disturbed the certainty with which they chose matrimony. Several of them were content to make the marriages planned for them by their parents to a greater or lesser degree; with gusto Richard Potter in particular entered into the part of matchmaker.

Lallie, the eldest, was the first to marry. Her husband, Robert Durning Holt, came from a respected Liverpool family, and knew Lallie's grandfather, Lawrence Heyworth. He was extremely acceptable to the Potters, but nevertheless a careful correspondence took place between Lallie and her mother while the courtship lasted. Lallie does not seem to have been romantically inclined towards her suitor, writing that she thought Robert Holt 'a nice, sensible, industrious man but I am sure I have no feeling for him at all approaching "being in love".'[15] But once the religious obstacles had been overcome (Robert was Unitarian and Lallie Anglican), the marriage took place in 1867, and was a fruitful one; Lallie had five sons and three daughters. Three years later Mary followed her example, marrying Arthur Playne, a local squire.

Beatrice's movements were often arbitrarily decided at the convenience of her parents, and in 1870 she was sent to stay with a family friend, Mrs Menzies, pursued by her mother's critical letters. Lawrencina was anxious that Beatrice should make friends with the Menzies's daughter. 'I hope you do your best to get on with your namesake,' chided Lawrencina, 'you know Mr and Mrs Menzies are very anxious that she should have a companion, so that they will be disappointed if you neglect her for the boys and it will be rather selfish to do so.'

Lawrencina worried that Beatrice, as so often, would fall ill and cause trouble to her hostess: 'I hope your eyes are quite well again, if they are not you should beg Mrs Menzies to see a doctor for you. If you feel the least ill you must tell her at once – there is nothing sillier or more selfish than to get ill, from neglecting to speak when you first feel out of order and when a simple dose would probably set all to right. I hope you go to bed early and are out of doors a good deal.'[16]

Beatrice's ill-health was a frequent topic in Lawrencina's letters; she had little sympathy for Beatrice's complaints, admonishing her sternly that 'all young people are better without wine'. Lawrencina did not find Beatrice as biddable as she would have wished, and Beatrice was not afraid to criticise her mother when she felt she had grounds, as was certainly the case over Lawrencina's handwriting. In adulthood Beatrice's own handwriting became almost illegible, but in 1870 it was reasonably neat, and she was able to write to Lawrencina in tones of superiority: 'Thanks so much for your long letter. Katie and Papa managed to make it nearly all out though there were one or two words which quite surpassed their understanding ... I hope dear Mother when you write a direction to Kate ... you will write a little clearer as Kate had a good deal of trouble to find out the name of the street you wanted to send to for the lace thread.'[17]

The relationship did not improve as Beatrice grew older, and although Beatrice usually wrote to Lawrencina with dutiful affection, she was capable of showing the same coldness as her mother. In 1878 Lawrencina replied from Rusland to one such letter with a touch of sarcasm: 'My dear Bee, [her usual opening was 'My dearest Beatrice'] A letter from my dear child is always welcome, even though it begins "Dear Mother" ... I still send best love to my cold little maiden ... I am your ever loving mother, Lawrencina Potter.'[18]

Fortunately, at this juncture Beatrice found a new ally, the fashionable philosopher Herbert Spencer who, in Beatrice's words, 'Alone among my elders was concerned about my chronic ill-health, and was constantly suggesting this or that remedy for my ailments; who encouraged me in my lonely studies; who heard patiently and criticised kindly my untutored scribblings about Greek and German philosophers, who delighted and stimulated me with the remark that I was a "born metaphysician", and that I reminded him of George Eliot.'[19]

There are similarities in the early lives of many of the Victorian pioneering women, and the influence of a male relative or close friend is often a significant factor. Barbara Leigh Smith's father gave his daughter £300 a year to enable her to become independent, and Elizabeth Blackwell's father was determined his daughters should have the same opportunities as his sons; in contrast Florence Nightingale's father combined with her mother to thwart her. Beatrice was at least compensated for her mother's lack of interest by her father's treatment of her as an intellectual equal and by Herbert Spencer's warm encouragement.

Herbert Spencer first met Richard and Lawrencina Potter at the Heyworth family home in Liverpool, and he was instantly attracted to the young couple. They 'appear to me the most admirable pair I have ever seen,' he wrote.[20] He had already heard that Lawrencina was something of a 'notability' for her learning and work for the Anti-Corn Law League, and was surprised to find that she did not appear particularly independent but was perfectly feminine with 'an unusually graceful and refined manner'. Richard Potter he admired from the start: 'He is, I think, the most lovable human being I have ever seen.' Spencer's interest in phrenology, learned as a boy at the Derby Philosophical Society, led him to sketch Lawrencina's head in profile and deduce from it her unusual character. Mr Potter's head he considered to be noble and democratic. 'The perfect agreement between his head and face is remarkable: the features are Grecian and their expression is exactly what a phrenologist would anticipate.'[21] What a phrenologist would have made of Spencer's cranium remains a matter for speculation, for his appearance was bizarre. Beatrice carefully noted his 'finely sculptured head, prematurely bald, long stiff upper lip, and powerful chin, obstinately compressed mouth, small sparkling eyes set close together, with a prominent Roman nose'.[22] He was particularly proud of his small hands and feet (a sign that he came high on the evolutionary scale, he believed), and he had perfect manners, precise and pedantic speech, and wore studiedly unconventional clothes, a habit copied from his father.

Although Richard Potter enjoyed intellectual companionship and delighted in welcoming to his house thinkers of note such as Thomas Huxley, Sir Francis Galton (author of Hereditary Genius), geologist and physician John Tyndall, and was honoured to join an afternoon walk with Thomas Carlyle, he was frankly bored by Herbert Spencer's 'synthetic philosophy', which was developed in the prodigious stream of books which poured from his pen.

Spencer was as influential as Darwin, and was the first evolutionist to coin the phrase 'Survival of the Fittest', ten years before Darwin perceived its brilliance and appropriated it for his own Origin of the

Species. But Richard Potter refused to read Spencer's books or to discuss his ideas. 'Won't work, my dear Spencer, won't work,' he would say laughingly, as Spencer attempted to walk against the tide of churchgoers on a Sunday to prove an abstruse point. When young Beatrice eagerly attempted to explain her teacher's philosophical 'laws' to her father, he brushed her aside: 'Words, my dear, mere words . . . Poor Spencer, he lacks instinct, my dear, he lacks instinct – you will discover that instinct is as important as intellect!' For intellectual debate Herbert Spencer had to turn to Lawrencina. 'Mrs Potter was scarcely less argumentative than I was,' he wrote, 'and occasionally our evening debates were carried on so long that Mr Potter, often playing chiefly the role of listener, gave up in despair and went to bed.'[23]

Like Beatrice, Herbert Spencer had been a lonely child who showed a marked distaste for normal school lessons, and was perceptive enough to see Beatrice's unhappiness. She was not an artistic child and had no aptitude for 'dancing or acting, painting or music, for prose or poetry'. Her ability to write, so patently demonstrated in her diaries, was unknown to her. The only talent of which she was aware was 'a tireless intellectual curiosity together with a double dose of will-power', which she already felt disqualified her for getting married: 'However useful intellectual curiosity and concentrated purpose may be to the scientific worker, they are not attractive gifts in a child or a marriageable young woman, and they are therefore apt to be hidden.'[24] Fortuitously, Spencer recognised Beatrice's analytical mind and from her early childhood encouraged her, praised her, and gave her life a new focus and purpose. He suggested new authors for her to try, and organised her aimless reading as his own father had done for him. He poked fun at the despised governesses who presided over the school-room, calling them, 'Stupid persons who taught irrelevant facts in an unintelligible way.'[25] Spencer was putting into practice the ideas he had expressed in his 1861 treatise, *Education*, in which he argued that education should lead from the simple to the complex, from the concrete to the abstract, and from the empirical to the rational. He compared the mind of a child to that of primitive man, observing that only when learning created a 'pleasurable excitement' in a child would it be permanent. Spencer had an instant success with his treatise; 'We have been reading Spencer's "Education" which we liked extremely,' wrote Beatrice from the Argoed six years later.[26]

Spencer advocated the study of science, bullying the Potter governess of the moment until she yielded, saying, 'You can go out this morning, my dears, with Mr Spencer,' because he himself had been encouraged as a boy to roam at will throughout the countryside and collect specimens. Science meant 'scouring the countryside ... for fossils, flowers and water-beasties which, alive, mutilated or dead, found their way into hastily improvised aquariums, cabinets and scrapbooks – all alike discarded when his visit was over'.[27] Beatrice was much more interested in discovering the method whereby 'the old philosopher', as she called him, collected illustrations to substantiate his theory of evolution. Spencer was selective in his gathering of facts, preferring to use those which fitted his previously conceived theory, and in this 'game', as it seemed to Beatrice, she became his apprentice, if not his accomplice. When the philosopher was short of a fact, his serious young pupil would struggle to find one suitable to illustrate his 'law' of nature, and if such a one was not forthcoming she would invent it. From this process she learnt two lessons: firstly that Spencer 'was the most gullible of mortals, and never scrutinised the accuracy of my tales', and secondly and more importantly, 'the relevance of facts; a gift said to be rare in a woman and of untold importance to the social investigator confronted with masses of data'.

It was Spencer's ideas as much as his method which influenced Beatrice's intellectual development as an adolescent. These ideas in their turn sprang from the industrial Nonconformist environment into which Spencer was born in Derby in 1820. He did not come from a privileged background but belonged to the lower-middle class. His schoolmaster father, William George Spencer, undertook the education of his only child himself, as Herbert was considered too delicate for school. He drew up a demanding scientific curriculum for Herbert, including elementary biology, botany, entomology, life drawing and mechanics, and encouraged him in his solitary rambles through the countryside collecting larvae, insects, butterflies, moths and wild flowers. Herbert was a willing pupil, writing that 'those who have never entered upon scientific pursuits are blind to most of the poetry by which they are surrounded'.[28]

Having no companions until his parents sent him to school at ten, Spencer became introverted, inhabiting his own private world of the imagination. Daydreaming or 'castle-building' (an expression Beatrice borrowed) was his favourite occupation. 'On going to bed, it was a source of satisfaction to me to think that I should be able to lie for a length of time and dwell on the fancies which at this time occupied me; and frequently next morning, on awakening, I was vexed with myself because I had gone to sleep before I had revelled in my imagination as much as I intended.'[29] It is no wonder that Beatrice's own isolation aroused the sympathy of the philosopher, who saw his own loneliness mirrored in hers.

Spencer's childhood was rooted in Dissent and Radicalism, and he reinforced the Unitarian and Radical influence upon Beatrice which stemmed from Lawrencina's own background. Richard Potter, like his wife, had had a Radical Nonconformist father, although he had himself adopted the Anglican faith. Spencer rejected his own father's Quaker faith, but deeply absorbed the ideology of Dissent 'where right and wrong were strongly contrasted, where benefit was strictly related to effort and deserving, where poverty was equated with improvidence'.[30] His Radicalism dated back to meetings of the Derby Philosophical Society, of which his father was secretary, and which was linked through the wealthy Strutt family to the famous Lunar Society of Birmingham, since William Strutt, leading light of the Derby Society, was a close friend of Erasmus Darwin, founder member of the Lunar Society and grandfather of Charles Darwin. To the Birmingham circle also belonged Samuel Galton, grandfather of Francis Galton, the father of finger-printing, and one of the scientific friends Herbert Spencer brought to the home of Richard Potter.

The significance of Unitarianism lay in its link with individualism, the belief that Spencer implanted most firmly in Beatrice, and which for so long retained its hold over her. Firmly rejecting state intervention, Spencer believed in individual liberty and self-help, the personification of his ideal being the successful businessman. 'How, in serving himself, does the merchant serve society. How wonderful is the scheme of things produced by the desire for gain.'[31] Spencer must have seen enlightened self-interest epitomised in Richard Potter, whose pursuit of wealth and power seemed justified in the Benthamite belief that the greatest good of the greatest number would be achieved by letting each man seek his own good in his own way. Certainly Spencer and Lawrencina, the ardent disciple of Adam Smith, Malthus and the economist Nassau Senior, found themselves in happy accord in the shared conviction that only by 'the persistent pursuit by each individual of his own and his family's interest would the highest general level of civilisation be attained'. This belief, as Beatrice observed, was held fervently by the majority of the middle class.

Radical and Nonconformist ideas created a climate which predisposed women to challenge the Victorian feminine ideal of subservient and self-sacrificing womanhood, and Beatrice was not the only woman growing up in such an environment. Harriet Martineau came from a strict Unitarian family, Barbara Leigh Smith's father was a well-connected Radical MP, Elizabeth Blackwell's father had been associated with the Anti-Slavery Campaign, as were many who then turned to social reform after 1833.

Spencer had met Carlyle, Huxley, and Tyndall at the soirées of the publisher John Chapman, whose offices were opposite those of the *Economist* where Spencer worked briefly as sub-editor. There he also met Marian Evans, then known as the translator of Strauss; there were rumours that he was in love with her, and certainly he found her 'the most admirable woman, mentally, I ever met'. By 1854, however, he had resigned his post and was writing *Principles of Psychology*. Spencer had no conventional academic training for many of the subjects he wrote about, and his theories were based on very little reading. He said he once tried to read Kant but tossed him aside as soon as he realised that Kant disagreed with his 'First Principles'. Beatrice suggested to Huxley that Spencer had worked out the theory of evolution by grasping the disjointed theories of his time and welding them into one. 'No,' said Huxley. 'Spencer never knew them; he elaborated his theory from his inner consciousness. He is the most original of thinkers, though he has never invented a new thought. He never reads; merely picks up what will help him illustrate his theories.'

Beatrice and her sisters looked forward with anticipation to the philosopher's visits, and found his eccentricity a source of amusement. Much troubled with 'cerebral congestion' or insomnia, he used to 'wet his skull with brine on retiring, covering it first with a flannel nightcap and then with a waterproof one to prevent evaporation'.[32] The highlight of his visits were always the nature rambles when the sisterhood would pin the helpless philosopher to the ground and pelt him with decaying beech leaves, until he fled from the 'little demons, all legs, arms, grins, and dancing dark eyes'. Their favourite ploy was to ask him: 'Are we descended from the monkeys, Mr Spencer?' His invariable reply, 'About ninety-nine per cent of humanity have descended and one per cent have ascended',[33] produced hysterical giggles.

'Mr Spencer's visits always interest me, and leave me with new ideas and the clearing up of old ones,' concluded Beatrice; they also left her conscious of the 'uselessness of my miserable little studies',[34] ready to sink back into depression and apathy. At times the stiflingly dull round of family life threatened to overwhelm her in the years before she was old enough to come out. 'Worse than physical pain was boredom, due to the incapacity of ill health, the ever-recurring problem of getting rid of the time between meals, and from getting up to going to bed; and worst of all, the sleepless hours between going to bed and getting up.'[35] She once stole a small bottle of chloroform from the family medicine chest, with the vague idea of ending the pain of family life; but she found the stopper loose and the contents evaporated, and was forced to abandon the idea.

CHAPTER

III

A LATER-BORN THERESA

*'Theresa's passionate, ideal nature demanded an epic life: what
were many-volumed romances of chivalry and the social
conquests of a brilliant girl to her? Her flame quickly burned up
that light fuel; and, fed from within, soared after some
illimitable satisfaction, some object which would never justify
weariness, which would reconcile self-despair with the rapturous
consciousness of life beyond self.'*
George Eliot, Prelude to *Middlemarch*

BY THE AGE OF TWELVE Beatrice had grown into an attractive child with
an oval face, glossy dark brown ringlets and serious eyes, so dark they
sometimes seemed black. Photographs show her as well-covered
without being plump. Stubborn and spirited as she was, she still had
little say in her own comings and goings; only Standish was a constant
in the shifting world, and Beatrice was often painfully homesick. 'Dear
Mama, I hope you will grant our wish,' she wrote miserably from
Yewtree to her mother. 'We have not seen Standish for seven months
and are dying to be there and I think it will be convenient to you, but
I do not know how the trains go but Georgie will tell you that.'[1]

Sometimes, though, Lawrencina's absence was the excuse for a
party, and for the older girls to flirt. 'Kate and Blanche are violently
in love with the Gzouskis, they are nothing as far as I can see very
wonderful,' Beatrice told her mother. 'Mr Gzouski is tall, rather stout
and decidedly prosi [*sic*] . . . We all hope to have a joly [*sic*] picnic on
Monday . . . We shall make a party of twenty-one.' Soon the
pre-pubescent Beatrice was warming to Mr Gzouski, who 'has told us
to [*sic*] or three very funny tricks, one of them being that if you put
two or three fingers of the right hand on the bend of the left arm
elbow, and then hold with the left hand the back of your neck, no
human's strength without tearing the flesh can divide them.' They all
had a go at the trick with howls of merriment, and then gave each
other piggy-backs.[2]

Such parties were flashes of light in a grey landscape. Generally
Beatrice was left alone, her constant illnesses the excuse for releasing

her from formal education once her elder sisters had come out, and Rosy had progressed to a nursery governess. The marked favouritism Lawrencina showed Rosy (and had also shown Theresa and Maggie) was obvious in the trouble and expense expended on Rosy's education compared to Beatrice's. When Rosy was twelve she was put in the care of a Newnham graduate who was to prepare her for the Oxford Junior Local examinations. Beatrice, on the other hand, in an attempt at self-culture, began copying extracts from books that she had read, writing reviews, and recording her own reflections. An early entry, probably written in 1868, was a criticism of the type of education commonly endured by girls of her own class:

> I am quite confident that the education of girls is very much neglected in the way of their private reading. Take, for instance, a girl of nine or ten years old, she is either forbidden to read any but child's books, or she is let loose on a good library; Sir Walter Scott's novels recommended to her as charming and interesting stories – 'books that cannot do any possible harm'. But the object of reading is to gain knowledge. The whole of their thought (for a child . . . spends little or no thought on her lessons) is wasted on making up love scenes, or building castles in the air, where she is always the charming heroine without a fault. I have found it a serious stumbling-block myself; whenever I get alone I always find myself building castles in the air of some kind . . .[3]

Guilt lay heavily upon Beatrice as she dreamed her romantic day-dreams in the country while her sisters were husband-hunting in London. Kate wrote cheerfully to their 'stray lamb, Bee', 'Have you begun your book yet and have you done any sketching of flowers and things about the Argoed? You should get a pony and go about with Fraulein over the wild land: make her ride. I wonder how she would look on horseback.'[4] But Beatrice, who preferred brooding alone to riding, and despised her governesses of whatever nationality, was too busy struggling with her adolescent sexuality to take Kate's advice. At fourteen she confessed, 'I have hardly learned anything in the way of lessons; honestly speaking, I have been extremely idle, especially during and after the company. But one thing I have learnt is, that I am exceedingly vain, to say the truth I am very disgusted with myself; whenever I am in the company of any gentleman, I cannot help wishing and doing all I possibly can to attract his attention; the whole time I am thinking how I look, which attitude becomes me, and contriving everything to make myself more liked and admired than my sisters. The question is, how can I conquer it, for it forwards every bad passion and suppresses every good one in my heart; the only thing I can think of, is to avoid gentlemen's society altogether. I feel I am not good enough to fight any temptation at present. I have not enough faith.'[5]

Beatrice regarded her awakening sexual feelings as wicked, animalistic, and to be denied. The two Egos, as she had christened the conflict between pleasure and her conscience, struggled for dominance in her teenage mind. At fifteen she was already marking out the path of her life, denying herself pleasure in the pursuit of a higher, heroic ideal. Her religious, puritanical instinct, inherited from Lawrencina, fought with her natural desire for enjoyment, and caused her great anguish.

'When I am indulging my vanity, I hear a kind of voice saying within me, "It doesn't matter at present what you say and do, if there is a God, which I very much doubt, it will be time to think of that when you are married or an old maid", and what is worse still I am constantly acting on that idea. Meanwhile I feel my faith slipping from me, Christ seems to have been separated from me by a huge mass of worldliness and vanity. I can no more pray to Him with the same earnest faith as I used to do, my prayers seem mockeries. I pray against temptations, which I run into of my own accord, and I complain secretly that my prayers are not answered. And intellectual difficulties of faith makes it impossible to believe. I am *very very* wicked; I feel as if Christ can never listen to me again.'[6]

One of Beatrice's main difficulties was that her analytical mind, trained by Herbert Spencer not to accept a statement without proof, found it almost impossible to accept the tenets of Christianity. She marvelled at their housekeeper Martha, who held 'the dogmas of the atonement, predestination, eternal punishment and of the literal infallibility of the Old and New Testament ... humbly and without question'. Beatrice found that Baptist creed primitive if not barbaric. She felt trapped in the contradictory situation whereby she cried out to Christ to hear her, while in the same breath she doubted his existence.

Beatrice became increasingly tormented, confessing to her diary: 'Vanity, all is vanity. I feel that I have transgressed deeply, that I have trifled with the Lord. I feel that if I continue thus I shall become a frivolous, silly, unbelieving woman, and yet every morning when I wake I have the same giddy confident feeling and every night I am miserable. The only thing is to give up any pleasure rather [than] go into society; it may be hard, in fact I know it will be, but it must be done, else I shall lose all the remaining sparks of faith, and with those all the chances of becoming a good and useful woman in this world, and a companion of our Lord in the next. December 23, 1872. Beatrice Potter. May God help me to keep my resolution.'

It was typical of Beatrice to choose renunciation. During the Season of 1873, when she was in London but not yet 'out', she kept her promise to herself to avoid the company of men. Instead she persuaded her sisters' admirers to obtain tickets for her for the Ladies' Gallery at the House of Commons, and spent her time listening to the debates of the political giants of the period, 'loathing Gladstone and losing my heart to Disraeli'. There was so little supervision over her movements that on one occasion she returned by hansom cab in the small hours and let herself in with her own latchkey to the house in Prince's Gardens.

The struggle against sin and temptation is a constant theme of women's memoirs in the Victorian age,[7] as it is of the heroines of Victorian fiction. George Bernard Shaw felt: 'Romance is always, I think, the product of ennui, an attempt to escape from a condition in which real life appears empty, prosaic and boresome ... The man who has grappled with real life, flesh to flesh and spirit to spirit, has little patience with fools' paradises ... [but] for all that, the land of dreams is a wonderful place.'

Much of this daydreaming had its roots in the dying Romantic Movement, and many young girls imagined themselves as Byron's Lara or as Catherine in *Wuthering Heights*, while boys saw themselves performing daring deeds in *The Castle of Otranto*. 'What was the Romantic Movement?' asked Shaw, and proceeded to answer his own question: it was 'a freak of the human imagination, which created an imaginary past, an imaginary heroism, an imaginary poetry ...' The Romantic Movement also demonstrated an almost pantheistic feeling for nature which for the first time was sensed to be at risk from the encroaching Industrial Revolution, and this landscape emphasised the Solitary and the Individual in his life-long quest for fulfilment.

Among Evangelical women self-loathing and disgust were common emotions. Taught to save their own souls and the souls of others, women felt acute guilt and sense of sin at the stirrings of a sexual nature. A lady was expected to be demure, submissive, and never provocative, a rule Beatrice, the possessor of a passionate nature, found particularly hard to follow.

'Dreaming always ... never accomplishing,' Florence Nightingale wrote, 'thus women live – too much ashamed of their dreams, which they think "romantic" to tell them where they will be laughed at, even if not considered wrong.' She believed that 'women often strive to live by intellect. The clear, brilliant sharp radiance of intellect's moonlight rising upon such an expanse of snow is dreary, it is true, but some love its solemn desolation, its silence, its solitude – if they are but *allowed* to live it.'[8]

Although Florence Nightingale antedated Beatrice by a generation, there are strong similarities. Both faced enormous obstacles in escaping from gender and class restrictions, and making the transition from the private to public sphere. Daydreams were the outlet for frustrated ambition, by which they indulged the longings for action. 'I cannot live – forgive me, oh Lord, and let me die, this day let me die,' cried Florence to the God whose voice called her to her vocation. Unable to escape 'the Devourers', as she called her mother Fanny and sister Parthenope, Florence became enslaved by daydreaming, her 'great enemy'. 'I see so many of my kind who have gone mad for want of something to do,' she wrote when she was foiled in her plans to train at Kaiserworth by the European Revolutions of 1848. Florence's daydreams became uncontrollable, and she fell into trances; in December 1850 she wrote, 'I cannot now deliver myself from the habit of dreaming which, like gin-drinking, is eating into my vital strength.'[9]

Beatrice's situation was never as severe as Florence Nightingale's, since her mother did not demand the social success that Florence's did, but the guilt was similar. Philanthropy, in different forms, was to provide both of them with a means of escape.

Like many friendless children, Beatrice turned to books for solace. She disliked *Jane Eyre*, writing, 'I do not think it is a pure book. The author's conception of love is a feverish almost lustful passion.' She preferred the moral and serious tales of George Eliot, in which woman's vocation is explored, and *Middlemarch* was her favourite. Beatrice identified closely with Dorothea, one of those 'later-born Theresas' of whom George Eliot wrote: 'Her mind was theoretic, and yearned by its nature after some lofty conception of the world which might frankly include ... her own rule of conduct ...; she was enamoured of intensity and greatness, and rash in embracing whatever seemed to have those aspects; likely to seek martyrdom, to make retractions, and then to incur martyrdom after all in a quarter where she had not sought it.'[10] Beatrice, like St Theresa, a favourite Victorian saint, demanded an 'epic life'.

Nevertheless the images of women created by George Eliot still largely conformed to the feminine ideal of the time. Although the tension within the ideal caused the split in characterisation between Dorothea and selfish, spendthrift Rosamund, woman's duty remained to serve man, and to teach other women their duty. Dorothea subsumed her own identity in that of her husband Casaubon, and although she aspired to professional work, saw her only path to it through Casaubon and their unhappy celibate marriage. Dorothea's later marriage to Will Ladislaw became the fulfilment of her vocation. Ladislaw was poor, foreign, a writer, and of a lower social station than Dorothea, but with her private income of £700 a year they could together work for social reform. Dorothea 'never repented that she had given up position and fortune to marry Will Ladislaw . . .' even though 'many who knew her, thought it a pity that so substantive and rare a creature should have been absorbed into the life of another . . .'[11] Years later Beatrice's private income enabled Sidney Webb, who shared many characteristics with Ladislaw, to leave the Civil Service so that he and Beatrice could devote themselves fully to social reform.

If Dorothea Brooke, in her plain dark dress, her stature and bearing dignified, and her mind uncommonly clever, was the heroine who impressed the adolescent Beatrice, her horror was that she was becoming something quite different: the artlessly chattering, seductively pretty Rosamund Vincey, whose only thought was to preen herself over the many conquests she made. Fortunately, at this point Beatrice's chance came to forsake her introspective dreams for a welcome change of scene: her father invited her to accompany him on one of his frequent trips to the United States, together with her sister Kate, and her sister Mary and her husband, Arthur Playne.

Two days before the party sailed for the States on 13 September 1873, the wedding took place of Beatrice's fourth sister, the witty, charming and 'granite hard' Georgina, to Daniel Meinertzhagen. In the autumn of 1872 Richard Potter had invited the young merchant banker to stay at Standish, but his appearance was unprepossessing, with full beard, Dundreary whiskers, and a monocle. Meinertzhagen had a fall hunting, and it was during his prolonged convalescence that Georgina fell in love with him.

It was to be a tragic marriage but, as Georgina, wreathed in orange blossom and clematis, walked up the aisle, the future seemed full of hope. Among her bridesmaids the fifteen-year-old Beatrice, standing with her cousin Mary Macaulay, and her other sisters, found it hard to concentrate on the ceremony. No sooner was the reception over than the little party of travellers, 'passed through the hall at Standish feverish with excitement and with longing to see the world, with sisters kissing and giving us tearful goodbye, with a file of wedding guests on each side, looking on with amusement and interest.'[12]

As President of the Grand Trunk Railway of Canada, Richard Potter travelled abroad several times a year. This visit was to him a matter of routine, but to Beatrice a source of endless delight, although she only liked the voyage 'pretty well', and felt twinges of jealousy as she saw how easily Kate made friends on board with an American artist, Mr Bradford. 'They were to be seen constantly walking up and down deck, arm in arm, evidently liking each other immensely, and sympathising in their views of people and things,' commented Beatrice.[13] Kate, whom Beatrice described as 'clever, kind, true, and rather plain', had a great gift for drawing people out. She had no desire to rush into marriage, and was already living alone in London and agitating to be allowed to work with Octavia Hill, the campaigner for housing reform, in the East End of London.

On 25 September they landed at New York. 'I was delighted with New York, there is such a cleanliness and elegance about the town, with trees all down its streets and no smoke; and then Central Park is so lovely, beats all our town parks to pieces,' recorded Beatrice.[14] They travelled on to Niagara, where they were joined by Arthur who claimed he was too tired to continue to Chicago. He certainly looked 'fearfully low and ill', but at length they persuaded him to go on. 'The poor fellow is so very low-spirited when he is ill, that he persuades himself and other people that he is going to die,' commented Beatrice, who had already decided that he was not a good travelling companion.

The equality between the classes surprised Beatrice, who found it 'so funny to see a common negro girl sitting between two well-dressed banker's daughters, and learning the same thing'[15] at school in Chicago. As sister Maggie had remarked on an earlier trip, 'Even the Irish, lately arrived from their native bogs give themselves great airs, serve for twice to three times the wages they would get at home . . . for the higher classes, equality is not so pleasant.'[16] However, Beatrice was protected from too much equality by the privileged surroundings of the private railway car as the train thundered across the prairie. Maggie had revelled in the luxury of the President's car, in which the French chef, Richot, provided them with cold woodcock and peaches. Beatrice, looking back in later life, criticised 'the elaborate accommodation and fittings . . . the over-abundant food; the extravagantly choice wines and liqueurs; above all the consciousness of personal prestige and power; the precedence of the president's car over all other traffic; the obsequious attention of ubiquitous officials; the contemptuous bargaining with political "bosses" for land concessions . . .'[17] For the first time was impressed on Beatrice the reality of her father's power, and it set her thinking about the morality of his wheeling and dealing.

There was a contradiction to be faced in that she loved her father, and defended him stoutly to herself, but she was beginning to question his methods. As a little girl Beatrice had listened uncomprehendingly to talk of 'capital' and 'labour', imagining the former to be made up of piles of gold sovereigns, and the latter in some mysterious way related to water, since both were so easily manipulated. As she grew older Potter explained to her that political and municipal corruption in the United States was due to the lack of a hereditary leisured class who were above the struggle for existence. He was, she saw, ready to adapt to new ideas, exclaiming after the 1867 Reform Act (which he vehemently opposed) extended the vote to the urban working-class, 'We must educate our masters, if necessary we must send our daughters to educate the masses.' Yet his god was personal power, and he was not adverse to the luxury that his power bought.

They reached the Yosemite Valley in California, where Beatrice took out her sketchbook, and wondered if she might ever be a great artist: 'Perhaps I shall find some day a solution to this great difficulty, of, how I ought to employ my time.' Meanwhile Arthur took the party to the Chinese theatre in San Francisco, but Beatrice found that 'being in such close quarters with John Chinaman was not exactly pleasant'. She suspected that every imaginable 'vice and disease'[18] existed in the Chinese quarter, and believed it was there that she caught the scarlet fever and measles which was to make her seriously ill.

No town in America excited Beatrice's interest more than Salt Lake City, the Mormon city built by Brigham Young and his followers. The wide streets, beside which flowed streams from the mountains twenty miles away, and the whitewashed wooden houses with neat gardens and green shutters and doors gave the city a fresh, innocent air. Apart from the Tabernacle the two most important houses belonged to Brigham, and were named the Lion and the Beehive; the polygamous arrangements of the Mormons fascinated Beatrice, who noted that Brigham was building 'a very pretty villa . . . for Mrs Amelia Young, his last and most beloved wife'. The other wives lived in somewhat inferior accommodation. Mrs Eliza Young, wife number seventeen, whom Beatrice met, was 'decidedly coarse when you examined her near', and in fact Beatrice decided the Mormon ladies 'most certainly had a dejected air . . . as if they had continually on their mind their inferiority to their lords and masters'. They lived very simply too, and Beatrice was surprised to find General Munro's wife with a servant's print on, as it was house-cleaning day.[19]

No sooner had the party returned to Chicago than Beatrice collapsed with scarlet fever, measles and rheumatism, and for four weeks she lay dangerously ill, 'nursed by Kate, spoilt by Papa, feared by everybody except a stranger', for Beatrice's strong will was already a byword in the family, as the teasing letter she received from her favourite sister Maggie shows. The date, 25 November 1873, was blotched, the result, joked Maggie, of 'tears . . . and mental collapse' at the prospect of not having her sister home for Christmas. 'To Bee,' it began, 'on hearing she had caught scarlet fever in America. But we are up to your dodges, you wicked thing, to go and catch a fever on purpose to stay out in America a month longer! At first we did not believe your letter (which by the way I was not allowed to see, Mother threw it in the fire on account of infection) so thought that you only wanted to make believe that you were not homesick and had persuaded Papa to stay out longer; but Arthur told us that you had exclaimed on hearing that you had scarlet fever, "Now I shall get my own way!" '[20]

Maggie's kindness bore fruit, and Beatrice made a new resolution, 'To make more a friend of Maggie. Hitherto I have lived a great deal too much apart from my sisters, partly from indolence and partly from my unfriendly disposition.' Beatrice had also become closer to 'dear Kitty'. 'I have got quite fond of her, she has been such a dear, kind devoted sister. I can't imagine why she does not get on better at home. Though we lived on the most intimate relationship for the last three months or more, I really have not found out one serious fault.'[21]

As Beatrice rested alone while Kate and her father went out to dinner, she wondered if she herself had altered, and if so, whether for better or worse; she consoled herself with the thought, 'I shall find my own level when I get home, that is one good thing in a large family.' It was with an awareness of being more 'grown up' that Beatrice looked forward to her return to Standish.

IV

SOCIAL BUTTERFLY

*'The Dance, oh how I did enjoy that! It was the first dance I
had ever been at as a grown-up lady, and I felt considerably
satisfied with myself, as I had two or three partners for each
dance. Ah vanity! vanity! unfortunately for me my ruling
passion . . .'*
Beatrice Webb Diary, 3 August 1874

WITHIN A FEW WEEKS OF her return from the States, Beatrice's anticipation
of a warm family welcome had turned to disappointment. The spoiling
she had received from Kate and her father had left her with an inflated
sense of her own importance, but once she was home at Standish, low
down in the family hierarchy, she received less attention than any of
her sisters. 'Then I was *the* important person but now I am the least
important of six or seven others, and naturally my interests and my
health cannot be considered first, and I am a great fool to think so,'
she confided to her diary.[1]

She turned again to her regime of self-education, occasionally going
to Rosy's governess to read Shakespeare in the evenings, but otherwise
labouring alone translating Goethe's *Faust*, and reading German
novels. Out of duty, and to please her mother, she practised the piano
for half-an-hour a day, and struggled to improve her drawing,
laboriously copying out the patterns in her School of Art book. The
long winter months at Standish passed slowly, and Beatrice spent many
hours alone in her bedroom becoming, in the opinion of her sisters,
increasingly a blue stocking.

Only her sisters' love affairs provided a diversion; it was now
Theresa's turn to fall in love, with Townsend Trench, who nearly
succeeded in 'carrying away our dearest sister', but who was finally
refused. Since he was 'personally the most attractive man I know',
Beatrice felt that she would have been too weak to refuse him, but
eventually she decided that Theresa had made the right decision, since
her suitor was too Irish, being overly rash and self-confident. Townsend Trench languished 'very ill and sad',[2] when he failed to gain
Theresa's hand. Was this another example of Mr Potter's success in
controlling the destinies of his daughters? As Beatrice pointed out, 'His

daughters married the sort of men he approved, notwithstanding many temptations to the contrary.'

The problems of Beatrice's isolated methods of study, the lack of any companion for a sixteen-year-old, or a teacher apart from Herbert Spencer with whom she might discuss her thoughts, became increasingly apparent as the spring of 1874 approached. Unsettled, discontented, and leading an increasingly introverted life, her diary became her only consolation. 'Sometimes I feel as if I must write, as if I must pour my poor crooked thoughts into somebody's heart, even if it be into my own,' she wrote in March.[3] Her sense of being different from the rest of the family, a feeling shared by Harriet Martineau and Florence Nightingale, continued to be strong. Although Maggie and Blanche were 'much improved' in the last four months, neither of them was the confidante that Beatrice needed.

Beatrice's prickly relationship with her mother continued to distress her. They had grown no closer. 'What is this feeling between Mother and me? It is a kind of feeling of dislike and distrust which I believe is mutual. And yet it ought not to be! She has always been the kindest and best of mothers, although in her manners she is not over-affectionate. She is such a curious character I can't make her out. She is sometimes such a kind, good affectionate mother, full of wise judgement and affectionate advice, and at other times the spoilt child comes out so strong in her.'[4] Lawrencina's cool ambivalence towards Beatrice aroused a sense of guilt in her daughter. 'Whatever she is, that ought not to make the slightest difference to my feeling and behaviour towards her. Honour thy Father and Mother was one of the greatest of Christ's commandments.'

Beatrice continually reproached herself; she was lazy at getting up in the morning, lazy about her drawing, lazy over her religious duties, and her studying lacked method. Worse than anything, she was still making castles in the air, this time about 'F.G.', probably Francis Galton, who was expected to visit the Potter household at Easter. 'And now my dear friend,' she admonished herself, 'I want to tell you something seriously ... You are really getting into a nasty and what I should call an indecent way of thinking of men, and love, and unless you take care you will lose all your purity of thought, and become a silly, vain self-conscious little goose.'[5]

In April good resolutions vanished into the background as Beatrice plunged into the maelstrom that was London Society in the 1870s and 1880s. Although not officially 'out', since she was still only a sixteen-year-old 'schoolroom girl', the ecstatic Beatrice was allowed to take part; as she wrote later, 'I enjoyed it immensely. It is seldom I have had so much pleasure in so small a space of time.' With a later, more critical eye, she came to see the London Season as nothing more than a cattle-market for women, the equivalent for daughters of the wealthy classes of the university education available to their brothers, since marriage was the recognised vocation for women not compelled to earn their own livelihood.

Beatrice and her sisters were secure in the knowledge that they were among 'the well-to-do folk who belonged or thought they belonged to London Society', that upper ten thousand whose doings were minutely chronicled in the *Queen*, the lady's newspaper. There were four distinct sets among the ruling class, as Beatrice noticed: 'The Court, representing national tradition and custom, . . . the Cabinet and ex-Cabinet, representing political power; there was a mysterious group of millionaire financiers representing money,'[7] and of course there was the racing set, led by Edward, Prince of Wales. The four inner circles crossed and re-crossed one another, dominated by certain particularly bright stars who figured prominently in the pages of the *Queen*, such as Lady Randolph Churchill, later Mrs Cornwallis-West, the Princess of Wales, Lily Langtry and Lady Dudley. Photographs of these beauties of the 1880s collected gawping crowds in front of shop windows, and were passed from hand to hand as eagerly as those of twentieth-century pop stars. Margot Tennant, later wife of H. H. Asquith, considered that, 'Of them all Princess Alexandra had a more perfect face than any of these I have mentioned . . . the frownless brows, the carriage, the grace of movement and gesture made her the idol of the people . . .'[8]

Surrounding the four inner circles was the British aristocracy, which Beatrice considered the most talented, the most energetic and the most vulgar in the world. Undeniably the British aristocracy was a more open caste than that of other European countries, its constantly shifting mass assimilating the new rich, such as American heiresses like Jennie Jerome, wife of Churchill, or Consuelo Vanderbilt, who married the Duke of Marlborough, injecting new wealth into older and bluer blood.

In the mid-1870s an agricultural depression had affected land-owners, whose profit margins fell under the onslaught of cheap American corn, but in London the social whirligig whirled even faster under the impetus of the new moneyed élite who dominated the London Season. Bankers, brewers, publishers, shipowners and merchant bankers mingled with the occasional star from the world of science or art. To add spice to this mixture of old money and new, literary 'lions' were for a short time taken up for the amusement of society. Thomas Carlyle at first found the unaccustomed luxury of life in a large Yorkshire country house overwhelming, and complained to his wife of the 'troops of flunkeys bustling and beckoning at all times, the meat jack creaking and playing all day . . . and such champagning, clareting and witty conversation. Ach Gott! I would sooner be a ditcher than spend my life so.'[9] However Carlyle was soon seduced by the attention he received into enjoying his lionisation. Even the deaf Harriet Martineau was prepared to go out in society any day but Sunday, after the success of her tales of political economy made her too a 'lion'.

Society was in a state of transition. During the earlier part of the nineteenth century social etiquette had become formalised. Upper-class women decreed whether aspirants to society would be accepted or rejected, and by mid-century the trend was growing towards greater exclusiveness and privacy, with the development of Gentlemen's Clubs and private rather than public dances. Certificates of Presentation were given from 1854 as a 'passport to Society';[10] Rituals such as leaving cards became a burdensome social duty, with a strict timetable to be adhered to: '3 p.m. to 4 p.m. for ceremonial calls, 4 p.m. to 5 p.m. for semi-ceremonial calls and 5 p.m. to 6 p.m. for intimate calls.' Not to call within three days of receiving hospitality was unforgivable.[11] Turning down the corner of the card indicated that a lady had called in person, rather than merely sending a servant. As Britain's imperial greatness grew, the formality and extravagance of Society increased, and in the 1870s when Beatrice entered Society, this trend was reaching its zenith. Although the power of the aristocracy was waning, the entry of commerce into London Society and the patronage of the Prince of Wales lent a new frenzy to the social scene. Into the limelight stepped the new families, 'the Rothschilds, . . . the Barings and Glyns, the Lubbocks, Hoares and Buxtons, who . . . represented money power in the London Society of the seventies and eighties',[12] in Beatrice's opinion. The Prince of Wales enjoyed the charm and lavish hospitality of his Jewish friends and since his marriage in 1863 to Princess Alexandra had freed himself from the control of the old Queen. It was, however, another matter to win a peerage for the Rothschilds from his indomitable mother. In 1869 Victoria refused this favour to Lionel de Rothschild: 'To make a Jew a peer is a step she could not consent to,' she wrote tartly to Gladstone.[13] But by 1885 she had changed her mind, possibly influenced by her affection for Disraeli, and Sir

Nathaniel de Rothschild became the first professing Jew in the Upper House.

Nor could Victoria stop her eldest son smoking, as the new rage swept Society, and in 1866 the Marlborough Club had been founded, with the Prince's encouragement, as a congenial spot for the fast set to smoke undisturbed. Smoking was gaining ground in private houses too, and Mrs Beeton suggested the provision of 'a little snuggery' for the purpose, with 'a couple of neat salivariums'.

Beatrice despised the worship of power and gold, the subservience of well-bred people to the South African millionaires with neither manners nor morals, but it was the thoughtless pursuit of pleasure which drew her greatest opprobrium. Women were the greatest offenders in dedicating themselves to pleasure, since most of the men continued to work while decorating Society in the evening (although there were some 'functionless males' and 'dancing men in my time were mostly fools'). For women however, the Season's rituals were all-consuming: 'The presentation at Court, the riding in the Row, the calls, the lunches and dinners, the dances and crushes, Hurlingham and Ascot, not to mention amateur theatricals and other sham philanthropic excrescences.'[14] Rotten Row was crowded every morning with fashionable riders whose purpose was to be seen rather than to ride, and even the Prince of Wales came to the meets of the Coaching Club beside the Serpentine.

The Prince of Wales could make or break a person in Society. Margot Tennant, whose father Sir Charles Tennant ('the Bart') had made the obligatory fortune and desired his daughter to shine in Society, had wit (she was a founder-member of the 'Souls'), charm and beauty, and was a nerveless rider to hounds to boot, but she attended comparatively few balls until she chanced to be introduced to the Prince of Wales at Ascot. She gave him a tip for the Wokingham Stakes, and the horse romped home. The grateful Prince presented her with a gold cigarette case and 'after that Ascot I was asked everywhere'. But the outrageous Margot caused a sensation when she arrived at a supper given for Lord and Lady Randolph Churchill wearing 'a white muslin dress with transparent chemise sleeves, a fichu and a long skirt with a Nattier blue taffeta sash. I had taken a bunch of rose carnations out of a glass and pinned them into my fichu with three diamond ducks . . .' To her horror she found all the other ladies in ballgowns and tiaras, and heard the whispers around her: 'Do look at Miss Tennant! She is in her nightgown!' At that moment the Prince of Wales arrived and the ladies made 'subterranean curtsies' but he came straight to

Margot and asked her to sit next to him at supper. Modestly she protested, 'Oh no, Sir, I am not dressed at all for the part! I had better slip away, I had no notion that this was going to be such a smart party. Some of the ladies think I have insulted them by coming in my nightgown.' But the Prince insisted, 'You are so original! You must dance the cotillion with me!'[15] From that moment her social success was assured.

Beatrice's first reaction to the Season was sheer delight as unaffected as Margot Tennant's. Amateur theatricals were the climax of her pleasure, especially when Maggie fell ill and it seemed that Beatrice might be catapulted into stardom as Kate Hardcastle in *She Stoops to Conquer* before two audiences of two hundred people. Fortunately – or unfortunately – Maggie got well in time 'and carried off the laurels'.[16] Amateur theatricals were a favourite occupation of the sisterhood, and the previous May when Beatrice had been too young to join in, Kate had written to her describing the family performance at their London home. The dress rehearsal had gone off 'excellently well' in front of a small audience including the servants: 'All the parts were well done, Mrs Stirling [the prompter] says the ladies were the best, in fact she was quite delighted with the family acting . . . As for Theresa . . . it was quite delicious, the moment she came in the audience brightened up visibly and evidently looked forward to her parts.'[17]

The fate of her sisters in the marriage mart fascinated Beatrice. The previous Season it had been Georgie who had been the belle of the ball and ended the Season successfully by marrying Daniel Meinertzhagen. This year Beatrice recorded that Blanche had started well and quickly found an admirer, but as the Season progressed her suitor's family had cold-shouldered the Potter girls, as it became apparent that Blanche did not care for the gentleman, who had turned 'gloomy and yellow'. Blanche, decided Beatrice, was 'handsome, downright', and she did not beat about the bush, as her suitor had probably discovered. As to Theresa, she 'had much more practical sense, [was] stylish to look at, clever to talk to, though not furnished with that easy flow of small talk which is so necessary in London', being 'totally unadapted to the shams and conventionalities of society, and therefore not a favourite generally at balls'. Poor Theresa was probably dismayed by the fickleness of her late admirer, Townsend Trench, who had married a young Irish girl only a month after swearing undying love for Theresa. Maggie, decided Beatrice, as she worked through the list of her unmarried sisters, was 'bright, lively, pretty, good-tempered', and would be 'a perfect success in society if she had just a little more polish'.[18]

Even at sixteen Beatrice could not subdue her critical eye. She was sickened by the relentless jockeying for position and the competitive scramble for social status; how quickly intimacy gave way to 'the cut' at the first hint of failure. Popularity was ephemeral. 'The rumour of approaching marriage to a great political personage would be followed by a stream of invitations; if the rumour proved unfounded the shower stopped with almost ridiculous promptitude.'[19] A Society lady would be invited everywhere while her husband lived, cold-shouldered before he was barely cold in his grave. A new marriage might undo a duchess.

Both competition and conspicuous consumption were most obvious in the giving of good balls. 'What is a good ball?' was the question on the lips of every hostess. The secret was not the simple spending of money, since wealth was everywhere in abundance. Electric light was superseding the soft gas lights of earlier decades, and its novel brilliancy made discretion in make-up essential. The number to invite was a considerable problem, since 'an over-crowded ballroom is not now considered the test of a ball being a good one – quite the contrary; yet people must not run away with the notion that a thin ball would be a success',[20] and this could be the mortifying consequence for a 'less smart' hostess if a more fashionable lady decided to give a ball on the date she had chosen. The élite would look in on the first ball for half an hour, and then progress to *the* ball of the evening.

A hostess had to be ruthless: 'Ladies who knew anything about ball-giving would rather run the risk of offending friends and relations – especially relations – than invite plain, ill-dressed, what is known as dowdy girls to their balls.' The most sought-after compliment was 'a great many pretty people were there'. It was necessary to spend extravagantly on banks of cut flowers, and flowering plants in every niche decorated the ballroom and sitting-out rooms. At 1 a.m. guests would expect to sit down to 'delicious cold entrées of fish or birds, salmon, lobster, soles and prawns presented in various disguises, in aspic and out of it; quails, ortolans, the humble but useful chicken . . . a hot entrée is given in the form of cutlets with a mysterious sauce; . . . the confectionery portion of a supper is an evidence of the triumph of ice, the champagne sharing the laurels.'[21]

The purpose of this reckless expenditure by parents on behalf of their daughters was to avoid the awful fate of those who failed to find husbands at the end of three Seasons: the old maids, that 'soured and disappointed section of society'. After thirty a woman was no longer marriageable, and was the object of pity by her married contemporaries. Since no vocation existed for a woman of the upper classes other than marriage, fear that she would fail to find a husband led Richard Potter to at first refuse Kate's request to withdraw from Society in order to work for housing campaigner Octavia Hill.

It was a dissipated and dyspeptic Beatrice who returned to Standish in August. Indigestion and insomnia had undermined her health, and she had become vain and cynical in the gratifying enjoyment of her own popularity. 'And yet at times one was hardly happy. One looked from day to day for some new excitement, and in the intervals between these excitements one hardly knew what to do with oneself.'[22] Her first Season had sowed the seeds of the love-hate relationship which was to bedevil her relationship with Society in the 1880s and ensure that even when she was one of its most glittering stars, guilt and contempt outweighed pleasure.

CHAPTER

V

THE SEARCH FOR A CREED

'I must make a faith for myself, and I must work, work,
until I have.'
Beatrice Webb Diary, 4 April 1874

THE DISCONCERTING KNOWLEDGE THAT man was not a fallen angel but merely a risen ape lay heavily upon the shoulders of the educated classes in the years following the publication of Charles Darwin's *Origin of the Species*. For many intellectuals the theory of natural selection exploded like a blaze of light upon the darkness of orthodoxy. Francis Galton, a frequent visitor to the Potters, confessed that the *Origin* aroused 'a spirit of rebellion against all ancient authorities whose positive and unauthenticated statements were contradicted by modern science'. For Galton, who shared a grandfather with Darwin, it snuffed out the last vestiges of religious faith, driving away 'my own superstition as if it had been a nightmare'.[1]

Beatrice recognised too that she had been born into an era which represented a watershed between Christianity and agnosticism. Her own experience of business morality convinced her that the Christian tradition 'had grown thin and brittle, more easily broken than repaired . . . We lived in a perpetual state of ferment, receiving and questioning all contemporary hypotheses as to the duty and destiny of man in this world and the next.'[2] Darwin had destroyed much of the faith in the tenets of religion, and science came to be seen as the tool which would unlock the secrets of the universe. Eugenics,[3] developed by Galton, would make the perfectibility of man possible. It seemed to Beatrice that the two most common assumptions were now that physical science could solve all problems, and that everyone could be his own philosopher.

Creeping secularism became the background to Beatrice's own personal search for 'a creed by the light of which I could live the life I had to lead'.[4] As the dying beech leaves fluttered damply earthwards in 1874 an autumnal gloom descended upon Beatrice, incarcerated again in Standish with her mother and Blanche. The girls were two rather broken crutches for Lawrencina to lean upon, since Blanche

44

was impractical and somewhat boring, and 'I am,' wrote Beatrice, 'as Mother says, too young, too uneducated and, worst of all, too frivolous to be a companion to her.'[5]

Depression and spiritual doubts, guilt at her sinfulness, led Beatrice to feel that the only solution was 'to go heart and soul into religion'. 'It is a pity I ever went off the path of orthodox religion, it was a misfortune that I was not brought up to believe that to doubt was a crime ...' Her problems were confounded by the contradictions inherent in her upbringing. Despite being raised as Unitarians, both Beatrice's parents went regularly to local Anglican churches, where not only did they take communion, although the Anglican clergymen knew that Potter had not been confirmed, but as a wealthy layman Potter was regularly invited to read the lesson, an example of Anglican hypocrisy shocking to Beatrice. One or two of the Potter girls would accompany their father to church each Sunday, but here, as Beatrice said, 'conformity ended'. In London they were exposed to quite contrary influences, since their father delighted every Sunday in discovering the most stimulating preacher possible. The preacher or lecturer might be of any persuasion, and the sisters were often taken to hear Frederic Harrison, the well-known Positivist. On the way home across the London parks the family would discuss the sermon they had just heard.

Meanwhile Galton had come to the conclusion that Darwin's natural selection was widely misunderstood, which led him to study heredity and the improvement of the human race. In the early 1860s little was known about heredity, and although it was generally thought that animals inherited bodily characteristics, this was not believed of man. One eccentric pursuit of Galton's was to classify the women he met into three classes of beauty, in order to make a 'beauty-map' of the British Isles, since he suspected that beauty, like intelligence, was inherited. He would prick holes unseen into a piece of paper shaped into a cross, which he carried with him and thus he classified all the girls he passed in the street as 'attractive, indifferent or repellent ... London I found to rank highest for beauty, Aberdeen lowest'.[6] Galton took a great interest in the Potter family and, in the opinion of Richard Meinertzhagen, Georgina's son, used them in developing his 'ancestral law' of 1879, which stated that a child inherited on average 'one quarter of the personal characteristics of the father; one quarter of the personal characteristics of the mother; and one half of the ... personal characteristics of the fraternity as a whole'.[7] By the 1880s Galton was developing his ideas on eugenics, the first object of which was 'to check the birth rate of the Unfit'.

Few young women can have been exposed to so many conflicting ideas to set against the tenets of orthodox Christianity as Beatrice was. 'F.G.' might lecture her that 'individuals appear to me as partial attachments from the infinite ocean of Being, and this world as a stage on which Evolution takes place'.[8] But from the Bishop of Gloucester, a favourite visitor to Standish, or Cardinal Manning, she heard the opposite case.

As autumn moved into winter Beatrice's spirits sank even lower. She was constantly 'poorly' and could not study. Her father was travelling in Canada with Maggie and Theresa, who were quite unequal to restraining his dissipation. 'The truth is we have been rather disarranged by dear Papa being rather knocked up through a too great propensity of champagne and lunches and speechifying, at both which things he excels,' Maggie told Beatrice. 'He has had a bloodshot eye and has felt thoroughly done, so we gave up the idea of going to Ottawa from Toronto, and came direct to Montreal.'[9] While Maggie and Theresa struggled to control their errant father, for Beatrice there was no respite from the companionship of Blanche and her mother.

Richard Potter never took Blanche abroad. Instead she was left behind to console Lawrencina, who found her daughters no substitute for her increasingly absent husband. Her complaints were, however, ignored by Richard Potter, who left Maggie to soothe her mother in a tactful letter from Montreal, 'Of course we all feel how disagreeable it must be to you to be so much alone at home. Papa feels it very keenly and he would do anything to make it better, but you yourself would hardly have wished him just in the middle of the battle to give up the Grand Trunk, and perhaps to lose success, . . . So I hope dearest mother, you won't allow yourself to be so miserable.'[10]

By the New Year even Lawrencina was becoming alarmed at Beatrice's melancholia. 'I have felt for the first time how much unhappiness there is in life,' Beatrice wrote. 'But one has not been given the choice of existing or not existing . . . I have come to the conclusion that the only real happiness is devoting oneself to making other people happy.'[11]

The decision was made to send the sixteen-year-old Beatrice to school for the first time, as a 'parlour boarder' at Stirling House, Bournemouth, a fashionable girls' school run by a Miss Tapp. Such private schools, usually run by a lady proprietor and modelled on the family ideal, were generally small, with no more than fifty girls. The teachers were unqualified middle-class women to whom no other occupation was open if they wished to preserve their gentility, and standards were low, as the Schools Inquiry Commission of 1866 had discovered. The Reform Movement began in secondary schools in 1841 when the Christian Socialists, Frederick Maurice and Charles Kingsley, founded the Governesses' Benevolent Institution to assist those in distress, and six years later lectures for governesses began. In the 1850s Miss Buss and Miss Beale founded the North London Collegiate School and Cheltenham Ladies' College, but the movement they spearheaded was barely beginning to filter through to the mass of girls' boarding schools. Even newspapers were not available to the pupils, in case topics such as the White Slave Trade were touched upon. The emphasis remained upon 'accomplishments', such as piano-playing and drawing, and when the first female candidates were admitted to the Oxford and Cambridge Local Examinations in 1863, every one failed in arithmetic.[12]

Beatrice had firm ideas about what she wished to study, and was soon admonished by Lawrencina to behave in a creditable manner. Miss Tapp, she told Beatrice, had kindly agreed to her requests, 'in a general form, and more I could not ask her to do. I will tell her what studies you wish to pursue, and that I do not wish you to apply yourself *too closely* until you are quite strong. I am sure you will find her very kind and considerate as well as very helpful . . . and I hope and believe she will find you equally considerate.'[13]

In fact Beatrice did as she pleased. Her thoughts were entirely occupied with religion, as she sought the comfort of traditional Christianity. Ignoring the High Church services the other girls attended, she discovered a Low Church evangelical preacher, Mr Eliot, and asked him to prepare her for Confirmation. Easter Eve found her full of religious feeling: 'May God grant that I may never cease remembering the vows which I have made before God and man, that I intend to become a true Christian, that is, a true disciple and follower of Jesus Christ, making Him my sole aim in life.'

It did not last. Hardly had Beatrice received the Sacrament for the first time before she began to question the doctrine of Atonement. Anxiously she searched the Gospels for evidence that Christ had said man should be saved by His death, and was soon writing vehemently, 'I cannot at present believe in that doctrine. It disgusts me.'[14] She did not mix with the other girls, with whom she found little in common. 'I must above everything endeavour not to think myself superior to the other inmates of Stirling House, because I have been brought out more by circumstances and encouraged to reason on subjects which other girls have mostly been told to take on faith.'[15] But Beatrice disliked gossiping and continued to hold herself aloof.

The summer at Standish passed off more happily than the previous autumn when she had felt 'all the responsibility for Mother's happiness on my shoulders', and it was with regret that she found herself back at Stirling House for the autumn term. Irritated by the continual din of pianos, petty rules, and a lack of interesting conversation, her only friend was her music master, Oscar Beringer, who abandoned the hopeless task of trying to teach her the piano and instead played his favourite pieces to her. Headaches plagued her, and her habit of exaggerating and telling lies made her feel increasingly guilty. 'Lied again today,' she recorded in October 1875. 'I will make a practice of noting lies, by putting a cross for every one to the day of the month.'

The 'repugnant' doctrine of Atonement continued to distress Beatrice, and finally she challenged Mr Eliot. The clergyman fell back on the argument that as the doctrine was found in the scriptures Beatrice ought to believe in it. Beatrice argued that the doctrine was not found in the Gospels but only in the Epistles, which were not 'the faithful record of Christ's own words . . . [but only] the writings of good men'. The defeated Mr Eliot lent her a book on the atonement, and withdrew. Soon Beatrice left Stirling House and within a few months had shaken off her belief in Christianity. 'And now that I have shaken off the chains of the beautiful old faith, shall I rise to something higher, or shall I stare about me like a newly liberated slave, unable to decide which way to go?'[16]

'I do not want to "come out", and I hope I shall have enough determination and firmness to carry my point. The family does not really want another come-out member, they are almost too many as it is,' Beatrice wrote in December 1875, but as the Season of 1876 approached she plunged into an exhilarating whirl of house parties and dances in Gloucestershire, followed by her presentation at Court at the age of eighteen. Soon she was busy riding, dancing, flirting and dressing up, and was revelling in the attention she received. The Potter girls, unusual in their sheer numbers even among the large Victorian families of the era, and noticeable for their outspoken and forthright ways, had made an impression in Society already, whether for their dark beauty, like Blanche, or for the loud laugh which first attracted Leonard Courtney to Kate; but Beatrice was exceptional. Christened 'the brilliant Miss Potter', after her sisters married, for her intelligence, quick wit and learning which made her stand out from the common herd, her glossy brunette hair, huge black eyes, and spirited manner attracted much admiration. The extrovert, gregarious and even reckless side of her nature, inherited from Richard Potter, ensured that she sparkled in Society.

It was during this London Season that Beatrice at last became close to Maggie, her elder sister by four years. As the age gap narrowed they became intimate companions. 'Warm-hearted and self-sacrificing towards her own family, a cynical gamine towards the rest of the world, an omnivorous reader ...' Maggie was 'the best of comrades in the hazards of the marriage market'.[17] But it was during the duller periods of her life that Beatrice really learnt to appreciate Maggie's worth. She was, thought her sister, the most intellectual of the Potter girls, and the only one with whom Beatrice could discuss her ideas.

Unlike Beatrice and Kate, Maggie never had the desire to break away from the conventional pattern of upper-middle-class life. 'Fate may decide in some way on its own. I am quite satisfied to abide by its decisions,' she wrote to Beatrice from Egypt in 1879. 'The truth is that one makes the grand mistake of expecting to be happy in life which is not the lot of most people.' Always a realist, she accepted that her holiday in Egypt with a troublesome Herbert Spencer and her cousins Charles and Mary Booth would merely be 'a sweet episode' to look back on. 'It cannot alter things at home, and the difficulties there must be overcome in time.'[18] Maggie was the most socially ambitious of all the sisters, with a sharp eye for the gradations of social rank. It was a pity, she told Beatrice, that she and Theresa had missed the best ball in Toronto on her visit with their father. It was given by a Mrs Harry Howland, '– or Mrs 'Arry 'Owland as she calls 'erself, 'ose first 'usband was 'Erbert 'Unt – that is the style', but it had been a mistake not to be there. 'Even Theresa has come round to my view of the case, but you know Theresa has a prejudice against balls in general, she was so badly treated at her coming-out ones, was not introduced to anyone ... I hope they won't treat me like that. To go to a ball and figure as a wall-flower, a mere decorator of chairs would be a mortification enough to sour a saint or a philosopher, even Mr Spencer were he a girl, could not stand it.'[19]

Fortunately for Maggie she did not have to, and found that when she went to stay with Lallie in Liverpool, she enjoyed all her dances 'pretty well'. Lallie, the managing elder sister, came in for much criticism from her younger sisters for the sharp-tongued but ineffectual anger she showed to her fast-growing brood of children, whom in

Maggie's opinion she spent far too much time looking after in a manner unbefitting to her class: 'I am now writing under difficulties as there is a general squallation around with Lallie's voice above the winds trying in vain by ferocious but unheeded anger to reduce order among the elements. Of course it is easy to criticise, but it seems to me that a woman has much more power with children by a *very gentle soft* impressive manner than by any amount of noisy insisting.' Maggie's opinion was that 'a kind of sacred myth'[20] should be kept around the mother.

Despite the ructions in the household, and Lallie's failure to 'cultivate herself', her house was 'magnificent and very prettily furnished', Maggie noted approvingly, and Liverpool offered possibilities for Beatrice. 'If you accept Lallie's invitation . . . there will be a dance at the Warrens and I will tell all my best partners about you, so that if you like to make a beginning in Liverpool it will be a good opportunity.'

Maggie's attitude to Society was most clearly shown in the boredom with which she met Kate's underprivileged tenants from the East End. 'Last night we went to one of Kate's poor people's parties . . . Mary Booth, Charlie and I adjourned to the house of a nice Mrs Hall in Onslow Gardens and had a champagne supper, which we kept up till two in the morning . . .'[21] Since she began working for Octavia Hill in 1875 Kate had firmly turned her back on Society: 'Mother is much better and is beginning to enjoy going out even to stupid parties . . . I am very quiet now and I find I can stand my work very much more comfortably for not going out much.'[22] Maggie however was truly her father's daughter, having the same taste for champagne and the social whirl. 'Tonight Georgie and I go to dance at Lady Campbell's,' she wrote to Beatrice in 1879; 'Tuesday to a dance at an old friend of Mama's, Wednesday Mrs John Holland's dance . . . On Monday I read the part of Lydia Languish at Mrs Walter Browne's.'[23] Maggie made the most socially desirable marriage of all the sisters in marrying Henry Hobhouse, nephew of Lord Hobhouse; ironically it was the socially unambitious Kate who introduced Maggie to her future husband.

If the spirit of fun which Maggie brought to the Season made her an ideal 'comrade' for Beatrice, their shared interest in sketching and reading brought a new intimacy Beatrice had never experienced before. 'Maggie and I particularly have had a perfect communion of pursuits and ideas. We had a delightful little trip among our sublime hills; . . . and this experience has inspired us with a wish to go sketching and reading tours together, should we remain lonely spinsters,' Beatrice recorded in the autumn of 1879. She and Maggie had taken a little cottage called Knab's Cottage at Grasmere, once lived in by Thomas de Quincey and Hartley Coleridge, elder son of Samuel Taylor Coleridge. There they spent an idyllic week or two, and when she left Beatrice wrote: 'I feel her loss terribly ... now she has gone it is a dreary blank ... I must go plodding on towards some goal that may never be reached.'[24]

Religion still preoccupied Beatrice. At nineteen she wrote, 'I might as well state what are my vague beliefs. I do not see that there is sufficient evidence either for believing in a future life or in a personal Creator of the universe. I at present believe ... that Christianity is in no way superior ... to the other great religions.' Beatrice came under the influence of an elderly neighbour in Gloucestershire, Brian Hodgson, a former diplomat in Nepal, who had fallen under official displeasure for urging the use of the vernacular languages instead of English in the education of the Indians. Under Hodgson's guidance Beatrice began to question the supremacy of Western over Eastern civilisation, and although she found Hodgson's own pedantic book unreadable, she devoured many volumes on Indian and Chinese thought and literature which 'threw into the shade for me the barbaric Jehovah of the Jews and the mean doings of the kings'. Soon she had reached a state of mind in which Buddhism seemed superior to Christianity: 'The mysterious Nirvana and the attainment of the unconditional blessedness by ridding yourself of your own personality, fascinated my imagination.' Finally, though, Beatrice came to believe that Buddhism was based on a falsehood, that man's aim in life was to 'rid himself of the evil of existence'.[25]

The spiritual void was next filled for Beatrice in 1876 by a new religion, that of science. 'The God was The Unknowable: the prophet was Herbert Spencer,' she claimed, as she threw herself exuberantly into Spencer's teachings. 'Mr Spencer's *First Principles* has had certainly a very great influence on my feelings and thoughts. It has made me feel so happy and contented ...' On first reading Spencer Beatrice became convinced she had reached a resting-place for her soul, and would be able to live her life according to reason, and the dictates of Science, 'without denying the impulse to reverence the Power that controlled the Universe'. Yet all too soon it proved a chimera, having little to offer her troubled spirit in which the impulse to pray was very strong. 'The religion of science has its dark side ... And to those whose lives are one continual suffering it has but one word to say –

suicide . . . it is a dreadful thought.'[26] For the next six years Beatrice struggled to find fulfilment in the religion of science, and failed. Her sense of mysticism was too strong to deny the reality of God's presence she experienced in prayer.

Spiritualism was also popular, and even a scientist like Galton dabbled in it for a while. Beatrice, Maggie, Theresa and Lawrencina experimented with table-tapping, until Beatrice's departure for Germany with Mary Playne, Arthur, and their adopted daughter Polly, ended their experiments. The Playnes had one natural child, a son called Bill. They were a strange choice of travelling companions for Beatrice, since Arthur had already been found wanting on the American trip, and Beatrice had little in common with Mary, who had 'a grudge against "intellectual people" and "learning" because she feels she is "inferior" or, rather, that they think her inferior. She has the same grudge against the family, particularly Mother.'[27] No sooner had they left London than Beatrice was regretting it, and feeling she was 'a long way on the road to absolute boredom'. By way of diversion she began a mild flirtation, only to receive a stern reprimand from Mary. Regretfully she dreamed of the London Season she was missing.

As the summer progressed their tour improved. Beatrice could only just tolerate Mary, who was prepared to talk of nothing but personalities, but she had made a new friend, in fact her first friend outside the family: Cary Darling, the Playnes' governess. Cary Darling was one of the first women to go to Newnham College, and shared Beatrice's interests in German and in particular in Goethe. 'At Wiesbaden our rooms opened on to each other; in her room we used to sit late into the night with our feet cocked high on the china stove . . . smoking cigarettes and talking philosophy.' Small and delicate, neatly and simply dressed, Cary Darling, whose 'breeding was somewhat mixed' and who therefore had to work for her living, offered an insight into a different way of life. Beatrice's tales of London Society were met with contempt, and Cary assured Beatrice that she preferred the life of a governess, 'hard though it be', to hers.[28]

As the leisurely tour continued, Maggie missed Beatrice increasingly. 'I shall indeed be glad to have you here. You may imagine how "hipped" I am getting all day among the lonely books and mountains, for we do not see a soul,' she wrote from Rusland where she was keeping her mother company in her father's absence. 'When Bee comes home she and I will develop into full-blown prigs,'[29] she told Theresa, and the two sisters planned to spend Christmas alone together. In November Beatrice returned, and with a final pitying thought for Mary

– 'how she can be happy with such an inferior man I cannot understand'[30] – thankfully said goodbye to the Playnes.

The quiet loneliness of Rusland Hall did not suit Beatrice after the stimulus of foreign travel, and the purposelessness of her life dogged her thoughts. It was 'the old story of anaemia; want of employment, which makes life almost torture, a silent misery, all the more painful because apparently causeless'.[31] Beatrice reproached herself for not sufficiently appreciating the walks in the beautiful countryside with 'my dearest old Father'. Why could she not enjoy life's simple pleasures? Was her loss of faith to blame? The hours dragged, as she read Goethe and Ruskin, and mooned over the hills. Theresa, happily diverted in London, was full of sympathy. 'You poor old girl, I so often think of you and wish you could be here,' she wrote, 'your bright mind and nature would find more scope and appreciation than it can in the solitary moors of Rusland; though *there is a great gain* in those perhaps rather dreary hours of thinking and pondering which will bring a great return to you someday.'[32] Theresa knew the dark demon of depression which haunted all her sisters. She sent 'a consoling note to poor dear little you, who no doubt are quite happy among your moors and untidy room, full of art and studies of stones and moss and figures and Grecian History and Shakespeare . . . A little gossip will keep you from growing into that dreaminess which is apt to induce biliousness and poor spirits, and Heaven defend you from those old enemies of the Heyworth-Potter nature. You see *I* am not in the grips of their clutches and can afford to imagine *you* are.'[33]

How Beatrice might have benefited from going to Newnham like Cary Darling; had Lawrencina and Richard Potter's son grown up, a spell at Oxford or Cambridge would have been his likely destiny, but although higher education was now increasingly available to girls, nothing could have been further from the Potters' minds for Beatrice, the most underestimated of their children.

VI

THE OPEN CAGE

'At present I feel like a caged animal, bound up by the luxury,
comfort and respectability of my position. I can't get a training
that I want without neglecting my duty.'
Beatrice Webb Diary, 31 March 1883

THE MARRIAGE OF MAGGIE to Henry Hobhouse in 1880 was a bitter blow for Beatrice. It left a hiatus in her life and exacerbated the chronic psychosomatic illnesses which had long plagued her. Although clever, Maggie had never shown the same disinterested love of learning as Beatrice, writing, 'I have rather come to Faust's opinion, that mere learning is not worth much, unless one has some particular aim which alas! poor women can hardly have, unless they could have some idea of their future; blessed spinsterhood and holy matrimony are equally on the cards, including every description of the states therein.'[1]

Knowing Maggie's intellectual capabilities, Beatrice had often chided her for not breaking out from Society life, but Maggie knew her own mind, and her plans did not include spinsterhood. She was of the firm opinion that Beatrice's best course of action would be to display herself in the London marriage free-for-all. 'It's a good thing you two are going to have a ball party,' Maggie wrote to Beatrice in 1879 when she was in Egypt. 'My being away will enable you to take the initiative, so that when I return you will be established as mistress of ceremonies – I shall be quite glad to resign to you. You ask if I am making up my mind to a change of life. No, not for a year or two, until I am near thirty and can see pretty clearly some line in which I might persevere and be useful . . . I feel more and more our right to keep one's heart pure and unhard, for it's a very unlovely thing to be withered and old of heart . . .'[2]

Maggie's waiting game proved fruitful. In Henry Hobhouse she found the rich and eligible mate she was seeking, and within a few weeks they were engaged. On her marriage in October 1880 she became mistress of Hadspen House, near Wincanton, and an estate of two and a half thousand acres, and was admitted to the ranks of the gentry. Hadspen House, dating from 1685, was a handsome mansion of yellow stone, approached through avenues of elms with a fine view over Somerset and Dorset. Five Henry Hobhouses in succession built up the family fortune, and it was the second Henry Hobhouse who, in 1785, bought Hadspen for £19,250.[3] Maggie had surpassed all her sisters in marrying well. Although Georgina and Daniel moved to Mottisfont Abbey, a thirteenth-century priory set amongst the water-meadows of the Test valley, which they leased from 1884, they could not match Maggie's splendour.[4]

The Hobhouses spent their honeymoon in Italy, and Beatrice joined them for a classical tour. She was following in the footsteps of her parents, but for Beatrice it was to be a less happy experience. In Rome she met up with Theresa and the Hobhouses, but she could hardly bear the happiness of the young couple. 'Henry and Margaret are here, silently happy. One would hardly know her to be the same woman as the discontented, original, interesting young person who used to be so fascinating to me . . . Now she has found in Henry Hobhouse just the man to complete her, a man utterly without worldliness or power to compromise with evil.'[5] Beatrice lamented both their lost friendship and her lost religion as she stood before the High Altar at St Peter's and was moved by the solemn beauty of the mass. The 'emotional faculty', as she called it, 'unceasingly insists that there is something above and around us which is worthy of absolute devotion and devout worship . . . the great Father and Creator, the perfect object for devotion'; yet her 'logical faculty' denied his existence. Spiritually confused, jealous of the Hobhouses' intimacy, and completely lacking in artistic feeling, Beatrice made dutiful notes on Giotto, Botticelli and Leonardo da Vinci and gazed unmoved upon their masterpieces. The Roman climate, which alternated between searing heat and intense cold, depressed her, and she hated being with Maggie, who was already queasily pregnant with her first son Stephen – 'the natural result of the conditions of married existence', as Beatrice observed.[6]

At Christmas all the museums closed, and Beatrice took to her bed for a fortnight to be nursed by Theresa. As she lay in bed in her queer-shaped room reading George Eliot and Balzac, she had the consolation of avoiding the 'different types of inferior English people' in the pension, but it was a disgruntled party which at last met Richard Potter at San Remo in April. Of them all Beatrice was the most disconsolate: 'The incapability produced by the relaxing climate, the deadly ennui from the absence of any occupation and of sympathetic companionship had forced me into an abnormal condition of both body and soul out of which I have not yet emerged . . .'[7] On closer acquaintance she had decided that Henry Hobhouse did not improve, and his deficiencies were 'acting like a wet blanket on Maggie's intellect. His own inferiority makes him disapprovingly suspicious of her great freedom, originality and variety of thought.' Beatrice mourned not only the loss of the sweet intimacy with Maggie, but also the limiting of her intellect to the level of Henry's.

Daffodils had pushed their heads through the dark earth when Beatrice returned to Standish, and its spring loveliness was balm to her homesick eyes. Her spirits revived rapidly and a temporary estrangement with her mother was overcome, but that summer Theresa followed Maggie to the altar, marrying a rising young barrister, Alfred Cripps, whose elder brother William Harrison Cripps had already married Blanche in 1877. Apart from Blanche, all the Potter girls had so far 'married well' by Victorian criteria, but Willie Cripps was a surgeon, a member of a profession of dubious respectability. Not only was he a surgeon, albeit an increasingly successful one, who later held a senior post at St Bartholomew's Hospital, but he had very little money, and in Potter eyes Blanche was marrying into poverty. Although from a respectable family, Willie was of unprepossessing appearance and manner, 'at first sight repellent, almost unclean looking, with the manners and conversation of a clever cad', as Beatrice, who was as snobbish as the rest of her family, wrote.[8] The Potters would never have countenanced him for Maggie or Theresa, but for the strange and fey Blanche he was acceptable. So absent-minded was Blanche that she once hailed a hansom cab to return home to 4 Stratford Place, just off Oxford Street, and instructed the driver to go to Oxford. Not until they were well into the country did she notice her mistake.

Blanche and Willie were grateful to be lent the Argoed for their honeymoon, and Willie tried his hand at fishing. 'Willie is trying to catch a trout . . . He has got a salmon licence this morning and we shall go to the Wye this afternoon.' Blanche added, 'Willie and I are on such perfectly easy terms together that we might have been married for centuries and the time when we were not husband and wife seems already quite traditional; there is no doubt that we are very happily suited to each other.'[9]

The marriages in quick succession of Blanche, Maggie and Theresa radically altered Beatrice's circumstances; no longer was she one of six or seven girls clamouring for attention but, since Kate was working in London, was now the only sister left at home with her mother and

Rosy. 'It is sad this last final break-up of the home life with all its ups and downs, through which we have been loving companions . . . Now I am left alone, with this "problematical" younger sister,' mused Beatrice,[10] for Rosy, who like Beatrice suffered from chronic ill-health, was considered difficult to manage. Lawrencina's efforts to make a scholar of Rosy had precipitated a nervous collapse; Rosy's periods stopped and she lost weight and suffered from 'manias',[11] such as the obsessive need constantly to look up the same words in a dictionary. Yet for Beatrice there was some consolation as the icy relationship between her and Lawrencina began at last to thaw. Increasingly Lawrencina came to understand that in Beatrice she had a daughter who shared her aspirations and abilities, and the same keen intellect animated them both. 'I shall know twelve languages before I die, said she to me with a triumphant smile, as . . . we paced up and down the measured span of gravel walk for a measured hour.' Lawrencina transferred her hopes to Beatrice, with 'a caressing glance and a sympathetic suggestion that I might succeed where she had failed, and become a writer of books'.[12]

The prickly and acerbic tone of their earlier correspondence had softened in a fresh appreciation of each other's qualities, and a new note of love crept into their letters. When Beatrice left for her Italian trip with Theresa she wrote affectionately, 'It is exceedingly kind of you, dearest Mother, to let me have this treat – but you may be sure that it will strengthen and not break my love for my parents and my home . . . If you feel at all low at being left, you must send for us.'[13] Hearing that her mother was not well, Beatrice was writing again on 5 November with a note of anxiety, 'I was so sorry to hear that you were not so well – You must please take care of yourself as all your nine daughters intend to have you with them a long time . . . I am sure, mother, if you would only consent to do as little and to take as much care of your health as the majority of your daughters are obliged to do, you would have many bright years of influence and love before you . . . ever best love, dearest Mother.'[14] By 21 November the depressed and homesick Beatrice was writing, 'Goodbye, dearest Mother, I constantly think of you and Father in England.'[15]

Lawrencina responded warmly to Beatrice's descriptions of Rome, which awakened old memories of St Peter's and the Vatican. 'It is delightful to think of you so interested in playing scenes so dear to our memory . . .'[16] Beatrice must have hidden her misery at Maggie's happiness from her mother, for Lawrencina wrote, 'I am glad, my dear child, that for once you discovered that life is worth living – I have always thought it so for the external pleasures it affords.' Lawrencina's thoughts were turning also to the 'moral forces' which increasingly preoccupied her as she grew older, and which 'are best seen,' she told Beatrice, 'when we keep ourselves secure from the urgent desires of worldliness in perfect confidence in the one master force in whom all other forces work together for good.'[17] This ascetic, puritanical streak in Lawrencina found an answering chord in Beatrice.

Although Lawrencina had 'a zest for living', in Beatrice's words, 'which left her at the age of sixty amazingly young alike in body and mind',[18] after Christmas 1880 her strength began to fade. She wrote to Beatrice, who was ailing in Rome, 'My dearest Bee, I am so glad to hear that you are stronger again . . . I have been ill almost ever since Xmas Day. I have been longing to write to you both but have only been equal to letters some days . . .'[19] Mary Playne, Beatrice's elder sister, wrote in February 1881, after Beatrice was again ill with ennui and the Italian climate, 'We are so very sorry to hear of your relapse . . . Mama is very well though certainly not so strong as she was a year ago. She is working awfully hard – doing a certain amount of list taking, writing to the papers about Ireland and generally doing about twice as much as would be within the capability of her daughters . . .'[20]

Religion provided a consolation for Lawrencina as she grew weaker, and as death approached she found the peace which had eluded her for most of her life. She continued to write to Beatrice in a fine spidery scrawl which covered every inch of the paper, turning the paper sideways to write over the top of her original script in order to save paper, a parsimonious practice which made her always illegible handwriting almost indecipherable. 'I have been so sorry to hear of your continued delicacy,' she consoled Beatrice. 'There is nothing for it but to rest that little brain and those eyes of yours.' Lawrencina wished that her daughter 'could be aprised [sic] that the source of life and light was *personally near* to you, waiting for your love, that He might enter in to cheer and support you both physically and spiritually, and to show you brighter glories than lie on the surface of things. I often find myself too weak to do much and to think much, but the weakness has results . . .' She was convinced that 'death does introduce one to a fuller consciousness of life'.[21]

In April 1882 Lawrencina became suddenly and seriously ill with kidney failure, and Richard Potter brought her home to Standish, where Kate and Beatrice did not at first realise how ill she was. They put her to bed and Beatrice slept with her that night, stroking and soothing Lawrencina, who was in pain until given an injection of morphia. Beatrice continued to nurse her mother with Kate, and Maggie Harkness, Beatrice's second cousin, was sent for to help. 'It was one continual strain to think and act,' Beatrice recorded. 'I was continually with Mother until Wednesday at 3 o'clock in the morning, when I left her for good, and only returned twice again for two short moments to give her the last farewell kiss and to take poor little weeping Rosy to her deathbed.'[22] On 13 April Lawrencina died peacefully; as Beatrice watched her mother in her last hours she became more convinced than ever of the impossibility of life after death. 'As I looked at our mother dying, I *felt* it was a final dissolution of body and soul, an end of that personality which we call spirit . . . a new and wondrous faith has arisen within me – a faith in goodness, in God. I must pray, I do pray and feel better for it . . .'[23]

Beatrice reproached herself for not loving and appreciating her mother more. 'Poor little Mother. Looking back I see how bitterly she must have felt our want of affection and sympathy and for that I feel remorse . . . I never knew how much she had done for me, how many of my best habits I had taken from her, how strong would be the influence of her personality when pressure had gone – a pressure wholesome and in the right direction, but applied without tact.'[24] For the first time Beatrice identified with her mother's solitary path: 'When I work with many odds against me, for a far distant and perhaps unattainable end, I think of her and her intellectual strivings which we were too ready to call useless, and which yet will be the originating impulse of all my ambition, urging me towards something better in action and thought.'[25]

Paradoxically, although Beatrice mourned her mother's death, it was to revolutionise her life. It released her from the frustration and boredom of behaving as a dutiful daughter, which by the age of twenty-four was largely responsible for her constant attacks of 'biliousness'. As she herself acknowledged, 'From being a subordinate, carrying out directions, and having to fit into the framework of family circumstance, studies and travels, friendships and flirtations, I became a principal, a person in authority, determining not only my own but other people's conduct.' For someone with Beatrice's strong personality, it was a blessed release from suffocating conformity to the wishes of others; it rescued her from further 'daydreaming' and the miserable ill-health which had assailed Florence Nightingale, who had to suffer for so much longer the demands of her mother, Fanny. Now Beatrice was free, deliciously free to indulge her own wishes and to bask in her new-found importance as 'a busy hostess in town and country, entertaining my father's, my own and my sisters' friends'.[26]

'My duty now lies clearly before me,' wrote Beatrice, '– to Father and Rosy first, secondly to the home as a centre for the whole family.' But it was because she was now in her mother's place as 'a person in authority' that she was able to find her duty congenial. Richard Potter, lonely and bereft at Lawrencina's death, allowed Beatrice a large role in decision-making, and she became his business confidante and secretary, being present at many of his meetings and taking notes, a skill she later found useful as a social investigator. Richard Potter left it to Beatrice to 'settle the why, when and wherefore of the expenditure of a considerable income; indeed he had more than once suggested that if I "did not want to marry" I might become his recognised associate in business',[27] a suggestion Beatrice found flattering. She had never been her father's particular favourite, but now she was his trusted counsellor to whom he turned in his silent grief.

The result of this change in Beatrice's circumstances was that overnight her illnesses vanished. From being sickly and depressed, 'An anaemic girl, always paying for spells of dissipation or study by periods of nervous exhaustion, often of positive illness, I became an exceptionally energetic woman, carrying on, persistently and methodically, several separate, and, in some ways, conflicting, phases of life – undergoing, in fact, much of the strain and stress of a multiple personality.'[28] For although Beatrice was determined to educate herself, she confined her studying to the hours between five and eight in the morning, as did many other intellectual Victorian women such as Harriet Martineau and Florence Nightingale. As Beatrice acknowledged, the Victorian code of feminine domesticity demanded that an unmarried daughter should spend all her time in either serving the demands of her family or in the social circle to which she belonged, entertaining and being entertained, paying calls, attending dinner parties and balls, in furtherance of the prospect of a 'good marriage'. Beatrice's feelings about her future life were ambivalent; she had not yet turned her back on Society, and she was determined to do her duty by her family.

A large part of this duty entailed being responsible for Rosy, although, as Beatrice confessed, 'I acknowledge that I am not equal to the position of mother to her, perhaps I confess, too, that my effort is rather a half-hearted one – that I am not willing to sacrifice my own interests to hers . . .'[29] Nevertheless, Beatrice was as concerned as the rest of the sisterhood about Rosy, and even if she had not been, there was a 'solid phalanx' of her seven married sisters, and seven brothers-in-law, standing by to see that she did not falter in her duty. Increasingly Beatrice began to resent her sisters' criticism and what she interpreted as their interference. Her blue-stocking tendencies particularly irritated Mary, who burst into her bedroom early one morning 'to find me sitting by an open window in an untidy dressing-gown, with dishevelled hair, and pale and spotty complexion, straining hand and brain to copy out and solve some elementary algebraical problems. "What nonsense this is," she began, half chaff, half compliment, "trying to be a blue-stocking when you are meant to be a pretty woman." "This is *my* room and *my* time – go away," I snapped at her.'[30]

Relations did not improve between Beatrice and Mary, and in November 1882 Mary wrote to apologise for the 'slight strain in their relationship'. 'Explanations are unsatisfactory as my inferior education puts me at a disadvantage with you but I will just say what I think . . . I was really sorry for what I said in the boudoir about your hair and know it is impertinent to remark to you upon your appearance and dress – but you gave me my rebuke, which I took in silence and acknowledged as just and I think it was strong enough for the occasion. I understand from your criticism of me . . . that you have a great objection to any criticism from any of your married sisters, or at least from me. Very well, dear, so be it – but you must please not ask me for my opinion on any subject about which you are sensitive. In this way you will be able to grow apart as you wish, unfettered by the discipline of rubbing up against a husband, and I think without the discipline and responsibility which children bring. We poor married women cannot order our lives by our own ideals, but must adapt ourselves to the practical necessities of our circumstances.'[31] But Beatrice did not wish to adapt any more to the domestic code her sisters supported, but to spread her wings, and no doubt was in their eyes strong-willed, hot-tempered and egotistical in making her wishes known.

Mary returned tentatively to the fray. 'The fact of your being in the position for the next few years of making Rosy what she is to be for the rest of her life is really the only excuse for the criticism of your married sisters, and in looking at the material this is a task which would strain the common sense and anxious care of any woman – at least if that child were thrown on my charge, I should feel desperately anxious.'[32] Undaunted by Beatrice's aloof attitude, she continued to ply her with advice about Rosy: 'She wants a certain amount of liberty to go her own way and make herself disagreeable, and then there will be a chance of her growing up, and in place of the mock humility will come real humility.'[33]

Although Beatrice was both conscientious and genuinely sympathetic towards Rosy, the seed of ambition was growing quietly within her. She was determined to find a purpose in life apart from a conventional marriage. As she put it to herself, 'The question remained, how am I to live, and for what object?' Only through study could she discover her aim. Painfully she struggled with mathematics, puzzling over geometry and algebra but, 'I might as well have attempted to turn water into wine.'[34] Reading Spencer's *Psychology* proved an easier task and Beatrice found that her three hours of study before the household came to life were the happiest ones of the day. Her sisters' scorn for her efforts at self-improvement was withering. 'Beatrice's intellect, or rather what she attempts to develop into an intellect,' Georgie snapped to Mary, 'what's the good of it? It's no use to her or anyone else – it's all done to make a show before old and young philosophers.'[35] Mary tried to be a little more tactful. 'I have every reason to believe that Mr Spencer's opinion of your intelligent and patient power of work is correct but I also know of my own experience that your social and practical powers are considerable and you have ambition and self control and I think you are well suited for a married life.'[36]

Maggie Harkness, Beatrice's envious cousin, was equally impatient with Beatrice's discontent. 'You are young, pretty, rich, clever, what more do you want? I expect you get on well in society, why can't you be satisfied? . . . I wonder if you would be perfectly happy if you married a man you loved and admired, rich enough and of good enough family and who would let you manage your own life and go your own way. I wonder if you would be perfectly happy! . . . There is no career – no profession for women.'[37]

Neither scorn nor persuasion had any effect on Beatrice. She burned with the need to find a career or 'craft', as she called it, which would satisfy her, and she toyed with the idea of writing a novel. The advantage of the profession of novelist was that there was no need for painful and time-consuming research, and writing was no more pretentious than the music or drawing to which women usually turned. Beatrice was aware that she had literary talent and an aptitude for hard work, and she was fascinated by the multitude of Londoners, the phantom figures who passed her by in the streets. Could she portray their secret lives in fiction? 'I have no ambition to be an intellectual scullery maid,' she wrote in her diary, 'but some natures have a taste for preparing food and the great multitude are intellectually toothless and require their meat minced.' In fact 'mincing meat', or the analysis of society, was where both her talent and inclination lay: 'Society should be to the novel-writer a laboratory in which he is hourly and daily engaged in observation and possibly in experiment.'[38] Beatrice's diary reveals her merciless pen and excellent gift for dialogue and characterisation, but she lacked psychological insight into fellow human beings, whom she saw as specimens rather than individuals.

Immediately after her mother's death Beatrice had reverted again to religion for consolation in her grief. As she shut up Standish in preparation for the family's departure for London, wandering through the familiar fields by the light of the setting sun, she found a mystical communion with God which, like the Romantic poets, she so often experienced out of doors. 'I paused, from above seemed to come some inspiration, I bowed my head. "Thy servant", words suddenly made real to me, and hallowed. Strange these feelings are, of an outward presence, this sense of down-coming help – this real answer to prayer.'[39] This new-found power of prayer helped her through the next ten years, a power she could not explain, although she continued to put her faith in the scientific method in her work. The religion of science had brought her no comfort; only in prayer did Beatrice feel conscious of an all-pervading spiritual force. Religion was not accessible to reason, as she would have wished, but she needed its support: 'Religion is love; in no case is it logic . . . for science is bankrupt in deciding the destiny of man.'[40]

During the 1880s the widespread faith in science as the solution to man's ills did not abate. Charismatic figures such as Charles Bradlaugh, the well-known atheist and 'most popular demagogue of the hour', commanded enormous support. Huge crowds flocked to hear him speak, especially when he was joined by Annie Besant, the greatest female orator of the day. The relationship between Bradlaugh and Annie was close but platonic; she was not free to marry after having left her clergyman husband, Walter Besant, and the custody of her children, to fall under the spell of the handsome and persuasive Bradlaugh. He and Annie bestrode the country, preaching scientific materialism and the 'Fruits of Philosophy', or contraception, a daring course which was to lead them to the law courts.

The working classes listened and were convinced. Halls of Science sprang up in working-class districts, for not only had the intelligentsia become intoxicated by the discoveries of science; man had become, it was believed, 'King of animals, lord of the elements, and sovereign of steam and electricity'. Optimism was unbounded in the power of science to suppress the forces of evil and man's base instincts, and this trusting faith in science elevated man's intellect to the status of a god who could transform the planet earth into paradise: 'Disease will be extirpated, the causes of decay will be removed, immortality will be invented. And then the earth being small, man will emigrate into space and will cross airless Saharas which separate planet from planet, and sun from sun ... Man will be perfect; he will be a creator; he will therefore be what the vulgar worship as God.'[41] Such Victorian faith in the perfectibility of man was to be shattered in the bloody carnage of World War I, but in 1882 Beatrice shared the conviction of many of her contemporaries that the scientific method of observation and experiment, hypothesis and verification could be applied to the study of the social problems.

Beatrice continued to study mathematics, although she was conscious of the paucity of her intellect compared to the powers of the 'really clever men' she met. 'All my duties lie in the practical direction. Why should I, wretched little frog, try and puff myself into a professional?'[42] she wondered. She persevered with her reading of Spencer's *First Principles*, finding it stiff, yet comforting in its primary truth, which was the indestructibility of matter. This meant that 'the fearful chasm between Life and Death in the imagination of the conscious being is but one little step in the universe of circles'.[43] Spencer's reputation was to dissolve in the next century, but in the 1880s his status had never been higher. Beatrice copied long extracts from his works into her diary and wrote careful criticisms, although admitting she found some of his theories unintelligible; she never ceased to believe in Spencerian evolution, and to retain an awed admiration for the members of the 'X Club', Huxley, Tyndall, and especially Francis Galton.

Beatrice's desire for some sort of scientific training even led her into the laboratory of her brother-in-law, the 'repellent' Willie Cripps, who was researching cancer of the rectum. The silent Beatrice stood beside Willie, puzzled but attentive, as he prepared microscopic sections for examination. She also took physiology lessons from a woman science teacher, enjoying the quiet study in a leafy corner of London, where, in the cool laboratory, she patiently pored over the microscope and enjoyed the business of dissection; the specimens 'do not distress me but give me genuine pleasure to pick to pieces'. But her thirst for knowledge was only partially slaked by this period of scientific study; part of the trouble was that she lacked the necessary time for any serious medical training, which, 'even when open to women, was flagrantly out of bounds for a woman who had my extensive and complicated home duties'.[44] Also, natural science bored her. Spencer urged her to study botany, but she knew in her heart it was the human animal that fascinated her and aroused her curiosity. The zeitgeist of the late nineteenth century led Beatrice, so she believed, to wish to study men and women, 'their past and present conditions of life, their thoughts and feelings and their constantly changing behaviour',[45] as they had never been scrutinised before.

When Beatrice left Standish in February 1883 for Prince's Gate to take up her duties as her father's hostess and a mother-substitute for Rosy, she thought she was aware of the strains of the rival demands on her time and energy involved in trying to satisfy all sides of her 'multiple personality'. Society could not be avoided, and to make time for her own interests would be difficult; therefore she had decided to follow the path of duty. 'On the whole the balance is in favour of Society. It is going with the stream, and pleasing my people.' It was a resolution she had found impossible to keep. Not only did her early morning studying spill over into the rest of the day, and occupy more and more of her thoughts, but Society, whose whirl she had enjoyed as a teenage girl, now became increasingly irksome to her. The whole burden of choosing the London house, moving the horses and carriages, buying the necessary elaborate wardrobe, and organising dinners, dances, picnics and weekend house parties all fell upon Beatrice's shoulders. But it was not merely the time-consuming aspect of Society which now irritated her, so much as the futility of a life of gossip and small-talk of which she became more and more critical. 'We are in the land of luxury, we are living in an atmosphere of ease, satiety and boredom . . .' she wrote in February 1883.[46] At a party at the House of Commons ('one or two such would last one a life-time') she found it impossible to make conversation to the empty-headed women of the upper classes, whose pea-sized brains were, she concluded, far smaller than those of their husbands. 'Could it be otherwise with the daily life of ladies in our society? What is there in the life which is so attractive? How can intelligent women wish to marry into the set where there is this social regime?' she demanded.

Her diary became decorated with conversational sketches of society women, whose days were spent bemoaning the servant problem, name-dropping, and boasting of their latest acquisitions. Beatrice's pen was as sharp as Margot Tennant's as she described how she interrupted 'Lady L, a great heiress of common extraction' complaining to stout, plain Mrs B, 'gorgeously got up', that 'the last cook who applied to me asked £250 per year, perquisites and freedom to buy his own materials, and his Sundays to himself . . . really the presumption and dishonesty of servants nowadays is preposterous. I found out only the other day that my cook was disposing of £14 of butter per week.' 'Good gracious,' exclaimed Beatrice, 'how very disgraceful!' 'But it is quite impossible to check it,' prattled Lady L. 'One's whole household is in the pay of the tradesmen who supply it.' 'The worst is that whatever you pay, for *that* after all one *does* not mind, you cannot get what you want,' complained her friend. 'Now *do* you think it a right thing for the butler to be out every evening, and not only the butler, but the first footman, and leave only the boy of the establishment to bring up coffee?'[47] And so on and so on, until Beatrice thought her head would burst.

Only into her diary could Beatrice pour her feelings of resentment and confusion; she felt, she claimed, like a caged animal. 'I can't get a training that I want without neglecting my duty.' Certain of her sisters' disapproval, she had become increasingly secretive. 'I silently withdrew all my own aspirations and plans for self-culture and self-expression from family discussion – a reserve which entailed isolation and loneliness.' Her diary served as a looking-glass for a life in which duty struggled with inclination, belief with unbelief, and the path ahead was still unclear. Surely, one day, prayed Beatrice, 'I shall have the veil withdrawn and be allowed to gaze unblinded on the narrow limits of my own possibilities.'[48]

VII

THE SERVICE OF MAN

'We have too long forgotten, that if man has been given the
bodily strength and the intellectual pre-eminence, it is the
woman who is the conscience of the world.'
Ellice Hopkins, rescue worker among fallen women.[1]

IN 1883 BEATRICE BELIEVED she was borne up by the Victorian 'time-spirit', that powerful mood of the 1880s which, in her own analysis, seized her and compelled her to turn away from Society and train as a social investigator. She was conscious of a new motive, 'the transference of the emotion of self-sacrificing service from God to man', which powerfully influenced the 'urban gentry'[2] and persuaded members of the upper-middle classes to live among and serve the poor in the East End of London. Some of those among whom Beatrice mixed experienced a sense of guilt at the chasm between rich and poor. Arnold Toynbee's confession to the working-class, 'We – the middle classes . . . we have neglected you; we have sinned against you grievously – not knowing always, but still we have sinned, and let us confess it . . .'[3] found an echo in the hearts of many of his contemporaries. Samuel Barnett, the frail and delicate vicar of St Jude's, Whitechapel, and founder of Toynbee Hall, turned down the offer of a comfortable parish in Oxfordshire. 'I can recall the realisation of the immensity of our task, the fear of failure to reach or help those crowds of people, with vice and lawlessness written across their faces,' wrote his wife Henrietta. 'Which way shall we decide? . . . Let us try it, but we may fail,' answered Barnett.[4]

At a time when orthodox Christianity was under attack, C. S. Loch, who earlier might have become a clergyman, instead found an outlet for his desire for service in becoming secretary of the Charity Organisation Society in 1875. Octavia Hill, a founder of the society, recalled her childhood distress as she gazed from the windows of her home in Russell Square on the poor: 'There the first knowledge of misery and poverty came to me, the first real feeling of poverty for ourselves . . . I had sat and watched, through the great windows, the London poor pass in rain and fog. There I sat and cried . . . at the remembrance of Tottenham Court Road on Saturday night, with its haggard faces.'[5]

A complex kaleidoscope of emotions underlay the surge in philanthropy in the second half of the nineteenth century. Class guilt, pity, fear and genuine religious sentiment all played a part, and from the late eighteenth century the devotion of women in visiting the poor had been marked. Many women agreed with Hannah More that 'Charity is the calling of a lady, the care of the poor is her profession'.[6] Woman's nature was seen as particularly fitted to charity; defined in fiction, poetry, advice books and medical textbooks as fixed on the affections rather than animated by reason; self-denying, modest, spiritual and morally superior to that of man, it was increasingly seen as complementary to man's in the exercise of philanthropy. 'We want her sense of the law of love to complete man's sense of the law of justice,' urged Frances Power Cobbe, philanthropist and member of the Langham Place Group. 'We want her genius for detail, her tenderness for age and suffering, her comprehension of the want of childhood to complete man's gigantic charities.'[7] Woman would be man's helpmate, her role a secondary one based on accepted gender differences, in which she might remain within her separate domestic sphere and not trespass into public life. Female philanthropy, however, from quiet beginnings, pushed out almost imperceptibly into the interstices of society, and for many women before Beatrice it proved the path to emancipation.

The mission to the poor which Hannah More opened up in the villages of rural Somerset set an example which an increasing number of middle-class women followed, finding in parish visiting an occupation which easily fitted into the domestic routine, a welcome escape, yet which exercised of the domestic virtues in which they felt themselves competent. But it was not only married women but also spinsters who found a solution to idleness in serving their fellow men. In 1861 there were estimated to be 750,000 spinsters over thirty.[8] 'Surplus' women, said W. R. Greg, made up 'a number quite disproportionate and quite abnormal . . . There are hundreds of thousands of women . . . who, not having the natural duties and labours of wives and mothers, have to carve out artificially and painfully sought occupations for themselves . . .'[9] These 'redundant' women spearheaded woman's mission in the workhouses, ragged schools and the slums. The qualities of compassion and self-sacrifice which, it was argued, belonged to women, were exercised in philanthropy, and women who did not find fulfilment in biological motherhood could become mothers in spirit of the poor. The model of the family, a powerful icon for Victorian society, validated this role for single women, and led them to claim, 'We cannot make a home for ourselves, but we can make ourselves a home for others.'[10] Florence Nightingale angrily claimed that 'the real mothers and fathers of the human race are NOT the fathers and mothers according to the flesh . . . for every one of my 18,000 children, for every one of those poor tiresome Harley Street creatures I have expended more motherly feeling and action in a week than my mother has expended for me in thirty-seven years.'[11]

Faith in Christ underpinned much philanthropy.[12] 'Charity' was the Greek word for love and, as such, meant bringing the transforming power of love into the homes of the poor in obedience to the example of Christ and other scriptural models such as Mary Magdalene and Mary the mother of James. Shame at the yawning gulf between the classes which was the by-product of capitalism fused with Christian teaching to form a powerful catalyst in the philanthropic movement.

In September 1884, while on holiday in Bavaria with Maggie Harkness, the twenty-six-year-old Beatrice read Comte's *Catechism of Positive Religion*, and copied in large letters: 'Altruism alone can enable us to live in the highest and truest sense. To live for others is the only means of developing the whole existence of man . . .'[13] Comte substituted Humanity, 'the only true Great Being', for God, and considered human history through theological, metaphysical and scientific stages; in the final scientific stage Comte saw a special role for the intelligentsia who would become 'Priests of Humanity', serving the working class and bringing about social regeneration.

The British Positivists made common cause with the trade unionists to fight for reform in the 1870s, and although their influence was waning by the 1880s, they provided a potent example to the Fabians of how a pressure group might bring about social reform as a possible prelude to social change. Edward Pease, secretary of the Fabian Party, recalled, 'The Religion of Humanity suggested a new heaven, of a sort, and it proposed a new earth, free from all the inequalities of wealth, the preventable suffering, the reckless waste of effort, which we saw around us.'[14]

Beatrice had discussed Positivism within her family circle, particularly regarding the novels of George Eliot, who had herself been converted to Positivism, but it was the close family friendship with Frederic Harrison, the Positivist leader, which led directly to Beatrice's decision to order all Comte's works from the London Library to read with her sister Maggie. In 1879 Beatrice and Maggie had spent a long day on the moors outside Rusland, striding through the mist with their packets of sandwiches and cigarettes in their mackintoshes, discussing Comte's ideas. Maggie, 'with genial smile, glittering black eyes and long wisps of lank brown hair flying in the winds', criticised Comte forcibly, as they sat on a dripping stone wall, dismissing him as a dreadful old French pedant who had kicked religion out of the front door of the human intellect, only to let it sneak in through the servants' hall. Beatrice listened as Maggie ruminated over the idea of a committee of bankers to rule the world, those 'dull but solid' Barclays, Buxtons and Hoares, 'just the sort father likes us to marry, and one likes one's sisters to marry'. What about the working class, who had the vote since 1867, protested Beatrice. 'My dear child, working men just don't count,' retorted Maggie. 'It's money that counts, and the bankers have got it. Not brains but money.' As they jumped off the wall Maggie had the last word. Each person should look after his or her own affairs, including family affairs, 'But there it stops ... As for the service of man, the religion of humanity; Heavens, Beatrice, what *does* it mean? It is just underbred theology with no bishops to bless it.'[15]

'So spake the Ego that denies,' concluded Beatrice sorrowfully. She fell deeply under the influence of Positivist doctrines, writing in 1884, 'Social questions are the vital questions of the day: they take the place of religion.'[16] She listened to Frederic Harrison's lectures at Newton Hall, to which she and her sisters had often been taken during the London Season by their father, and took his opinions increasingly seriously. Once she had dismissed the Harrisons for being too personable and worldly, although the Potter and Harrison families enjoyed mutual dinner parties in London and picnics in the Cliveden Woods, but Frederic Harrison was sympathetic to 'unrecognised intellectuals' (as Beatrice considered herself). Later he taught her to appreciate the importance of the trade union movement and factory legislation, to rediscover the medieval social organisation, as socialists such as William Morris and his Pre-Raphaelite friends were doing, and he became a close friend.

Nevertheless, Beatrice did not take the final step of joining the Positivist Church, which took no account of her own mystical feelings of the presence of God. In 1889, after dining with the Frederic Harrisons and listening to Harrison's address at the Positivist Hall in the City on the text, 'Live for Others', she concluded, 'His address seemed to me forced – a valiant attempt to make a religion out of nothing; a pitiful attempt by poor humanity to turn its head round and worship its tail. Practically we are all positivists; we all make the service of man the leading doctrine of our lives. But in order to serve humanity we need inspiration from a superhuman force towards which we are perpetually striving.'[17]

If Positivism influenced the more angst-ridden members of the leisured classes like Beatrice and the young Charles Booth, a sociologist and future husband of her cousin Mary Macaulay, far greater numbers were motivated by fear, rather than by thoughts of service, when they considered the poor in the early years of the 1880s. The worry that industrial capitalism had created a creature all of its own, a Caliban, who might issue from the cramped and squalid dwellings of the urban working class, and destroy the system that had created it, was increasingly voiced from 1881. Englishmen looked across the Channel to where the revolutionary mob had surged across the barricades during the Paris commune of 1870, and the suspicion grew that the mistreated helot of English industrial society might similarly seek to cast off his chains and emerge from that unexplored hinterland of fashionable London, the East End, to overturn the civilisation which had brought unprecedented wealth to one class, misery and degradation to another.

It was not a new theme: Dickens had satirised Coketown and the dehumanising work done there, Mayhew had described the noisome rookeries of London, and Arnold, Ruskin and John Stuart Mill had all recoiled from the evils of industrial society. As the century waned and, from 1875, agricultural depression followed mid-century prosperity, warnings that the wrong path had been taken increased. Had society based on the 'cash nexus', as Carlyle called it, paid too high a price for wealth creation? In his nostalgic *Merrie England*, which sold one million copies, Robert Blatchford preached of the factory system: 'The thing is evil, it is evil in its origin, in its progress, in its methods, in its motives, and in its effects. No nation can survive whose motive power is greed.'[18]

Poverty was particularly acute in London where the dock labourers were vulnerable to the effects of a hard winter on the declining shipping industry. The dockers, English, Irish, Scottish, German and a few French among them, worked as casual labourers in the five docks, but of twenty to twenty-five thousand, only three or four thousand were in regular employment. Their earnings were 7s 6d a week on average, and rents averaged 2s as against a 'poverty line' of 21s 8d a week. Thousands starved and many applied to the workhouse in the bitter winter of 1861.[19] The anger of the starving poor boiled over, and the mob attacked the barbers' shops in Whitechapel Road and Commercial Road East, until the alarmed shopkeepers shut up their premises. Protests at unemployment grew as the depression bit deeper in the late 1870s and early 1880s, and the shipping and silk weaving industries continued to decline. Only in the casual or sweated trades such as tailoring or jam making were there jobs available, while the housing crisis grew as the Cross and Torrens Acts led to the clearance of the rookeries in which the poor had huddled together. The new railway lines cut a swathe through the most over-populated areas adjoining the City, such as Southwark, Clerkenwell, Finsbury, Shoreditch, Bethnal Green and Whitechapel. Slum housing was ruthlessly levelled to make way for new roads, and the building of New Oxford Street alone displaced over five thousand persons.[20]

Fear and guilt combined to create the Socialist Revival of the 1880s; the poor were perceived as an ever growing menace as their numbers mushroomed (the population of London had doubled between 1841 and 1881).[21] The catalyst for the revival was the American Henry George, whose rousing lectures alerted the élite to the sad paradox of poverty in the midst of plenty. He argued in *Progress and Poverty* that destitution must follow economic growth since wages did not increase as fast as rents, and he saw the landlord as the villain who had reduced the free labourer 'to the helpless and degraded condition of a slave . . . The unequal distribution of wealth is the curse and menace of modern civilisation.'[22]

Socialist societies sprang up all over London, dedicated to what George Bernard Shaw called 'a tremendous smash-up of existing society'.[23] Henry Mayers Hyndman, a top-hatted Old Etonian, had been convinced through his readings of Marx, and many erudite conversations throughout 1881 and 1882 with the Doctor, as he called him, that revolution in England was not only necessary but possible. As the 'powerful, shaggy, untamed old man' denounced the system of wage-slavery, Hyndman, representative of that very class for which Marx reserved his bitterest and most personal hatred, became convinced that Marx was a genius. Determined to popularise Marx's ideas, he wrote *England for All*, which led to the founding of the Social Democratic Federation, a revolutionary Marxist society determined to lead the way in the coming 'convulsion'.

Hyndman fell out with his former colleague, the Pre-Raphaelite artist William Morris, who left to form his own Socialist League, but he reserved his greatest scorn for the Fabian Society, which was formed in 1883 by those, in the opinion of Hyndman, unable to accept Marx's ideas or mix easily with the working-class. Members of the Fabian

Society[24] regarded Hyndman's Social Democratic Federation with equal suspicion. Shaw avoided the 'manual-working pseudo-Marxists', as he contemptuously called them, in favour of the more congenial milieu of the Fabian Society, made up of the middle-class intelligentsia. Despite their squabbles, however, in the early days the differences between the societies were not as great as their shared anger at the capitalist thieves who had oppressed the working class; together they talked revolution, anarchism and insurrection, and although their numbers were small, alarmed the upper and middle classes with their fiery talk. 'Modern civilisation', cried Annie Besant, who by 1883 had deserted atheism for Fabianism, 'is a whited sepulchre in very truth, with its outer coating of princes and lords, of bankers and squires, and within filled with dead men's bones, the bones of the poor who builded it.'[25]

'Educate, Agitate, Organise,' were the Fabian watchwords, but they might not have caused so much unease among the prosperous classes were it not for the sensationalistic disclosures of writers and journalists of the horrors of the slums on the doorsteps of the rich. An anonymous penny pamphlet, *The Bitter Cry of Outcast London*, shocked the middle classes with its tales of incest among the poor; the author, the Rev Andrew Mearns, a Dissenting Minister, had intended to show the connection between religious apathy and slum living, but his revelations that 'seething in the very centre of our great cities, concealed by the thinnest crust of civilisation and decency, is a vast mass of moral corruption ... The vilest practices are looked upon with the most matter of fact indifference,'[26] led to a wave of indignation, pain and sympathy, and even disturbed the consciences of the Queen and the Prince of Wales. At the subsequent Royal Commission on Housing, Lord Shaftesbury gave evidence that the overcrowded conditions in which the poor were forced to live after slum clearances led to sexual promiscuity, and 'ten- or eleven-year-old children were endeavouring to have sexual connection in imitation of their parents'. Sins 'condemned in savages were practised in the heart of the Empire', he told his shocked audience,[27] making an increasingly common comparison between the 'wild races' of the East End and the tribes of the Dark Continent.

Many writers were of the opinion that it was the urban environment which reduced men to the level of brutes, and led them to flock to the gin palaces whose light and glitter held more appeal than their wretched homes. 'Drink is sustenance to these people,' argued G. R. Sims, 'drink dulls their senses and reduces them to the level of the brutes they must be to live in such sties.'[28] But for how much longer would the poor bear their misery uncomplainingly? 'Your slaves are beyond caring for your cries,' warned Shaw, 'they breed like rabbits; and their poverty breeds filth, ugliness, dishonesty, disease, obscenity, drunkenness and murder. In the midst of the riches which their labour piles up for you, their misery rises up too and stifles you . . .'[29]

In 1875 Beatrice's elder sister Kate had left home to be trained by the model housing pioneer Octavia Hill, who was always in need of lady rent-collectors to manage her buildings. Kate was in emotional turmoil, having turned down the proposals of two suitors, but she wrote in her diary that she was 'glad that the pain drove me into a life of independent thought and action'.[30] To begin with she was secretary to Octavia Hill, writing, 'I was taken with a great enthusiasm for her, and expected her to love me in return, but she did not.' Soft words were not a characteristic of Octavia Hill, who was born in 1838 and was twenty years older than Beatrice. She was the granddaughter of Dr Southwood Smith, whose Sanitary Report on the condition of the poor in 1842 had begun to awaken the consciences of the rich to the need for public health reform. Her concern with the housing of the poor was first aroused when she was responsible for Ragged School children who were toymakers, and was shocked by the condition of their homes in Marylebone. In the late 1850s Octavia became secretary of classes for women run in connection with F. D. Maurice's Working Men's College, and could find no satisfactory housing for young families, so when John Ruskin, who had earlier encouraged her to paint, was looking for a suitable cause to which to devote his inheritance, she suggested that he finance the purchase of three houses in Marylebone. Her plan was not to build new model housing blocks, as other benefactors had done, but to do up run-down houses gradually, and not to too high a standard.

Earlier housing organisations such as the Society for Improving the Condition of the Labouring Classes, led by Lord Ashley with the Prince Consort as President, had built from scratch in the 1840s, with a net return of five to six per cent to the investor. In the 1860s Angela Burdett Coutts, who was more concerned with space and comfort for her tenants than a return on her money, built four blocks in Bethnal Green which even welcomed costermongers and their donkeys, and only yielded two and a half per cent. The wealthy American philanthropist George Peabody gave a generous donation in 1862 to set up a housing trust, and within six years was housing two thousand people. Yet none of these housing projects accepted as tenants the very poorest victims of the slum clearance schemes; Peabody's tenants came from the artisan class. The Royal Commission of 1884 to 1885, chaired by Sir Charles Dilke, found that only a little over fifty thousand were living in 'model' dwellings or Octavia Hill's houses. Already the battle lines were drawn up for the developing struggle between the individualism of Octavia Hill and the interventionist view of her opponents, such as the London Trades Council, who argued that 'what the individual cannot do the State and Municipality must accomplish'.[31]

Octavia Hill ran her housing in an efficient if authoritarian manner, pinning her faith in the beneficent effect of her band of lady rent collectors upon the poor which, combined with improved conditions, would, she hoped, build better characters in the tenants. She offered a five per cent return to the investor, and her empire grew as both individuals and organisations such as the Ecclesiastical Commissioners offered her more property to manage. Octavia's 'steadfast mind and dauntless spirit' fired others with enthusiasm, although Henrietta Barnett was sometimes exasperated by her seriousness, complaining that some of her husband's best stories were spoilt in the telling as the unresponsive Octavia fixed her eyes on him, and 'expected high ethics even in a joke'. 'She was small in stature,' recalled Mrs Barnett, 'with a long body and short legs. She did not dress, she only wore clothes which were often unnecessarily unbecoming. She had soft and abundant hair and regular features, but the beauty of her face lay in her brown and very luminous eyes . . . Her mouth was large and mobile, but not improved by laughter. Indeed Miss Octavia was nicest when she was made passionate by her earnestness.'[32]

Kate Potter soon found that the 'strain of life' with Octavia Hill was too much, and went down with bronchitis, which forced her home to Prince's Gardens; in 1876 she took two rooms in Westminster, and made her work among the poor the focus of her life, although she never questioned the causes of poverty.[33] For eight years she worked for Octavia Hill as a rent collector, bringing in her wake a host of friends and her two sisters, Theresa and Beatrice. Kate's friends, wrote Henrietta Barnett, 'were not of the "goody" sort, but were people holding the world's plums, of wealth, high social position, . . . but she brought them all to tender their need of service to the poor, and compelled them to face conditions usually hidden from the comfortable.'[34]

From 1878 Kate formed a close friendship with Leonard Courtney, a Liberal MP and friend of Samuel Barnett. Courtney did not press his suit, being unsure of his financial standing, but at last Kate blurted out her feelings and they came to an understanding which resulted in their marriage on 15 March 1883. 'Leonard was nervous that night and much excited,' recorded Beatrice. 'No wonder. Marriage at their age is rather a leap in the dark – curious to see how it turns out . . .'[35] (Leonard was then fifty-one and Kate thirty-six). Kate had chosen to be married at St Jude's among her 'own people', and so at the reception the costermonger sat down next to the Member of Parliament, but this mixing of social ranks was not, according to Henrietta, forced or awkward, since all the guests were united in their love for the bride.

Following Kate's example, Beatrice decided to work in the East End, joining the Soho Committee of the Charity Organisation Society, which had been founded in 1869 by Octavia Hill, the Barnetts and C. S. Loch, to co-ordinate the many charitable societies helping the poor, and also to stem what the founders believed was the demoralising flood of charity handouts to the poor. Beatrice had more opportunity than ever before to do practical work; she had, with difficulty, persuaded Rosy to go to school in France. Guilty that she could not show Rosy more love, yet irritated by Rosy's jealousy of her closer relationship with their father, it was with relief that Beatrice saw her sister sail.[36]

When Beatrice joined the Charity Organisation Society in April 1883, it was only one of her occupations and it was not great concern for the poor as individuals that motivated her, 'But the experience I shall gain from it will work in well with my "human studies". One learns very little about human nature from society.' Her motives were both similar to and different from those of other society women who ventured into the slums, an occupation that became increasingly fashionable after Mearns' *Bitter Cry* and the subsequent popularisation of the poverty problem by W. T. Stead in his *Pall Mall Gazette*. To some extent it was the expected behaviour for women of her class, and for others of the leisured classes it was merely a way of alleviating boredom.

Many middle-class women discovered that visiting the poor in the East End represented a sense of adventure akin to the freedom their brothers found in the colonies. Escaping the conventions of polite society, women like Beatrice were able to go about the narrow streets of 'darkest England',[37] as General Booth of the Salvation Army called the East End, with comparative anonymity. Safe from assault, unmistakably a lady, yet dressed neatly in 'a close bonnet, black preferable, a black cloak, a plain black dress to clear the ground with no trimming'[38] a middle-class girl could find the excitement missing from the rest of her life. As Octavia Hill pointed out in 1889, 'It used to be difficult for a girl to walk alone, and it was considered almost impossible for her to travel in omnibuses or third class trains',[39] but by the time Beatrice joined the Charity Organisation Society these barriers had fallen.

Kate Courtney and Henrietta Barnett became deeply attached to the poor families they visited, and Octavia Hill was convinced that there was no panacea for poverty but personal friendship across the classes. She urged that 'real deep lasting friendships may be formed that will link the visitor to her people . . . the rich with the poor, the young with the old, the educated with the less trained'.[40] For the visitors themselves, friendship with the poor could compensate for the lack of children, and of course visiting was a source of status, even of power, conspicuously lacking elsewhere.

Beatrice described the Charity Organisation Society as 'my friend the enemy', a description revealing her ambivalence towards an organisation she later considered reactionary; but in 1883 it 'appeared to me as an honest though short-circuited attempt to apply the scientific method of observation and experiment, reasoning and verification, to the task of delivering the poor from their miseries'.[41] Intellectual curiosity, and the opportunity to apply Spencer's vaunted 'scientific method' to a different section of society than the privileged sector with which she was already familiar, drew her to offer her services.

The Charity Organisation Society was inspired by the Rev Henry Solly, a Unitarian minister, and from its earliest beginnings its aim was to reduce pauperism and 'repress mendicity' among the poor. Hill, the Barnetts and C. S. Loch, the Society's secretary from 1875, were all united in the belief that the flood of private charity from rich to poor had demoralised the character of the poor and undermined self-help and independence of character. 'Charity . . . infects the people like a silent working pestilence,' said Loch,[42] while Barnett declared that 'the poor starve because of the alms they receive'.[43] Poverty was seen as a failure of character, a moral flaw, which resulted in the stern distinction being made between the 'deserving' who might be helped, and the 'undeserving' who should be abandoned to a punitive Poor Law.

These ideas were controversial even then,[44] and the Society was acutely unpopular almost from the beginning. The first meeting was dominated by the nobility, with the Earl of Derby in the chair, but it soon became clear that the ideas of those who regarded themselves as professionals in the field, particularly Loch, would be dominant. Octavia Hill soon had thirty-five visitors organised, mostly women, and all applications for help received by the Poor Law Relief Committee were vetted by the district visitors; the Charity Organisation Society was already working hand-in-glove with the hated Poor Law authorities. One of its main aims was to co-ordinate the many rival charitable societies. The earliest visiting society run by women was probably the Lying-In Charity established in 1791 in Tottenham and by the 1860s virtually every parish church in London had a visiting society.

Although Beatrice began social work almost accidentally, by May it was occupying much of her thoughts. Her initial impressions were favourable, and she considered the Charity Organisation Society an improvement on the old state of things, although her faith in *laissez-faire* led her to doubt the wisdom of helping the weak, because favouring the weak could harm the stronger members of society. But Beatrice concluded that these economic facts were unimportant 'when we come face to face with individual misery'. Significantly, as Margot Asquith found, she appreciated from the first that it was the giver of charity who often benefited more than the recipient from their relationship: 'One thing is clear to my mind,' Beatrice wrote, 'it is distinctly *advantageous to us* to go amongst the poor . . . the study of their lives and surroundings gives us the facts wherewith we can attempt to solve the social problems; contact with them develops on the whole our finer qualities, disgusting us with our false and worldly application of men and things and educating us in a thoughtful benevolence.' Charity should never, she concluded, be the cause of self-congratulation and pride.[45]

As a lady visitor Beatrice followed the rules in the *Handy Books for Visitors* prepared by Bernard Bosanquet, the first secretary of the Charity Organisation Society, which told the visitor how to write up her cases. Visits were to take place once a week between 9 a.m. and noon, or 2 p.m. to 4 p.m., and all applications were to be noted on a visiting form, a number allocated to the case in the record book and, after the case had been investigated, the decision taken recorded in the decision book. A register and index book also recorded all cases of relief from local charities. In addition to this paperwork there were many other forms, for subscribers and for enquiries to schoolmasters and to employers, revealing the Victorian passion for classification and codification, which also appealed to Beatrice's own desire for facts.

The principles of casework in which the lady visitors were trained at first seemed sensible to Beatrice. Temporary help was only to be given if it would result in permanent benefit, not merely because the applicants seemed 'deserving'; thrift was to be encouraged as was the repayment of help; and the assistance of friends and relatives was to be sought. Beatrice had to note carefully the applicant's employment or lack of it, past addresses, relatives, membership of clubs, rent, articles in pawn, and health; all replies to enquiries from employers, clergy, or schoolmasters, would be entered in the applicant and decision book and, after interviews, letters and visits, a careful decision would be taken.

For Octavia Hill the 'dole demon' was her greatest enemy. 'Do you think the old dole demon is dead?' she asked in 1889. The answer was no. Free dinners were handed out by the thousand, weakening the parents' sense of responsibility and encouraging fathers to waste money on drink and mothers to gossip instead of doing the cooking.[46] The middle-class standards in which Octavia believed so firmly were also Beatrice's standards, and as a Charity Organisation Society visitor she was engaged in imposing them upon the working class.

Many patient visits were made to help put families upon their feet, and every case was assessed on its own merits: a sick dressmaker was given £1 to help buy a sewing machine, to be repaid at 1s a week; the parents of a boy of thirteen who had lost his kneecap in an accident were given money for a surgical boot; a gardener was given money to buy seeds; and widows were often given mangles or sewing machines so that they might take in work. An old couple who depended on their horse and cart for their livelihood were given a loan to buy a new horse when their old one fell lame. Whenever possible loans were given rather than money.

Beatrice carried with her form 28, a formidable deterrent to the work-shy. It trumpeted that help was only available to those doing all they could to help themselves. 'Persons of drunken, immoral or idle habits,' it warned, 'cannot expect to be assisted unless they can satisfy the committee that they are really trying to reform.'[47] A widow who applied for relief in 1873 after breaking her collar bone in an accident was refused when it was found 'she resorted to a public house every night and broke her collar-bone when under the influence of drink'.[48]

But there was a problem with 'deserving' women married to 'undeserving' men. On 20 May 1883 Beatrice wrote up in her neatly cross-referenced visitor's book the case of Pavey, 'Had been dispenser, took to opium eating, now unfitted for work'. Opium was a favourite drug of the 1880s, often diluted in laudanum and given as a sedative to fractious babies who were farmed out, neglected and left to die. Beatrice was touched by the wife who was earning 15s a week, out of which she had to support her husband and three children. Of her other children two were cared for by relatives, and one was boarded out at 4s a week. 'Still clings to her baby, poor woman,' wrote Beatrice. 'Why should I be separated from my children as if I were a bad woman? What will they think of me? They will hear whispers against me and I slaving all the while, night and day. I cannot bear it much longer. I must give way.' Beatrice did not hasten to make a moral judgment upon the husband, as Octavia Hill would have done, although she felt contempt for 'the wretched man, standing sulkily in the corner, twisting his thumbs, cursing the existing order of things, talking of his better days and good education ... had a smattering of Greek and Latin. All to no purpose! One is tempted to a feeling of righteous indignation against the man, but did he not make himself wretched and is he not on the whole pitiable?'

Beatrice's observations show her talent for the quick and penetrating character sketch: 'Look at the two faces. An expression on the one of dogged discontent and misery, ever-present disgust of the world and himself; marking the woman's face, deep lines of unselfconscious effort, of perhaps agonising struggle, agonising in those moments when she felt herself face to face with the fact that in the end she *must* succumb; but still she loved, and the little one for whom she is giving away strength and maybe life, smiles sweetly and stretches its tiny arms longingly towards her.'

Her social work made Beatrice disgusted with the superficial preoccupations of society. 'I walk down Piccadilly, meeting the well-dressed men and women who had been praying to Jesus of Nazareth that he should forgive them for having twirled and whirled and chattered through the last week – "sensitively" ignoring the huge misery around them.'[49] Her experiences as a visitor made her call into question assumptions she had previously accepted, and increasingly led her to compartmentalise her life.

By July 1883 Beatrice realised some survey was needed of 'capabilities and wants' of each district, already anticipating the task Charles Booth was to take upon himself. The need for accurate statistics was apparent, as was the need for the poor to be informed of the job opportunities and benefits available to them. 'London is so huge,' Beatrice wrote, 'and the poor are so helpless and ignorant ... The clergy, as an adequate organisation, are worked out. Some secular body must take their place.' Her revulsion at the self-centredness of society grew: 'Why do these hundreds and thousands of cultivated people go on boring themselves with unrealities when there is near to them this terrible reality of tortured life?' Beatrice toyed with the idea that she might concentrate on social reform, although aware it was not poverty alone that preoccupied her. 'If only I could devote my life to it I might do something, that is not my fate! Perhaps I stand now on the eve of a new life, shall watch the sun rise and disappear behind a black cloud extending out into a grey sky cover. I shall not be deceived by its glory. If it is to be so, there is work and the influence that work brings, but not happiness. Am I strong enough to face that?'[50]

1883 was a pivotal year, for not only was it the year in which Mearns's *Bitter Cry* was published, but in April that year Samuel Barnett published an article entitled 'Practicable Socialism', the first indication that his work in Whitechapel was turning his mind towards socialism. From that date the Charity Organisation Society was caught in the cross-fire of the collectivism/individualism debate, and in its adherence to the deterrent ideas of the Poor Law, was fighting a rear-guard action.

Beatrice could not help loving Samuel Barnett, although, with his 'diminutive body clothed in shabby and badly assorted garments, big knobby and prematurely bald head, small black eyes set close together, sallow complexion and a thin and patchy pretence of a beard, Barnett, at first sight, was not pleasing to contemplate!' Barnett had no grasp of logic, was a muddled thinker who often irritated fellow reformers, had few gifts as a preacher and no particular artistic talents, but his deep and enduring love for his parishioners, his humility and determination to bring to the people of Whitechapel not just the necessities of life but some of its pleasures, impressed Beatrice profoundly. It was Barnett who argued that the best things in life should be free, that East Enders should have baths and wash-houses, swimming-pools, public libraries, picture galleries, and parks, 'so that every man, woman and child might sit in the open air and see the sky and the sunset'. His ideas were considered advanced, but he knew from his own experiences that 'poverty cannot pay for the pleasure which satisfies, and yet, without that pleasure, the people perish'.[51]

Henrietta Barnett, young and pretty, supplied the practical and businesslike qualities her husband lacked, together with a brazen self-confidence, and the conviction that the rich required a good 'spanking', which served her well in organising her many schemes to help the poor. Despite the fact that she and Barnett were both tone deaf, and hardly knew when to rise if 'God Save the Queen' was being played, she assiduously arranged concerts and oratorio services in St Jude's, and the long brown pews were filled with the parishioners who, despite their vermin and 'sickening odour', were so moved by the *Messiah* that they often broke into sobs. Lectures were given in the church, mothers' meetings arranged, a Maternity Society formed, and the parishioners were frequently entertained at the vicarage where all classes were energetically mixed together, having first been sent a formal invitation. 'St Jude's and Toynbee Hall [which he later founded] . . . are all built on my wife's tea-table,' said Samuel Barnett.[52] One of Henrietta's most successful schemes was the Children's Country Holiday Fund, begun in 1877, sending nine children into the country for a holiday that first summer, thirty-three the next, until thousands were leaving the slums every year for their annual holiday, afterwards writing their hostess touching letters: 'The cow has large thoughtful eyes and is an oblong animal.'[53]

Beatrice's early enthusiasm gave way to increasing scepticism at Charity Organisation Society methods, as she realised that the investigative case work which was claimed to be an innovative feature of Octavia Hill's methods was no more than a cloak for the old division of the poor into the 'deserving' and 'undeserving', the sheep and the goats. By 1886 the term 'undeserving' had been changed to 'not likely to benefit', but this did not obscure the fact, as Beatrice soon discovered, that the reality of the situation was that 'good character' bore no relation to need; those who through chronic sickness or poor housing had most need of help were least likely to be offered it. The lady visitor was forced into the unpleasant role of snooper in the attempt to discover which case could be made self-supporting and which could not, and the so-called 'hopeless' cases, those with no prospect of ever being self-sufficient, were refused all aid even if their characters were blameless.

During the prosperous years of the mid-century the principles of the 1834 Poor Law had been loosely applied. The Poor Law guardians had been loath to force abandoned mothers or the elderly into the workhouse, but as the poor rate became an increasing burden on the middle classes, pressure grew to reduce it. In London before 1867 each Poor Law Union was responsible for the relief of its own poor, an arrangement only workable when a balance between rich and poor existed in each district. By the 1860s the flight of the rich from the East End had created an imbalance of classes, with the result that the poorest district had the highest rate to pay, while the charge on the rich districts was nominal. In 1867 complete Poor Law breakdown occurred, when the rate could not be got in in Mile End and Bethnal Green. Instead the local boards left poverty to be relieved by the charitable impulses of the conscience-stricken rich, allegedly creating such a cornucopia of charity that it was blamed for tempting even the honest poor to copy loafers and idlers.

In 1867 George Goschen, chairman of the Poor Law Board, decided that the poor should only be offered the workhouse, and a strict division should be made between Poor Law relief and charity. The movement gained momentum with the establishment of the Charity Organisation Society and the growing obsession, as Beatrice believed it to be, that the misery of the great cities was entirely due to doles and handouts to the poor. Professional social commentators were convinced that dole undermined the urge to work in 'the average sensual man' who became servile and greedy, but Beatrice suspected the truth lay in 'the sub-conscious bias of "the Haves" against taxing themselves for "the Have Nots" '.[54]

Inevitably the refusal of relief to the poor who had been accustomed to receive it led to the widespread unpopularity of the Charity Organisation Society, although Beatrice told of a committee member furtively slipping sixpence to a poor woman applicant for relief, while Octavia Hill was lecturing her on self-help. In reality, as Beatrice recognised, the visitor's power rested mainly on the stick, with the threat of the workhouse as her back-up. C. P. Bosanquet urged lady visitors to tell the Relieving Officer of the workhouse, 'if you find that persons receiving outdoor relief are in the habit of drinking to excess, begging, or otherwise show themselves unworthy of what is unquestionably a favour.'[55] Beatrice was repulsed by the hypocrisy of Octavia Hill who paid lip-service to the principle of personal service, instructing her visitors to the poor, 'You might gladden their homes by bringing them flowers, or, better still, by teaching them to grow plants; you might meet them face to face as friends; you might teach them, you might collect their savings; you might sing for and with them; you might take them into the parks, or out for quiet days in the country ... You might teach and refine them and make them cleaner by merely going among them,'[56] and who believed that to make the poor self-supporting required no more than 'sweet subtle human sympathy and the power of human love'. In the meantime the lady visitors, as Beatrice saw to her dismay, attracted to themselves dislike and distrust.

Beatrice knew that although she had gone into the slums as a well-meaning idealist, she and her colleagues were 'transformed into a body of amateur detectives, in some cases initiating prosecutions of persons they thought to be imposters, and arousing more suspicion and hatred than the recognised officers of the law'. She began to fear that philanthropists had made an ominous discovery: 'By rudely tearing off the wrapping of medieval almsgiving disguising the skeleton at the feast of capitalist civilisation they had let loose the tragic truth that, wherever society is divided into a minority of "Haves" and "Have Nots", charity is twice cursed, it curses him that gives and him that takes.' Disillusioned, Beatrice decided that philanthropy was a lie. Almsgiving, which should be an expression of the love of God, had turned into a witch-hunt, in which the only loser was the poorest and weakest of humanity.[57]

When she looked back later, Beatrice recognised that Octavia Hill never shared the same consciousness of sin as she and the Barnetts had done. Hill and Loch accepted unthinkingly the superiority of the capitalist system and never questioned the structure of society nor looked for causes of poverty beyond improvidence or laziness on the part of the poor. It was this 'narrow and continuously hardening dogma'[58] which eventually drove Samuel and Henrietta Barnett to break away from the Charity Organisation Society in 1886, as they became aware that there was a greater evil than indiscriminate charity: unrestricted capitalism, in which evil landlords and greedy employers could exploit the poor.

It is no coincidence that Beatrice approved of the Society's principles when she first joined, as its stern individualism had been stated in its most uncompromising form by Herbert Spencer in *The Man versus the State* in 1884. Beatrice's intellectual journey from the individualism imprinted upon her in her youth to collectivism and ultimately to Fabian Socialism mirrors the shifting mood of the 1880s in which many questioned the role of capitalism in causing the mass misery which they saw around them. Individualism and collectivism were terms which fell into disuse by 1918 (and had very little currency before the 1880s), but during that turbulent decade they presented a neat antithesis in the minds of the intelligentsia. Spencer defended the liberty of the individual, arguing that the state was only justified in restricting this liberty to prevent a man harming his fellows. In the tradition of the classical political economists, he assumed the economy to be a self-regulating mechanism which only functioned efficiently when there were no limits upon competition. He compared society to a biological organism, arguing that competition was the mechanism

of progress in both the animal and human worlds. Moderate individu-
alists combined in their opposition to such measures as progressive
taxation, state pensions, or a legal minimum working day.

At the opposite end of the political spectrum was collectivism, with
its uneasy bedfellow, socialism. Collectivism embraced 'any attempt
to implement social reform through the legislative and executive
powers of the state',[59] and this minimalist definition meant it was
possible to be a collectivist without calling oneself a socialist. Although
the terms were to merge, socialism, with its French origins, had
continental and implicitly dangerous connotations, suggesting the
abolition of private property, class warfare and the proletarian
revolution. Yet many who called themselves socialist did not visualise
violent revolution, but aspired to a more equal society based on
co-operation rather than competition.

Both sides approached the problem of the demoralised poor with
the same serious and alarmist tone, as the middle classes sought to
instil in the poor their own bourgeois standards of cleanliness,
righteousness and deferred gratification. The individualist argument
that state aid undermined character backfired as increased awareness
of the size of the problem led Beatrice and others to suspect that only
the state had the power to improve the environment and thus make it
possible for the working class to develop suitable moral habits.

Within three months of joining the Charity Organisation Society
an entry in Beatrice's diary recorded, 'Wretchedly wasted week. No
hard work done. Sick headache from over-eating and under-exercising.
Met sundry distinguished men, among others Joseph Chamberlain. I
do and I don't like him. Talking to "clever men" in society is a snare
and a delusion . . . Much better read their books.'[60] This terse entry
hid a momentous event in Beatrice's life, for from that first meeting
with the Radical leader her life was never to be the same again.

VIII

THE WHIRLPOOL

*'It is indeed an Eve for me. Two distinct ways open to me, one
of which, it seems inevitable that I must take.'*
Beatrice Webb Diary, New Year's Eve 1883

BY THE END OF 1883 Beatrice had come to a significant conclusion: 'The
most hopeful form of social service was the craft of social investigator.'[1] Optimistically she wrote, 'The die was cast, the craft was chosen.'
It was not a simple decision but one arrived at only through conflict
and suffering, for the instinctive, passionately experienced desire
Beatrice felt for love, marriage and maternity, had to be denied if she
was to realise her intellectual and reforming ambitions and develop
her craft.

By the age of twenty-five she was a strikingly beautiful woman
whose slim figure, imperious manner, flashing eyes, and abundant
dark hair, coupled with a spirited wit, had earned her the title of 'the
brilliant and beautiful Miss Potter'. Charles Macaulay, the father of
Beatrice's close friend and cousin, Mary Booth, wrote in February
1883 that he sent his love 'to dear Beatrice. Tell her I would give a
pretty penny to see her in her crimson satin and white lace dress, but
tell her not to be proud of the power of her beauty. It is a grand
possession but it has its dangers and should make her extra careful in
her choice of mate.'[2] So far such a prospect had not exercised Beatrice's
judgement, nor had romantic love done much to disturb the equilibrium of her life.

Youthful romances had stirred her emotions too little to merit
inclusion in her diary. 'All the small *affaires de coeur* of past
years I have left unmentioned, simply because they have not interested
me,' she wrote in March 1884.[3] The only exception was the young
professor of mechanics, Professor John Main, whom she met on a visit
to Germany and Switzerland after her mother's death. He was, Beatrice
noted, 'promising . . . a clever and sensitive man – short in stature
with a pleasant open sympathetic face', and she approved of the fact
that he was conscientious: 'He is devoted to work, never feeling quite
content when out of it.' However, the twenty-eight-year-old professor

was content to neglect work while they wandered together over the Alpine meadows, talking earnestly, but as the days passed Beatrice began to feel increasingly guilty at neglecting Rosy and her father, since the purpose of the trip was to distract him from his grief following the death of Lawrencina. Rosy was aware of the professor's attentions, noting in her diary, 'Dr Main fell violently in love with Beatrice and made her an offer before we left.' His swift courtship impressed Rosy, but left Beatrice confused. 'A week spent with nature and alas! with the young professor. After four months of loneliness it was delightful to have the companionship of a refined and sympathetic mind, deeply appreciative of nature and yet steadfast in devotion of work and duty ... But still in looking back there is bitterness in the consciousness of having given way to pleasure, thoughtlessly ignoring what pain might come of it ... altogether the last week has been spent unworthily.'[4]

'Giving way to pleasure' was, in Beatrice's eyes, a sin she equated with neglect of duty. 'If a weakly mortal is to do anything in the world besides eat the bread thereof, there must be a determined subordination of the whole nature to the one aim – no trifling with time, which is passing, with strength which is only too limited.'[5] Beatrice determined that the one lesson she would learn from the experience was self-control and she chastised herself for allowing pleasure to overwhelm her. She wrote a letter of apology to Professor Main, whose reply showed he was on equally 'susceptible' terms.

23 July 1882

Dear Miss Potter,
I have nothing to forgive you. On the contrary I ought to ask and do ask your forgiveness for having intruded upon you with my own wishes and desires, more especially at this your time of sorrow. The fault is all mine, may the suffering from it be all mine too. For the friendship you have given me, and which I hope ever to retain, and for having afforded me a clearer insight into the aims of a noble mind, inspired by a high ideal, you have my abiding thanks. Your words will not be forgotten; much that you have said will be a moral tonic for me all my life, and the remembrance of you as I have known you will help and invigorate me in the labours that lie before me in the world.

If you can find a place for me in your memory, think of me kindly, as one who has wished and will ever wish the best things for you, who would gladly come from the world's end to serve you and who will remain all through his life,

Your very sincere friend,
John Frederick Main

By the time Beatrice read this letter, her admirer had left on the next stage of his travels, but she did not forget him. Two years later, chancing to meet a mutual friend, Professor Roberts, outside the South Kensington Museum, Beatrice enquired of him whether Professor Main was still at the Institute. 'Ah, . . . an exceedingly able, brilliant young man, a charming fellow; but now in consumption', and living abroad, she was told. Beatrice remembered with regret the happy interlude at Murren: 'Two young human beings on the threshold of life and on the verge of an ever-uniting love. Parted for ever – one to die, the other to live a life of . . .?'[6]

In fact Beatrice's closest relationship had been with another woman, Cary Darling, the governess to Mary Playne's children. She was, Beatrice wrote in 1878, 'A dear little woman, a person it is impossible not to be intimate with . . .'[7] and soon the two were meeting frequently in London. Cary was the daughter of the illegitimate son of a squire, and had always had to earn her own living, but they had a common love of culture, and became close. Their intimacy was shattered by a family crisis which forced Cary Darling to accept a headmistress-ship in Australia in order to support her impoverished family.

It was an emotional relationship but both Beatrice and Cary were heterosexual. Beatrice worried that in Australia Cary was forgetting her, but her friend told her that this was not so: 'You are not becoming "phantoms in the far distance". Every day I look at your picture which . . . occupies the most conspicuous place in my room . . .'

When Beatrice began to suspect she was falling in love with Joseph Chamberlain, Cary played the role of confidante, and the anxious letters flew between London and Queensland. 'Beatrice dearest, I know you will get married but don't don't say goodbye to me in consequence,' implored Cary in November 1883. By May 1884 Cary sensed the change in Beatrice: 'Your letter tells me how much you have learned of life since I saw you. Woman cannot live *happily* alone. That I know to my bitter cost. [Cary had an abortive affair with a married master at the boys' grammar school] . . . I am determined to show that she can live *usefully* alone . . .'[8] As Beatrice's letters grew ever more distraught, she gave Cary the choice of returning them or destroying them, and Cary took the latter course, assuring Beatrice that her confessions about Chamberlain lay in thousands of pieces in the wastepaper basket.

Beatrice was introduced to Joseph Chamberlain, leader of the Radical wing of the Liberal Party, and President of the Board of Trade in Gladstone's ministry, at a dinner party given by Miss Williams, a neighbour. Chamberlain and Beatrice lived only a few doors away from each other, he at 72 Prince's Gate and she at 47.

Chamberlain made an instant impression upon Beatrice; he was twenty-two years older than her, already twice a widower, but his polished and cutting wit, his charismatic personality, the hint of deep emotions hidden behind a mask of reserve, attracted Beatrice in a way wholly new to her – her previous admirers might have amused her, flattered her, but her own sharp intelligence had been too great to have any respect for them, apart from Professor Main. Impressionable and inexperienced, she was awed by the Minister's reputation for belligerent and fiery speeches, for sarcasm and biting epigrams, which had made him enemies in the House of Commons. Yet neither enemies nor friends among the Whigs and Radicals of his own party, nor the Conservatives on the opposition benches, dismissed this provincial politician whose popular following in the country was greater than that of any other politician but Gladstone. Passionate, arrogant and impatient, Chamberlain denounced inherited wealth and the inequalities of a society ripe for reform. Gladstone's retirement was anticipated at any time and Chamberlain and his close ally Sir Charles Dilke were seen as likely rivals to the succession.

Chamberlain's good looks and forceful personality had already won him two wives – Harriet Kenrick and her cousin Florence Kenrick – both of whom had died in childbirth, leaving him the father of six children: Beatrice and Joseph Austen by his first wife, Neville, Ida, Hilda and Ethel by his second. Chamberlain mourned deeply the death of Florence, his beloved 'helpmate and companion', submerging himself in work. 'I am at least undergoing it without unmanly weakness,' he wrote, but it was at this point that he lost his Christian faith.

Chamberlain was proud of his luxuriant black hair, which even at fifty had no hint of grey; from his twenties he had disguised his short sight with a monocle, now his indispensable accessory, and together with the orchid he invariably wore in his buttonhole, sent direct from his glasshouses at Highbury in Birmingham to London when the House was sitting, gave him the air of a man who, if not a dandy, took a pride in his appearance. His laconic manner was not merely an accident of nature, but was as studied as the hooded eye and curling lip perfected in many amateur dramatic productions, and now pressed into service in his oratory.

When Chamberlain and Beatrice met, it was known in society circles that the Radical leader was in the market for a new wife, and was one of the most eligible men in London; as a politician he needed that essential adjunct, a loyal political wife. Although he had been an intensely lonely man after the death of Florence in 1875, there is no evidence that Chamberlain ever took a mistress. The position of the third Mrs Chamberlain had a certain allure for the socially ambitious side of Beatrice's nature she could not ignore, and for him, to win the young and brilliant Miss Potter would be a feather in the cap of an ambitious provincial politician eager to make his way in the London establishment. The situation caused Theresa to write a letter of caution to Beatrice: 'If, as I hear from most quarters, Mr Joseph is on the look out for a good wife, and one who would forward, as you would, his most ambitious views, don't you be carried away by any ambitious ideas yourself, or any feeling that your life would be worth more in such a position than it is in the quiet pursuit of science which is *really* congenial to you . . . Look at the *man* himself as a man, and if, apart from his whole connection with the Radical party and politics he is not congenial and companionable to you in the highest sense, look at something or somebody else.'[9]

It was not easy advice to take, and Beatrice's thoughts turned continuously to Chamberlain. In May 1883, just before she met Chamberlain, she had spent a whole day with Herbert Spencer at a private view. 'He worked out, poor man, a sad destiny for one whose whole life has been his work. There is something pathetic in the isolation of his mind, a sort of spider-like existence, sitting alone in the centre of his theoretical web, catching facts, and weaving them again into theory.' Beatrice saw Spencer's predicament as a warning of the dangers of a life devoted only to work. 'It is sorrowful when the individual is lost in the work . . . and then when working days are past, left as the husk, the living kernel of which is given to the world.'[10]

Spencer was instrumental in forwarding Beatrice's friendship with Chamberlain, since he invited her to his annual picnic in June, near Weybridge, at which Joseph Chamberlain's younger sister Clara was present. Beatrice 'spent most of the afternoon with Miss Chamberlain – a really genuine woman, who is somewhat perplexed and bored by

London Season life'. Beatrice found Clara Chamberlain 'essentially provincial in the good and the bad sense', but she relished the opportunity to learn more about Chamberlain himself. A further opportunity presented itself later when, wrote Beatrice 'Mr Chamberlain joined us in the evening and I had much conversation with him. His personality interested me . . . Gradually sinking into a do-nothing worthless life. Ah me!'[11]

By July Beatrice alternated between being excited and disgusted by Society, and struggled to balance the demands of her 'multiple personality'. It was an almost impossible juggling act, and Beatrice was sometimes confused by the competing influences upon her, one of which was Eleanor Marx, daughter of Karl Marx, whom Beatrice met in May. They discussed Christianity, for which Miss Marx had little use, and socialism, which she found impossible to explain to Beatrice. Although 'comely, dressed in a slovenly picturesque way with curly black hair flying about in all directions', Beatrice was suspicious of the free-thinking Miss Marx, who mixed with radical politician Charles Bradlaugh, and whom she suspected of practising free love. Beatrice feared that the chances were against her remaining long within the pale of 'respectable society'.[12]

Beatrice enjoyed holding her own in the cut-and-thrust of political conversation, and sharing a joke with Chamberlain: at a dinner Beatrice was amused by a faux pas made by Lady Campbell, who did not recognise Chamberlain. 'Mr Chamberlain,' Beatrice wrote to her sister Mary, 'took Lady Campbell down and when they got to the table she remarked, "Here's my name. They haven't put yours. Who are you?" "Well, I believe I am Mr Chamberlain, you will see my portrait in some of the recent periodicals," replied the distinguished guest.'[13]

In April 1884 Beatrice and her father moved from Prince's Gate to the imposing former royal residence of York House in Kensington Palace Gardens, set in its own grounds with two lawn-tennis courts, herbaceous gardens, a paddock and rookery; writing in her diary of Beatrice Rosy noted, 'By theory she is an ascetic and lives up to her ideas, but she loves comfort and even luxury.'[14] In fact Beatrice and Richard Potter both had a tendency to extravagance which only Lawrencina's puritanical habits had restrained. Rosy recalled later that Beatrice never looked better than she did at this time; she appeared to her younger sister, 'strikingly handsome, her features lit by her keen intelligence. Above the broad, intellectual forehead and dark, glowing eyes, her brown hair grew in profusion.'[15] Beatrice, meanwhile, was not so secure, writing in her diary in February 1884, 'I was not made to be loved, there must be something repulsive in my character.'[16]

On 18 July Beatrice entertained Chamberlain to dinner, placing him next to her; on the other side was a Whig peer, and since the Whigs were old enemies of Chamberlain, she may have planned the ensuing heated conversation. 'Whig peer talked of his own possessions, Chamberlain *passionately* of getting hold of other people's – for the masses. Curious and interesting character, dominated by *intellectual passions* with little self-control but with any amount of *purpose*.' It was soon clear to Beatrice that the views of Herbert Spencer and those of Joseph Chamberlain were diametrically opposed. Spencer had already given Beatrice his crushing criticism of Chamberlain: 'A man who may mean well, but who does, and will do, an incalculable amount of mischief.' Chamberlain was equally sarcastic in his opinion of Spencer's philosophy. 'Happily,' Chamberlain told Beatrice, 'for the majority of the world, his writing is not intelligible, otherwise his life would have been spent in doing harm.' There was, decided Beatrice, 'no personal animus, but a fundamental antipathy of mind'[17] between them. Despite her conversations with him, Beatrice could not understand the 'reason for Chamberlain's passion', eventually deciding, 'The motive force which moves the man of action is seldom rational.' 'How I should like to study that man!' she admitted in her diary.

There were greater differences in their backgrounds than there were similarities. Chamberlain's family had been shoemakers in Cheapside, and he was proud of his English middle-class stock. One of the earliest traceable Chamberlains, Daniel, had kept a malt house in Lacock near Bristol, but his descendant William Chamberlain had set off for London to seek his fortune, and had become apprenticed to a cordwainer. As such he considered himself superior to a mere cobbler, who only mended shoes, and was soon successful enough to set up his own business in Milk Street, Cheapside. Joseph Chamberlain, the third in a line of three of that name, was born on 8 July 1836, in Camberwell Grove, and Caroline Harben, Joseph's mother, had contributed a more spirited temperament to the sober Chamberlain blood, which surfaced in Joseph. It was a happy childhood, and soon he was making his mark at University College School, the leading public school for Dissenters, partly chosen by his father because it had abolished capital punishment.

But Joseph's idyllic childhood was cut short when his father decided that his eldest son should start work in the family business at sixteen.[18] In vain Caroline pleaded that he might be allowed to enter University College. Joseph became a conscientious apprentice who learnt his craft diligently and could mix easily with his fellow shoemakers, giving him an insight into the minds and emotions of the working class he could never have acquired at university. Instead Joseph went to evening science lectures and studied French at night school.

Joseph Chamberlain had Nonconformist roots, being the product of five generations of Dissent, descended from a clergyman called Sargeant who was one of the 'ejected ministers' expelled from their livings in the seventeenth century by the Act of Uniformity. Chamberlain as a Unitarian came from the extreme left of Dissent. During his boyhood he worshipped at the Unitarian chapel near St Paul's and the doctrines he learnt, the rejection not only of the Trinity but of the Atonement, and the grudging admission that Christ was, at most, not the son of God but a prophet who showed the way to heaven, left him with not only a sense of separateness from other Nonconformists but a fierce antagonism towards the established Church.

At eighteen a change came in Chamberlain's life as a result of a crisis in his uncle John Nettlefold's screw-making business. It was the time of the Great Exhibition, where an American inventor was exhibiting a new automatic machine for making screws by steam power; John Nettlefold's old-fashioned business in which the screws were made by hand was threatened with extinction, so Nettlefold appealed to his brother-in-law, Joseph Chamberlain senior, to help raise the capital of £30,000 to purchase the British rights to the invention. He agreed, stipulating that his son Joseph must keep an eye on the business, and so in 1854 Chamberlain found himself travelling to Birmingham to become sales manager in the screw factory.

Chamberlain's sales methods were dynamic and modern; as the cashier put it, 'Money was made very rapidly after Mr Joseph came.'[19] In order to conquer the French market he arranged to have a Frenchman talk to him every morning at breakfast, until his French was fluent, and to meet market demand he had the screws packaged in blue packets all of one size. Sales figures soared, and other screw businesses went bankrupt or were sold out. He was popular with the men, for whom he started a Working Men's Institute, a Benefit Society and Debating Club, thinking nothing of walking the three miles home to his lodgings when the meetings ended.

In 1865 Chamberlain joined his local Liberal association, where few failed to notice 'Pushful Joe'. Three years later he became the leader of a pressure group for universal compulsory education, the National Education League, which he founded in 1869. He was outmanoeuvred by Gladstone, who produced a uniquely British compromise in Forster's Education Bill of 1870 which set up a dual system of local Board Schools to co-exist with the existing voluntary system. Outraged, Chamberlain asked Charles Dilke to help him 'in smashing up that whited sepulchre called the Liberal Party'[20] which appeared to him to ignore the pressing social problems of the day.

None of Chamberlain's Progressive ideas were particularly original, but his skill lay in articulating them in a way which fired the Nonconformists of Birmingham. In 1873 he called in the *Fortnightly Review* for the 4 Fs – Free Schools, Free Land, Free Church and Free Labour (the right to picket) – and in the same year he was elected Mayor of Birmingham and began a programme of civic works which left the city 'parked, paved, assized, marketed, Gas-and-Watered and *improved* – all as a result of three years hard work'.[21] The Birmingham reforms laid the foundation for the reputation which took him into Parliament in 1876 as the representative of his city, after an earlier failure at Sheffield.

At home at Standish in August 1883, Beatrice tried to gather her thoughts together about the 'whirlpool' in which she had so recently been swimming helplessly, a metaphor not only for society life but for the strong current of her emotions which had carried her into dangerous new waters. 'The whirlpool is past for the present – the current of my life may bring me again within the sphere of its attraction but now I again swim freely; with green banks of tangled verdure on each side I look dreamily into their depth and pick out for curiosity the quaintly coloured forms.'[22]

In September Beatrice spent a week with Miss Chamberlain, who was a 'quiet, genuine woman not attractive or interesting in person or intellect'. Beatrice's only motive in staying there was to learn more about Joseph Chamberlain and his character. Since Clara Chamberlain tried to live by high principles, in Beatrice's opinion, she deduced that 'coming from such honest surroundings he surely *must* be straight in intention'.[23] But she burned to know the principles behind his ideas, and it was at this time her diary first showed a growing interest in politics.

Should government be merely the interpretation of the wants of the people, demanded Beatrice, or should it be direction by the 'ablest minds ... irrespective of the longings of the patient?' Her own bias towards Spencerian *laissez-faire* is revealed by the comment 'possibly the wisest physician will leave most to nature'.[24] Yet she feared that if the instincts of the people were not gratified, it might lead to revolution. Was this Chamberlain's principle, she wondered, to encourage the populace in its demands, to 'increase the hunger . . . until it could no longer be appeased without injury to the whole nature?'

Beatrice's suspicions of Chamberlain's political ideas were influenced both by her sisters and by outspoken political comment, which found in the speeches and appearance of Chamberlain a ready target for the cartoonist's pen and journalistic satire. Beatrice probably read the *Pall Mall Gazette*, the paper to which she sent her first letter on unemployment. It is also likely that she listened to her sister Kate, who since her marriage to Leonard Courtney was inclined to doubt Chamberlain's honesty and regard him with hostility.

Kate had met Chamberlain in Liverpool in 1881, when he delivered a 'clear and able speech', and she found him 'chatty and pleasant'. After the meeting she walked in Sefton Park with him, and had some 'queer frank talk . . . Mr C. interested me very much but I could not altogether admire his character', she wrote in her diary. 'I doubt his being an all round great man – rather too narrow in feeling and with little understanding of other classes than the one he belongs to.'[25] Kate felt that Chamberlain was representative of a provincial middle class to which the Potters, albeit subconsciously, felt superior. 'Anyhow, he is painted black enough by his enemies, Tories and Whigs,' concluded Kate, 'and dislikes them in return.' After her marriage to Leonard in March, Kate went down to Liskeard to hear her husband speak on Proportional Representation, an issue dear to his heart, which Chamberlain feared was a vote loser which might split the Radical Liberals, and which ultimately did lead Courtney to resign from the government in 1884. In December Kate was invited to stay with Chamberlain at Highbury, his neo-Gothic house in Birmingham, and her reaction was unfavourable. Chamberlain was 'agreeable' enough, but the house was 'overcoloured, I thought, and certainly overheated, rather a gloomy atmosphere about the inmates – suppressed I should say – many relatives to dinner all too much of the same way of thinking to be good for their "Joe".'[26]

Beatrice spent three weeks in November at the Argoed musing over her future. '*If* I remain free (which alas is a big if) I see pretty clearly where the work is which I *would* do.' She knew now that it should be work connected with social diagnosis, which would 'satisfy the restless ambition of my nature'. If she remained unmarried for the time being, her duties in caring for her father and Rosy would fulfil the nurturing side of her nature; Beatrice was convinced, 'It is almost necessary to the health of a woman, physical and mental, to have definite home duties to fulfil: details of practical management and, above all things, someone dependent on her love and tender care. So long as Father lives and his home is the centre for young lives, I have mission enough as a *woman*.' Beatrice still accepted the Victorian domestic code enough to consider this her '*most* important work', but what she sought also was another type of work which could fit in with her domestic commitments and yet be worthwhile enough to justify the sacrifice. 'If I could not honestly say, "the work was good", I should bitterly regret the absence of human ties, the neglect and disease of those powers for good which belong to all women alike.'[27]

One evening it suddenly occurred to her that at Bacup, the mill town near Rochdale from which her mother's relations had originally come, she might test her gift for social diagnosis. Their old nurse Martha, or 'Dada', was herself a poor relation who could give her the entree to this unknown world of artisans and weavers. But when Beatrice begged Da to take her, Martha protested, 'My friends would be astonished to see a Miss Potter coming along with me; they are not accustomed to such grand folk. I think they would be what they called "flayed" by you.' Beatrice was not put off: 'Oh! cried I, jumping up with the delightful consciousness of an original idea, "I wouldn't be Miss Potter, I would be Miss Jones, farmer's daughter, near Monmouth." '[28]

Beatrice's first visit to Bacup was more than merely an outlet for her sense of adventure; it was an imaginative step which gave the opportunity to live among and study a different and self-sufficient section of the 'respectable' working class who would, as she anticipated, provide a marked contrast to the experience of poverty, misery, and unemployment among the 'demoralised' residents of the East End. It was a significant step in her move from social reform towards social diagnosis, a move she was almost unique in making among the pioneering women of the 1880s. Many campaigned but few had the same faith as Beatrice had researching the underlying causes of poverty through the application of scientific methods.

'It was a wet November evening 1883, when Mrs Mills and Miss Jones picked their way along the irregularly paved and badly lighted back-streets of Bacup,' wrote Beatrice, with a sense of the dramatic. She was received into the 'charmed circle' of respectable working-class life, making friends with John Aked, an unemployed reed-maker, and her grandmother's nephew. The inherent tendency to depression in the Heyworth family became more apparent to her, as she learned that a brother and sister of her grandmother had committed suicide, and two or three others had been threatened with suicidal mania: 'Perhaps it is from that quarter that we get our Weltschmerz,' wondered Beatrice.[29]

The Akeds and their friends accepted her without suspicion. John Aked innocently told Beatrice that she had a look of Mrs Potter, 'far more like a male than a female to talk wi'.' One old man was suspicious and asked Beatrice whether her father was a Lord, but she convinced him otherwise with her quick answers on farming topics.

Her visit left a deep and lasting impression on Beatrice; as she sat in a rocking-chair by the kitchen fire, after a supper of oatcake and cheese (she had brought the butter with her), and drew on a cigarette, she was touched to be so completely accepted by these self-sufficient Nonconformists, who lived on £1 a week, and with whom she felt strangely at home. It was an antidote to the generally hopeless impression of the working class she had gained in the East End, and served as a useful basis for comparison. Beatrice concluded it would do politicians and philanthropists good to live amongst these sturdy artisans instead of concentrating on the 'ne'er-do-wells'. She was particularly impressed with the Co-op store which she went round, and after carefully studying the manager's books (on the pretext that her father wanted to start his own Co-op) and learning that the dividend was never less than twelve per cent, deduced it was a useful way of teaching working men self-government: co-operation was to be later the subject of her first book.

Beatrice visited also several mills in Bacup, which made her see that *laissez-faire* in practice needed restraint in the form of the factory acts, which forbade women and children to do overtime. Although at that time she saw organisations such as the Co-op as a preventive against 'the socialistic tendency',[30] in fact the visit was to eventually point her in the direction of socialism. It also impressed her with the value of a simple religious life, based on nightly prayer readings from the Bible, Sundays in chapel, upon which the daily round of the mill-workers was still based.

Bacup life had been all engulfing but the moment Beatrice was home again the attraction of Joseph Chamberlain began to lure her in the opposite direction to her avowed aim to make a life as a social investigator. Chamberlain's attention to her was no secret within the family, and Beatrice had already written to her sister Mary disclaiming her suitability for the role of the third Mrs Chamberlain. 'If, as Miss Chamberlain says, the Right Honourable Gentleman takes "a very conventional view of women", I may be saved all temptation by my unconventionality. I certainly shall not hide it. He would soon see that I was not the woman to "forward" his most ambitious views.'[31] Privately however, Beatrice feared that she would not be able to prevent passion and inclination overcoming her true character. It was the old war between the denying and assenting Egos reasserting itself: should she follow the path of duty, or that of love?

To renounce the chance of Chamberlain as a husband might mean giving up her only chance of happiness. Beatrice had quoted the historian James Froude in her diary in October: 'Those that seek for something more than happiness in the world must not complain if happiness is not their portion.' In reality Beatrice hungered for new sensations, for that taste of physical passion which at twenty-five she had not yet experienced. As she sat on the stone bridge overlooking the Wye, watching the water beneath her, she felt she too was being involuntarily carried into a new realm of emotion and feeling, which part of her welcomed. 'Consciousness of sensation,' she wrote, 'is the bridge by which we cross over into the mysterious world of emotion and thought.'[32]

Torn by her contrasting feelings, Beatrice invited Chamberlain to stay in the New Year. Originally she asked him to join the Potters for a dance, but Chamberlain replied with an attempt at humour.

> Dear Miss Potter,
> I do not despise dancing and I have a great respect for King David who continued the exercise to a late period in his life, but what would the Tories say?
> Nero fiddling while Rome burned would be making a sybaritic President of the Board of Trade . . .

Regretfully the Minister concluded that he 'must sacrifice his inclination to the prejudices of the British philistine', although he accepted for 5 and 6 January.[33]

The days passed in a fever of anticipation for Beatrice. 'Alas! The whirlpool. Only two months and I shall be sailing past it for weal or for woe,' she had written in November. But as Christmas approached she resolved 'not to give way to a feeling, however strong, which is not sanctioned by my better self'.[34]

The threat of Chamberlain's visit hung like a sword of Damocles over the Christmas party, who held differing views about what Beatrice called 'a possibly *coming* question'; Mr Potter was particularly uneasy, and Beatrice felt guilty that she was 'entertaining with no *un*tender feeling the arch-enemy'. 'My tortured state cannot long endure. The "to be or not to be" will soon be settled,' she recorded, '. . . as the time approaches I *dare* not *think*, but trust that the energy stored up in days of though*tless*ness will suffice for the last struggle; . . . Perchance some current arising within the "whirlpool" will drift me outward,'[35] she wondered, but the water roared about her ears and she felt herself sucked inexorably towards the vortex.

CHAPTER

IX

RADICAL JOE

*'And last of all came passion, with its burning heat; and
emotion, which had for long smouldered unseen, burst into
flame, and burnt down intellectual interests, personal ambition,
and all other self-developing motives.'*
Beatrice Webb Diary, 15 October 1884

CHAMBERLAIN'S VISIT PROVED AN anti-climax. At first Beatrice was so
nervous when she heard his name announced, that she almost pressed
into his hand £6 just presented to her. Mr Potter resolutely ignored
his unwanted guest, and returned to his game of patience.

Beatrice soon recovered her equanimity, and after dinner the
Radical leader began to delicately hint his requirements. They remained
on 'susceptible terms' until an argument over state education arose;
this was a subject close to Chamberlain's heart, and one which had
made his early reputation. Free education was a pillar of the new
Radical programme about to burst before the public in the *Fortnightly
Review*, and apart from land reform and the Irish problem, there were
few topics on which he felt more strongly. Beatrice dared to defy him
and quote Herbert Spencer. 'It is a question of authority with women,'
Chamberlain told her sternly. 'If you believe in Herbert Spencer you
won't believe in me.'[1]

Battle was declared in the garden; Chamberlain informed her that
'it pains me to hear any of my views controverted', before explaining
his political beliefs to her. Silently she listened, without acquiescing.
Beatrice was a political ingenue at this time. Her new-found interest
in politics stemmed from her growing infatuation for Chamberlain
and, through her sister Kate, a recent friendship with Liberal MP
Leonard Courtney. But while 'the People's Tribune' presented himself
to Beatrice as the champion of the masses, and while she still clung to
the old order, and Spencerian *laissez-faire*, there was little common
ground between them.

It was not merely his convictions but his manner of presenting them
that annoyed Beatrice. Noticing her silence, Chamberlain remarked
that he required ' "intelligent" sympathy' from women. 'Servility, Mr

Chamberlain, think I, not sympathy, but intelligent servility.' Beatrice decided to state her objections as sincerely as she could, but Chamberlain brushed them aside as he vehemently tried to convince her of his mission to undo upper-class privilege and improve the lot of the people.

Chamberlain had made a bid for her sympathy, and he had failed. Beatrice had no understanding of the pressures he was exposed to in Gladstone's divided cabinet, and no awareness of the political situation, with the clamour for social reform, the fate of Ireland and the gathering mood of Jingoism, all surging in conflicting currents around the feet of Gladstone. Chamberlain found the Prime Minister was a hard master to serve under; one who looked for moral absolutes in politics, and saw himself as the instrument of God, carrying out His purpose in an amoral world. And although Gladstone believed that he stood for Liberty (he called his home, Hawarden Castle, 'Liberty Hall'), and Nationalism, in reality he adhered to the old Liberal ideas of self-help and balanced budgets, and was firmly opposed to spending government money on righting social wrongs or foreign adventures. Chamberlain's easy social success irritated Gladstone immensely, who disdained to mix with party members in the smoking room of the House of Commons, and clung to the lonely eminence of his position.

If Chamberlain was riled by the insensitive authoritarianism of the Prime Minister, so was his sovereign, who protested with feeling, '*She* has felt that Mr Gladstone would have liked to *govern* HER as Bismarck governs the Emperor . . . she always felt in his manner an overbearing obstinacy and imperiousness . . . which she never experienced from *anyone* else, and which she found most disagreeable.'[2] One of Chamberlain's greatest sources of aggravation was not knowing when the Grand Old Man would retire. He had already done so once in 1875, only to return to protest at the Bulgarian atrocities. As he grew older Gladstone became convinced that he could not and should not give up until he had found a solution to the Irish question. Meanwhile Chamberlain and Dilke manoeuvred for the position of heir apparent, and Liberal popularity plunged before foreign disasters at Majuba Hill and in Afghanistan and Egypt.

Besides Gladstone and Chamberlain, the other colossus upon the political stage of the 1880s was Charles Stuart Parnell, the Irish Nationalist leader. Certainly Chamberlain had served Gladstone well in negotiating in April 1882 the Kilmainham Treaty, by which the Irish leader was freed from gaol in return for his promise to moderate terrorism; although no sooner was he free than Lord Frederick Cavendish, Gladstone's nephew and the new Chief Secretary for Ireland, and his under-secretary Burke, were murdered in Phoenix Park, leading Gladstone to rush through the new Coercion Bill.

By Christmas 1883, as Beatrice's thoughts dwelt on Chamberlain's coming visit, the storm clouds were gathering over the Sudan. In November the Egyptian army was massacred at the hands of a religious fanatic called the Mahdi. The Queen, who well represented the Jingoist mood of her subjects, urged Gladstone to take revenge, but he dithered, and it was at this juncture that Chamberlain, beset by cares of state, came to spend a few days with Beatrice, who was nervously antici-pating his proposal. Decisive and arrogant, he must have imagined that he could wrap up his business with Beatrice in a few brief conversations, before returning to London. He soon learnt that he had underestimated his hostess.

Beatrice was convinced that Chamberlain wished only to dominate her. 'I felt his curious scrutinising eyes noting each movement as if he were anxious to ascertain whether I yielded to his absolute supremacy,' she noted. If she ventured to protest he 'smashed objection and qualification by an absolute denial'. At the end of the discussion in the garden Beatrice felt exhausted, and Chamberlain remarked that he felt as if he had been making a speech. The next day they walked again in the garden, but pleasantries soon turned into a discussion of the 'woman question'. 'I have only one domestic trouble,' Chamberlain complained to Beatrice, 'my sister and daughter are bitten with the women's rights mania.' But, he added, he allowed them to take no action on the subject. 'You don't allow division of opinion in your household, Mr Chamberlain?' 'I can't help people *thinking* differently from me.' 'But you don't allow the expression of the difference?' 'No.'[3] That single negative made it clear to Beatrice what her position would be as Chamberlain's wife; nor, to her chagrin, did he attempt to propose.

After Chamberlain's departure Beatrice began to regret that she had wasted the opportunity of getting to know him better. She considered that 'the political creed is the whole man', and began to think more carefully what that creed meant. Chamberlain was the leader of a crusade, whose power rested on his intuitive knowledge of the desires of the lower classes, but she doubted whether the gratification of these desires would benefit the country. Nevertheless, she recognised his real sympathy with the lower classes in their misery, despite his despotic nature. 'Running alongside this genuine enthusiasm is a passionate desire to *crush* opposition to *his will*, a longing to put his foot on the necks of others . . .'[4] Beatrice felt that Chamberlain preferred 'the adversary who regards him as the incarnation of the evil one and answers his cold sneers with virulent abuse'. There is little doubt that Chamberlain was both ambitious and arrogant, but Beatrice was not aware of the deep loneliness and unhappiness which gave an extra edge to the vituperation he heaped upon his opponents, and which led him to write, 'This life is a d—d bad business for me and I wish I were out of it.'[5] Unable to express his grief, Chamberlain had developed a protective shell of cynicism and he was at first unpopular in the Commons. An eye-witness wrote after watching him at a public meeting, in terms similar to Beatrice's, 'His face I thought disagreeable when I saw it for the first time close at hand, his mouth taking on a sneer more readily than a smile. The tones of biting sarcasm . . . gave force to the oration but they did not endear the man.'[6]

The meetings between Beatrice and Chamberlain were too few for her ever to know him well, and there is something two-dimensional about her descriptions of him; his letters to Morley and Dilke give the impression of a loyal friend rather than a despot. Nevertheless Beatrice went ahead with a visit to Highbury in March 1884.

'Received a pressing letter from Miss Chamberlain, and feeling convinced that the negotiation was off, I saw no harm in going for two days to Birmingham to watch the great man at home,' her diary states, for Beatrice could not resist the temptation to see Chamberlain and the Caucus in action. Her first impressions of Chamberlain's elaborate red-brick residence, flanked by orchid-houses, were not favourable. Inside there was very much *taste* and all very bad, decided Beatrice, who was soon longing for a plain deal table. The Highbury drawing room attracted the full weight of Beatrice's criticism; she found its elaborately-carved marble arches, satin paper, rich hangings and many watercolours, unrelieved by books or music, horribly nouveau-riche; the two Miss Chamberlains, the Minister's sister Clara and elder daughter Beatrice, sat dowdy and uncomfortable amidst the splendour. The whole family were waiting to greet Beatrice, apart from the Minister himself, who eventually emerged from the greenhouses and welcomed Beatrice with polite constraint. Are we about to take part in a funeral procession? she wondered. The only cheerful note was sounded by John Bright, the respected Radical elder statesman, who warmly welcomed her; he remembered Lawrencina Heyworth, and told Beatrice tales of her early vivacity and charm.

Chamberlain and Bright were to speak that night in the town hall, and were restless and apprehensive. Peremptorily Chamberlain asked Beatrice to allow him to show her the orchid-house the next day, remarking that he did not want his sister to take her there. He retired to his library, only emerging for dinner. It was a subdued meal, during which a guest from Liverpool, a friend of Beatrice's eldest sister Lallie, fawned upon Chamberlain till Beatrice felt like shrieking with irritation. Radical Joe, as everyone called Chamberlain, departed for the town hall leaving Austen, the son of Chamberlain's first marriage to Harriet Kenrick whose birth caused his mother's death, to escort the women. Austen placed them in good seats in the front row of the balcony and all around them were Chamberlains and Kenricks; to Beatrice these earnest Unitarian families appeared utterly provincial. She decided that Chamberlain's brothers had a bit of the cad about them; the women, plain and unpretentious, might be labelled 'for use and not for ornament', and were treated accordingly.

Beatrice sat next to Chamberlain's brother Arthur, who pointed out to her the serried ranks of the Caucus, those members of the National Liberal Federation who were the lynchpin of Chamberlain's popular front. These were the men who had challenged the monopoly of influence long held by the Whigs at Westminster, and under Chamberlain's skilful leadership given Radicalism a new voice and made it a major force in the country. The Caucus was the prototype of the modern party machine, and has been one of Chamberlain's most enduring legacies. As Arthur explained the theory of the organisation to Beatrice, she stared around her at the vast audience packed tight together, mesmerised by the sheer numbers. The audience hummed and swayed, cheering faintly when neighbouring MPs or delegates took their seats on the platform. The band struck up and the three MPs for Birmingham entered, Bright, Chamberlain and the elderly Philip Muntz.

To deafening shouts Chamberlain, 'the master and darling of his town', advanced to the platform. 'The Birmingham citizen . . . adores "Our Joe", for has he not raised Birmingham to the proud position of one of the great political centres of the universe!' declared Beatrice. While Bright spoke she gazed at Chamberlain, who seemed lost in intent thought. The crowd grew increasingly restive, until at last he rose and stood perfectly still before them. The crowd went wild, waving hats, handkerchiefs, even coats, cheering Chamberlain to the rooftops. As he spoke the audience fell silent, borne away by the sound of his voice; the mesmeric passion in his voice was reflected in the faces of the crowd. 'It might have been a woman listening to the words of her lover!' wrote Beatrice.

Beatrice did not lose her suspicion of Chamberlain and compared the crowd to a mistress, with whom a wise man does not argue, preferring merely to assert his will, flavouring it with flattery and appeals to moral feeling. She concluded it was no wonder Radical Joe preferred the sympathy of an uneducated mob to the debates of the educated House of Commons – and if Joe manipulated the crowd as a man manipulates a dependent woman, did that not make him an amoral and unprincipled demagogue? This was the conviction that Beatrice took home with her from Birmingham but it was an unjust one. Despite the later accusations of betrayal made against Chamberlain as the Judas who split the great Liberal Party over Home Rule before crossing the House to join the Conservatives, in the early 1880s he had a genuine desire to improve the lot of the working class, based on the conviction that the great wealth of the landed proprietors was unjust. His social conscience owed much to his bourgeois roots, but although he wished to remedy the abuses of unrestrained *laissez-faire*, he did not wish to sweep the system away. His socialism was merely reformist, although to his enemies his passion sounded alarmingly revolutionary.

That night Beatrice noted Chamberlain's peremptory treatment of his lieutenant Schnadhorst, secretary to the National Liberal Federation. His despotic tendencies, as Beatrice perceived them, were exercised in different ways, sometimes by high-handed arbitrariness, sometimes by manipulation, but they rested squarely upon the support of the powerful clan of Kenricks and Chamberlains to which he belonged. 'There is one eternal refrain in a Chamberlain–Kenrick household,' wrote Beatrice with amusement, 'Birmingham society is superior in earnestness, sincerity and natural intelligence to any society in the United Kingdom.' But although she poked fun at the earnest simplicity of the Chamberlains and their kind, she found a similarity between Birmingham society and that of Bacup, where she had been struck by the deep religious faith of the millhands, 'The same quality of one-idea'dness is present in the Birmingham Radical set.' But in Birmingham it was political conviction which took the place of religion. It seemed possible to Beatrice that the spiritual instinct in Englishmen was now being gratified by politics instead, and she suggested as much to Chamberlain. 'I quite agree with you, and I rejoice in it,' he replied. 'I have always had a grudge against religion for absorbing the passion in man's nature.'

Chamberlain possessed both passion and diplomacy; yet he applied neither *à la recherche d'une femme*. 'But then possibly he does not consider our sex worthy of manipulation,' thought Beatrice. She attempted to analyse her relationship with Chamberlain which, she acknowledged, had affected her in a way no earlier relationship had done. 'Joseph Chamberlain with his gloom and seriousness, with absence of any gallantry or faculty for saying pretty nothings, the simple way in which he assumes, almost asserts, that you stand on a level far beneath him and that all that concerns you is trivial; that you yourself are without importance in the world except in so far as you might be related to him: this sort of courtship (if it is to be called courtship) fascinates, at least, my imagination.'

Although the power Chamberlain exercised in Birmingham fed his egotism, which Beatrice professed to dislike, for a woman with as strong a personality as she possessed, there was an attraction in being courted by a man whose own will was equally strong, if not stronger. Her instinctive desire to be dominated, and to find a father figure as successful and charismatic as her own father had been, was fulfilled in Chamberlain. The other side of her personality, which wished to assert its independence and find intellectual fulfilment, was thwarted by him.

The morning after the political meeting Chamberlain and Beatrice met in the orchid-house. The 'great man', as Beatrice invariably called him, was no longer so constrained, and, 'I had no longer any desire to dispute with him. I no longer cared to adjust my mind to his: I wished only to watch him.' Together they wandered amongst the orchids, Chamberlain, a keen gardener, proudly showing off the different specimens; a bloom from his own glasshouses was always in his buttonhole, the only time when it was absent being after the Phoenix Park murders. Beatrice noted that Chamberlain was 'curiously piqued because I said that the only flowers I loved were wild flowers'. At dinner he 'apologised to me for my own want of taste!'

It was Beatrice's impression that that evening, after their second meeting, 'susceptibility was increasing', although 'it did not show itself in any desire to *please me*, but in an intense desire that I should *think and feel like him* (even in small details of taste), by a jealousy of other influences, especially that of the old philosopher . . .' So the visit ended, leaving Beatrice uncertain of the future, but full of foreboding. 'I don't know how it will end. Certainly not in *my happiness*. As it is, his personality occupies all my thought, and he occupies a too prominent position for me not to be continually reminded of him . . . And if the fates should unite us (against *my will*) all joy and lightheartedness will go from me.'

Beatrice thought that if she married Chamberlain she would be swallowed up in the life of a man whose aims were not her aims, who would refuse her all freedom of thought and to whose career she would have to subordinate her whole life, without believing in its usefulness. Marriage to him would mean her intellectual suicide: 'When feeling becomes strong, as it would do with me in marriage, it would mean the absolute subordination of the reason to it . . . the "pure intellect" would die. I should become *par excellence* the mother and the woman of the world intent only on fulfilling practical duties and gaining practical ends. And that, as Mary would say, is a consummation devoutly to be wished for.'[7]

The next month Beatrice drove over from Mary Playne's home, Longfords, to shut up Standish for the last time; the house where she had spent so much of her childhood was to be finally given up, since she and her father had taken York House in London. She wandered nostalgically along the old walks, reliving her childhood loneliness. For the first time in her life, realised Beatrice, she had just experienced 'the *deliciousness* of life', and known what it was to revel in her own sensations.

As she picked wild flowers, which she later pressed, 'These flowers of all memories, whether bitter or sweet, were clothed with the beautiful sadness of the setting sun . . .' The garden seemed to reflect the struggles which had so far characterised her life, and to remind her of past friendships and the strong ties which bound the nine sisters together under the beneficent hand of Richard Potter. She knew she stood on the threshold of a new life and must choose which path to take, yet she could only resolve to watch and pray.[8]

By 22 April 1884 Beatrice and her father were settled at York House, but her thoughts continually reverted to her inconclusive relationship with Chamberlain. 'My own mind is not made up,' she wrote. 'I have been meditating over the question for five months, have done little else but think about it; now I am no nearer solving it. Practically I have resisted, have refused to take the line of subordination and absolute dependence which would have brought things to a crisis. Possibly my refusal to consent to the conditions will have cured all desire on the other side. Then, though mortified, I shall be relieved.'

Beatrice was forced to admit that the attraction of being 'the wife of a great man', rather than a spinster or an ordinary married woman, was very great. With obsessive fascination she turned over in her mind the part she would play, were she to become the Minister's wife. Alternately attracted and repelled, again and again she reverted to the same stumbling block: the Radical Leader's overpowering and, in Beatrice's eyes, unscrupulous ambition; it followed from this premise that the wife he required was one who would not criticise him, nor contradict his opinions. 'He desires a woman who is personally attractive to him, who will sympathise and encourage him, be a continual rest to him, giving him the uncompromising admiration which the world withholds.' Another time she admitted, 'His temperament and character are intensely attractive to me. I feel I could relieve the gloom, could understand the mixed motive and the difficulties of a nature in which genuine enthusiasm and personal ambition are so curiously interwoven.'

Beatrice was certain she would find the life of a politician's wife distasteful and demoralising. 'Do I believe in the drift of his political views and do I believe that the means employed are *honest*? ... If I do not believe that the end is pursued without deviating from the first moral principles ... I should be selling my soul and should deserve misery.' She acknowledged that once married she would subordinate her views to her husband's and accept his views of right and wrong; she was not a feminist, and accepted the conventional wisdom that the wife should defer to the husband. But until Beatrice had taken that irrevocable step of marriage she would use her own judgement.

Like Chamberlain, Beatrice believed social questions had taken the place of religion and cried out for a solution, but the nagging fear that in Chamberlain's personality the lust for power overrode all other considerations alarmed her; if he bent the facts in his own interests, then he was a traitor to the society which he professed to serve. And if she married him she would have to acquiesce in wrong-doing, perhaps become an accessory to crime, and then 'where could I turn to for peace, that peace which passeth all understanding, the peace of a satisfied conscience?' Beatrice knew she could never influence Chamberlain. 'When I have been absolutely honest with him he has turned away. That is not what he wants and *I know it*. It is only when I have simulated *la femme complaisante*, turned the conversation from principles to personalities that he has desired me.'

If only the man could be separated from his politics. For it was the man she wanted, frankly acknowledging the fundamental need which would be met by Chamberlain's 'great personal attraction and the immediate gratification of a woman's instinctive longing for love and support'. Anxiously Beatrice reproached herself for immodest behaviour: 'My action and thought have been wanting in dignity and nicety of feeling. I have *chattered* about feelings which should be kept within the holy of holies. The only excuse has been the extraordinary nature of the man . . .'[9] As spring turned to summer, Beatrice became increasingly weakened and depressed, leafing hopelessly through her books, unable to concentrate.

Plagued by self-doubt, Beatrice fell under the influence of her friend and cousin Mary Booth who had expressed her contempt at 'any vain attempt to leave the beaten track of a woman's duty'. Mary, like Beatrice's sisters, did nothing to encourage Beatrice's inarticulate but deeply felt aspirations towards an independent life of her own, although she was a well-read woman herself. Instead she led Beatrice to feel that her ambition towards public life was no more than some strange fancy. Mary's disapproval of any breach of the Victorian domestic code which confined woman to her 'proper' private sphere, her veto of Beatrice's dimly felt desire to cross into the forbidden, public, male world, through 'another highway to prominence' apart from marriage, social investigation, discouraged and dispirited her cousin. Hopelessly Beatrice wrote, 'I prayed for light and I *have* it. I see clearly that my intellectual facility is only mirage, that I have no special mission.'

As she contemplated the last few months, Beatrice became bitterly conscious of failure, a failure which spanned the realms of feeling and reason, of love and work. Her diary entry for 9 May contrasted the luxury of her physical surroundings with her inner desperation: 'There is glitter all around me and darkness within, the darkness of a blind desire yearning for the light of love. All sympathy is shut from me. I stand alone with my own nature now too strong for me.'[10]

During the season of 1884 Beatrice met 'the great man', as she called him, once or twice, 'There was a little flicker of feeling and then it died, died a natural death from the unfitness of things.'

The growing acceptance of the 'new woman' of the 1880s gave professional women increasing confidence to pursue careers of their own and the embryonic women's movement had attacked the double standard of Victorian society, a standard which condoned the exploitation of working-class women and girls to meet the sexual needs of men, but demanded virginity of 'pure' middle-class girls. Feminists argued the purest relationship between the sexes was a celibate one, enabling men to rise above the 'animality' and women to find an outlet for their talents outside marriage. Annie Besant, who in 1877 had argued that celibacy was harmful to women, causing hysteria, and shortening their lives, had abandoned this position by 1891. After her conversion to Theosophy she claimed that the sexual instinct that man held in common with the brute should be held in complete control.[11] Empowering celibacy was coming to be seen as a new and positive concept, and was one which influenced Beatrice.

The belief that the highest relationship between the sexes was one in which sex only existed for procreation merged into the belief that marriage itself involved the annihilation of a woman's personality in continual, often unwanted childbearing. It was this belief which led a significant proportion of women to remain single by choice. In addition the continuing imbalance in the population made it inevitable that some women must remain spinsters.

Beatrice's refusal to accept that 'behind *his* destiny woman must annihilate herself' echoes the attitudes of other Victorian women pioneers, at a time when marriage, despite recent Acts of Parliament, such as the Married Women's Property Act and Infants Custody Act, still entailed the merging of a woman's identity into those of her husband and family. In refusing Chamberlain Beatrice had rejected the version of domesticity which she saw in the marriages of sisters Mary, Georgina, Maggie, Theresa and Blanche. The marriage Kate had found with Leonard Courtney became Beatrice's ideal, in which common aims were shared, and the fact that other independent women like Elizabeth Wolstenholme Elmy and Frances Swiney had also advocated celibacy, and were becoming increasingly visible in public life, supported Beatrice in her decision.

By August Beatrice was certain that her relationship with Chamberlain was at an end; as her depression deepened she wrote instructions in her diary that in the event of her death she wished all her diaries to be sent to Cary Darling. The death wish, which is a recurrent theme in her diaries at times of emotional stress, found expression in the notes Beatrice left about the disposal of her effects. On 13 June 1882, two months after her mother's death, Beatrice had willed her 'little property' to her nephew, Alfred Standish Cripps, born in 1881 to her sister Blanche. 'If I do die I hope no one will regret it for me, as I shall not regret it for myself,' she said. The diaries were a particular source of concern to her – 'I don't want any of the *sisters* to see them,' she wrote vehemently. In a further note on 26 September she asked her father to burn all her notebooks after he had read them, but changed her mind and instructed him to send them to Cary Darling, as she did again in 1884.[12]

'I know we are as truly united as ever,' Cary tried to comfort Beatrice in May 1884, 'I think of you constantly and only hesitate about writing lest my letters should find you married and disinclined to talk with me.' Cary still suffered her own 'heavy affliction' after the break-up of her affair with a married master at the boys' grammar school in Queensland, and knew, as she told Beatrice, that 'no one can enter into the secret bitterness of another's heart'.[13] Beatrice found some relief in helping her father, who found it hard to adjust to life as a widower, and he relied upon Beatrice, the only one, apart from Rosy, not absorbed into 'the dearer ties of the wife and mother'. From Summerhill, near Ulverston, where he had rented a house in August near his business in Barrow-in-Furness, he took comfort in sending Beatrice an almost daily account of his doings,[14] and the closely-written pages continued to follow her on her travels abroad.

For in the late summer of 1884 Beatrice went holidaying in Bavaria with Maggie Harkness, who was attempting to earn her living as a freelance writer. Nevertheless, despite the companionship of an intimate friend, day and night Beatrice wept.[15]

Although Beatrice did not write in her diary daily, often allowing several days or even weeks between entries, she found writing it up provided greater therapy than travel. In October, at Summerhill with her father, Beatrice considered the part her diary played in maintaining her equilibrium. 'I don't suppose I shall ever again take that interest in myself to make me much care to tell my thought and feelings to this impersonal confidant – my diary,' she wrote. 'And yet I am loath to bid goodbye to an old friend, one who has been with me since I first had experiences, and wished to tell them to someone, though it were only to a phantom of myself.' Who was it she wrote her diary for, she wondered. In her childhood Beatrice recalled her diary had been her only confidant, and had been the mechanism by which she had survived Lawrencina's rejection. 'Well do I remember, as a small thing, sitting under the damp bushes and brooding over the want of love around me (possibly I could not discern it) and turning in upon myself and saying – "Thou and I will live alone, and if life be unbearable, we will die." Poor little meagre-hearted thing! And then I said – "I will teach thee what I feel, think and see, and we will grow wise together. Then shall we be happy." '

Beatrice's diary became the 'Unknown One' in whom she could confide when surrounded by hostile or neglectful adults. Eventually she found friends in whom she could trust, yet the diary remained a vital prop. Another entry written at midnight at Summerhill in October 1884 shows the extent of her misery: 'Up with pain. The last sleepless nights I had were those terrible ones at York House. Sitting in blank misery on my sofa looking at the two candles burning lower and lower. Darkness is unbearable when in pain. But how much more difficult to bear mental misery than physical pain.'[16]

Wracked with neuralgia and insomnia, she spent a miserable October and November, only diverted by a stay with Theresa and Alfred Cripps, and visits from the Playnes and Kate and Leonard Courtney. As usual Beatrice made swift judgements on her family, finding Theresa 'faintly depressed . . . but sweetly happy'. Alfred's success at the Bar continued, but he had decided not to go into politics, and Beatrice dismissed him peremptorily as 'not a leader of men'. She reserved her approval for the Playnes, Arthur struggling to make a success of his mill, Mary full of schemes to inspire the millhands with *esprit de corps*. Leonard she found more of a puzzle, but her assessment of him was correct: a character full of integrity but lacking in humility. Accurately she prophesied that he would fail on 'the battlefield of politics'.[17]

The rising crises both at home and abroad led Beatrice to analyse the confused political situation. Excitement was mounting over the fate of General Gordon besieged in Khartoum, and soon the 'Grand Old Man' would be vilified 'Gordon's Own Murderer'. In Parliament the new Reform Bill enfranchising rural labourers was limping through the Lords, revealing divisions within the Liberal Party magnified by the antics of the Randolph Churchill's Fourth Party. Beatrice reserved her greatest scorn not for Churchill, but for those leaders who appealed to the passions of envy and class hatred of the masses; in the category of those who manipulated the Will of the People she included Joseph Chamberlain.

Had Chamberlain been able to convince Beatrice of the sincerity of his beliefs, it is probable that they would have married; in 1884 her desire for him was greater than her desire for independence, and it was not until after three years' work in the East End that she felt confident enough of her abilities to be sure that they were more than mere wishes and dreams. But Chamberlain failed: by the late autumn Beatrice was convinced that her relationship with him was finished and the simple happiness of wifehood and motherhood was closed to her. Morbidly she brooded over 'a certain physical deformity overtaking me' and wondered if death were near. 'Have seldom felt more strangely ominous than I do now,' she wrote at York House on 26 November, 'as if death were approaching. Personally it would be welcome.' In her misery she longed for the comfort that Lawrencina had so often failed to give her, and had a dream in which her mother kissed her, while she sobbingly begged her forgiveness for her lack of tenderness; Lawrencina kissed her a second time, and signified forgiveness. 'What would I not give for a mother now; just to lay my head down, tell all – and cry,' wrote Beatrice despairingly.[18]

As Beatrice stared down at her strong, healthy body, she tried to throw off her morbid fancies. But her frustrated desire demanded satisfaction; unlike Kate, who had experienced celibacy with quiet equanimity before her late marriage to Leonard, for Beatrice celibacy was an unnatural and painful state. Only to her diary did she dare confess the passionate longings which threatened to overwhelm her as she struggled helplessly to find a solution to her dilemma. 'But nature is strong and cries out for its natural fulfilment . . .' were words wrung from the depths of her misery. She scratched out the rest of the entry, fearful that her sisters might guess at her agony.

X

A LITTLE KINGDOM OF RIGHTEOUSNESS

*'You will unite the loving-kindness of the friend to the control
of the landlord ... you will rule a little kingdom of
righteousness, and help to eradicate evil by slow but
thorough ways.'*
Octavia Hill, *A Few Words to Fresh Workers* 1889[1]

IN DECEMBER BEATRICE FOUND a way out of her impasse. Canon Samuel
Barnett offered her the management of Katherine Buildings, a bleak
new block of model dwellings in Cartwright Street, near St Katherine's
Docks. Once again she was following in the footsteps of her sister
Kate, after whom the block was named, for Kate herself had intended
to manage it before marriage to Leonard Courtney intervened. Katherine Buildings was the product of the idealism of Samuel Barnett and
a small group of fellow philanthropists who had met in St Jude's
vicarage in 1883 to form the East End Dwellings Company,[2] with a
capital of £200,000, to house those dispossessed dock labourers, 'the
poorest of the poor', who could not afford the rent charged by the
Peabody Trust. Their inspiration was Octavia Hill; Beatrice, and her
new colleague, Ella Pycroft, a country doctor's daughter, now became
part of the corps of lady rent collectors.

Once again Beatrice began charitable work with high hopes,
convinced that this time she would not be dealing with the failures of
the East End, but a representative cross-section of people who would
repay study. Her job was closer to that of social worker than rent
collector or housing manager, based as it was on the firm upper-class
belief that friendship across the classes would bring about the moral
reformation of the poor. From the Ladies Association for the Diffusion
of Sanitary Knowledge to Octavia Hill herself, it was assumed that
nothing but benefit could accrue to the working classes from the
attention of their superiors. Beatrice had no scruples about her
intrusion into the lives of the poor, and was pleased that 'From the
outset the tenants regarded us, not as visitors of superior social status,
still less as investigators, but as part of the normal machinery of their
lives, like the school attendance officer or the pawnbroker.'[3] She was

full of hope that she would not meet the hostility she had encountered as a Charity Organisation Society 'snooper'.

Beatrice and Ella Pycroft's first task was to choose the tenants for the two hundred and eighty rooms, to learn how to size up those likely to prove sober, trustworthy and prompt with the rent. Busily they followed up references, interviewing medical officers, sanitary officers, relieving officers, and School Board visitors, conscientiously visiting tenements in the rabbit warren of streets in Whitechapel and around the docks. From the beginning it was tempting to pick the artisan in regular work, but Beatrice and Ella knew the intention of the founders was to house the lowest classes of East End society whose homes had been demolished. Octavia Hill's buildings, although offering shelter to a class below Peabody's artisans, were usually beyond the reach of those earning less than a regular 16s to 18s a week. Classes C and D, to use Charles Booth's categories, could afford her rents, but they were beyond the reach of the very poor, class A, the lowest class of semi-criminals and loafers. It seems from Beatrice's evidence that class B (casual labourers) were sometimes accommodated in Katherine Buildings, where they presented a multitude of problems.

Katherine Buildings had to be both sanitary and cheap, in accordance with the firm principles laid down by Octavia Hill, who did not believe in spoiling the working classes. 'Primarily I should not carry the water and drains all over the place,' she told the 1885 Royal Commission on Housing. 'I think that is ridiculous. If you have water on every floor, that is quite sufficient for working people.'[4] The result of following Octavia Hill's guidelines was a building remarkable for its ugliness, poor design and hideous decoration. The long double-fronted block, five storeys high, looked out over a street to the front and to a high blank wall at the back, behind which was the Royal Mint. Inside open galleries ran the length of the building, opening out into narrow passages from which led sets of five identical rooms. 'All the rooms were "decorated" in the same dull, dead-red distemper, unpleasantly reminiscent of a butcher's shop. Within these uniform, cell-like apartments there were no labour-saving devices, not even a sink and water-tap!' wrote Beatrice in horror.[5]

The new rent collector reserved her harshest criticism for the sanitary arrangements, which, like the sinks, were concentrated on the landings between the galleries and the stone staircases. There, 'behind a tall wooden screen were placed sets of six closets on the trough system, sluiced every three hours'. Below in the yard stood lines of dustbins. From a sanitary point of view it was a 'super-economical structure', but six hundred men, women and children tramped up and down stairs morning, noon and night, to use the lavatories, which became the focal point of the building. Round the water closets the inhabitants of Katherine Buildings flirted and fought, gossiping and groping in the dimly-lit galleries, 'all decency'[6] sacrificed to the need for low rents.

Katherine Buildings had been built with high ideals. 'At last good houses have replaced hovels,' wrote Barnett exultantly '. . . in the broad streets with their clean tall dwellings it is almost impossible to recall the net of squalid courts and the filthy passages which went by the name of streets . . .'[7] But by 1887 Barnett was arguing that 'to treat one's neighbour as oneself is not to decorate one's own house with the art of the world, and to leave one's neighbour's house with nothing but drain-pipes to relieve the barrenness of its walls.[8] His conclusion came too late for Katherine Buildings, which remained one of the least popular blocks of new housing and by 1890 had a large number of vacancies.

Ella Pycroft soon became a valued friend to Beatrice. 'Plain, very strong-looking, and unattractive except for sincerity of expression', she had a somewhat similar background to Beatrice, coming from a free-thinking family who did not mix with their neighbours; like Beatrice she too idolised her father and had several sisters. Unlike her new colleague however, Miss Pycroft felt her looks were inferior to those of her sisters. 'We shall get on and we are anxious to have no other workers on the block,' wrote Beatrice, who was eager to have no interference in her management of the block.[9]

'Work is the best of narcotics, providing the patient be strong enough to take it,' Beatrice decided in March. Only by throwing herself into her Whitechapel work, trudging through the narrow streets until she was overcome with exhaustion, could she forget Chamberlain. The confusion of the past year when she attempted to combine society life and Charity Organisation Society work had subsided. 'Real work brings society into its proper place – as a rest and relaxation, instead of an effort and an excitement.'[10] Avoiding the temptation to make a good story out of her East End experiences during her West End evenings, she vowed to conquer egoism, to humbly serve those around her rather than coldly to make them the subject of her observation and analysis.

Beatrice's approach to the inhabitants of the slums was less emotional and more detached than that of many of her contemporaries, but it was almost impossible for her to step outside the reactions of a woman of her class to the throbbing, pulsating mass of humanity which was the East End. The slum dwellers seemed to her, 'a constantly decomposing mass of human beings, few rising out of it but many dropping down dead, pressed out of existence in the struggle.'[11] The image of decaying matter was one which frequently presented itself to her. Edward Denison, one of the first young intellectuals to come and live in the East End, had written with a similar note of horror in 1867, 'I passed for the first time up Petticoat Lane and through Ragfair. You never saw such a place; humanity swarms there in such quantity, of such quality, and in such streets, that I can only liken it to the trembling mass of maggots in a lump of carrion.'[12]

When not perceived as crawling larvae, the poor were regarded as savages, inhabitants of a dark continent more unknown than Africa, whose natures were bestial, whose passions were animalistic, and who were separated from the middle classes by a yawning chasm almost impossible to bridge. General William Booth of the Salvation Army, bitter opponent of the Charity Organisation Society, likened the poor to the inhabitants of the jungle. 'Civilisation, which can breed its own barbarians, does it not also breed its own pygmies?' he asked. 'May we not ... discover within a stone's throw of our cathedrals and palaces similar horrors to those which Stanley has found existing in the Great Equatorial Forest?' Booth divided the Africans into two types, which he considered also present among the 'natives' of the East End: 'The baboon type of pygmy ... a very degraded specimen, with ferret-like eyes, close-set nose, more clearly approaching the baboon than was supposed to be possible, but very human,' was, like the 'handsome dwarf' type, represented in darkest London by 'the vicious lazy lout and the toiling slave'.[13] 'The lot of a negress', argued Booth, was happier than that of many a Christian orphan who fell into prostitution until she sank to the depths of the 'Woolwich dusthole', where the prostitutes stood in sad groups at the pierhead, willing to sell themselves for the price of a crust of bread.

The language of colonialism was shared by Beatrice, who referred to her own tenants as a 'rough lot – the aborigines of the East End'.[14] Class contempt for the very poor, who were regarded as a separate race, merged into another fear, that they might infect the prosperous classes with disease.

Fear of the slum-dweller as a source of contagion had increased with the ravages of the cholera epidemics in 1831, 1848, 1853, and more recently in 1866, when thousands of people had died. Typhus and typhoid were also endemic, the result of overcrowding and polluted water supplies, although between 1858 and 1865 Bazalgette laid down his great sewer system in London, eighty miles in length, which had improved London's sewerage. The air-borne diseases such as tuberculosis, the 'white plague' (which accounted for a third of all deaths in Victorian England), diphtheria, measles, scarlet fever and smallpox, were all widely feared, and lent fuel to the environmentalist argument for social reform.

Although the general death rate had dropped from 22.5 per thousand in the 1860s to 18.9 in 1881, the infant death rate remained stubbornly high at 153 per thousand even in the 1890s. In London alone twenty thousand infants under one died each year in London during that decade, showing the enormous gulf between the middle-class Victorian ideal of 'motherhood' and the working-class reality. The working-class mother was made the scapegoat for infant deaths, blamed for working when she should be breastfeeding, for quieting her baby with fatal opiates such as Godfrey's Cordial, for leaving it with childminders, which amounted to infanticide, and for overlaying when drunk.

In Katherine Buildings Beatrice and Ella Pycroft waged war on dirt and immorality, attempting to impose their own bourgeois standards upon the 'natives', who were, in the main, impervious to their earnest efforts. 'Feel so utterly *done* when I come back from Whitechapel,' complained Beatrice. 'Too tired to think or feel, which possibly under present circumstances is the most comfortable state. So long as I have strength enough to go on, don't much care, but dread idleness as if it were Hell.'[15] The 'bigness of my work', the sense of responsibility for the occupants of Katherine Buildings, worries over Rosy and her father, left her feeling 'rather dizzy'. Although Beatrice claimed to welcome work and dread idleness, rent collecting in the East End was a hard and demoralising experience, physically draining for a woman of her leisured and sheltered background. 'When over-tired the tenants haunt me with their wretched, disorderly lives. Wish I had started with more experience, and had taken the thing more regularly in hand,' she wrote, 'half-hearted work is always bad.'[16]

The truth was that Beatrice was still drawn to Chamberlain, despite her protestations to the contrary. She had confronted but not conquered the duality in her nature which caused her constantly to juxtapose the ideal of love and marriage against that of an independent working life. The struggle between the affirming and denying Egos continued to occupy her conscious mind, causing her to ask,

'What will the next entry be – in the rapids – or out of them? either *for ever.*'

In January 1885 she had allowed herself to return to Birmingham. Chamberlain's name was on everyone's lips as he launched his Radical Programme with a furious attack on the rich who, 'having annexed nearly everything that is worth having, expect everybody else to be content with the crumbs that fall from their table . . . I ask what ransom will property pay for the security which it enjoys?' he thundered.[17] This provocative question brought the expected storm of criticism from the Whigs. The climax of Chamberlain's campaign came at a meeting at Bingley Hall which Beatrice attended. 'I have been the subject of torrents of abuse and of whirlwinds of invective . . . If it be blackmail to propose that the rich should pay taxation in equal proportion to the poor, what word is strong enough to describe the present system under which the poor pay more than the rich?' Chamberlain asked his audience.[18] In Birmingham the cult of 'Radical Joe' had reached unprecedented heights and Chamberlain received a standing ovation even before he began to speak. As Beatrice watched the master orator on the platform before her, the object of adoration to the cheering masses who had at last, so he told them, come into their inheritance, her infatuation increased. 'A warm moonlight night with soft west wind, thinking of a crowded hall, deafening shouts, dead silence except for one voice – the voice of the people's tribune,' she wrote that night.

Beatrice was reading the letters of George Eliot, and her thoughts of Chamberlain were curiously confused with memories of Herbert Spencer, through whose affection she felt she and George Eliot were closely bound: 'A great lover and a small soul linked by a great mind,' she wrote.[19] The 'great lover' was in the forefront of Beatrice's own mind, but there is an element of wish fulfilment in her diary entry, as it seems probable that at this critical point in his career politics claimed Chamberlain's entire attention. But in Beatrice's imagination the next day held the secrets of her fate: 'Tomorrow I shall know how my fate is to be unravelled. No longer in my hands. If the answer be yes I am in honour tied. If no, I am free and *will* be free in body and mind, free until another binds me. I will not bind myself again and wake up and find myself unbound. Do most people shut their eyes wilfully as *I* have done and drift, drift, drift they know not whither even with a dim dark dread of a whirlpool ahead? God help thee child; this will be thy last childish day – tomorrow will make thee a woman, a woman to love or a woman to work while others love.'[20]

The next day proved an anti-climax to Beatrice's secret imaginings;

if a critical meeting with Chamberlain did take place, again no proposal ensued. Instead Beatrice had to console herself with a long talk with Clara Chamberlain, who had become engaged to be married. Clara explained to Beatrice the loneliness of her life as the great man's sister, 'My brother absorbed in his sorrow and his politics, and only the little children to care for.' Disappointed, Beatrice turned back to George Eliot's 'dull' letters. She was amused by Spencer's romantic interest in Marion Evans – although attracted to Evans in a cerebral sense Spencer was said to think her too ugly to take the relationship further – which had led him to consult Beatrice on the impression the letters gave of their relationship; he had even asked Cross, the editor of the letters, to insert a denial that there had been a relationship between himself and George Eliot. But the most enduring lesson Beatrice drew from her reflections was that man must accept his fate. '*Renunciation*, that is the great fact we all, individuals and classes, have to learn. In trying to avoid it we bring misery to ourselves and others.'[21] Renunciation was the path that Beatrice's conscience urged her to follow, but not her heart.

In the intervening months Beatrice read the essays of Ralph Emerson on Fate. Learn 'fatal courage' was Emerson's injunction: 'Go face the fire at sea, or cholera in your friend's house . . . knowing you are guarded by the Cherubim of Destiny.' Beatrice doubted Emerson's belief that every man or woman had a special mission to fulfil; surely it could not be true of the ordinary man, she wrote scornfully, 'unless serving as manure be the special mission of some men and women', but, 'Emerson speaks as a great man to great men. He inspires you at the risk of inflating your ego.'[22]

Still she wavered over Chamberlain. Later in January, after visiting a private view with Herbert Spencer, Beatrice had gone on to Dolly Tennant's. In the little sitting room were portraits of great men, including most of the radical ministers. 'Leonard Courtney used to be a great favourite' (no doubt before his fall from favour in November 1884); instantly Beatrice noticed one of her hostess's other portraits, of 'another great man whom I recognised and somewhat envied the likeness of . . .' It was a signed photograph of Chamberlain.[23]

The turning-point in Beatrice's relationship with Chamberlain came in July 1885, again a critical point in the Radical leader's career; on 8 July Gladstone's government had fallen. In February the nation had been shocked by the news of the death of General Gordon, but the Liberals had rallied when Gladstone sent Garnet Wolseley to crush the Mahdi, the nationalist leader in the Sudan. No sooner was this crisis surmounted than news came that the Russians had attacked Afghanistan. There was a crisis on the London Stock Exchange, echoed throughout Europe, but fortunately the issue was resolved through arbitration. All was overshadowed by the Irish question, in which few were more deeply involved than Joseph Chamberlain. Captain O'Shea, claiming to be in the confidence of Charles Stuart Parnell, negotiated with the President of the Board of Trade on behalf of his master, but O'Shea was never privy to Parnell's real feelings, which remained committed to an Irish Parliament. Chamberlain's own plan for a National Council for Ireland merely held out the hope of Irish control over local government, and as such fell far short of Parnell's hopes and aims.[24] Even so, it was too ambitious a scheme to please the Viceroy, Lord Spencer, the 'Red Earl', as the Irish nationalists called him, who swung the peers behind him to vote against Chamberlain's scheme in Cabinet. Chamberlain, his ally Charles Dilke and the Prime Minister himself, were all threatening resignation when at last the shaken government finally fell over the unpopular duties on beer proposed in the budget.

Chamberlain was now 'unmuzzled'. Elated, he and Dilke saw new power and influence opening before them, if Salisbury's Conservative government should prove short-lived. Surely now the seventy-six-year-old Gladstone must retire and leave the field for younger men? But the Radicals had committed themselves to the Irish proposals which appeared in the *Fortnightly Review* as part of the Radical Programme, proposals now the subject of vicious attack in Parnell's mouthpiece, *United Ireland*. The 1884 Reform Bill and single-member redistribution of seats made it clear that after the General Election Parnell would, as Chamberlain had calculated, have eighty, not sixty, followers in the House of Commons, and therefore be in a new position of strength. It was an electric situation politically; it was also the point at which Kate Courtney decided to bring Joseph Chamberlain and her sister together again at a picnic at Burnham Beeches.

It is curious that Kate should have attempted to further the relationship between Beatrice and Joseph Chamberlain, since she bore him considerable resentment for his part in her husband's disgrace. Earlier in July Chamberlain had dined with the Courtneys and Beatrice. 'He said, looking at me intently to see how I took it, "Your brother-in-law is an ass. Proportional representation lost him his chance of distinction in political life. *This* lost him his seat",' wrote Beatrice. (Courtney had voted against the medical relief bill, thereby defying Chamberlain.) When the picnic was suggested, Chamberlain had requested that the date be changed in order that he might be able to come, and a party was made up which included not only the Radical leader but his daughters, as well as Beatrice. Despite the lovely weather, the day proved a fiasco. 'That day will always remain engraved on my memory as the most painful one of my life,' wrote Beatrice. 'The scene under the Burnham beeches, forcing me to tell his fortune – afterwards behaving with marked rudeness and indifference. The great reception given to him at the station, returning back in the evening, we all running after him like so many little dogs . . .'[25]

She wrote an account of the occasion to her sister Mary: 'I suppose you will want a "notice" of our last entertainment – the great man and I are painfully shy when we are alone and very anxious that nothing shall be noticed when others are there – a state of affairs which seems destined to lead to endless misunderstandings. It certainly brings a good deal of unhappyness [sic] to me – and I can't imagine *he* finds much amusement in it – I should think one or the other of us must break off this impractical relationship this autumn, by refusing to see more of each other. I shall try to let the matter rest now and turn my thoughts to other things – perhaps he will do so too and then the relationship will die of inanition . . .'[26]

Kate wrote in her diary, 'Mr. Chamberlain talked a good deal and very frankly about politics but his tone about them was detestable and made me feel that if he becomes as he threatens to be the dominant power in the Liberal party, we shall have no such thing as real freedom in political life. It will become an organised petty tyranny . . .' Kate blamed Chamberlain for Leonard's downfall, and denounced him for making speeches, 'Openly bidding for the leadership and throwing out socialistic suggestions to catch the popular vote.'[27] Leonard's position was now, Beatrice considered, 'very pathetic . . . I am pretty sure he will be an absolute failure as far as success is concerned – and that will be. a sad business,' she told Mary.[28]

To Beatrice Kate wrote anxiously, 'Dearest Bee, . . . I wonder what you thought of yesterday? You may know something I do not but to me there was no sign or trace of any other feeling than an intense personal ambition and desire to dominate at whatever cost of other people's rights – I do not even see any room in his nature for such an affection as would satisfy one of us. It would be a tragedy – a murder of your independent nature.'[29]

Mary Booth too hurried to comfort Beatrice, writing on 25 July, 'I can't tell you the feeling of relief that your letter has given me. Even in the midst of feeling sorry – very sorry that you should have all this pain and disturbance of thought; – the worry of worries that the need to decide finally a crucial question must bring; – I do rejoice to know that the decision is "No". In my mind the conviction has been growing and deepening that you could never be happy; – and would be increasingly unhappy with that man in such a relation to you. However you know how I feel; and what you tell me of him in your letter only confirms what I have felt before. As for your future happiness; – it is no doubt natural that as I have not had your suffering to go through in person, I should take a more easy minded view than you seem to do. It has been the decision; – the constant recropping up of the most inauspicious connection which has taken away your peace. But that is over, and now that you can feel that you have given yourself every motive for determining to turn your back on it all, I think you will begin to mend.'[30]

Mary Booth's optimism was to prove ill-founded; Beatrice's depression was to deepen before it mended. But Leonard Courtney's advice to her to follow the inner promptings of her conscience and to put moral principles before ambition, befitted a man who had sacrificed his own career over principle. Leonard had never approved of the planned picnic, which he had not attended, and 'only knew by report what happened in the afternoon, but as we came home in the saloon carriage you looked to my eyes a little distraite,' he wrote on 28 July. 'Was I over anxious or am I more than brotherly in wishing we could get clear of these uncertainties and embroilments?'

Hesitating to interfere, Leonard now feared that he was being cowardly. 'After all, a word may not be grossly impertinent. Can there be any real happiness except in the satisfaction of our deeper wants and the fulfilment of better ideals? – You sometimes declare a politician must pursue his ends (if they are noble) by ignoble means; but even if there be a necessity, which I deny, there is no paramount necessity on anyone of us to be a politician or a politician's wife. I do not believe you could be happy in being less than yourself, especially if you find yourself left to live a splendid life without real companionship or sharing aims and plans. So I have been sad, or sorry if sad is too strong a word at what might prove a preparation for barren brilliances. . . . Wit and the capacity for a noble life should not be sacrificed at meaner altars . . . You see, my dear Beatrice, I don't want you to be unhappy anyway, but there is a choice in the forms of unhappiness and the lower is always the lower.'[31]

Beatrice took her brother-in-law's advice to heart, knowing that the 'higher' unhappiness of a life of work and study suited her nature better than the 'barren brilliance' of being Chamberlain's wife. After the meeting in Burnham Beeches the element of fantasy evaporated, although Beatrice was unable to help herself constantly thinking of Chamberlain and from following his career with close interest. But for many months after Burnham Beeches she did not meet him.

Philosophically she wrote again to Mary Playne from Rusland, where she was staying with her father and Rosy. 'I think it is better to stick to my work and try to forget the past and the sympathy of sympathetic sisters tends to keep useless feelings alive. During my fortnight's holiday I have thought very seriously about my own fortune and especially about my relationship to Mr Chamberlain and I think I have arrived at definite conclusions. I certainly do not intend to be forlorn . . .' There was, she decided, enough work to be done to make life worth living, 'Even without personal happiness – and who knows either how personal happiness comes to us. What are the conditions which bring it and destroy it? . . . Better to be guided by a sort of sobered instinct.'[32]

When Beatrice returned to London on 8 August, she threw herself whole-heartedly into her work at Katherine Buildings. Kate and Leonard Courtney had bought a house in Cheyne Walk in Chelsea, after some initial misgivings over the drainage, and Beatrice was glad to stay with her sister and travel conveniently to work by the ferry to Tower Pier. In the evenings she lay on the sofa, exhausted by her work with the recalcitrant tenants, watching the river and the barges floating by, while Maggie Harkness, who was also staying with the Courtneys, played the piano and they talked of old times. Once, as schoolgirls, they had visualised a married future, 'prophesying we should in ten years be talking of cooks and baby linen'. Instead both were struggling to forge a working life, one as a novelist, the other, despite 'her cook and big establishment', committed to that 'service of man' which best fulfilled Positivist ideals. Both, said Beatrice, had 'passed through the misery of strong and useless feelings'.[33]

Soon after her return Beatrice visited Emma Cons, who was in charge of another working-class tenement called Surrey Buildings, noting that, unlike the majority of the voluntary rent collectors, Miss Cons was 'not a lady by birth . . . the face and manner of a distinguished woman, a ruler of men . . . Certainly not a lover of fact or theory. Was not clear as to total number of rooms, unlets or arrears. No description of tenants kept.' Beatrice decided she would gather accurate facts and statistics about the South London Building Company, who managed Surrey Buildings, and about Katherine Buildings and its tenants, and even about the docks after a visit to the Albert and Victoria Docks in November. 'But I should like to master the whole thing,' she wrote. 'The courteous old gentleman seemed somewhat taken aback by my questions and demand for statistics. But I shall get them if I have patience.'[34] And so she did; such was her energy and persistence that after their initial surprise her informants usually gave her the information she wanted.

From mid-1885 Beatrice came more and more to identify with the celibate, philanthropic women who had in some way deviated from the Victorian domestic ideal of the 'angel in the house'. Miss Cons she categorised as one of 'the modern class of *governing women*'. 'Their eyes are clear of self-consciousness and bright with love and the pity from which it springs. They have the dignity of habitual authority. Often they have the narrow-mindedness and social gaucherie of complete absorption, physical and mental, in one set of feelings and ideas.' She contrasted this type with the 'pure organiser' such as a hospital matron, 'to a certain extent unsexed by the justice, push, and severity required'. Not that Beatrice despised these qualities, but to guide men, she concluded, feeling more than thought was required.

Working in tandem, Beatrice and Ella Pycroft launched a variety of schemes designed to civilise and moralise their tenants. However they were attempting to realise an unrealisable ideal, even if their vision of the working-class home was not as patronising nor as sentimentalised as Octavia Hill's picture of 'the pretty little home, small, but so happy, where the cradle stands by the fire, and where the wife sits working till father comes home, where every shilling of raised wages means fresh little comforts, worked for and valued'.[35]

It was a strange paradox which found two unmarried middle-class women acting as 'mothers' to hundreds to working-class families, the majority of whom rejected the much-vaunted 'friendship' offered them. The robust working-class culture of the tenants proved provokingly resistant to change, despite scoldings[36] on the part of Beatrice and Ella, until their energy and enthusiasm eventually gave way to disillusionment and capitulation. As Ella complained to Beatrice the following February, when they held a concert for the men, 'They sang songs I very much disapproved of, and Mr Aarons brought forward a friend to sing and dance though Mr Paul and I had distinctly said we would not have it.' Ella Pycroft's 'black looks' stopped them, but then, 'Elliott came forward . . . and made a speech most insolently finding fault with my conduct, and I had to answer him and assert my authority; and Mr Aarons appealed to the people to know if he hadn't succeeded in amusing them, and all the low set applauded him.' Ella had no alternative but to leave 'with my friend Miss Black, the only lady who was there, and I got hissed by the rough set as we went out'. Undefeated, Ella called a meeting, and Aarons and Elliott agreed that they 'ought to try and raise the tone of the people . . . without vulgar jokes or worse'. 'We parted with smiles. It was a grand conquest,' recounted Ella with pride, secure in the knowledge that she held the whip hand with the men as the club room was let to her.[37]

'Raising the tone' of the tenants occupied all Beatrice and Ella's time; soon they were on first-name terms, and in each other's absence they ran the building methodically. It was with satisfaction that Beatrice wrote, 'Took over the whole work from Miss Pycroft . . . Arrears diminished; rooms let; first-rate broker engaged; caretaker's work observed; amount of repairs done by him estimated. Morality enforced on buildings . . .'[38] Maurice Paul, one of Octavia Hill's helpers, started a Boys' Club and ran a Reading Room, Beatrice began to plan the introduction of a committee of men who might take part in the management of the buildings, and Ella ran a savings bank for the tenants and soon had forty depositors whose savings amounted to about £1 a week – they did 'pretty well for these bad times'.

Enforcing middle-class standards of sobriety and morality was more difficult. Beatrice had to report that she had 'failed in respect of Roadnight [a porter] . . . Suspect him of drinking; not sufficiently to be a scandal, but too much to keep respect of tenants'. The gin palaces of the East End offered the poor an escape from their squalid tenements, as many reformers recognised: 'Gin is the only Lethe of the miserable,' wrote General Booth. He estimated that there were fourteen thousand drink shops in London alone. 'The tap-room in many cases is the poor man's parlour. Many a man takes to beer, not from the love of beer, but from a natural craving for the light, warmth, company and comfort which is thrown in along with the beer . . .'[39] Drink and immorality – I have to wage an incessant war against – not always a pleasant occupation,' Beatrice told her father. She tried firmness, making use of that natural air of authority which was part of her character, part the hallmark of her class, but nevertheless she had a 'disagreeable row with one of Miss Pycroft's tenants, and had to use summary measures'. She decided that 'softness would have paid better than hardness', but it was not easy to enforce respect for the law,[41] and the tenants needed constant watching. As she explained to her father, 'I am here every day but Saturday and Sunday. I sleep here on Monday – I think it would really pay to sleep here oftener as it gives me a better chance of watching the tenants and finding out the bad ones. The caretaker is a good man *if* he does not drink – of that I have a slight suspicion – I mean to keep a steady look out.'

The tenants' habits proved impossible to remedy. 'I have turned out two women this week for leading bad lives – and I am quite aware there are a dozen more,' Beatrice complained to her father. Ella too found the tenants a trial in Beatrice's absence, writing to her colleague, 'Mrs Taylor is as bad as ever, and I am going to give her notice on Monday, and county court her for every penny she owes when she leaves,' as a warning to the others.[41] As for the trough system, 'it has led to indecencies of which I should never have dreamed', but Ella and Maurice Paul had put their heads together, and, 'He proposes that when the keys come to the latrines for men and women they should be kept on separate balconies, and he thinks most of the men would approve.'[42]

Beatrice was scandalised by the behaviour of the police, who cohabited with the female tenants when the opportunity presented itself. A police inspector regularly visited a young married woman when her sailor husband was away. 'I am afraid the police down here are far from immaculate – in spite of the ultra respectability of their uniform – and take advantage of their position of authority.'[43] The moral standards of the middle classes had little meaning or relevance for the urban working class, and prostitution often appeared the only way of supplementing the starvation wages open to a seamstress. Vice, as General Booth said, 'offers to every good-looking girl during the first bloom of her youth and beauty more money than she can earn by labour in any field of industry open to her sex.'[44] Records of the Salvation Army Rescue Homes showed that many new entrants into prostitution were orphans to whom no other asylum was available but the Workhouse, and the 'friends' whom they encountered on the London streets frequently hoaxed them into entering a brothel.

Few of the tenants in Katherine Buildings were in regular work. They were lazy, complained Mrs Ansing, who came from a Prussian Catholic family of sweaters, middlemen between the hands who made men's clothing and the retail outlet. Beatrice agreed with Mrs Ansing, who often spent the whole day hunting for her employees in pubs. The tenants were, 'On the whole a *leisure* class; picking up their livelihood by casual work, poor in quality; by borrowing from their more industrious friends, and by petty theft. Drunken, thieving and loose in their morality.' Ella too considered the tenants workshy. 'If a man is constantly out of work it is generally his own fault,' she told

Beatrice, giving as an example the case of Gibbs, who was given a ticket for a day's work at the docks by a friend who was a Preferable, a regular dock labourer, but failed to get out of bed in the morning.[45] Yet the tenants were not all bad, Beatrice decided; they were also 'generous-hearted and affectionate, capable of self-control when once you have gained their affection'.[46]

Beatrice decided to become an authority on artisan dwellings; she was, she told her father, amazed that her sister Kate had remained so in the background while working as a rent collector. 'It is a wonder to me how Kate kept so clear of excitement – and felt content to stick to her own little bit, without an attempt to master the whole question of artisan buildings.' Beatrice, on the contrary, was determined to master the facts, but she was shy of her new enthusiasm, requesting that her father did not show her letter to anyone staying in the house. 'I wish you would talk about *all* your daughters *except* me,' she told him. 'An interesting hard working life with *just a touch* of adventure! is so delightful, so long as one does not get stamped with that most damaging stamp, "Eccentricity"! . . . So my darling old Father, you must wipe me clean out of your conversation! And then if Rosebud will get strong and blooming and be prepared to take more of my duties in home and society life – I shall feel myself free to devote a good portion of my time and energy to the "question of the day" with what results time will show.[47]

Although Katherine Buildings dominated Beatrice's mind, she never forgot her family; her father was speculating unwisely on the Stock Exchange, and she worried that he would not provide satisfactorily for her sisters. 'I don't feel quite happy about money matters with all those speculative investments. I can't help wishing you could see your way to fulfilling your promise of making up the married sisters' portions and Kate's. They are all getting on in life and would be glad of the extra income . . . I think Mother would have thought it a wise and right step to take – now that you are getting on in life . . . Of one thing I am quite certain: it is wisest to make up your mind what you *really intend to do* – assert it – and stick to it.' Her homily bore fruit, and in September she was able to thank her father for sending her married sisters £500 each, although disclaiming it for herself and Rosy. 'We really have no more right to it than we have to the initial £500 settled on the girls – We both of us enjoy the luxury of your home and are liberally provided with everything we require; handsome allowances for our dress – Rosy has her horse and I give from out of your pocket to my charities . . . Of course when we marry we shall be given the same amount as the others possess at that time.' Beatrice was extremely concerned to be fair yet generous, as she told her father: 'The only way, in a big family like ours is to keep a thoroughly nice feeling about money matters – is for every member to be generously indifferent how much others get and scrupulously fair just how much they receive themselves . . . Gifts should be given where there is a want, without having to give all the others the same amount – (If ever I marry a poor man and want £200 to get over some crisis – I shall accept it with gratitude).'[48]

The strain of her life as she tried to juggle running a large house, entertaining, and the responsibility of her father and Rosy, made Beatrice complain to her father in November that she was exhausted after spending the whole of Saturday interviewing thirty maids, finally selecting three to come back from whom to make her final choice. The happiness of the household at York House revolved around Rosy, who seems to have been suffering from anorexia nervosa,[49] and who was a constant source of worry to her sister. 'I shall give the one I choose clearly to understand that her place depends on pleasing Rosy and doing well for her and that she goes with her everywhere and looks after her thoroughly,' Beatrice told her father.[50] To Mary Playne she partly blamed her father for Rosy's chronic illness and unhappiness, and governesses came and went without any academic progress on Rosy's side. 'The latest governess failed to get hold of Rosy in any way – in fact so long as she is with father the ablest woman in England could not do it.'

Beatrice decided Rosy should be separated from her father, and suggested abandoning her work temporarily to take Rosy to the Argoed, 'so long as I get her to myself and have a fair chance of success and return for my sacrifice'.[51] Mary agreed that something must be done, 'There will be a danger of this hysteria getting control over her. It is a ticklish time when a girl gets into this state and she needs a firm and kind hand over her – There is always a danger of a girl getting into a chronic state of wilfulness and ill-health.'[52] Rosy herself was understandably resentful of her 'handsome and brilliantly clever' sister, who made her feel inferior. 'We were fond of each other after a fashion,' she wrote, 'and I had a great opinion of her abilities as she had no doubt a contempt for mine. She used to call me a sweet young thing and always advised me to look upon marriage as my destiny.'[54] Yet although Beatrice found the ineffectual Rosy endlessly infuriating, she was sympathetic. 'Poor little Rosy,' Beatrice said to Mary, 'after all everything has been against her from the very beginning when Mother felt so miserable and resentful and thoroughly worried about Dicky. She has really been sacrificed to the failings of her two parents.'[55]

As her knowledge of the tenants at Katherine Buildings grew, Beatrice became inspired by a new project: to make a book of all the tenants, past and present, including details of 'number of family, dead and alive; occupation of all members; actual income from work, charity or private property; race; whether born in London, if so, belonging to London stock? If not, reason for immigration, and from what part of the country; religion . . .'[55] This survey, which was to include all Miss Pycroft's tenants as well as her own, was part of her 'special aim' to understand working-class housing by applying the 'scientific method' for which Spencer had taught her to have so much respect.[56] Beatrice was defensive about her plans, writing in her diary: 'And why should not I have the enjoyment, now that I am young, of a thoroughly congenial pursuit? Through the management of men, one will always get the opportunity of studying them.'[57]

Beatrice was beginning to impress people with her ability and she was surprised to find that the Directors of the East End Dwellings listened to her criticisms of Katherine Buildings and took them into account when planning a new model dwelling. Samuel Barnett eagerly seized on her suggestion that an association should be formed of all the agencies concerned with housing the poor, of whom there were now about one hundred and fifty thousand in model housing according to Beatrice's estimate. She was surprised to find that even the most unlikely young men were drawn by her enthusiasm into offering to help; 'Young S——, a meek and mild pretty-looking young man, who I have always put down as a dancing idiot . . . half-promised to help me with the boys' club . . . It is extraordinary how much earnestness there is in the air, and how shy every one is of owning to it.' A major, who had commanded the Black Watch when it was quartered at the barracks in Church Street, Kensington, next to York House, offered to pay the arrears of those tenants who were behind with the rent. In fact, Beatrice wrote to her father, the gallant major also wanted to know whether Beatrice was 'at home' any other day but Sunday, and whether she and her father could come down to Aldershot, 'to which I replied my profession tied me absolutely to London'.[58]

Beatrice was growing in confidence and the devoted Ella Pycroft was the perfect partner for her. 'She and I are cut out to work with each other, as she has the practical ability and power to carry things through with steady work, and I have more initiative and power of expression,' Beatrice explained to her father. 'What I lack is method and strength; both fail me in critical times. I have much greater *show* of ability than reality, arising from my audacity of mind and plausible way of putting things. My dear old Father, I am a sort of weak edition of you! There is no doubt about it. I enjoy the planting, but don't care for the tending!'[59]

Many well-meaning idealists like the Barnetts or Octavia Hill distrusted the gathering of information which was to be such an important catalyst for reform, but Beatrice had enough faith in her own ideas to persist even when Octavia Hill told her that her plan to keep accurate descriptions of the tenants was so much 'windy talk . . . There was a slight clash between us, and I felt penitent for my presumption. But not convinced.'[60]

Beatrice and Octavia Hill only met once during this period, at dinner at the Barnetts in May 1886. 'A small woman, with large head finely set on her shoulders; The form of her head and features, and the expression of the eyes and mouth have the attractiveness of mental power. A peculiar charm in her smile,' was Beatrice's description. Ella Pycroft was less complimentary, feeling jealous of the higher class of tenant at Octavia Hill's buildings, and the better cleanliness, although she consoled herself by remarking, 'They have none of our space and light and fresh air.' As for Miss Hill, she 'is a wonderfully powerful woman. I know she could manage me, and there aren't many people who could. There is a sort of deliberately ponderous strength in her face and manner. I am not sure that I like her. I feel as if I should be afraid of her if she set her will against mine.'[61] That indomitable will which had won Octavia Hill such a respected position in the housing movement had not protected her from emotional trauma, as Beatrice knew, for Octavia Hill had been in love for many years with Edward Bond, a leader of the Charity Organisation Society; it was with sympathy and a certain sense of identification that Beatrice recalled first meeting Miss Hill when she came to dine at Prince's Gate with the Potters fourteen years earlier: 'At that time she was constantly attended by Edward Bond. Alas! for we poor women! Even our strong minds do not save us from tender feelings. Companionship, which meant to him intellectual and moral enlightenment, meant to her "Love". This, one fatal day, she told him. Let us draw the curtain tenderly before that scene and enquire no further. She left England for two years' ill health. She came back a changed woman.' Beatrice blamed Octavia Hill for allowing her thoughts and feelings to have become crystallised by sorrow into a rigid mould which forbade the acceptance of new ideas, until love of power came to dominate her character: 'This she undoubtedly has, and shows it in her age in her despotic temper.'[62]

Gradually, Beatrice's immersion in the lives of the casual labouring poor led to an 'ethical revulsion' towards capitalism, which was instrumental in guiding many socialists, including the Fabians, towards the collectivist ideal.[63] 'This East End life, with its dirt, drunkenness and immorality, absence of co-operation or common interests, saddens me and weighs down my spirit . . .' she wrote a year later when she took over Ella Pycroft's work and her room in Wentworth Dwellings, another block near Katherine Buildings. 'I could not live here; I should lose heart and become worthless as a worker.' Wentworth Dwellings, like Katherine Buildings, she condemned as an 'utter failure', the water-closets serving again as a grotesque meeting-place for the boys and girls to meet and flirt, the lady rent collectors 'an altogether superficial thing'.

Beatrice realised that bourgeois philanthropy was impotent in the face of the East End population, an 'ever-increasing and ever-decomposing mass', vast and yet atomised, those with the slightest pretensions to respectability keeping rigidly apart from their fellows. 'Why resist the drink demon?' asked Beatrice with new cynicism in November 1886. 'A short life and a merry one, why not? A woman diseased with drink came up to me screaming, in her hand a quart pot, her face directed to the Public [House]. What could I say? Why dissuade her? She is half-way to death – let her go – if death ends all.' The futility of her own and Ella Pycroft's efforts to change the habits which were a product of a degraded environment became evident, and it was with compassion and sadness that Beatrice wrote, 'Alas! *there* is the pitifulness in this long chain of iniquity, children linked on to parents, friends to friends, and lovers to lovers, bearing down to that bottomless pit of decaying life.'[64] Disillusioned, Ella confessed to Beatrice, 'I am coming to see more and more that it is useless to try and help the helpless, that the truly kind thing is to let the weak go to the wall and get out of the strong people's way as fast as possible.'[65] In October 1886 Ella was to return to her father's home to 'settle down west' in accordance with his wishes.

Beatrice hoped her proposal for an association of all the housing agencies would attract 'stronger and finer women' into the profession of rent collector. 'I admire and revere women most who are content to be among the "unknown saints" – but there is no use shutting one's eyes to the fact that there is an increasing number of women to whom the matrimonial career is shut and who seek a masculine reward for masculine qualities. There is in them something exceedingly pathetic and I would give anything to open careers to them in which their somewhat abnormal but useful qualities would get their own reward . . . I think these strong women have a great future before them in the solution of social problems. They *are not* just inferior men. They may have masculine faculty, but they have the *woman's temperament*, and the stronger they are the more distinctively *feminine* they are in this.'[66] Femininity did not mean the neglect of the 'masculine' faculty of reason, but its combination with women's own moral and spiritual qualities was a new conception of the feminine ideal. Beatrice's experiences at Katherine Buildings with her network of friends crossing the invisible line separating the private from the public sphere mediated her ideas in new ways, so that she began to visualise the closed matrimonial door as a positive way towards a higher goal.

In the week beginning 15 November 1885 Beatrice had worked a forty-hour week, culminating in seven hours on Friday spent on her tenants' book; on 26 November disaster struck. Polling in the General Election had begun on 23 November, and on the morning of the 26th Richard Potter went out to vote. Beatrice became alarmed when he and Rosy did not return, and went out into the street: 'There [came] Father, leaning heavily on poor little Rosy, dragging his leg, his face drawn down . . .'

At once Beatrice called their general practitioner, Dr Tyrell, who diagnosed a stroke and advised her to send for Sir Andrew Clark, Chief Physician at the London Hospital, a close friend. That evening her 'beloved physician' told her that Richard Potter was unlikely to recover, and in fact over the next few days he deteriorated, sending out for fifty or sixty pairs of slippers from different shops on 5 December. 'There is something gone – some part of his mind sleeping or dead?' wrote Beatrice.[67]

After anxious consultations with Mary Playne, it was agreed that the little party should travel to Longfords, Mary's home, just before Christmas. 'I am afraid it would mean bringing his new man who comes tomorrow,' said Beatrice. 'I should suggest his man slept by him and looked after him at night and that Mr Thompson helped him in the day . . .'[68] Rosy, who blamed herself for her father's stroke, was despatched abroad to winter with friends, and by February Beatrice and her father were settled in Bournemouth to spend the rest of the winter quietly in lodgings. 'Companionising a failing mind – a life without physical or mental activity – no work. Good God, how awful,' Beatrice wrote in her diary.[69]

It was a dramatic change of circumstances for Beatrice, and it affected her psychologically. She missed her friends and 'was deprived of the narcotic of work, and, for the first few weeks, this abstinence was tormenting'.[70] Overwhelmed by depression, her thoughts became suicidal; she marked the New Year by making another will, leaving her small estate of £600 to Leonard Courtney to help him in his political career, and ordering her diaries to be destroyed. 'If Death comes it will be welcome – for life has always been distasteful to me,' she wrote.[71]

It must have seemed to Beatrice, as she wheeled her incapacitated father along the bleak sea front, that her hopes of a career were blocked irrevocably. Later she called this period the 'dead point' of her working life, as she tried to 'beat back feeling into the narrow rut of duty . . . Religion, Love and Ambition have died . . . I look out tonight on the beating of that hateful grey sea, the breaking and vanishing of the surf on the shore; the waves break and vanish like my spasms of feeling, but they return again and again – and behind them is the bottomless ocean of despair. Eight and twenty! Living a life without hope . . .'[72]

Reworking the feminine ideal in Victorian times frequently resulted in feelings of conflict, depression, and the expression of the death wish. To attempt to transcend ascribed sex roles was to confront the ideal of womanhood which still assumed women's containment with the home as the 'angel in the house'. Therefore the acute depression Beatrice suffered after she had finally broken with Joseph Chamberlain in the summer, only to find that in November 1885 she had to abandon her fledgling career as a rent collector, cannot be seen in isolation. Other women's autobiographical writings express similar themes and present images of women as passive, suffering and martyred; as victims rather than victors. For many autobiographers the 'unresolved problems of self-advancement, of narrative progress, slide towards a dramatic contemplation of death, frequently in tension with fraught terms of sexuality'.[73]

Yet although her first reaction was one of despair which led to her heartfelt 'wail of egotistical misery', Beatrice's enforced leisure had a positive side. Released from the responsibility of York House and from the care of Rosy as well as the exhausting emotional and practical demands of her tenants, Beatrice was free to study and reflect. In

January she began to study English history, law and economics as a background to housing, rising early and working for three hours before breakfast. The rest of the day was spent writing letters for her father, reading aloud the morning papers, taking her father for walks in his bath-chair, culminating in peaceful evenings reading aloud again from Jane Austen or Walter Scott. Beatrice loved her father deeply, and did not find it so irksome to care for him once she had become used to her new life. When she looked back she claimed that 'this compulsory withdrawal from the distracted and diversified life I had been leading was, on the whole, a gain'.[74]

XI

JUDAS MISJUDGED

*'But if we recognise the existence of this duplex or manifold
personality, surely we, by the added presence of the Will, may
ensure success to one or the other? The battle was long and
terrible because my Will was undecided which side to elect . . .
But now Fate . . . has built strong barriers . . . And womanly
dignity and reserve side with Fate and forbid the inroads of
Passion.'*
Beatrice Webb Diary, 10 December 1886

WHILE BEATRICE REMAINED IN Bournemouth with her father, London was
hurtling towards the social crisis long anticipated by journalists and
reformers. In 1886 the depression which had begun in 1884 deepened
and the numbers of unemployed rose, the industrial downturn exacerbated by the lengthy agricultural depression and the decline of
old-established businesses in the centre of the capital. February 1886
was the coldest for thirty years and pea-souper fogs hung over the
capital. In the docks the mood of the unemployed became increasingly
hostile and truculent, whipped up by the orators of the Social
Democratic Federation, the only Marxist socialist organisation among
the embryonic socialist groups.

Fear of the revolutionary potential of the 'residuum' or casual
labouring sub-stratum of the population was long-standing.[1] Hopes
that the degradation in which this class lived would be solved by the
activities of Octavia Hill and other social reformers were revealed by
the 1885 Royal Housing Commission to be futile. As Beatrice had
discovered at Katherine Buildings, poverty was not easily cured, and
on 8 February 1886 the bubbling resentment and misery of the
unemployed overflowed into a violent riot in London involving the
Social Democratic Federation and the Fair Trade League, which was
funded by the Tories and run by Trade Unionists demanding protec-
tionist tariffs to prevent unemployment, both organisations claiming
leadership of the East End unemployed.

Although Henry Mayers Hyndman, wealthy Old Etonian leader of
the Social Democratic Federation, and Henry Hyde Champion, an
ex-artillery officer, both spoke to the crowds, it was John Burns, a

rough but good-looking young workman, who led the protest meeting against the Fair Traders. Burns despised Peters and Kelly, leaders of the London riverside workers, whom he called parasites on the Labour movement, and his behaviour was deliberately provocative. Waving the red flag, he climbed the balustrade in front of the National Gallery, and made an inflammatory speech attacking the MPs in nearby Westminster as capitalists fattening on the labour of working men, who were no more likely to reform society than wolves were to help lambs.[2] With venom he attacked the loungers in the West End clubs who sat at their ease, not caring whether the people starved. With the rallying cry that it was better to die fighting than starving, he led a motley mob composed of Social Democrat followers and many Fair Traders down Pall Mall. A riot followed, as the mass of men swarmed up St James's Street, to be jeered at by members of the Carlton Club, while at the Reform Club members threw missiles at the crowd; the mob hurled stones, breaking the club windows, before looting shops in Piccadilly.

The upper classes were shocked beyond belief by these riots in the heart of the capital. The indifference which the majority had shown towards the plight of the poor changed to 'swift born pity quite indistinguishable from craven fear',[3] and within forty-eight hours £75,000 had been received by the Lord Mayor's Mansion House Relief Fund, which up to then had only been worth £2000 to £3000. The newspapers fanned the terror, with wild reports of seventy-five thousand socialists on the march from Deptford. On 5 April the trial opened at the Old Bailey of Burns, Champion, Hyndman and Williams on a charge of seditious conspiracy; they were found not guilty, and during the summer the agitation waned. Unemployment was largely seasonal, which was the reason for the Poor Law Board collecting the figures of those receiving relief on only two days of the year, 1 January and 1 July; it was assumed that pauperism would be at its height on the former date.[4]

The uneasy peace lasted through the summer and Queen Victoria's Golden Jubilee, but with the approach of winter the misery of the 'people of the abyss' increased again, and demonstrations by the unemployed became almost a daily event. A huge meeting was planned for 9 November, after the Lord Mayor's Procession, but on this occasion Hyndman and Burns encountered stiff opposition, and Sir Charles Warren, the new Commissioner of Police, forbade the meeting and cleared Trafalgar Square. The infuriated Social Democrats advertised another meeting for Sunday, 13 November. Warren ordered four thousand police to be stationed at the square, with five hundred Life Guards in reserve.

On 13 November, the way to Trafalgar Square lay barred from the south, a heavy cordon of police surrounded the square, thousands were inside, and both cavalry and foot soldiers stood by.[5] Socialist processions converged from different directions; George Bernard Shaw, William Morris and Annie Besant coming from Clerkenwell and being attacked by the police in Holborn. By mid-afternoon the mêlée in the square was out of control: Annie Besant, who at this phase in her life was one of the best-known Fabian orators, attempted to organise a laager-like ring of wagons, which broke up in confusion, and between sixty and seventy people had to be taken to Charing Cross Hospital. The square continued in a state of siege for the next fortnight, and on 28 November a demonstrator named Alfred Linnell was so badly beaten by police that he died on 3 December, and hundreds of thousands of spectators turned out to watch the funeral cortège. William Morris, Cunninghame Graham, Annie Besant and W. T. Stead, the editor of the *Pall Mall Gazette*, acted as pall-bearers, and the vast crowd sang a 'Death Song' composed by Morris.

Beatrice was far from the scene of the action, but she wrote a letter to Stead in which she gave her own analysis of the situation based on her experiences in the East End, and to her surprise and delight received a letter by return offering its publication. With pride Beatrice stuck this letter into her diary on 13 February, and headed it 'A Turning Point in my life'. Her article was given the title 'A Lady's View of the Unemployed', and for the first time she saw her name in print in Stead's crusading paper which sold for 1*d*.

With her experiences at Katherine Buildings fresh in her mind, Beatrice wrote of her knowledge of the poorest of the poor, the dockers, building labourers, fish porters, and hangers-on to the numberless small industries of East London. She explained that new machinery, cheap fares to the suburbs, and the increase of metropolitan rates and taxes had increased unemployment. Old waterside industries such as sack-making and gun-making which relied on labour by hand had moved out to the suburbs or country. The docks were in decline but still casual labour flocked to their gates.

Beatrice, like so many of her class, believed the character of the people was partly to blame for unemployment. The East End was composed, she argued, of a nucleus of original inhabitants, many foreigners, and also those who had thoughtlessly drifted into London, attracted by the glitter of the metropolis, and who did not want to work. 'It is a mistake to think that existence in one room, with little clothes, less food, and in the midst of dirt, so long as it is tempered by leisure, society, amusement and dissipation, has not more attractions to many minds, even of the lower classes, than a monotonous working life in a good cottage, surrounded by an allotment, and if need be provided with a cow.'[6] It was a point that had been made before, for since the mid-century more than half of the population had lived in cities. Not only the gin palaces and public houses, which led to accusations of drunkenness, but the music and dance halls presented attractions to the crowded, migrant population of the East End. Beatrice had become aware of the vibrant leisure culture which existed among the urban poor, and was in conflict with bourgeois values.

Beatrice's analysis brought an unexpected result as it led to the renewal of her relationship with Chamberlain who, after much political manoeuvring and parrying with Gladstone over the Irish Home Rule question, had eventually reached an uneasy compromise with the Premier, and was now Pesident of the Local Government Board in the new cabinet.

Chamberlain had barely read himself into his new department before the Trafalgar Square riots burst upon London, and a deputation of Social Democratic Foundation leaders demanded to know what he would do about the unemployed. He refused to receive Burns and Champion, but accepted their written resolutions; the continuing upset kept the unemployment problem near the forefront of his mind. Although the Irish question overshadowed all other issues, and the civil unrest provided the occasion or the excuse to reopen contact with Beatrice. She, however, was feeling particularly humiliated and vulnerable after an incident the previous November when she had opened her heart to Clara Chamberlain (now married to Frederick Ryland) about her feelings for her brother. Clara had told her bluntly that she was mistaken: 'the brother had never thought of me'. This was hard to believe for, as Beatrice remembered, Clara had quizzed her intensively as to her intentions only a year ago, but naturally it undermined her confidence.

With difficulty Beatrice was recovering from the 'terrible nightmare of absolute despair' which had haunted her since her father's stroke, and led her to again make her will on 1 January 1886, when the letter from Chamberlain arrived at Kildare, the guest-house in Bournemouth where she was wintering with her father. 'When I saw the Great Man's handwriting I was ominously excited. I knew it was the old torture coming back again . . .' she wrote.[7] The letter was brief and to the point.

25 February 1886

Dear Miss Potter,
Will you be at home on Sunday afternoon, and if so may I come and talk to you about the distress at the East End? I read your letter with great interest and agreement, and should very much like to know your experiences. I hope Mr Potter is stronger again.

I am, Yours very truly, J. Chamberlain.[8]

Beatrice replied guardedly that her knowledge was superficial, and that she was in any case at present living outside the East End. It seems probable she was suspicious of Chamberlain's motives in writing to her, but she pointed out that practical workers like herself wished for a systematic investigation of unemployment and the requirements of the labour market. She condemned also the harmfulness of the Mansion House Relief Fund, 'which did an incalculable amount of mischief', an opinion shared by her fellow-workers in the field.

Beatrice's article caused a furore at Katherine Buildings, with many residents upset by her remarks that the buildings were 'designed and adapted for the lowest class of workmen'. Beatrice sent an apologetic letter to her old tenants as 'a peace offering', and eventually they came to the conclusion that she was a 'brainworker'. Writing articles, or filling in the rent book was, they informed Ella Pycroft, much easier to do than hauling about casks in the dock-yard. 'People say the rich don't know how the poor live; but it is equally true that the poor have no idea how the rich live,' was Ella's opinion.[9]

Samuel Barnett was pleased at Beatrice's literary success, but added she had ignored one of the greatest needs of the poor – proper medical attention. Unable to afford the fees for respectable doctors, the children of the poor died in huge numbers. 'The poor can live with third-rate food and parsons but not with third-rate doctors,' he argued. Like Beatrice, he saw no solution in the Mansion House Relief Fund, which was just a 'Big Bold advertisement – the rich proclaim £60,000 to be given away. The poor loafers who think themselves hardly treated hurry up from the country . . . the dissolute and idle crowd into the offices opened for relief.' The applicants, according to the police, were 'low and brutal types', and fights for the handouts were common. 'Here in the parish people beg who have never begged, lose heart and become angry . . . others become evil and rude,' Barnett claimed. The result of the Fund was the demoralisation of the respectable poor. At Toynbee Hall, he said, his helpers were working from 9 a.m. to 2 a.m. to prevent the 'lightly given gifts from doing harm'. Charity, repeated Barnett, must be regular, or else all their work was spoiled.[10]

Barnett, in day-to-day contact with the poor, was convinced he knew what should be done in the face of distress. Chamberlain, new to the job of Poor Law overlord, was sure that he did not. Eagerly he replied to Beatrice on 28 February, brushing aside her excuse that her knowledge was superficial: 'Pray do not think that I can have too much information on the subject on which I consulted you. I know that you have much experience, and that you are not "crotchety" . . .' Although his department knew 'all about paupers and pauperism', it had no official knowledge of distress above the pauper line. Yet Chamberlain was sure that the suffering of the 'industrious non-pauper class' was very great and increasing.[11]

In reality the Local Government Board, which had superseded the Poor Law Board from 1870, was remarkably ignorant of the true extent of poverty, despite collecting a plethora of statistics. It knew how much it spent, but not how many people were relieved, nor how many were chronic cases, who might return repeatedly for help.[12] The main thrust of the New Poor Law Act of 1834 had been to deter the 'able-bodied' scrounger from applying for relief by the practice of 'offering the workhouse', but the term 'able-bodied' had never been clearly defined, and was loosely applied to all those between sixteen and seventy. Nor was the distinction clear between the 'indoor paupers' in the workhouse and 'outdoor paupers' who remained in their own homes, for many new and overlapping institutions had arisen such as homes for the feeble-minded or orphans in which 'indoor' pauper children were cared for. The conundrum which faced Chamberlain was this: if the number of paupers was falling (and the official figures showed a steady downward trend from 1.26 million in 1834 to 800,000 in 1880), why were the people rioting in the streets? In fact women, not men, made up the majority of paupers; widows, deserted wives, mothers of illegitimate children, and the old and sick claimed relief far more frequently than 'able-bodied' men.[13] But both women and men disliked the Poor Law 'bastilles' so fervently, with their policy of separating families and the stigma of pauperism which was a mark of shame to any 'respectable' working-class family, that they preferred to live on the margin of starvation rather than enter the workhouse. Thus the 'less eligibility' principle merely masked the results of the economic depression which had brought subsistence living to increasing numbers of the poor.

Although Beatrice, like other middle-class social reformers, clung to the lingering belief that 'bad character' was the prime cause of unemployment, she was observant enough to see that the prime cause of unemployment in London was not moral but economic. It was the decline of industries in the centre, and the fact that employment was seasonal, which affected the 'industrious non-pauper class', as Chamberlain called them, and led them to take to the streets in alarming numbers.

Chamberlain did not, however, appreciate Beatrice's suggestion of introducing some form of labour exchange. 'I do not quite follow your suggestion,' he wrote. 'Surely the reason for the distress is that there is an actual insufficiency of employment and not merely that the workers do not know where to find work which actually exists somewhere for them . . . I cannot think that any registration of labour would be more than a trifling convenience. Wherever there is work wanted, the workers find it out very quickly for themselves.'[14]

'If the distress becomes greater, something *must* be done to make work. The rich must pay to keep the poor alive,' he insisted. Although determined to keep the test ('offering the house') for the old, infirm, and lazy, Chamberlain cast around for some simple 'spade labour' for the ordinary workman who was out of work through no fault of his own. 'Works of sewage, extra street cleaning, laying out recreation grounds . . .'[15] was all he could suggest which was available in the metropolis. He did not realise, as Beatrice did, the unpopularity of such work among the casual labourers for whom it was intended. The Mansion House Relief Committee, Ella Pycroft reported to Beatrice, had been offering the men 2s. a day for sweeping the streets. 'In three days one hundred and thirty men [were] offered the work, thirteen had accepted it, eleven had gone to it, and about half of those threw down the brooms and left.' Her men were divided, said Ella; some thankful for the work, others saying they would never be offered work in their trades again if they took it.[16]

To Canon Barnett the pitiful human specimens who applied for money or relief work were 'broken creatures, many evidently suffering from malformation or disease, many the slaves of drink and vice'. The lesson he drew from their ill-health and incapacity was that the environment should be improved, with the government enforcing the 'sanitary laws' and providing open spaces for Londoners. The population, he argued, needed 'sufficient air, light, water and space . . .

reading rooms, libraries, and a system of education', even if some of its unfitness for work resulted from 'vice and wilfulness'. Barnett knew that Beatrice would argue that a better environment would bring 'more workers than work', and anticipated her objections by a plea that land should be reclaimed, for example from the fens, so that labourers could become possessors of the land.[17]

Beatrice's reply to Chamberlain was a stark restatement of the principles of *laissez-faire*. Despite her Charity Organisation Society experiences, she was still a hostage to Spencerian and Malthusian ideas. If 'natural checks' did not prevent the population breeding, it would outrun the means of subsistence, and harm the whole community, and therefore the State should not interfere, notwithstanding the suffering which might result. Beatrice was also suspicious of Chamberlain's motives in asking her to step outside the subservient and intellectually dependent feminine role of which she knew he approved. 'You take me out of my depth! ... As I read your letter a suspicion flashed across me that you wished for some further proof of the incapacity of a woman's intellect to deal with such large matters ... I agree that "the rich *must* keep the poor alive" ... I fail to grasp the principle "something must be done". It is terribly sad that 100 men should die in semi-starvation – should prefer that slow death to the almost penal servitude offered them by the workhouse – but ... Death after all is a slight evil compared to life under many conditions ... I have no proposal to make, except sternness from the state, and love and self-devotion from individuals – a very sad and self-evident remedy.'

She taunted Chamberlain with his earlier remarks on women's inferior intelligence indicating how deeply she felt her previous humiliation at his hands: 'But is it not rather unkind of you to ask me to tell you what I think: I have tried to be perfectly truthful. Still, it is a ludicrous idea that an ordinary woman should be called upon to review the suggestions of Her Majesty's ablest minister, especially when I know that he has a slight opinion of even a superior woman's intelligence in these matters – I agree with him – and a dislike of any independence of thought ...'[18]

Doubtful whether Chamberlain was taking her seriously, Beatrice alternated between a careful statement of her views and a denial that she had the wit to have any. But Chamberlain misread her mood, and taking her letter at face value, wrote a terse and sombre reply. He found her swiftly changing moods perplexing, and her abrupt switches from encouragement to rebuff left him bewildered and only able to fall back on conventional courtesies and a blundering and defensive statement of his views.

'Dear Miss Potter,' he wrote on 5 March, 'I thought we understood each other pretty well. I fear I was mistaken. In the hurry of this life it is not easy to get a clear conception of any other person's principles and opinions. But you are quite wrong in supposing that I undervalue the opinions of an intelligent woman. There are many questions on which I would follow it blindly, although I dislike the flippant self-sufficiency of some female politicians. Neither do I dislike independence of thought . . . I hardly know why I defend myself, for I admit it does not matter what I think or feel on these subjects . . . On the main question, your letter is discouraging, but I fear it is true. I shall go on, however, as if it were not true, for if we once admit the impossibility of remedying the evils of society, we shall all sink below the level of the brutes. Such a creed is the justification of absolute unadulterated selfishness . . . And so we must go on rolling the stone up the hill, even though it is almost certain that it will roll down again, and perhaps crush us . . . If men will starve rather than dig for 2s a day I cannot help them and I cannot greatly pity them. It will remove one great danger, viz. that public sentiment should go wholly over to the unemployed and render impossible that state sternness to which you and I equally attach importance. I thank you for writing so fully and do not expect any further answer.'[19]

The final dismissive sentence brought a heartfelt response from Beatrice. As she wrote in her diary, she had felt, 'He of course did not wish for my opinion for its own sake. I was not such an arrant fool as to think I could inform him; I thought that he wished to know my mind literally to see whether it would suit him.'

In the agony of the moment Beatrice opened her heart. 'Now I see I was right not to deceive you,' she wrote to Chamberlain impetuously. 'I could not lie to the man I loved. By why have worded it so cruelly, why give unnecessary pain? Surely we suffer sufficiently – thank God! that when our own happiness is destroyed there are others to live for. Do not think that I do not consider your decision as *final* and destroy this.'[20] The fear that prying eyes might read her diary led her to omit the line 'I could not lie to the man I loved' when she copied this letter into her diary, although she added on the day she posted the letter, 'And so the agony of two years ends.'

For the next few months Beatrice and Chamberlain did not meet. It had been a hurtful correspondence in which Beatrice and her 'evil genius' showed the same capacity to misunderstand one another as they did in conversation. 'Double-mindedness ... [the] perpetual struggle between conscience on the one hand and feeling on the other' had waged a bitter battle, a contest in which again neither element had gained the victory. On his side she detected 'hatred of insubordination and personal attraction tinged with pity, for I believe the man believed I loved him – so I did!' Her infatuation or 'delusion about the Great Man', as she called it, was too powerful to be conquered, and she turned again to the consolation of religion, and to her friends. 'Now I feel comforted: for the first time I live harmoniously with myself,' she wrote on 15 March 1886. 'My great love for him is acknowledged before God, but it is chastened by truthfulness and absolute honesty.'[21]

In her distress Beatrice turned to her cousin Mary Booth, eleven years her senior. Mary had always thought Beatrice 'a good sort of girl', although too inclined to be bothered by the 'Weltschmertz'.[22] Their friendship dated from the many shared holidays when Mary had come to stay at Standish. Mary's mother, the daughter of 'Radical Dick' Potter, had made no objection to her daughter becoming absorbed into the Potter circle. Mary was deeply attached to her father, Charles Macaulay, who was a member of the Clapham Sect and had been influenced by his own father's determined opposition to slavery; Mary, therefore, was part of the liberal-minded 'intellectual aristocracy', learning to read at the age of three, and devouring Plutarch's lives soon afterwards. It was 'such a relief', she said, 'when the search for something to play with was ended by the solace of books.'[23] At Standish Mary met Charles Booth, her future husband, who was a guest at the wedding of Lallie Potter to Robert Holt. An enthusiastic Radical from a Unitarian family, Charles Booth was a founder of the Booth Steamship Company.

Charles had married Mary in 1871, notwithstanding some opposition from the Macaulay family who took exception to the young shipowner's Liverpool accent. Charles's health soon gave cause for concern and his weight dropped alarmingly due to 'nervous indigestion', and following a period abroad he and Mary moved to Kensington in London.

Now mother of five children, Mary neither condoned nor understood Beatrice's desire for a professional ideal; Beatrice had miscalculated in thinking Mary understood her, and this miscalculation was to bring her heartache in the future. But nevertheless it was to Mary that Beatrice turned for consolation, and she was quick to give it: 'I wish I was a man and could relieve my feelings with respect to the conduct of the CHM [Chamberlain] a little more emphatically than decorum would allow me to do. We are both of us utterly revolted; asking, inviting your opinion, and then going into a childish pet because it is not what he expected or wanted. One thing, however, in the midst of this painful affair comes into my mind as good. You see him as he is; and, depend upon it, a man so dependent on flattery; so impatient of contradiction; so sensitive in regard to his own feeling; and so indifferent to those of others; must be at bottom a very poor and shallow creature. You are well rid of him!'[24]

Beatrice could not share this opinion. 'I am afraid I shall never think of him as you do,' she told Mary. 'I shall always be ready to help him even if I *do* get a slash in the face in return. I have no proper pride!' Mournfully she asked her diary, 'How shall I resist the querulous grief at missing the greatest happiness of a woman's life?' and haunted the ladies' gallery of the House of Commons during the Home Rule crisis.

Leaning from Kate's seat, which her sister let her use, Beatrice could just make out Chamberlain, pale and nervous, talking to 'that beast, Sir Charles Dilke', who was then in the throes of the divorce case which would lose him his reputation. Beatrice's heart went out to Chamberlain, in his brave and dignified defence of his resignation from the Cabinet in March. She sensed the heartsearching which preceded his decision to defy Gladstone, that angry old lion who stood quivering with passion in the chamber. Chamberlain had seen one of his dearest friends, John Morley, succumb to the lure of the Chief Secretaryship of Ireland which Gladstone dangled before his eyes. The tide was flowing towards Gladstone, and for the moment Radicalism was forgotten. Should Chamberlain go with the tide, waiting his moment to supersede Gladstone? It was the obvious, politic choice. But Chamberlain could not countenance the separation of Ireland from England, whatever the personal cost to himself. From April his prime objective was to kill the Home Rule Bill. Isolated and friendless, Chamberlain sat late at night turning over the mountain of correspondence supporting or chastising him. The final blow came when he learnt that Dilke would not vote against the Second Reading of the Bill. For the first time in their political life the two allies were to be separated. Chamberlain was not deterred, and he marshalled his small band of fifty Radicals who, influenced by the knowledge that John Bright intended to vote against the Bill, followed their leader into the 'No' lobby. Parnell's cry, 'There goes the man who killed Home Rule' rang in his ears, and Liberal claims that he had acted the Judas were heaped upon his head. Still, he had changed the course of history; Ireland, 'squalid, dismal, sullen' as she seemed to Morley, was still inextricably linked to England.

As the country plunged once more into a General Election, Beatrice reproached herself for her unworthiness. Chamberlain was vastly superior to her and stood on the high-ground of independent political action. She had been wrong to demand personal attention from him at a time of political crisis. Now she longed to give him a word of sympathy, even though she considered his behaviour contributed to his downfall. But she neither saw him nor wrote to him, although she continued to meet Beatrice Chamberlain.

In April 1886 Beatrice attended the first meeting held by Charles Booth at his City office of his new Board of Statistical Research, the impressive name behind his novel plan to use the census returns to create a complete picture of the people of London, their lives and employment. It instantly appealed to Beatrice, who considered it just the sort of work she would like to do if she were free from the burden of caring for her father. The next day Canon Barnett poured cold water on the scheme, which he considered impossible, but Beatrice valiantly, defended it, arguing that accurate facts could influence policy. The idea grew in her mind to write an article on social diagnosis, which would prepare her for possible work with Booth. Encouraged by Charles Loch, secretary of the Charity Organisation Society, she carried home some heavy volumes from the Statistical Society and set to work.

Not until Beatrice took her two invalids, Richard Potter and Rosy, down to the Argoed, was she able to begin serious work. And serious it proved: 'Political economy is *hateful* – most hateful drudgery,' she complained at the beginning of July. In January she had written to her friend Arabella Fisher, asking for advice on how to study. 'Take a topic which puzzles you and make up your mind to write an article upon it as if for publication,' was Bella's advice. This was how she had 'got up' Darwin's *Descent of Man*: 'I had never been published and had no thought of publishing what I wrote but it *was* published as has been everything I have written since.' She recommended the London Library as a good source of books, but was more doubtful about finding Beatrice someone to study with. 'I am not a good guide in this as I always prefer hammering out for myself . . . I fancy you will have to grope first for yourself and find out your difficulties.'

It was good advice and Beatrice took it. As the month progressed, and Rosy, a 'changed mortal', proved sweet-tempered and unselfish, Beatrice was able to break the back of her studies. An insatiable reader, she devoured J. S. Mill, Adam Smith, Ricardo, Jevons and Marshall, and by September had finished her essay on English economics. Her friends were impressed by her diligence: Charles Booth protested that he could not possibly undertake such a long course of reading, and Ella Pycroft was convinced that if she had twenty books of political economy, nineteen would remain uncut. Mary Booth marvelled that Beatrice could study in the hot, brain-dulling weather they were having, and with all she had to do caring for Rosy and her father. 'I know you are plucky and don't shirk carrying your burdens, but they weigh just as heavily on brave as well as faint-hearted people,' wrote a worried Ella.[25] Apprehensively Beatrice parcelled up her 'little thing of my own' and sent it to the Booths for approval. Their reaction was guarded, though kind.

'The paper is *never* dull,' wrote Mary, 'some parts of it, in spite of the intrinsic heaviness of the subject, are remarkably lively and bright.' She advised Beatrice to put it to one side for a month or two. Charles equally tactfully cautioned against publishing the paper straight away: 'Let it stand awhile. It is good wine, but new, and needs to mature in bottle!' Beatrice was not deterred, and plunged into Karl Marx's *Kapital* in French, there being no English translation available. But continual intellectual study with no diversion but her comatose father and Rosy, whom she continued to find dull and irritating despite her efforts to busy herself visiting the neighbouring poor, left its mark. Try as she might to bury the past, the old craving for love returned, and she had visions of children, 'little ones . . . of flesh and blood, dependent on one and upon whom one might in old age depend'. With relief she accepted her sisters' offer of a working holiday, and returned to York House.

Back in London Beatrice's first action was to make a flying visit to Highbury to see Clara Ryland, Chamberlain's sister. Chamberlain and his daughter were away, so the place only carried memories of his presence. Ruefully Beatrice recalled that it was the news that Chamberlain was to be married to her which brought Ryland to the point of proposing to Clara. She wondered if the pain of her feelings for Chamberlain would ever cease.

In search of peace of mind, Beatrice retraced her steps to Bacup in October, but her earlier adventure had lost its freshness and 'Miss Jones' her former bloom. She was so changed that some of her former friends hardly recognised her. By the end of the visit Beatrice found her incognito impossible to sustain, and confessed her real identity. Her Aked relations were not angry, but they were unable to stir her from her melancholy frame of mind. Depressed Beatrice returned to autumnal London. The dark side of her personality dominated her moods: the 'despondent vain, grasping person . . . doomed to failure'. Yet this *'nether* being' rubbed shoulders with the sceptical, questioning Ego, whose roots were sensual and physical. Beatrice expressed it: 'If I were a man, this creature would be free, though not dissolute, in its morals, a lover of women . . . the strong physical nature upon which the intellectual nature is based would be satisfied.' As a woman, there could be no physical satisfaction for her except within the conventions of marriage.

As the year turned and her twenty-ninth birthday approached, death and decay seemed all around Beatrice. Regular visits to Herbert Spencer, old and alone in his lodgings in Brighton, led her to feel universal euthanasia had its merits. His request that she would be his literary executor led to a meeting with Thomas Huxley, another friend of her youth and contemporary of Spencer's, now a broken-down 'old lion', conscious of failure.

Struggling with toothache, neuralgia and a gum abscess, Beatrice found it impossible to avoid thinking of Chamberlain whose name was on every lip. Kate took her down to Liskeard, Leonard's constituency, to hear her husband speak on Ireland. During the seven-hour train journey and the drive in an open carriage through the cheering crowds, the talk was all of Chamberlain and his disloyalty. Beatrice ached to defend him, but dared not.

Hiding her feelings was a source of mounting stress. Reason dictated that Beatrice kept her distance from the 'great man', but frustrated passion weakened her resolve, and when Chamberlain again made overtures to her in May 1887 she found it impossible to resist him. He had met Charles Booth at breakfast, who had told him Beatrice was now researching dock labour. Perhaps Chamberlain was genu- inely short of information, perhaps he was simply seeking an excuse to reopen negotiations with Beatrice. It was, as Beatrice wrote wearily, 'another act of the old, old story'.[26]

The crowd was smaller at the political meeting where they met, the mood sombre, the leader white and agitated; but his voice retained its old charm for Beatrice, and at dinner at Arthur Chamberlain's she was unable to prevent herself inviting Joseph to stay at the Argoed in six weeks' time. She felt that in Chamberlain's manner to her there had been 'a strange lack of chivalry and honour. In mine to him, of womanly dignity'. He had behaved like 'the triumphant lover, the man who is sure of his conquest'. He irritated her exceedingly, yet she burned with anticipation as the weeks unrolled. The visit was put off as Chamberlain wished to attend the Queen's golden jubilee naval review. A new date was made. When at last he came to stay Beatrice, unable to contain her feelings, confessed her love for him and then, in a fit of mortification, asked him to go. Chamberlain found her too strong and volatile to venture a proposal of marriage as Beatrice perhaps still hoped he might, and she, attracted yet repulsed by his pride and arrogance, resolved to banish him from her life.

Chamberlain wrote asking if they could not remain friends. Beatrice agreed, but repeated that they must not meet. In his final letter of 7 August the bewildered politician said reproachfully: 'The concluding part of your letter has given me much pain. Did I do wrong in accepting your invitation? If so forgive me and allow me to tell you frankly what I feel. At your own request I destroyed your letter of March 1886. There was one passage in it on which I did not presume to put a definite interpretation, and which I thought at the time was rather the outcome of a sensitive mind, overstrained by suffering and work, than the expression of settled feeling. I thought you had forgotten it and wished me to forget it also. So much for the past – now as to the future. Why are we never to see each other again? Why cannot we be friends – 'comrades' – to use your own expression? I like you very much – I respect and esteem you – I enjoy your conversation and society and I have often wished that fate had thrown us more together. If you share this feeling to any extent why should we surrender a friendship which ought to be good for both of us? I have so much confidence in your generosity as well as in your sense that I am encouraged to make this appeal to you in what I feel to be a very delicate matter.'

He confessed that he often felt depressed and discouraged, that past circumstances had made him solitary and reserved, and that he valued her sympathy and support. 'I cannot say more. You must decide, and if it is for your happiness that we should henceforth be strangers I will make no complaint. I return your letter, as you wish it, but there is surely no reason why you should be ashamed of feelings which are purely womanly and for which I have nothing but gratitude and respect.'

His letter was a final plea for the understanding which Beatrice could not give. Chagrined and indignant at Chamberlain's failure to propose marriage, Beatrice wrote in her diary, 'This letter after I had, in another moment of suicidal misery told him I cared for him passionately. This after he had pursued me for 18 months and dragged me back into an acquaintance I had all along avoided. To insist on meeting a woman who had told you she loved you in order to humiliate her further.'

After the General Election of July 1886 Lord Salisbury had again formed a government. Chamberlain's hopes of Liberal reunion were dashed against the rocks of Gladstone's intransigence; for eight more years Gladstone was to refuse to step down, clinging to the hope that the country would accept Irish Home Rule. His personal and political life alike in ruins, Chamberlain accepted Salisbury's invitation to become one of the three Commissioners appointed to arbitrate in a fisheries dispute between the United States and Canada. In October 1887 he sailed from Liverpool towards the new world where the woman who would become his third wife awaited him.[27]

XII

A GLORIFIED SPINSTER

'I long every day more for the restfulness of an abiding love . . .
I must check those feelings which are expression of the physical
instinct craving for satisfaction; but God knows celibacy is as
painful to a woman . . . as it is to a man. It could not be more
painful than it is to a woman.'
Beatrice Webb Diary, 7 March 1889

RESOLVED TO BREAK HER chain of misery, Beatrice fled to the new home of the Booths, Gracedieu Manor, an idyllic country house on the edge of Charnwood Forest in Leicestershire.[1] The long grey stone house had been bought by Charles as an escape from London the previous year. There Mary claimed to live a life of 'continual sunshine', surrounded by her children and the precious woods she insisted on opening to the local people to her keeper's horror.[2] Sometimes she felt isolated: 'One misses the equal or still better the superior mind; – and when I have been long here I get a sort of elephantine feeling . . . If I don't soon encounter someone with a full-sized brain I shall become a hopelessly didactic and prosy old lady.'[3] And Beatrice, although she still found the Booths close and loving friends who 'become each year more near to me. Perhaps they are the only persons who really love me', had begun to patronise 'dear sweet little Mary, with her loving ways and charming motherhood!'[4]

Since her involvement in the research for *The Life and Labour of the People in London*, Charles's massive seventeen-volume investigation into the condition of the people, Beatrice saw Charles and herself as fellow-workers, both inspired by the same intellectual desires. 'We are very fond of each other, a close intimate relation between a man and a woman without sentiment (perhaps not without sentiment but without passion or the dawning of passion).'[5] Her feeling for him had run ahead of that for his wife. Leaving Mary behind with the children, Beatrice and Charles travelled to Manchester to spend two days looking at an exhibition of Pre-Raphaelite pictures, discussing the sweating system among the East End tailors as they feasted their eyes on Burne-Jones, Millais and Rossetti.

Beatrice was unwise to underestimate Mary, whose editing of her husband's survey played a vital part in its success; probably she too felt closer to Charles Booth than he did to her, for he was essentially an independent man whose overriding priority was his great work, which had to be fitted round his shipping interests. This meant commuting between London, Gracedieu and Liverpool, with annual trips to New York as well. All day he did office work, spent the hour after dinner with his family, and began work on the inquiry at 10 p.m., sometimes walking the East End streets, at others writing up his notes for three hours or more. He barely ate, munching a piece of fruit at his high office desk for lunch. Train journeys were never wasted, for he would line up a row of candle-ends along the carriage windowsill in order to read.[6] He found refuge from stress by periodically going to live among East End families living on the 'poverty line', as he christened it.

To Beatrice, Booth epitomised the *Zeitgeist* of the 1880s. He was, she recognised, a man without bias and prejudice, one who by fifty had 'passed through a period of terrible illness and weakness, and who has risen out of it, uncynical, vigorous and energetic in mind, and without egotism'.[7] Always ready to consider the most far-fetched or seemingly irrelevant suggestion, his open mind, combined with the Positivist desire to serve his fellow men, spurred him on to finance his survey through seventeen years of unremitting toil. It was to prove a landmark in social science; until 1887, when the first results appeared, the government had no idea of the facts regarding poverty in London. It was also a watershed in Beatrice's life; the years between 1883 and 1887 she considered her 'apprenticeship' in which she was transformed from a good looking society girl into a professional career woman. It was the mark of Booth's greatness to spot the potential in his wife's cousin, the analytical mind behind the turbulent emotions and handsome face. In setting her to work he released all her pent-up desire for a professional challenge, one which made best use of her talents for interviewing, collecting facts and making pertinent deductions.

Booth's intention was to obtain an exact cross-section, as on a microscope slide, of the four million people of London at a given moment: to do this he investigated their lives, their homes and their employment. He had a suspicion of statistics, writing to Beatrice: 'Most single facts, and strings of statistics *may* be true, demonstrably true, and yet entirely misleading in the way they are used.'[8] Working on the assumption that every fact he needed was already known to someone, he adopted the suggestion of Joseph Chamberlain of using

School Attendance Officers, who went from house to house, and could flesh out the bare facts about each family. Finding this method worked well in Tower Hamlets, he combined it with the census returns and adapted it to the whole of London.

Early in 1887 Charles was hard at work every evening with three paid secretaries, and Beatrice promised to spend her March holiday undertaking 'Docks', one of the occupations he wished to know about. Since her father's illness had stabilised she had persuaded him to give her brother-in-law Daniel Meinertzhagen power of attorney, which released her from worry about her father's speculations on the Stock Exchange. Her sisters insisted now that they took turns in looking after their father for at least four months of the year so that Beatrice might amuse herself in society. Instead she spent the time in the East End, staying either at the headquarters of the Quakers, the Devonshire House Hotel, or with her sister Blanche and Willie Cripps, her surgeon husband, off Portman Square.

Beatrice started work apprehensively, feeling 'the little bit of work I will do will be very superficial', but soon she wrote, 'I *feel* power, I *feel* capacity even when I discover clearly my own insufficiency . . . *Nous verrons!*'[9] She pitied the East Enders in their stunted environment: 'a million poverty-stricken men, women and children, working, sleeping, eating, mating and being born under the perpetual shadow of buildings belching out smoke, sweating vermin, and excreting filth . . .',[10] although she relished the freedom and stimulus of working-class life. The 'Friends' hotel was the perfect base from which to venture out along Billingsgate to the London Docks. Beatrice met an old tenant from the Katherine Buildings called Dartford, who was a Preferable, or permanent employee, and who told her that the daily payment at the docks caused trouble: 'It is always a mistake not to give the woman the money once a week instead of at odd times.'[11]

Soon Beatrice was getting up early to watch the daily ritual of the 'cage' in Nightingale Lane, where the low-looking casuals congregated within the iron bars in the hope of being given a ticket for a few hours' work by the foreman. He, the petty tyrant of the docks, would strut up and down, teasing the desperate men. A fight might break out; one labourer once tore off another's ear in the life and death contest for a ticket. Yet having won it 'Jack' would sell it to 'Tom' for a few coppers and go drinking and gambling, Beatrice noted.

She was quick to realise why 'the tide of commerce turned against the greatest port in the world'.[12] The great sailing ships no longer came in on the tide to line the quays of the London and St Katherine, the

West and East India, and the Millwall Docks, providing weeks of work for the stevedores. Instead steamers came and went against wind and tide, and the owners now wanted their ships turned round in a few hours. Tonnage which a few years ago took weeks to unload was sent to the warehouses within a night and a day. There the coopers plugged and mended casks, sugar was bulked after being washed and coloured, the old men and boys sorted spices. 'The fine lady who sips her tea from a dainty cup, and talks sentimentally of the masses, is unaware that she is tangibly connected with them, in that the leaves from which her tea is drawn have been recently trodden into their case by a gang of the great unwashed,' wrote Beatrice with cynicism. Tally-clerks, the product of the new board schools, noted the weights and measures and copied invoices. But all in all fewer hands were needed, and the lot of the casuals had become a hard and uncertain one, the last refuge of jailbirds and men without character. The good days after the opening of the Suez Canal, when trade and profits were up, were long since gone, and in 1865 the directors of the London and St Katherine Docks had introduced piecework. Now there were ten thousand casuals in Tower Hamlets alone, but only enough daily work for three thousand, and while the 'preferable' might take home 20s to 25s a week, the casual could only expect 5d an hour, adding up to a bare 2s 9d a day.

Beatrice spent evenings at the Working Men's Club where even the preferables told her how scarce work was, only enough for two or three days' work per man. She mingled easily with the working men, smoking and laughing, finding the same acceptance that she had done in Bacup. A socialist labourer confided that the wives of working men were no sort of companion to them: 'If a working man gets a good mother, and a woman that does not drink, as his wife, that is as much as he can expect.'[13] The inference was that Beatrice was something more.

She interviewed Kerrigan, one of the School Board visitors, who told her that the worst scoundrels among the casuals were the cockney-born Irishmen. Like the circle of suicides in Dante's *Inferno* they moved round from lodging to lodging, living within easy reach of the dock gates, treating their friends if they had earned a few pence, living chiefly on noxious 'tobacco' concocted of sugar, vinegar, brown paper and German nicotine. 'The teapot is constantly going – bread and a supply of dried haddòck which goes through a domestic preparation: dried in the chimney and acquiring a delicate flavour by lying between the mattresses of the beds.'[14] Kerrigan invited her for a day out at Victoria Park, and Beatrice went with Ella Pycroft to listen to the speakers on every subject from Primitive Methodism to the Fruits of Philosophy. Kerrigan asked them back to his home, one of the 'small two-storey houses of the genteel type' where he gave them tea and first-class cigarettes.[15]

During the summer Beatrice wrote up her experiences as an article on 'Dock Life', published in the *Nineteenth Century* in October 1887. '*The* work I have always longed to do ... the realisation of my youthful ambition,' Beatrice wrote proudly.[16] Although Beatrice protested that she had no talent and little literary faculty, she knew she had originality and persistence. Yet she saw her new craft as one forced on her by circumstances; she had longed for married happiness and would have married Chamberlain had events been otherwise; she would have gone on as a rent collector had not her father's illness forced her to leave London. But her article had good reviews, and when she went to a meeting of dock labourers in Canning Town she was cheered. 'I was the only woman present,' she wrote, relishing her role as a surrogate man.[17] She lunched with Sir James Knowles, the editor of the *Nineteenth Century*, and an old friend of Herbert Spencer's. Knowles offered to take anything she could write, and with a new touch of self-complacency she decided there was no reason why she should not rise further in the literary world.

Together Beatrice and Booth decided on her next topic, the sweating system. He had begun to recognise her potential. Unlike other early enthusiasts, only Beatrice showed staying power, and a clear idea of what she wanted to do. Other earnest women who wanted to help were only 'worth a rotten apple' in Mary Booth's opinion, although Clara Collett, one of the first women graduates from London University, was also part of Charles's team.[18] As Beatrice, temporarily banished again to Bournemouth with her father, pored over blue books and periodicals on sweating, she determined this time to make a dramatised picture of the sweating industry, in which Jewish contractors with a staff of fixers, basters, fellers, machinists and button-hole hands, turned out coats by the score, and were accused of putting out of business the English journeymen tailors with their regulated pay and restricted hours. Forming in Beatrice's mind was the idea of disguising herself as a trouser-hand and finding work under false pretences, which would allow her to cross class barriers and be accepted by the working girls of the East End. She had done it successfully in Bacup; why not in the East End?

On 14 October 1887 Beatrice returned to the Devonshire House

Hotel and five days later, having recovered from a cold, she set off for Stepney to try her luck. She was venturing into a close-knit, crowded community where the accents of Yiddish, Polish, or German were heard more frequently than those of the Irish or cockney English. In Whitechapel alone there were nearly forty thousand Jews and nine hundred Jewish coatmakers. Stepping along the streets, where steam rose from the down-trodden filth, and 'Jewish girls with flashy hats, full figures and large bustles; furtive eyed Polish immigrants with their pallid figures and crouched forms; and here and there poverty-stricken Christian women swarmed about the pavements', Beatrice stopped at the sweat shops to ask for work. Dressed in buttonless boots, a short bedraggled skirt, ill-fitting coat and a tumbled black bonnet which sat ill at ease over her unkempt, black hair twisted up on top of her head, she looked the part. 'Do you want a plain 'and?' was the question she asked, awkwardly affecting a cockney accent. 'We're suited,' came the reply on all sides. Feeling horribly sick and ill, Beatrice stopped in front of a placard which said 'Trouser and Vest Hands Wanted Immediately'. Advancing towards the long work table, she asked Mrs Moses, the woman in charge, dishevelled in dirty cotton velvet and a gold eye glass, if there was any work for a trouser finisher, and was hired at once. She was to start the next morning at eight.

The next day found Beatrice standing in front of the sign MOSES AND SON: CHEAP CLOTHING, and a window in which coats and vests were on display for 17s and trousers for 4s 6d. Thirty women and girls hurried in, hanging their bonnets and shawls on nails, each settling in front of her bundle of work and an old tobacco or candle box holding her cottons, twist, gimp, needles, thimble and scissors. The Factory and Workshop Regulations were prominently displayed on the wall, and at two high tables sat the pressers and basters; at a long low plank table the trouser finishers crouched, and under the sky light the machinists and vest hands sat at two other tables. Within half an hour the two English lads who worked as pressers had lit up the gas jets and begun preparing the irons.

Beatrice had brought no trimmings, but she made a new friend who lent her some. As she fumbled over the cloth, she explained that she was long out of work. 'Ah, that accounts for your being a bit awkward-like,' remarked her friend innocently. As they worked the girls sang music hall songs against the monotonous whirr of the sewing machines:

Why should not the girls have freedom now and then?
And if a girl likes a man, why should she not propose?
Why should little girls always be led by the nose?[19]

Beatrice worked slowly, and had done little when the dinner hour was called. Some women wandered into the street, others pulling out baskets from under the table and spreading out cracked mugs, bits of bread and butter, cold sausage and salt fish on dirty newspaper. Beatrice went out for a bun and cup of tea, only to return to a telling-off from her employer. 'You must work sharper than this,' Mrs Moses told her brusquely, and Beatrice coloured in embarrassment. By the afternoon she had pricked her fingers several times, and her back was aching. By Friday morning she was hopelessly tired, and shaky all over. 'This will never do,' muttered Mrs Moses, pulling her work to pieces. Beatrice's eyes filled with tears and Mrs Moses put the disgraced workgirl between two young girls who were to show her what to do; one of them offered her a nip of brandy.

As she set to again, Beatrice was horrified by the tales of incest and promiscuity to which she was forced to listen. Laughingly her companions chaffed each other about having babies by their fathers and brothers. Yet these companions were 'in no way mentally defective . . . were on the contrary just as keen-witted and generous-hearted as my own circle of friends'. The casual nature of these conversations, the references to small children being violated, brought home to Beatrice that sexual perversion was 'almost unavoidable among men and women of average intelligence crowded into the one-room tenement of slum areas'.[20] Incest was a subject ignored by the majority of Victorian writers and select committees, although to Shaftesbury the link between overcrowding and incest was clear. There were, he had told the House of Lords in 1861, 'Grown-up sons sleeping with their mothers, brothers and sisters, sleeping very often not in the same apartment only, but in the same bed . . . incestuous crime is frightfully common in various parts of this Metropolis.'[21] It may have been an integral part of the Victorian culture of poverty,[22] demonstrating the huge gap between middle-class ideals of the home as a 'sacred place, a vestal temple, a temple of the hearth watched over by the Household Gods'[23] and working-class reality. Ignored by Parliament, which had swept away Cromwell's death penalty against incest during the Restoration, it was a silent vice fermenting below the surface of Victorian life until at last brought out into the open by the 1908 Incest Act, which made it punishable by up to seven years' imprisonment.

Beatrice was shocked that the girls of slums 'unburden themselves in promiscuous love-making' but she did not condemn them, since they had no consciousness of sin and lived 'in the garden of Eden of uncivilised life'.[24] She struggled on felling sleeves into coats, while Mrs Moses washed her haddock in the back yard, and Mrs Irons, Beatrice's Scottish friend, slipped her some bread and butter for lunch. It was ill-paid work. Mrs Irons only took 1s 6d a day, and Mrs Moses, who had taken a liking to Beatrice, advised her to find herself a good husband. 'You're fit for more than to be making your own living in this sort of place,' she told Beatrice, who was pleased to leave after four days.

This time Beatrice had a popular success with her account of her adventures, entitled 'Pages from a Work-Girl's Diary'. Knowles paid her two guineas a page, and she achieved a certain notoriety as a society girl who had penetrated the sweater's den. Beatrice became even more of a public personality when she was called before the House of Lords Select Committee on Sweating in May 1888. It was her first experience of media attention, and she was distressed when the *Pall Mall Gazette* criticised her dress and appearance, and the peeresses came to stare at her during lunch. There were hurtful accusations that her evidence was false, that she had been given special treatment in the workshops. Although Beatrice knew her disguise had not been penetrated, in her confusion she exaggerated the number of weeks she had worked in different sweatshops. Beatrice agonised over how to retrieve the situation, and in the end surreptitiously altered the proofs of her evidence to the correct figure. It was a small sin but one which caused her sleepless nights.

With the help of the Chief Rabbi Beatrice turned the Quakers' Hotel into a headquarters from which to interview a never-ending stream of contractors to the tailoring trade, masters, middlemen and workers. From this four-month investigation grew her spirited defence of the Jewish race, whom she saw not as villain but victim in the struggle for survival. To the charge that the Jewish middleman destroyed the market for the Englishman, Beatrice replied that there was in fact no competition between the Jewish contractor who supplied the wholesale houses with ready-made clothing, and the native bespoke tailor who made a coat which lasted three times as long and fitted far better, and supplied the West End and City trade in 'ordered coats'.[25] The competition was not between English trade unionists and immigrant foreigners, but between the Jew and the provincial factory, and between Jewish and female labour. For the first time Beatrice was beginning to interest herself in the conditions of working women, as she uncovered the true story of the tailoring trade.

English tailors, she told the peers, worked regular hours on tailors' premises for good wages of £2 10s a week, but they were being displaced by journeymen, English, German or Jewish, who worked at home for long hours with their wives and daughters as their helpmates, and therefore could undercut bespoke prices. Among the coatmakers of Whitechapel many 'sweated' their workers in overcrowded 'slo shops', 'noisome habitations' with less than ten workers who slept on shake down mattresses on the floor when their day's work was done, but, she warned the 'imaginative journalist', there was worse over-crowding in the bespoke shops. The large Jewish contractor employing twenty-five hands offered his workers more comfort and regular hours than did the small master. Beatrice admired the Jews: 'the strongest-motive of the Jewish race – the love of *profit* as distinct from other forms of money earning' led to the rise of the individual Jew, although the race depressed the industry through which they rose by taking on the worst work, accepting the dirtiest lodging, charging the lowest prices until they had bettered themselves. Then it was the turn of the newest immigrant to start the process again, ever burrowing upward. The Jews, said Beatrice, were 'mentally and physically progressive', and no inquiry was needed. It was a bold statement to make to the backwoodsmen of the House of Lords, but one she defended vigor-ously.

Beatrice's sympathy lay with the women of the East End, the 'struggling wives and mothers of drunken husbands and starving children [who] slave day and night for a pittance which a greener would despise'.[26] They were the wives and daughters of the poorest and most worthless labourers. Since these destitute women would accept any work for any wage, earning only 3/4d to 2d an hour, working for tallymen who paid them in instalments, or in the retail slopshops, it was they who threatened the livelihood of the bespoke tailor. Forever condemned to remain plain hands, unlike the male 'greener' apprentice who would soon be on his way to becoming a small master, these women had no choice but to beg for work at any price. It was the capitalist system which allowed sweating to exist, decided Beatrice, which was the villain of the piece, 'the evil spirit of the age, unrestrained competition'.[27]

She had come to a disturbing conclusion. Individualism and self-help, *laissez-faire* and minimal state interference, which Herbert Spencer had taught her to accept as her creed, suddenly seemed a cruel and wicked ideology. She had defended it to Chamberlain when he told her the rich must pay a ransom to the poor, but now she began to call 'state sternness' into question. Her change of heart led to a fundamental parting of the ways from Charles and Mary Booth, for Charles was no socialist; the spark which triggered his inquiry had been the claim made by Henry Hyndman, the Social Democratic Federation leader, that twenty-five per cent of the population lived in extreme poverty.[28] Outraged, Booth called on Hyndman and accused him of 'incendiary statements' which encouraged the rioting in the West End. 'I have never yet been shown to be wrong in my statistics,' Hyndman informed him. Booth then announced he would be beginning his own inquiry which would demonstrate the truth.

The truth turned out to be the opposite of Booth's expectations. Not only was Hyndman right, he had underestimated the number living below Booth's poverty line, defined as the minimum income sufficient to keep a couple and four or five children – 18s to 21s a week. Not twenty-five per cent but thirty-five per cent were living at subsistence level. But Booth never followed his findings to the same conclusion as Beatrice, and this was the root of their difference. His ideas developed in a similar direction to Samuel Barnett's, who considered that a strict dividing line needed to be drawn between the 'respectable' working class and the demoralised casuals. Get rid of the casuals and there would be work enough for the true working class. As Barnett put it, 'it is a shocking thing to say of men created in God's image, but it is true that the extinction of the unemployed would add to the wealth of the country.'[29] His solution to the problem was to send the casual labourers to farm colonies in the countryside where they could be trained in agricultural skills and settled on the land. Similarly Booth argued that class B, the casual labouring class which he put just above the semi-criminal class A, should be taken charge of by the state. 'The entire removal of this very poor class out of the daily struggle for existence I believe to be the only solution to the problem.'[30] Preferably they should be taken into 'state slavery' in labour colonies out of London. Since slavery as such was impossible in a free country, their lives would be made impossible until they submitted to entering the technically voluntary colonies where they would lead 'a disciplined existence, with regular meals and fixed hours of work (which would not be short)'. By practising this 'limited socialism', Booth believed the capitalist system would operate more efficiently, and a serious danger would be averted.

It was, as Beatrice pointed out, a breathtakingly ambitious and ruthless scheme, since class B numbered over three hundred thousand in London alone, and it found few supporters. But the problem of what to do with the unemployed was one which occupied the minds of many as the economic depression deepened. Lord Brabazon suggested that they should be sent overseas and settled in the Empire, but, as Samuel Smith remarked, 'While the flower of the population emigrate, the residuum stays, corrupting and being corrupted, like the sewage of the Metropolis which remained floating at the mouth of the Thames last summer.'[31] A more prophetic scheme was Booth's call for a universal, non-contributory pension to be given as a right to all those who reached the age of seventy.

While Booth toyed with these schemes Beatrice was questioning the basic premise of Herbert Spencer's thought: that the capitalist system belonged to the natural order of things, and any attempt on the part of the state to interfere with profit-making was doomed to failure because it was inherently artificial. At last she realised that to the workers there was another side of the picture. To Beatrice in the past the new experiments of free state education, first begun in 1870, factory acts and trade unionism, even the use of a police force, had seemed 'against nature'. Now it came home to her that they were made at the cost of her own class to benefit another class. Were they perhaps, after all, right?[32]

As she continued to work for Booth, Beatrice developed a new professional persona, attending conferences at Toynbee Hall, exchanging opinions with Hubert Llewellyn Smith and Maurice Paul, her fellow workers, dining with working men such as Benjamin Jones, a textile worker and a co-operative organiser, and John Burnett, secretary of the engineers' union. She saw Annie Besant, whom she admired as a great orator, but condemned for her brashness in speaking in public, thinking 'it is not womanly to thrust yourself before the world'. Beatrice excused Mrs Besant on the grounds that she had been unsexed by the loss of her child, and wished to know her better.[33] Gradually Beatrice was withdrawing herself completely from Society. When she did venture up to the West End at a dinner given by her sister Kate, where Arthur Balfour, Lord Salisbury's nephew and then Secretary of State for Ireland, was present, she was not impressed. It was all froth, she decided. 'No one said what they thought, and everyone said what they thought to be clever.'[34]

In April 1888 Rosy became engaged to Arthur Dyson Williams, a nephew of the Miss Williams who had first introduced Beatrice to

Chamberlain. Although he was a barrister, Beatrice considered him 'not up to the mark of the other brothers-in-law, but then Rosy is the least gifted mentally and physically, of the whole sisterhood'.[35] With Rosy's marriage that autumn, Beatrice's responsibilities were changing. The winter of 1888 was the last she spent at Kildare, the quiet Bournemouth boarding house where she cared for her father. Beatrice moved him to Box House in Minchinhampton, Gloucestershire, a small house belonging to her sister Mary Playne just five minutes' walk away from Longfords where the Playnes lived, and it remained her home until her marriage.

Marriage and the feminine ideal were still very much in Beatrice's thoughts, although she protested 'passion lies at my feet dead. At first I stood over it and wept bitter tears. Now I have buried it and think of it tenderly.' As her thirtieth birthday approached she wrote: 'I have lived through my youth – it is over.'[36] As the year's end approached she mused over the past. She had been tossed on 'the ocean of passionate feeling' but now she was safe in calm water. As Bella Fisher told her, she was entering a new phase in her life, as a working woman, for which she must equip herself. Thoughtfully Beatrice examined her new ideal of work; it was important to remain warm-hearted, to keep up ties of friendship, not to become a disappointed spinster. She must show love and sympathy towards other women: 'Every woman has a mission to other women – more especially to the women of her own class and circumstances.' But although sisterhood was possible with other women, helping men was harder because emotion and sexual attraction got in the way. Beatrice debated whether as she grew older this would wear off. So great was the unwritten barrier between the upper and lower classes that she could already sympathise with working men without any 'unpleasant consequences'.

Beatrice's efforts to forge a new pathway as a working woman were made immeasurably harder by the news of Chamberlain that trickled back across the Atlantic. The *Etruria* had brought the new commissioner to New York, where he dexterously parried reporters' questions and quoted William Cowper to the New York Chamber of Commerce before moving on to Washington where the Commission was to sit. There he stayed at the Arlington Hotel, and was swept up in a whirl of engagements, the high point of which was an 'orchid banquet'. Sir Lionel Sackville West, the British Minister, introduced him to President Cleveland who was then fifty years old, eight months older than Chamberlain. Cleveland, a corpulent bachelor, had recently married his twenty-four-year-old ward, Florence, an example not lost on his visitor.[37]

Chamberlain's days were occupied in negotiations over the 'three mile limit' allowed American fishermen when fishing in Canadian territorial waters, but his nights were spent in pleasure. American women had made a very favourable impression on him, for he wrote to his daughter Beatrice: 'I am compelled to admit that as far as I have seen the average of American female beauty is higher than ours.' A month later his enthusiasm had grown: 'I never saw so many bright and pretty women . . . I have taken to dancing and revived my waltzing and polking . . . All anxious they say to have my secret of perpetual youth. I give them my receipt freely, "No exercise and smoke all day".'[38]

The secret of Chamberlain's new-found enthusiasm for American beauty was Mary Endicott, the tall, fair twenty-three-year-old daughter of Judge Endicott, Secretary of War in Cleveland's cabinet, who made an instant impression upon him when Sir Lionel gave a sumptuous ball in his honour at the British Legation. Her New England background was impeccable: her Puritan ancestor John Endicott had left Devon for Salem in the *Abigail* in 1628 and had risen to become Governor of Massachusetts.[39] His descendants had intermarried with other New England families and were leaders of Washington society. More important was her character: Mary was able to give Chamberlain the 'intelligent sympathy' he craved on the subject of Home Rule, having visited England with her father when Chamberlain was President of the Board of Trade, and this was balm to his soul at a time when so many former friends had become apostates.

Soon the newspapers were buzzing with the rumours of his devotion for Mary Endicott, from whom 'he fairly chased all the young men away'.[40] They became secretly engaged, as Cleveland was afraid that the Democrats' chances in the autumn election would be harmed if Irish-American voters knew that the Secretary of War's daughter was to marry the chief opponent of Charles Parnell. After signing the fisheries' treaty, Chamberlain sailed home from New York sporting a red rose in his buttonhole instead of his usual orchid, but on 3 November 1888 he crossed the Atlantic again to claim his bride, travelling under the name of Willoughby Maycock, his assistant secretary. Secrecy had been in vain: Cleveland fell in the election but the ex-President was present at Chamberlain's marriage to Mary Endicott at St John's Church, Washington. On this occasion the bridegroom wore white violets on his black coat, at the bride's request.[41]

At home in London Beatrice had heard the rumours of Chamberlain's new attachment, but hardly believed them. In April the story had broken in the *Pall Mall Gazette*, and 'Chamberlain's Marriage' was on every newspaper placard. 'A gasp, as if one had been stabbed, and then it is over,' recorded Beatrice.[42] But it was by no means over for her. On 29 July she wrote, 'This day last year I spent with J.C. Now we have each gone on our way – parted for all Eternity (?).' Her depression deepened during a miserable August at the Argoed, despite a short stay with Dr Mandell Creighton, Professor of History at Cambridge, and his wife. She passed nights of 'self-torture', dreaming of Chamberlain, her heart palpitating, her mouth dry. Again she thought of suicide, and the laudanum bottle tempted her to end her misery for ever. While she suffered, Chamberlain was writing to his fiancée, 'I look back on the last thirteen years as a bad dream . . . I have been so lonely, there has never been a time when I would not have accepted a sentence of death as a relief.'[43]

As his loneliness came to an end, Beatrice's became a heavier burden. She spent the eve of his marriage praying in Westminster Abbey, listening half-dazed to the solemn chanting of prayers and the voices of the choristers lifted in the anthem. She prayed for his happiness, 'That the love of a good woman might soften and comfort him . . . If he could only *feel* my sympathy and *understand* it.'[44] At 2 a.m. she lay awake thinking of Chamberlain's future, wondering whether he would become a Tory, and a pleasure-loving English gentleman under the influence of his new wife. By 5 p.m. she wrote desolately, 'It must be over: and they are man and wife.' Willie Cripps, with whom she was staying in London, did his best to comfort her, and she spent long mornings at St Paul's, finding consolation in Holy Communion. But nothing could prevent the week of nervous collapse which followed, when Beatrice took to her bed, marvelling that someone who in the future would be a stranger to her could inflict such intense pain. She wrote an 'epitaph' for Chamberlain, analysing his political career and personal life. Had he found 'a mate to his nature' who, unlike herself, would see only through his eyes? And would this bring him happiness unless he also found the power he believed was his birthright?[45]

Chamberlain's marriage spelt the end of the hope that somehow they might have been reconciled. The news of the engagement of Ella Pycroft to Maurice Paul signalled a different kind of desertion, for

Beatrice had felt certain that Ella, like Cary Darling, Maggie Harkness and herself, was a 'glorified spinster', the name given to the 'new race of women not looking for or expecting marriage' featured in *MacMillan's Magazine*.[46] In October 1886 Ella had refused Maurice Paul although by autumn 1888 she had cautiously agreed to marry him. 'I must confess it would grieve me sadly if there were any prospect of giving up any of my work, glorified spinsterhood plus a future to look forward to – even at the cost of its losing its halo – is a very jolly form of life.'[47] Ella's decision meant the loss of an old friend who had been at the very hub of Beatrice's network of supportive, celibate friends, and who had validated her own chosen way of life and shared her sense of mission. When Beatrice heard that Cary Darling too was getting married to her old love, Mr Murdoch, she was scathing. 'Oh, woman, you are passing strange,' she wrote. 'God preserve me from a lover between thirty-five and forty-five. No woman can resist a man's importunity during the last years of unrealised womanhood.'[48]

Beatrice's feelings about spinsterhood were confused. 'Ah, poor things,' she had exclaimed, when she read the article about 'glorified spinsters'. Her feeling of pity was one shared by many complacent married women when they contemplated the fate of their unmarried sisters, traditionally condemned to a life of soured virginal self-sacrifice, surviving on the margins of society as helpmates to married sisters or the poor. The popular image of the spinster was of a woman wholly alone. Her dread, as the bathos of contemporary fiction showed, was that 'most likely it will be strangers only who come about the dying bed, close eyes that no husband ever kissed, and draw the shroud over the poor withered breast where no child's head has ever lain'.[49] In fact Beatrice, caught up in the excitement of re-interpreting the celibate working life in a new and positive way, which allowed her to experience comradeship with working-class men and women, and escape from the domestic life she had found stifling, wrote: ' "Glorified spinsterhood" is at present gilded, gilded by the charm of novelty and youth.' She was honest enough to articulate her fears too: 'Dark times will come again; days of weary loneliness, of physical depression, of the decay of all personal charm (the most precious gift of womanhood).'[50]

It was time to move on. At the beginning of 1889 she completed her work for Booth and was looking for a new subject to research in her own right. Beatrice was drifting away from both the Booths. Mary had discouraged her from calling and when Beatrice did eventually come by appointment for a private chat with her she was disappointed to find the room full of other friends. Beatrice left, deeply upset. 'Charlie I could have given up but *she* has been so much to me.'

Charles Booth had suggested to Beatrice that she should look more thoroughly into the problems of women workers, who so often fell into prostitution with its appeal of easy money, but Beatrice hesitated. At the Creightons she met Professor Alfred Marshall, the Cambridge economist, who asked her to lunch and quizzed her on her tentative plan to look at the Co-operative Movement which, with its ideal of worker rather than capitalist ownership of capital, seemed to Beatrice to provide a small-scale alternative to the capitalist system. 'Do you think I am equal to it?' Beatrice asked Marshall. 'Now, Miss Potter, I am going to be perfectly frank,' he replied. 'Of course I think you are equal to a history of Co-operation: but it is not what you can do best.' Her field must be female labour. He paid Beatrice the compliment of saying, 'You have, unlike most women, a fairly trained intellect, and the courage and capacity for original work.'[51] Beatrice was not convinced and decided, 'I shall stick to my own way of climbing my own little tree.'

Part of Beatrice's reluctance to research women's work was that despite professing to believe in women's mission to other women, she was known at the time as an anti-feminist, having thoughtlessly signed the manifesto of Mrs Humphrey Ward, the novelist, against female suffrage. Beatrice felt that she herself had never suffered any discrimination as a woman and had in fact benefited through being a woman in carving a career in research. Had she been a man she would have been pushed into making money and might have aroused more suspicion as an investigator. Frederic Harrison had influenced her against votes for women, and in July begged her to reply to the 'dry democratic formulas' of Mrs Millicent Fawcett, the leader of the National Union of Women's Suffrage Societies. Two thousand signatures had been collected to support Mrs Ward, but even so Harrison urged Beatrice, '*You* are the woman most fitted on every ground to take up the task . . . I really think it is a duty you owe to the public. It is criminal to bury your talent in a napkin in Monmouthshire.'[52]

When Beatrice sat down and tried to write a defence of the anti-suffrage position for Harrison and Knowles, who joined his pleas to Harrison's, she saw its impossibility. Her awkwardness was increased by the reproaches of her working men-friends: when she went to the Pickwickian White Horse Inn at Ipswich for the Co-operative Congress held every Whitsun, she had to face the united wrath of John

Mitchell, the chairman of the Manchester Wholesale Co-op Society, Benjamin Jones, and J. J. Dent, a bricklayer from the working-men's clubs. Professor Marshall had come to the conference too, but the men left their conversation with him to turn on Beatrice, whose stand had just become known. 'There is another question Miss Potter has to explain to us, one for which she is far more responsible,' remarked Dent gruffly. 'Why she has lent her influence to that appeal against the suffrage.' He went to the heart of the matter: 'I believe it is just this: she is satisfied with her own position, because she is rich and strong. She does not see that other women need the power to help themselves which would be given by the vote.' There was too much truth in this accusation for Beatrice not to feel embarrassed, and her embarrassment increased when the Professor sprang to her defence, saying that she understood that men would not marry women if their wives became their competitors. With a scornful glance at Marshall's own wife, a badly-dressed Newnham graduate with protruding teeth, Beatrice indignantly defended herself, saying she was the personifica- tion of emancipation. But Jones was not easily deterred. 'It is pure perversity on your side, to say one thing and act another.'[53] Although Beatrice tried to retrieve the situation by telling fortunes in the smoking room that night and sharing cigarettes with her old friends, her reputation was tarnished. She did not publicly change her mind for nearly twenty years.

Beatrice had found no difficulty in getting her work published, and she lacked understanding of the obstacles faced by less privileged women. She had not troubled to think of the civil and political disadvantages which faced women because they lacked the vote. Yet paradoxically she was aligning herself more closely with other celibate women, suggesting in March 1889 that they formed their own trade union of working women. Beatrice saw her love of cigarettes as a symbol of emancipation, by which women adopted 'mannish ways'. The cigarette was, she wrote, 'the wand with which the possible women of the future will open the hidden stores of knowledge of men and . . . become the leading doctors, barristers and scientists,' and she prophes- ied that 'a female Gladstone may lurk in the dim vistas of the future'.[54]

Despite Beatrice's brave protestations of emancipation, the emo- tional vacuum in her life left by the final loss of Chamberlain and the cooling of her relationship with the Booths, could not be ignored. She found troublesome the attentions of another professorial admirer, Francis Edgworth, a statistician from Oxford University, who began to dog her footsteps. He sent her plaintive, admiring letters, telling her that her speech was 'better than silver and your words do seem gold to me and your confidence and appreciation the most precious things which I have on earth'.[55] 'The man is pathetic,' wrote Beatrice, when he came to pay his addresses to her at the Devonshire Hotel. 'He bores me.' She despised the forty-four-year-old bachelor, with his pedantic ways, his little stories gleaned from *Punch* to amuse her, his 'furtive glance of unsatisfied desire'.[56] Undeterred, Edgworth followed her to Ipswich, but she found the agonised expressions of romantic feelings from 'a statistical measuring machine' made her self-conscious, and led other women to give her the cold shoulder.

Even unwelcome admirers produced a physical response in Beatrice, one she tried hard to bury. 'Those relations with men stimulate and excite one's lower nature, for where one can give no real sympathy strong feelings in another seem to debase and drag one down to a lower level of animal self-consciousness.' She was ashamed of her sexual feelings. 'How one despises oneself, giving way to those feelings (and over thirty too, – it would be excusable in a woman of twenty-five), but that part of a woman's nature dies hard.'[57]

Beatrice knew her emotions required an outlet. She had never expected that, despite good looks and high spirits, at over thirty she would still be a virgin, nor increasingly unlikely to become a mother like her sisters. She saw sexual feelings as an expression of maternal longing: 'It is many variations of one chord, *the supreme and instinctive longing to be a mother.*'

In addition she was beginning to doubt her intellectual abilities as she struggled with a mountain of information on the Co-operative Movement, and seemed to make no headway. 'I am unfit for the work I have undertaken,' she wrote in June. 'Brain-sick', feeling 'cold as steel', she knew she needed help, and asked Maggie Harkness to recommend someone from whom she could learn the early history of Co-operation. At once Maggie thought of the Fabian, Sidney Webb, and arranged a meeting. It was to herald a momentous change in Beatrice's life, one which would undo the sad future she had forecast at the beginning of the year when she quoted Matthew Arnold on the first page of her new diary: 'Thou hast been, shalt be, art, alone.'

XIII

BEAUTY AND THE BEAST

'Our years are beads, blown by uncertain fate;
At birth strong on the narrow film of time;
Each bead is coloured by the chequered state,
On youth's gay show, or sunset's winter rime,
Till Death with pallid smile and calm sublime,
Does burst the film alike for small and great.

O happy they who tell their beadlets right,
Dropping like gold into the silent sea,
Their deeds live on to all eternity.'

Sidney Webb, 4 May 1883[1]

SIDNEY JAMES WEBB was an unlikely candidate for the affections of an upper-middle-class girl of wealth and beauty; indeed he had few outward qualities to attract a girl of his own class, lacking as he did social assurance, good looks and sexual appeal. His qualities were inner ones: idealism, sincerity, a powerful intellectual appetite, and ambition, qualities appealing to a woman of ability but lacking in confidence, who was cast adrift from her natural social milieu and was in need of both an ideology and a husband.

Born on 13 July 1859 in Cranbourn Street near Leicester Square, Sidney grew up in very different circumstances from his future wife. His was a London childhood, which left him with a cockney accent, the shiny petit bourgeois suit of the clerk, and the diffidence of not belonging. His family origins are indistinct, but it seems that his paternal grandfather was a Kentish inn-keeper, and one of his cousins a professional cricketer. His maternal grandfather had a small property in Suffolk. Despite the frequent assumption that he was Jewish, on account of his appearance and surname, there is no evidence that his family was other than English.

Sidney was a middle child, having an elder brother, Charles, and younger sister Ada. His father was an ardent intellectual, an admirer of John Stuart Mill, and a keen Radical. He earned a precarious income as an accountant, but spent most of his time in unpaid work, as a vestryman and Poor Law guardian. It was little, rosy-cheeked Mrs

Webb who provided the main part of the family income, running a small but efficient hairdressing business. Left an orphan as a young woman she had refused to live as a parasite upon her East Anglian relatives and, borrowing money from her brother-in-law, set up the shop which was already a going concern when she married in 1854.

Neither of Sidney's parents were worldly people. They belonged to the 'superior' section of the lower-middle class which 'kept itself to itself', and did not mix with the neighbours. Lively political arguments took place, for Mrs Webb's Evangelical leanings were at cross purposes with her husband's Radicalism, but generally Sidney slaked his hunger for knowledge in books. 'After a few lessons at my mother's knee, which I do not remember, I had taught myself to read at an early age, very largely from books and notices displayed in the shop windows,' he recalled in 1928. 'I found more instruction in the reputedly arid pages of Kelly's London Directory, then already a ponderous tome, than in any other single volume to which my childhood had access,' he remembered.[2] He loved London and one of his earliest memories was watching the Lord Mayor's Show from the steps of St Martin's Church, and he declared there was nowhere else on earth that he would rather live.

As soon as he could read Sidney began to win prizes at school, first at day school in St Martin's Lane and then at the City of London School. He retained an affection for his prizes in later life, refusing to throw them away when Beatrice later complained about dusting them at their home in Grosvenor Road. Unusually, his mother sent Sidney and his brother Charles abroad to learn languages, first to Switzerland to learn French, then to the home of a pastor at Wisnar, near Hamburg, to acquire German. When family circumstances dictated that Sidney left school at sixteen, he was able to get a job as a clerk in the City office of a Colonial broker on the strength of his languages, but his prodigious gift for memorising facts meant he did not stay there long. After a day's work he went to London University evening classes, and in 1878 sat the Open Competitive Examination for the Civil Service, passing into the War Office as a Second Division Clerk. A year later, after excelling in another exam, he moved to the Inland Revenue, and from there into the First or Administrative Division of the Colonial Office. By 1885 Sidney estimated that he had won £450 in prizes, and he had reached the same Civil Service grade as those who, like his close friend Sydney Olivier, had come in via university. It was a triumph indeed for the hairdresser's son, and explains something of the passion with which he later fought for the Education Bill which set up the scholarship ladder for poor men's sons. For his own satisfaction Sidney studied for an external law degree at London University, graduating in 1886.

Sidney stayed in the Civil Service until 1892, supplementing his wages by prolific freelance journalism and unpaid tract writing for the Fabian Society, but even after he left the Colonial Office he retained the habits and manner of thought of a civil servant. He never desired to be a public leader but was prepared to work extraordinarily hard without recognition, oblivious to monetary rewards or fame, although he so sparkled in committee that he earned the nickname 'Wily Webb'.

In the winter of 1879 Sidney attended a meeting of the Zetetical Society, an offshoot of the Dialectical Society founded to discuss John Stuart Mill's *Essay on Liberty*.[3] It was before the socialist societies sprang up like mushrooms all over London, and the Zetetical Society was atheistic; as Edward Pease, founder member of the Fabian Society, explained, there was an intellectual gulf between the young generation who had absorbed and accepted Darwin's *The Origin of Species*, and their parents, who continued to believe the Old Testament story of creation.[4] That winter there were many women at the meeting, taking an important part in the debate and protesting against the inadequacies of the Married Women's Property Act. Their anger was also directed against the Lord Chancellor who had allowed Annie Besant's children to be torn from her because she was an atheist. The Zetetical Society was a young, excitable society, and to its members socialism was nothing more than 'an exploded fallacy of Robert Owen's,[5] the socialist leader whose socialism had died with Chartism in the Hungry Forties.

A few weeks previously an Irish clerk named James Lecky had brought a friend to a meeting, George Bernard Shaw. At age twenty Shaw had come to London from Dublin in 1876 in pursuit of his mother, Bessie Shaw, who had left her husband, the drunken George Carr Shaw, to find musical success with her music teacher. Success eluded Bessie, and for a long time it also eluded her son, who claimed to have only earned £6 in nine years as a journalist, in between writing five unpublished novels. In 1885 Shaw began reviewing books for the *Pall Mall Gazette*, and by 1888 was music critic of the *Star*. But he found it impossible to escape the imprint of his early years as the son of 'an Irish Protestant gentleman of the downstart race of younger sons'.[6]

During the debate Shaw was struck by Sidney Webb. 'He was about twenty-one, rather below middle height, with small hands and feet, and a profile that suggested an improvement on Napoleon the third, his nose and imperial moustache being of that shape,' Shaw noted. 'He had a fine forehead, a long head . . . and remarkably thick, strong, dark hair.' Webb's encylopaedic knowledge impressed Shaw instantly. 'He knew all about the subject of debate: knew more than the lecturer; knew more than anybody present; had read everything that had ever been written . . . he used notes, read them, ticked them off one by one, threw them away, and finished with a coolness and clearness that seemed to me miraculous.'[7] Shaw decided Webb was 'the ablest man in England'; later he was to write, 'Quite the wisest thing I ever did was to force my friendship on to him and to keep it.'

Controlled and diffident, 'the simplest of geniuses', as Shaw called him, Webb was the perfect complement to that more complicated wordsmith Shaw, and together they formed the nucleus of the Fabian Society Old Gang.

Neither Webb nor Shaw was a founder member of the Fabian Society, which had come into existence on 4 January 1884 in the rooms of Edward Pease at 17 Osnaburgh Street in Regent's Park. The society was the result of a split in the idealist Fellowship of the New Life founded by the wandering scholar, Thomas Davidson. Dedicated to vague spiritual aims, such as the 'cultivation of the perfect character' and 'the subordination of material things to spiritual', the Vita Nuova was an expression of the yearning for a more spiritually satisfying way of life which characterised the 1880s. The desire to live in a community away from the competitive materialist world activated the twenty-six-year-old Edward Pease, a disenchanted stockbroker. Inspired by the socialist writings of William Morris, Pease had left the City to become a 'worker with his own hands', or cabinet-maker, in Newcastle until he became secretary of the Fabian Society.

One night while Pease was watching for ghosts in a haunted house in Notting Hill Gate with Frank Podmore, who shared his interest in Spiritualism, they began discussing Henry George's *Progress and Poverty*. The ghost never appeared, but they decided to call a meeting of those members of the Fellowship of the New Life interested in social as well as spiritual progress. The new society was called the Fabian Society after the Roman general Fabius Cunctator who, Podmore told his fellow Fabians, waited 'most patiently, when warring against Hannibal though many censured his delays; but when the time comes you must strike heard, as Fabius did . . .'[8] Pease and Podmore, a young clerk called Percival Chubb, Havelock Ellis the sexologist, and Hubert Bland were present, among others. A resolution was passed that the aim of the fledgling society should be the 'reconstruction of society in accordance with the highest moral possibilities'. There was no mention of socialism.

On 4 April 1884 the pamphlet committee decided to print two thousand copies of the first Fabian tract, *Why Are the Many Poor?*, by W. L. Phillips, a house painter, and the only working-class Fabian member. It was the beginning of a long educative tradition in accordance with the Fabian motto, 'Educate, Agitate, Organise', for despite the protests of Shaw that in the early days the Fabian Society was 'just as anarchistic as the Socialist League, and just as insurrectionary as the [Social Democratic] Federation',[9] from its first beginnings the society was a middle-class drawing-room society. Shaw, who had become a socialist after reading Henry George, like so many of his contemporaries, was elected to the Fabian Society on 5 September 1884. Ignoring talk of the 'reconstruction' of society, Shaw decided the Fabian aim was 'to bring about a tremendous smash-up of existing society, to be succeeded by complete socialism'.

On 2 January 1885 Shaw was elected on to the Fabian executive, and by 1 May he had persuaded Sidney Webb to join, together with Sidney's closest friend, Sydney Olivier. Olivier was Oxford educated, had become close friends at university with Graham Wallas, an Evangelical who underwent the spiritual crisis so common to Victorian intellectuals and lost his faith. In 1884 Wallas became classics master at Highgate School, and within two years had joined Webb, Olivier and Shaw in the Fabian 'Politbureau', as Shaw called it. Other members considered Webb, Olivier and Wallas as the Three Musketeers, with Shaw as their D'Artagnan.[10]

There were other, overlapping circles, among these young and idealistic men and women. Among the most flamboyant was Mrs Wilson, a Girton graduate who lived on the edge of Hampstead Heath in Wildwood Farm which she 'simplified' into a cottage; there she founded the Karl Marx Club in 1884, which soon became the Hampstead Historic. She appeared to Webb as a 'Rossetti young woman' with dense hair, who astounded him by reading an elaborate analysis of Marx, which Webb 'gaily' danced upon and demolished.[11] Emma Brooke the novelist, who interested herself in 'the woman question', and was the author of the controversial bestseller, *The Superfluous Woman*, was secretary to the Hampstead Historic, where the young Fabians argued and developed their public speaking skills. With Charlotte Wilson's election to the Fabian executive a 'sort of influenza of anarchism soon spread through the society', according to Shaw, for she was an ardent supporter of Prince Kropotkin and editor of the anarchist journal *Freedom*. In 1887 Charlotte resigned from the executive, but Emma Brooke continued her Fabian connection, as well as interesting herself in the Men and Women's Club, in which the eugenicist writer Karl Pearson was a central figure. There the topic of discussion was the relationship between the sexes and the desirability of free love.[12]

By the Thames at Kelmscott House, Hammersmith Mall, the most famous 'Rossetti woman' of all, Janey Morris, the one-time lover of Dante Gabriel Rossetti, presided over the headquarters of the Socialist League. Her husband William Morris, artist, writer, poet, and leader of the Arts and Crafts movement, as well as being the possessor of a private income and a successful businessman, had become a socialist as he approached fifty. Throwing himself heart and soul first into the Social Democratic Federation and then into the Socialist League, which he founded after falling out with Henry Hyndman, Morris spoke at open-air meetings all over the country, edited *Commonweal*, converted his coach house into the meeting-house of the Hammersmith branch of the Socialist League, and told his disciples: 'I want a real revolution, a real change in Society: Society a great organic mass of well-regulated forces used for bringing about a happy life for all . . . the revolution cannot be a mechanical one, though the last act of it may be civil war.'[13] Among his disciples was Eleanor Marx and her lover Edward Aveling, with whom she lived in a free union for fifteen years, before committing suicide at the age of forty-two. By night Eleanor and May, daughter of Morris, posted bills in secret, by day they ran social events such as Christmas parties for the children of members, giving the 'little Socialists' a tree and a 'good romp' in honour not of Christmas but the Pagan Festival of Light.[14]

Then there was the back-to-nature impulse shared by Henry and Kate Salt in the Surrey hills. Salt was an Eton housemaster who left his post voluntarily, retiring to a labourer's cottage with his wife, where she, together with Shaw, would play duets on the old grand piano, a relic of Eton days. Salt, who was vegetarian, founded a Humanitarian League, and he, the homosexual poet Edward Carpenter and Shaw spent happy weekends at Tilford. Kate Salt was a lesbian who had no objections to this strange ménage. Shaw nicknamed Carpenter the 'Noble Savage' for his adherence to the simple life, but refused to wear sandals like Carpenter after returning from a walk with bleeding feet.

Beatrice was unaware of the Fabians during the first years of the society's existence. In 1885 it had only forty members, and operated as an intellectual discussion group while Hyndman's Social Democratic Federation and Morris's Socialist League occupied the limelight. It was during this period, boasted Shaw, that the Fabians learnt to laugh at themselves, and to despise those orators who 'stoked up' the working class by dwelling on their woes. 'There was far too much equality and personal intimacy among the Fabians to allow of any member presuming to get up and preach at the rest in the fashion which the working classes still tolerate submissively from their leaders,' wrote Shaw with a touch of complacency.[15] It was just this intimacy and intellectual bias which attracted Beatrice to the 'small set of able young men' she felt the Fabians to be by 1890.[16]

The Fabian Society had become more clearly defined after it split with the Social Democratic Federation over the so-called 'Tory Gold' scandal after the November 1885 election. The Federation ran two candidates in London, whose expenses were paid by the Conservatives in order to split the Liberal vote. When Hyndman was attacked for corruptly accepting Tory money, he responded with a classical quotation: '*Non olet*.' [It does not smell.] But to London Radicals smell it did, and from that date Fabians were hostile to the Federation, as was Morris. Hyndman's aim, said Morris, had been 'to make the movement seem big, to frighten the powers that be with a turnip bogie which perhaps he almost believes in himself: hence all that insane talk of immediate revolution, when we know the workers in England are not even touched by the movement.'[17] While the Social Democratic Federation preached class war and marched in the streets, the Fabians decided to work through the normal political channels.

The Fabians were still not sure what kind of socialists they were. The tract *What Socialism Is* attempted to address the question, concluding that there were two strands to continental socialism, anarchism and collectivism, but English socialism was still undefined. After a noisy meeting at Anderton's Hotel, from which the drunken Fabians were hounded in disgrace, the society parted company with the Anarchists. Annie Besant, the most flamboyant of the Fabian orators, was appointed to the executive committee in 1885, and grew impatient with the caution of the fledgling society, which in June 1886 still had only sixty-seven members and an annual income of under £40. But Sidney Webb was not to be pushed into violent tactics; in June 1887 he quietly produced the new 'Basis', a test of admission for new members. It remarked sagely that 'The Fabian Society consists of Socialists', and its aim was to reorganise society by freeing land and capital from private ownership, without saying how this might be achieved. So nebulous a document allowed every shade of socialism to co-exist under the Fabian umbrella, and for this reason the 'Basis' remained unchanged for thirty years.

Sidney's other great achievement in 1887 was to write *Facts for Socialists*, the fifth Fabian tract and a bestseller. Hard-hitting facts, such as that the infantile death rate at Bethnal Green was twice that of Belgravia, made sure that the pamphlet 'went off like smoke', as Shaw put it. The Fabians, who had been unsure whether to print one thousand copies, found they sold twenty thousand, and when *Fabian Essays* burst upon an unsuspecting public just before Christmas 1889 the seven essayists were astounded to find their work selling forty-six thousand copies in English alone, even though none of the contributors had ever been published before.

When Beatrice read the slim green volume with a frontispiece designed by Walter Crane, and a cover by William Morris's daughter May, she was as impressed as many of her contemporaries, and was eager to meet the contributors whom her friend J. J. Dent told her were haranguing the Radical clubs, and spreading socialist propaganda. Her own thoughts had been independently turning in the same direction as she travelled the county from end to end interviewing co-operators in the Midlands, the North and in Scotland. Sometimes Beatrice stayed with working-class families such as the widow of an ironfounder in Hebden Bridge, Yorkshire; at other times she took rooms in lodgings as in Manchester where the old maid lodging-keeper gloated over the exhausted Beatrice as she sank wearily into an armchair on her return from Burnley. 'See, you are completely knocked up,' she told her lodger. 'You're only a woman: in spite of your *manly* brain, you're just as much a woman as I am.'[18]

Beatrice often dined with the co-operators, where the food was not to her taste: 'a higgledy-piggledy dinner,' she noted disapprovingly in March 1889. 'Good materials served up coarsely, and shovelled down by the partakers in a way that is not appetising.' But she never allowed her fastidiousness to show, responding pleasantly to joking references to a match between herself and John Mitchell, chairman of the Wholesale Co-op Society, and sharing cigarettes with her working friends in an atmosphere of 'business camaraderie'.[19] Her natural upper-class confidence allowed her to undertake the work of winkling out stray information without embarrassment or self-doubt.

In November 1889 Richard Potter had what appeared to be his final crisis, and Beatrice felt his death was near. 'Darling father!' she wrote.

'How your children have loved you: loving even your weaknesses, smiling over them tenderly like so many mothers . . . With what gentle dignity you have resigned your grasp on life . . .' But Potter rallied, and as Beatrice bent over him, he told her, 'I want one more son-in-law', a remark which surprised her, as he had always discouraged her from marrying before. 'A woman is happier married,' he pronounced. 'I should like to see my little Bee married to a good strong fellow.' Beatrice was conscious that she was no longer his 'little Bee' of long ago.[20]

When she had finished reading *Fabian Essays*, she sent her copy on to a friend, remarking in a letter, 'By far the most significant and interesting essay is the one by Sidney Webb; *he has the historic sense.*' By coincidence Sidney, when reviewing Charles Booth's first volume in the *Star* the previous spring, had remarked, 'The only contributor with any literary talent is Miss Beatrice Potter.'[21] Beatrice claimed that Sidney's persuasive treatment of 'the inevitability of gradualness', a phrase he coined to show that society was evolving towards socialism, impressed her most, but she may have identified with the author when she saw the names of her own youthful heroes, Comte, Darwin and Herbert Spencer, for Sidney, like Beatrice, was influenced by Positivism.

In the New Year of 1890 Beatrice's father was stronger again, and her sister Kate begged her to return with Leonard to London. Beatrice was glad to accept, knowing that she urgently needed historical background for her book. Dent had already told her that there were some clever speakers among the Fabians, but the man 'who organises the whole business' was Sidney Webb. It was Beatrice's problematical friend Maggie Harkness who brought the two together; Maggie, who had been trying to make her way as a journalist, had not been loyal to Beatrice. Piqued when Beatrice was in the limelight over her work for Charles Booth, Maggie spread rumours that Beatrice had lied to the House of Lords Select Committee about her sweating experiences; 'a false friend', wrote Beatrice sadly.[22] Nevertheless she continued to see her, visiting Maggie in her little room in Gower Street, and even lent her £50 in 1889 to pay compensation to a former lover she had libelled. 'Though I do not trust her, I love her and she loves me,' Beatrice concluded.

At last Maggie was able to repay Beatrice her debt of friendship. 'Sidney Webb . . . is your man,' she informed Beatrice. 'He knows everything: when you go out for a walk with him he literally pours out information.'[23] A meeting was arranged at Maggie's rooms in

Beatrice aged five *(Lord Parmoor)*

Lawrencina and Richard Potter
with Beatrice, 1865 *(Lord Parmoor)*

Beatrice, 1885
(Lord Parmoor)

Rt Hon. Joseph Chamberlain, MP, circa 1880
(*The Hulton-Deutsch Collection*)

Beatrice and Sidney working at their desk at
41 Grosvenor Road in the 1890s *(above)* and the 1920s *(below)*
(Passfield Papers, LSE)

The Webbs on their way to Russia for their
first visit in 1932 *(Passfield Papers, LSE)*

The Fabian Window, ordered by G.B. Shaw in 1910 and
designed by Caroline Townshend *(The Fabian Society)*

Sidney Webb in his sixties
(Passfield Papers, LSE)

Beatrice in her sixties
(Passfield Papers, LSE)

The Webbs in their garden at Passfield Corner, 1942
(Passfield Papers, LSE)

January 1890, and by the time Beatrice left she had in her hand a list in Sidney's faultless handwriting of all the sources she needed which could be found in the British Museum. Full of gratitude Beatrice went to work in the domed Reading Room which she felt had a 'homey feeling', even though it was full of life's failures, 'decrepit men, despised foreigners, forlorn widows and soured maids',[24] all knitted together by the feeling of communion with the great immortals whose books they read. As Beatrice burrowed among old Chartist papers she felt she was at last making progress. Sidney Webb meanwhile followed up his initial introduction with a Fabian pamphlet, which led, as he hoped, to a regular exchange of letters between them.

Sidney's early love-life had met with a singular lack of success. He was an unassuming man when young, aware of the class difference between his new friends and himself. 'I hope you will allow me to continue to see something of you,' he wrote humbly to Graham Wallas in May 1885, 'I am just now very much cast down, partly on being left alone [Olivier was away] and partly I suppose by the reaction from the excitement of my last week's examination.' Shy of asking Wallas to visit him in case he would be bored, Sidney suggested 'when you do have a blank coming you might come for a walk together over Hampstead Heath'.[25] When Wallas proposed a day for their walk, Sidney accepted with alacrity, almost unable to believe his luck. 'If you should perchance be busy, do not scruple to cast me adrift,' he told his new friend. With shy pleasure he accepted Wallas's offer to accompany him on a trip to Germany in 1885.

Foreign trips usually brought disastrous romantic entanglements for Sidney. In Brussels a woman called Ilse broke his heart, although he told Wallas with dignity, 'As to Ilse, she is very well, but I am not in love with her, and leaving out of account this inexplicable emotion, which "bloweth where it listeth" beyond our ken or reason. I don't think I should have married her. She was not reasonable enough.' He was probably right, but he remained cast down. He knew nature had not favoured him physically. Girls were not attracted to him as they were to the dark and dashing Olivier who was, Sidney told Wallas jealously, 'unreasonably and inhumanly happy' in his marriage to Margaret Cox, sister of a school friend. Despondently Sidney decided individual happiness was not attainable at all, and therefore 'a logical deduction would be a) alcohol, b) opium, c) suicide . . . Don't be like me,' he told Wallas, who had lost his job at Highgate and was in low spirits, 'wanting at each step to see my whole life in advance (though this has landed me in the *Impasse du bureau des Colonies* instead of on the *Avenue directe à Mondesir*).'

A visit to Salisbury that July caused Sidney to reflect on his boyhood, which he compared with Ruskin's. 'Though a *happy* family, we have always been in the thick of the fight, and I feel now that one of the great influences I have missed is this peace, which I have never known,'[26] he told Olivier. Sidney protested that he was glad that he had had a London boyhood, which had prevented him growing up a Conservative. Better his own father than 'a High Church, porty, Tory father'. Yet it is likely that Sidney's turbulent childhood led him to long all the more for the ideal of domestic peace, the hearth and home guarded by a loving wife, which seemed to be denied him. Certainly he reacted with even greater misery to his next blow. The object of his affections, a girl called Annie Adams, jilted him for a barrister, and Sidney wrote pathetically to Wallas, after a missed meeting with his friend, 'I wanted to talk to you. I did not know I should have felt so bad ... I feel very desolate indeed. Why *did* God put such a thing into life? PS. I don't think I told you yet that she is engaged to Corrie Grant – the woodblock.'[27]

By August Sidney's spirits had sunk even lower. 'Everything, great and small, has gone wrong with me this year, down to my losing 5s at cards the other night – quite unusual for me. It is my Pechjahr [year of bad luck]. My star has gone out, and from being a child of fortune, I am reduced to an ordinary mortal.' He found a diversion in teaching German to Shaw, 'the embryo novelist', using volume two of Marx – 'not the easiest of books' – but the pangs of love were hard to bear. He had been down into Hell, he told Wallas, although, 'I have no *impulse* to suicide, though the thought has never been totally absent from my mind for years ... it is interesting to notice how man is still 9/10 an irrational animal – how little influence intellect has, compared with that exercised by the emotions. It has been a lesson to me.' Rejection had destroyed his faith in God also, and Sidney claimed that he had become distinctly more atheistic, and had fallen back into his old life 'reading and loafing, and playing cards'.[28] An autumn visit to Germany found him susceptible to the 'beaux yeux' of Ela Sonntag, to whom he was soon writing.

Despite his troubles, Sidney found time to suggest a new career for a 'model boy' of Graham Wallas's. In December 1885 he drew up a careful list of possible openings: '(1) The City – cunning,' he wrote, '(2) Manual labour, will not produce more than £100 a year at best. (3) Literature is too uncertain and difficult. (4) The army is not for a poor man. (5) The Church requires some taste for it, or at least a grain of belief.' After thought, he recommended 'the City at once . . . if there is *no* money',[29] an interesting recommendation, from one who had himself rejected the City for the Civil Service. Meanwhile Sidney was busy studying for his law degree, coming 'rather a "mucker" (for me!) in the Honours Exam, as I am only in the third class'.

Always good to his friends, Sidney continued to worry about Wallas and suggested that the schoolmaster should read for the Bar. It only cost £130, and meant dining in hall four times a year which left plenty of time to go to Germany. In a more jocund mood he told Wallas, 'It qualifies you for several things which might come your way in after life, when *we* all get into power!' His spirits rose at the prospect of a trip to America, for which he was given extra leave from the Colonial Office, and September 1888 found him with Edward Pease in New York, where the damp heat reduced him to 'pulp'. He found New York 'exceedingly depressing': their friends were out of town, the buildings were 'ramshackle', with just a few new blocks which im- pressed him, 'all else mean and untidy: pavements *worse* than a small German town, telegraph poles undressed and unpainted pinestems'. But first impressions changed, and Sidney liked Boston better, and Harvard he praised as 'the most ideal academe that I have ever seen'. Most of all he was amazed at the 'typewriter girls' in all the offices.[30]

Sidney's return to England and news of Edward Pease's engagement produced a melancholy mood again. He had begun to fear that there was some fundamental flaw in his personality which made people recoil from him. He wrote to Margery Davidson, Pease's fiancée, a sad and introspective letter. 'I have the greatest desire for your friendship, with the very smallest capacity for acquiring it. (I have often envied the ease with which others "catch on" to congenial spirits. E.R.P. [Pease] is one such lucky or clever person.) where I simply remain outside. I am of course very busy, somewhat serious, very analytic and introspective – but, I hope, passably honest, sincere, and not obviously hateful or repulsive. Yet I seem "left out" in more than one case, and in more than one department of life.'[31]

Anxiously Sidney wondered why love was missing from his life, when it came into the lives of his close friends. 'I am nearly thirty,' he told Margery, 'and during the last five years (just *those* five) I have lost five intimate friends by marriage.' Why did he have so little luck, Sidney asked himself. When he looked in the mirror he had his answer.

* * *

While Sidney suffered the pangs of unrequited love, Beatrice was exorcising her old infatuation for Chamberlain. Unsure as to how she should behave towards the Chamberlain family, she asked Bella Fisher for her advice. 'I say, *do exactly what you would have done* if there had been nothing more than simple friendship,' Bella urged her firmly. 'I should respond when advances are made, but not make them.' She advised Beatrice to ask Mrs Ryland to stay, and to see Beatrice Chamberlain, but to let the acquaintance 'by and by become more casual'. Beatrice should *not* call on the new Mrs Chamberlain 'because as an unmarried woman I fancy it is not required'. 'But I should allow her to call upon me and I should return the call, just as if there was nothing behind. I should meet them at dinner if asked, but I *think* I should not accept an invitation to dine there . . . *Feel superior* to the situation and you will show that you are so.' Bella understood the depth of Beatrice's feelings, telling her: 'You have something to *kill*, kill it deliberately and you will gain strength for work and future happiness. Take the practical matter of fact view that what you dreamt *was* only a dream, or has now *become* such. Face the reality, and remember that every phase one passes through in life is an education. Do not meet him more than you can avoid and force yourself, when meeting him, to recall nothing beyond the fact that he is married.'[32] It was sound advice, and Beatrice took it, asking Beatrice Chamberlain for a visit, but still in her dilemma she wished she had a mother or sister to confide in. She felt she was doing penance for her lack of 'womanly reticence and self-control. God help me, and make it not *too* hard for me,' she pleaded to her diary.[33]

But ignoring the new Mrs Chamberlain was not easy when all London was whispering about her. Beatrice's sister Maggie Hobhouse told her that Mary Chamberlain was perfectly dressed, quiet and dignified, with a retroussé nose, blue eyes, and not much behind them. Kate Courtney also comforted her sister by assuring her that if she were not Mrs Chamberlain the new bride would be 'a pleasant nobody'. 'A little Puritan', 'might have come out of a country rectory', 'the affection is most on her side', were the remarks flying about society. Beatrice felt sick and faint when asked whether she had seen the bride, but managed to reply with placid indifference, 'No, I have not seen her but I hear she is charming.'[34]

Fortunately Beatrice's curiosity about her successor in Chamberlain's affections was diverted by her intense interest in the Dock Strike of 1889, which followed hard on the heels of the Match Girls' Strike, and signalled the birth of 'New Unionism'. In July 1888 Annie Besant had called out fourteen hundred matchgirls, many of them teenagers, all of them unskilled, at Bryant and May's factory. Annie's article, 'White Slavery' in *The Link*,[35] the paper she started with W. T. Stead, had drawn the public's attention to the twelve-hour day the girls worked for only 4s a week, the dangers of 'phossy jaw', the disease caused by the phosphorus fumes into which the matches were dipped, and the fact that the workers had no union to protect them. Her success in challenging Bryant and May emboldened the gas workers and dockers, similarly unskilled, who were excluded from the New Model Unions of the artisans and were considered incapable of organisation. Beatrice's heart lifted when she saw her old docker friend, Ben Tillett, marching with John Burns at the head of thousands of labourers through the streets of London, the men controlled and dignified in a way which won round public opinion. At first just five hundred casuals had marched out of the West and East India Docks; now a general strike was taking place in support of the dockers' demand of 6d an hour.[36]

Beatrice was fascinated by the strike because of her personal experience with the dockers. She was amazed to see them uniting in their demands instead of being apathetic and indifferent, and when in September the men won a great victory, aided by £50,000 of public subscriptions (including £24,000 from Australia), she rejoiced with them although she was doubtful whether the benefits would be permanent. London seemed to be in a ferment, and Beatrice longed to be in the midst of it, taking part in the great movement sweeping the men into the arms of the new trade unionism, animating the Radical clubs, her friends the Co-operators, and led, so it seemed to her, by the Fabians. 'I feel . . . exiled from the world of thought and action of other men,' she wrote in frustration, feeling that she was wasting time caring for her father who still lingered on in an apology for life. The contrast between the stirring, tumultuous scenes she had seen at the Trades Union Congress at Dundee, where Henry Broadhurst, the Liberal MP, fought off his socialist critics, and Cunninghame-Grahame – 'a *poseur* [and] unmitigated fool' – whispered that he had a letter from Prince Kropotkin demanding that John Burns and his eight thousand men make a revolution forthwith, and the quiet of Box House was hard to bear.

In February 1890 Beatrice returned to the Devonshire House Hotel for a fortnight. Her thoughts were ripening and changing, and a kaleidoscope of impressions fought for precedence in her mind: the 'East End crowd of wrecks, and waifs and strays', among whom she had worked and for whom she had come to feel sympathy; her friends among the Co-operators, condemned to the treadmill of manual labour; the luxurious homes of her sisters and brothers-in-law: Daniel Meinertzhagen, the City financier, Willie Cripps, the fashionable surgeon, and Alfred Cripps, the youngest QC at the Bar. Beatrice was distancing herself from her social origins, and the 'picked men of the individualist system'. A new Utopia rose before her eyes, where men would be free and property would be held in common, where the class slavery she saw around her would be abolished. 'At last I am a socialist!' she wrote triumphantly on 1 February 1890.[37] It was a strange and significant decision for a girl of her class and upbringing, but it was, as Beatrice observed, 'where observation and study have led me', the natural conclusion of the 'apprenticeship' which began as a lady visitor for the Charity Organisation Society.

Beatrice did not trumpet her conversion, and after a dinner meeting with Lord Thring, a lawyer, and Lord Monkswell, a Liberal, to discuss the Dunraven report on sweating, she noted cautiously: 'I am suspected of socialism.' She realised she needed to keep the trust of the *laissez-faire* economists if she were to do any good as a reformer, and Beatrice was much concerned to reform the sweated industries of London. Despite her nominal opposition to women's suffrage she wished to make women's work an important subject of research in the future. She kept her own counsel therefore, but to one person she revealed her new convictions: Sidney Webb.

On 14 February Beatrice asked Sidney to dinner to meet Charles and Mary Booth, whom she still saw despite the cooling in their relationship. In her diary she recorded her impressions of him. 'A remarkable little man with a huge head on a very tiny body, a breadth of forehead quite sufficient to account for the encyclopaedic character of his knowledge, a Jewish nose, prominent eyes and mouth, black hair, somewhat unkempt, spectacles and a most bourgeois black coat shiny with wear; regarded as a whole, somewhat between a London card and a German professor. To keep to essentials: his pronunciation is Cockney, his H's are shaky, his attitudes by no means eloquent, with his thumbs fixed pugnaciously in a far from immaculate waistcoat, with his bulky head thrown back and his little body forward he struts even when he stands, delivering himself with extraordinary rapidity of thought and utterance and with an expression of inexhaustible self-complacency.'

Beatrice was still a social snob, instantly conscious of Sidney's dropped H's and the clerk's suit which placed him irrevocably among her social inferiors. She was also aware of the lack of physical appeal and to someone who had felt the stirrings of passion for the charismatic Chamberlain, Sidney's 'very tiny body' was a strong deterrent.

'But I like the man. There is a directness of speech, an open-mindedness, an imaginative warm-heartedness which should carry him far. He has the self-complacency of one who is always thinking faster than his neighbours, who is untroubled by doubts, and to whom the acquisition of facts is as easy as the grasping of matter; but he has no vanity and is totally unselfconscious,' added Beatrice.[38]

She felt a rapport between her mind and Sidney's, and was quick to pay her debt, writing to him in May: 'It was in my first conversation with you last winter that it flashed across my mind that I was, or ought to be, a Socialist – if I was true to the conclusion that I had already reached; and by this sudden self-revelation you saved me months, perhaps years of study.'[39] In her conversion to socialism Beatrice at last found the faith, albeit secular, for which she had yearned so long.

XIV

THE MIRAGE OF LOVE

'Marriage to me is another word for suicide. I cannot bring myself to face an act of felo do se *for a speculation in personal happiness . . . Though I am susceptible to the charm of being loved I am not capable of loving.'*
Beatrice Webb Diary, 1 December 1890

BEATRICE'S CONVERSION TO SOCIALISM became the cornerstone of her spiritual and intellectual life. John Bunyan wrote in his self-lacerating autobiography, *Grace Abounding to the Chief of Sinners*, 'My dear children, the milk and honey is beyond this wilderness. God be merciful to you and grant that you be not slothful to go to possess the land.' From 1890 Beatrice wished only to be a Pilgrim in the service of Socialism, and the rest of her life was to be dedicated to finding the 'milk and honey' of the promised land. Like other Victorian autobiographers of the hermeneutic genre, Carlyle, Ruskin and Harriet Martineau, Beatrice visualised her life in terms of escape from the bondage of youthful beliefs.[1]

For Beatrice Sidney Webb was the key to Socialism and he knew this was his ace card in a poor hand. His looks, his background, his fortune, were all against him, but he did not hesitate to play the ace in his pursuit of his quarry. It was a tortuous courtship in which Beatrice's belief that in Sidney she had found a creed and a 'loving comrade' fought a bitter battle with her physical repugnance for him. Beatrice's Socialism was not a milk-and-water ideology aimed merely at ameliorating the lot of the masses but, as she stoutly told the Booths that February, the economic system of 'communal or state ownership of Capital and Land'. Without the cushion of private property to protect them, the upper classes would be thrown into competition with the rest of society; absence of ability would become obvious and individual effort would be maximised. Thus, argued Beatrice, Socialism was perfectly compatible with Individualism, and she would stand on a barrel and preach it. The Booths were unimpressed.[2]

From April 1890 Sidney was deeply in love with Beatrice. His visit to Box House that month left them with widely differing impressions of each other. To Beatrice Sidney's body was repulsive, as well as ludicrous when coupled with his conceit. 'A London retail tradesman with the aims of a Napoleon! a queer monstrosity to be justified only by success,' she confided to her diary. Yet she was impressed by his sensitivity and quickness. He was, above all, 'a loophole into the socialist party; one of the small body of men with whom I may sooner or later throw in my lot for good and all'.[3]

For Sidney, Beatrice was the woman he had been seeking all his life. He poured out his life's story to her, the youthful struggles to pass exams, the law scholarship at Cambridge he was unable to take up, his dreams for the future, his belief in his 'star'. On his return home to Park Village East, in Camden, he wrote to tell her what a deep impression her 'frank friendliness' had made upon him. 'I really must have a Mentor outside the working circle, a looker-on who seems most of the game,' he begged. In reply Beatrice sent a swift warning which should have prepared him for the rapids that lay ahead. Women's maternal instinct and intellectual dependence on men drew the sexes together in friendship, she informed him, but when such a friendship was 'blurred by the predominance of lower feeling' then it became a source of pure evil.

The superhuman effort Beatrice had made to repress her feelings for Chamberlain had left its mark. 'That terrible time of agonised suffering seems to have turned my whole nature into steel – not the steel that kills, but the surgeon's instrument that would save,' she wrote in May.[4] It was a theme to which she constantly returned: she was steel, an instrument fit not for love but only to serve humanity. The people around her seemed only so many shadows, and Beatrice's vision often seemed more real to her than these phantom figures. Sidney, meanwhile, wanted a flesh-and-blood Beatrice to love.

Beatrice set up a pattern of encouraging Sidney, and then punishing him for his presumption in making plain his feelings. She invited him in to accompany her to the Co-operative Conference in Glasgow – 'Do you not feel inclined to come too?' – and they travelled up together in a third-class coach, Beatrice surrounded by her working-class friends, Sidney squatting uncomfortably on a portmanteau at her feet. That night she and Sidney wandered through the Glasgow streets, and he began to hint at his feelings for her. During the next twenty-four hours Sidney let Beatrice know that he hoped for marriage, and she told him that the chances were a hundred to one against it. On the second night in Glasgow they struggled through the crowds of drunken Scots and, in Beatrice's inimitable prose, 'with glory in the sky and hideous bestiality on the earth, the two socialists came to a working compact'. Not for the first time, Sidney used the persuasive argument that together they could accomplish more than they could apart. Beatrice was almost persuaded, but was alarmed by the physical aspect of his devotion to her. She gave him a solemn caveat: ' "One word more," say I. "Promise not to let your mind dwell on the purely personal side of your feeling. I know how that feeling unfulfilled saps all the vigour out of a man's life. Promise to deliberately turn your mind away from it – to think of me as a married woman, as the wife of a friend." '5 It was an impossible request, and Sidney refused to promise. Instead he agreed, for the sake of his health, to try and suppress his feelings and concentrate on the working tie between them.

There is a further story behind Beatrice's diary entry. Clearly she hurt Sidney cruelly by her rejection of his advances, and in his fevered state he sent her a passionate pencilled note. 'You tortured me horribly last night by your intolerable "superiority",' he wrote. '. . . And you blasphemed horribly against what is highest and holiest in human relations. I could not speak my mind last night, but this agony is unendurable. You will at any rate not be indifferent to my suffering. I do not know how to face another night such as I have passed.'6 Carefully Beatrice pinned this note into her diary, and thought about it. When she was home in London, she unsealed Chamberlain's letters which she sealed up in 1887, and pondered over her deep humiliation at his hands, a humiliation in which he had seemed to glory and prolong. Looking back, she admitted her own faults: opinionated, over-emotional, she must have confused him, led him to dread a refusal. And still she was haunted by him, listened to gossip, combed the newspapers for news of him, learned that he had become the darling of the London drawing rooms. Could she ever vow to forgive and forget? It seemed improbable that Sidney could blot out the memory of that passion with his own, but she sat down to write to him.

She began her letter to Sidney with a lie: she claimed that she had never granted friendship before to a man who desired something more, although there is no indication that Sidney had any inkling of her past relationship with the Radical leader. His references to Chamberlain are wholly innocent and it is ironic that soon Sidney was to be compared to Chamberlain, in attempting to do for London what Chamberlain had already done for Birmingham. Indeed, Sidney often said he had no wish to know Beatrice's past. 'Personal happiness,' Beatrice told Sidney, 'to me is an utterly remote thing.' She claimed she was 'heartless' in that everything to her must be subordinated to serving the community since she had been 'forced through the fire and forged into a simple instrument for work'. He might find the love of a young life; she was bruised and scarred, and therefore he must not regard their friendship as a means to an end. He must not hope for 'complete union'.[7]

Sidney responded with desperation. 'I cannot be any deeper in the stream,' he told her. '. . . I am through and through yours already. Nor can you take from me that week of happiness. *Ich habe genossen das irdische Gluck: ich habe gelebt und geliebt.* [I have known earthly happiness: I have lived and loved] . . .' Beatrice must not be indifferent to personal happiness, he told her. She must feel 'the throb of life'. He too had known the fire, even if it was not as hot as hers. He too had crept about with a broken wing. How could he survive, 'now that I am plunged head and heels in the stream I then only sipped?' There was no going back for him, even if she could not return his 'hurricane of feeling'.

The flowing, regular handwriting covered the pages, as Sidney poured out his feelings: 'Now you are to me the Sun and Source of all my work . . . I now realise what Comte was driving at when he apotheosised woman . . . You are making all things new to me. You are simply doubling my force . . .' Sidney begged for some 'personal intercourse', a more detailed Concordat, although he promised not to pester her with his feeling. 'I shall be very hungry but I can be very patient . . . No God can be so sacred as you will be to me . . . I will not seek to remind you that I am your slave also.' Sadly Sidney admitted, 'No one could be less skilled than I am in "making love". I could not woo you by my manner even did I wish.' So he would be in love without the desire for possession, content just to know that she was there, 'to be touched by your tactful sympathy like the cool fingers of a nurse'. Without this, 'you can torture me horribly . . . When I think how much I am in your hands I am almost ashamed to have fallen so low'.

Sidney sent also a warning of his own – one to which he was frequently to return. 'You said some horrible things on Friday night . . . You almost posed as being willing to sacrifice everything for your intellectual work.' This, he told her firmly, would be a mistake. 'You would be making an idol of yourself. Your altruism would become an egoism. And your work would unconsciously suffer . . . You would have dried up "Warmheartedness" in order to get Truth – and you would not even get Truth.' It was a telling argument, one which Beatrice was ultimately to find convincing. What was the point of excluding personal relationships with the opposite sex in order to fulfil her ambitions, if she were then to discover herself soured and stunted, turned in upon herself, lacking the sympathy to be a successful sociologist? Ramming home his point, Sidney begged her to believe that he was not a conventional man who would expect a conventional marriage. 'I am capable of sacrificing more than you dream of. I could be as great an adjunct to your intellectual life as you are to my moral being . . . *Together we could move the world* . . . I cannot believe you will commit this emotional suicide.'[8]

Sidney received an icy response. Although Beatrice confessed to being deeply touched by his letter, she told him, '*It must be the last word of personal feeling.* I shall try to grow worthy of that reverence you are giving Woman through me,' but she did not desire it in its present form. 'I shall only wish to serve as a stepping-stone to a more perfect service of suffering Humanity,' she added priggishly. She would withdraw her friendship from him unless he could limit it to 'camaraderie'.[9] That afternoon she went to Westminster Abbey and prayed that she might be worthy of Sidney's soul which was in her keeping.

A more profitable tack for Sidney was to make himself indispensable to Beatrice in her writing. Beatrice still lacked confidence in her abilities, and depended on Sidney for advice and criticism. That June she had an article published in *Nineteenth Century* on 'The Lords Committee on the Sweating System'. Sidney, although tactfully praising its 'swing and go', pointed out that it was politically ineffective. Beatrice had wanted to fix a sixty-hour working week for women in workshops and factories in London, but to Sidney this seemed impossible to enforce. Beatrice was grateful for his advice, although she protested that 'drafting clauses is not my *Fach* [department] in life'. She was sure she would be an utter failure as a practical politician.

In June Beatrice went on a summer walking tour in Austria with her friend, Alice Green, the widow of a historian, who had taken pains to make herself agreeable to Beatrice. One day Beatrice warned Sidney of his growing reputation for political manipulation. He was edging himself into different organisations, she wrote, and people were talking about him as someone not perfectly sincere – a false impression, she hastened to add. She was concerned too that he tended to boast of his small successes.[10] Beatrice's thoughts oscillated between Chamberlain and Sidney on that holiday, and she returned to Cologne Cathedral, where she had prayed before that she might pass through the 'fire' of her love for Radical Joe. Now, six years later, she realised that her prayer had been granted. She had come through fire to find a measure of peace on the other side. And she should not live without love, the 'dark and bright side of tenderness ... And thus I thought of the worship a man is giving me – not me – but Woman through me – and I prayed again that I might make my life a temple of purity wherein to receive. And I, so vain, so impure – God help me.'[11]

Sidney responded gratefully to her advice, promising to be less egotistical in future: 'Do you not realise that your real *Fach* in life is to run me?' he asked her. Sidney was not so much of a 'new man' as to be without lingering feelings of male superiority and female dependency: 'I, as a man, can execute so much of what you can only conceive.' She must cut herself free from her sisters and trust to her instincts. 'Shall we continue to count each for one, or is there no way of making our forces count for eleven? You have it in your hands to make me, in the noblest sense, great ... Let us, at any rate, walk reverently in the Garden of these Gods, the awful possibilities opening before us ... Between us two let there be at any rate perfect soul union.'

Sidney's references to 'soul union' rang alarm bells in Beatrice's mind, and she hurried to reprimand him, reminding him that they were simply friends. 'Beware how you tread!' This did not prevent her asking him to join her for dinner, so long as they were both agreed to discourage the degrading love of personal power in advancing their cause. Beatrice was no doubt thinking of Chamberlain when she said that political life was horribly dangerous, tarnishing the nature of politicians with its glare and glamour. Chamberlain's great ambition had led Beatrice to see him as unprincipled, and it was important to her that Sidney should appear disinterested and only concerned to advance the truth.

As Beatrice returned to London from Cologne and high summer approached, Sidney's passion became all consuming, despite his vow to Beatrice after his thirty-first birthday on 13 July, that, 'I will put the woman in and beyond the work ... I could not love thee, dear, so well, loved I not honour more.' He had been reading Goethe's autobiography and thinking about George Eliot's Maggie Tulliver; he decided its message was that 'we have no *right* to live our own lives'. Beatrice took these remarks at face value, and recorded in her diary: 'I think I realise that the worship is not of me, but of the Ideal for which I serve as the chosen Temple.'[12] Ruskin's image of woman as a vestal temple in 'Sesame and Lilies' was a pervasive one, deep rooted in the Victorian psyche. Both Beatrice and Sidney, for all their protestations of radical thought, retained an image of woman as spiritually and morally superior to man. As Beatrice put it, 'it is the spiritual function of a woman to be the passive agent bearing a man's life'.[13]

But spirituality was far from Sidney's mind, and his control was slipping when they spent a Saturday together in Epping Forest. As they lay together under the trees economics were for once forgotten, and he read poetry to her aloud, Keats and Rossetti. Beatrice was unaware of Sidney's strong emotions until they parted, when he burst out with a confession of his feelings. Primly she reminded him of their compact, that she must never oust work from his mind. Once home, Sidney sent another letter in which he poured out his frustrated love: 'You were so *ravissante* and angel good, that I had all I could do not to say goodbye in a way which would have broken our Concordat. I had to rush away from you speechless to hold my own. Do not punish me either for the impulse or for my self-control. I have no lover's arts . . . Frankly I do not see how I can go on without you. Do not now desert me . . . Do not despise me because I am at your feet.'

Sidney was doubly unhappy because he had discovered the extent of Beatrice's fortune and that one day she would be rich. It was a new barrier between them – 'one more step in that noble self-sacrifice which you must make to pick me up'.[14] The theme of his letter and her response was that of sacrifice – the sacrifice to be made by Beatrice should she marry Sidney, poor, lower class, and not favoured by nature. And in reply to Sidney's declaration of love, Beatrice made it horribly clear that it was a sacrifice against which her whole nature revolted. The tone, as much as the actual words, reveal Beatrice's physical revulsion from the man who offered her total devotion. 'Another time, write such a letter if you like, but do not post it,' she told him. Was it honourable of him to use their friendship as the excuse for the 'constant and continuous pressing forward of wishes of your own which you know are distasteful to me – and which simply worry and distress and rob me of all the help and strength your friendship might give me?' The word before 'distasteful' she scratched out, nearly scoring through the paper. 'You speak of the "self-sacrifice" . . . but, whether it be a sacrifice or not, I have refused to make it . . . Is this not a stupid selfish device to complete your own life without any thought of the risk to mine?' Sidney's 'abominable letter' was the result of his need to relieve his own feelings and have his own way, not the desire to add to her happiness. It was, in fact, 'gross impertinence'. What did love mean to a man's mind, she asked. To a woman, 'Love . . . has in it some element of self-control and self-sacrifice . . . Don't provoke me again. You talk of "obeying" but what extraordinary obedience – almost as marvellous as to Love! There – now – I have done.'[15]

It is hard to understand the extent of Beatrice's sternness to Sidney. Although the terms of their 'Concordat' might seem reasonable to her, just as it was impossible for Sidney, she showed a lack of sensitivity in her demands of him. Sidney replied with sad dignity: 'I desired to "take" nothing, and I knew that nothing was given to me. If you only realised how much I have repressed you might not perhaps judge me so harshly. I will not offend again. You shall not need to write to me another such letter: a terrible letter.'[16]

In the same letter in which she harshly rebuked his fervour, Beatrice asked Sidney for his help in explaining the economics of Alfred Marshall. Sidney's reading speed was impressive: when Massingham asked him to review Marshall's *Principles of Economics* in a hurry, he sat down and read the six-hundred-page book overnight. Beatrice, by contrast, spent ten days carefully reading Marshall and was still perplexed by it. Could Sidney explain the diagrams, which she found horribly hard to follow, and parts of the text? With her somewhat shaky hold on mathematics, she asked if it would be all right to ignore the curves in the diagram and treat them as straight lines.

Sidney sent a patient reply, drawing neat diagrams to explain Marshall's theory of 'Consumer's Rent' and showing her how to calculate the rent in England at that time. She was also relieved to receive an earlier letter he had sent from Oberammergau, where he was holidaying with Shaw, in which he revoked some of that earlier, frightening emotion: 'Even if you dismissed me abruptly, I should not die,' he had written calmly. 'I intend firmly that I should not spoil my life over it. You would knock me to pieces for a time, physically and mentally, and perhaps morally, and I should suffer horribly. The light of life would be extinguished from me . . . The springs of hope would be dead. But you may decide quite freely at your leisure . . .'[17] Already Beatrice was repenting of her frightened defence of her virginity. Written words were desperate instruments, she told Sidney, promising not to 'cut so deep' next time, but to act by his suggestion that if he went too far she would remind him that *noblesse oblige*; it would be their watchword against future transgressions.[18]

Awkwardly Sidney tried to explain the strength of his physical desire to Beatrice, in order that she might understand and sympathise with his predicament. 'I wonder whether a woman ever adequately realises the dreadfully "tearing" nature of a man's real love . . . I suppose I have a strong nature . . . *C'est plus fort que moi* . . . This is not merely a close friendship between a woman and a man, but one between a woman and a man very deeply in love with her.'[19] But Beatrice did understand lust: she had experienced it herself, and taken the decision to bury her own sexual needs. It was the sad fact, still unknown to Sidney, that she could only accept his love by spiritualising and apotheosising it in terms which far diverged from the reality of Sidney's feelings.

Soon they were back on the old terms again. Beatrice developed a proprietary interest in Sidney's social development. If she were his sister, she told him, she would give him three small pieces of advice:

> However old your coat may be (and that is of no importance) *brush* it.
> Take care of your voice and pronunciation: it is the chief instrument of influence.
> Don't talk of 'when I am Prime Minister', it jars on sensitive ears.[20]

Clearly Beatrice's was the sensitive ear upon which Sidney's cockney accent and lack of humility continually jarred. 'Look after the breadth of the English vowel!' she told him briskly in a later letter. 'Do not refuse to recognise the individual existence of or, ir, ow, a, and confound them all in a common er.'[21] Sidney remained grateful for her advice, and strove to do better.

That summer both Beatrice and Sidney witnessed the Passion Play at Oberammergau, which produced differing reactions in them both. When Beatrice saw it in June it appeared to her as a 'vivid representation of the revolt of the workers and the women, led by a great socialist, from the tyranny and false conventions of the moneyed and official class'.[22] Sidney was surprised at her reaction. To him the Passion Play was not so much a Peasants' Revolt as an exaltation of womanhood. The Virgin Mary brought tears to his eyes, and he felt guilty that he had only sent his mother a quick note for her birthday. He told Beatrice, 'I do not greatly worship the Jesus type . . . he ought to have "taken it fighting" . . . the least bit of energetic defence would have enabled Pilate to save him',[23] but the figure of Mary brought home to Sidney the moral inferiority of man to woman and the martyrdom of motherhood. Sidney's comments on woman's nature reveal the interaction between his stereotyped notions of women as spiritual, morally superior, suffering and passive, and the new ideas of the early 1890s which filled the novels and periodicals of the time.

. He had been reading Grant Allen, whose novel *The Woman Who Did* was to cause a sensation in 1895, with its advocacy of free love.[24] Sidney was sympathetic to the aspirations of 'advanced' women for self-fulfilment and emancipation from old shibboleths; one lesson he learnt from the Passion Play was that women should be less docile towards men.

In July Sidney spent a weekend with his friends, the American Pearsall Smiths, who lived at Friday Hill, near Haslemere, and played host to many intellectuals; Alys Pearsall Smith, one of the Pearsall Smiths' three children, later the first wife of Bertrand Russell, was to write a spirited defence of the desires of daughters not to be 'dwarfed and thwarted' in 1894.[25] Beatrice spent August 1890 with her friends the Mandell Creightons at Worcester College. Louise Mandell Creighton had written the Anti-Suffrage Appeal with Mrs Humphrey Ward, which Beatrice had signed in 1889. In their home, said Beatrice, new thoughts lived among old traditions, but Louise Creighton was unlikely to be an influence of which Sidney approved. 'I think you will one day feel the need of more obviously and actively "repenting" about Women's Suffrage,' he told her,[26] questioning whether she was acting honestly. Why did she not join a Liberal Association? Was she giving her full 'rent of ability' to the world? He could not help feeling a little suspicious of the luxury in which Beatrice lived, her enthusiasm for her rides on her cob Dorcas over the soft turf round Minchinhampton, her walks with Don, her dog, which were so far removed from his own London boyhood. Sidney was confused too by the contrast between Beatrice's emancipated ways, as she went unchaperoned among her working men friends in the Co-operators, and her demands for old-fashioned respect and sexual deference. Sometimes he wondered whether she was indeed a Socialist, or just an upper-middle-class woman playing with advanced views.

In fact Sidney was doing Beatrice a great deal of good. She felt stronger than she had done for years, and on 26 August began work on her book on Co-operation. Beatrice had asked Sidney to find her a publisher, pleading that she was no good at bargaining and needed his help. Sidney had come up with Sonnenscheins, and happily Beatrice calculated that she would make between £60 and £100 out of the book. In addition Mrs Humphrey Ward invited her to lecture on Co-operation at University Hall, in Bloomsbury, to working men. 'Five lectures at £18,' wrote Beatrice proudly, 'so you see I am beginning to earn an honest penny.' Sir James Knowles, the editor of *Nineteenth Century*, had given her £42 for her article. Sidney, although equally busy with a commission to write a book on the Eight Hours Movement, was feeling unhappy and full of self-doubt. He had embarrassed Beatrice by speaking in a 'rattling clever' way at a meeting of the British Association which they attended together in Leeds, irritating and bewildering his audience, and in September he had to leave her to begin a whirlwind tour of Lancashire. A wealthy Fabian named Henry Hutchinson had donated £100 to subsidise a lecture tour, the second edition of Fabian essays was re-printing, and a reluctant Sidney travelled north with Wallas and Bernard Shaw to spread the Fabian word.

While he was away Sidney bought Beatrice her first present: a book of Rossetti's poems. Not daring to give away their relationship, about which Beatrice had sworn him to secrecy, he did not put any special inscription in it. At Beatrice's suggestion he kept a diary in red 'commonplace' books, which he posted to her as he filled them up. 'Do you know, I think I am too much in love to be a lover,' he wrote. 'You see I *must* talk to you about this, because I may not confide in anyone else.' It was hard for Sidney. Wallas suspected nothing – 'Poor Wallas, he is not very "sharp" in his insight, – though the most "loveable" of men,' Sidney explained. Breaking into German, as he often did to express his emotions, he wrote her a poem:

> *Was willst du heute sorgen*
> > *Auf morgen;*
> > *Der Eine*
> > *Steht allein fur,*
> > *Der gibt auch dir*
> > *Das Deine.*
> *Sei nur in allem Handel*
> > *Ohn' Wandel.*
> > *Steh feste.*

[Don't worry about today, or tomorrow; one stands alone, but there is another one for you. Don't change your mind. Remain steadfast.][27]

It was a punishing tour, as he hurried to Rochdale, late for his lecture after a five-and-a-half-hour journey and no supper, dashed off an article for the *Speaker* in two hours, then travelled to Oldham to speak on the Eight Hours Movement. In Manchester he felt ill-tempered and irritable; the irregular life and constant meeting of new people told on his nerves, but that evening his spirits lifted when Shaw rounded off the evening for him with a rousing ten-minute speech which won many converts.

Meanwhile Beatrice was holding court among the Fabians at Box. Sidney was jealous that Graham Wallas, who had become a firm 'comrade' of Beatrice's, had been allowed to stay the night, and begged for the same privilege. He had always to visit with a chaperone in order not to arouse suspicion, and this time Alice Green was invited with him. Mrs Green found him 'a dear little man, one could get quite fond of him', and Beatrice recognised that he was 'certainly extraordinarily improved and becoming a needful background to my working life and I the same to him'.[28] Encouraged, Sidney began to plan a Fabian party, ostensibly to say farewell to Sydney Olivier who was about to leave for a new post in British Honduras, but in reality to introduce Beatrice to his friends. She told him not to have the party on her account, yet invited Pease and Shaw to Box House. Shaw was not impressed, protesting that he could not afford the 17s fare: 'You, with the insouciance of a millionaire, calmly order me down to tell you about Lancashire. Never – by Heaven – will I suffer any created woman to lead me about in this fashion. No: You may reduce the rest of the Fabians to slavery – they prattle from morning to night about Beatrice Potter in a way I despise – but if I am to go through my amusing conversational performances for you, you must come up to town: this lion is untameable . . . To think I should have lived to be sampled – to be sent down on approval or return – to be inspected by daylight by a fastidious young lady in search of an eligible socialist society to join! . . . Turn no more Fabian heads with your wiles.'[29]

For whatever reason, Beatrice came up to town. She was testing the water as she knew the relationship between her and the Booths had faded, but they were long-standing friends, and she was anxious to have their opinion of Sidney. But he failed to ingratiate himself with them over dinner. Mary wrote damningly to Beatrice that she did not care for opinions: 'I do not care a fig if they can be shown to be held honestly, and are not such as in themselves to brand a man a fool . . .' and she left little doubt in Beatrice's mind that she considered him such.[30] Charles was both vehement and perceptive in his condemnation of this unsuitable mate for his brilliant helper: 'I find I don't like him at all; and neither Mary nor I can bear to think of you as his wife or of him as your husband . . . If you cared for him, it might be different – would be very different – but, if you do not, I believe you would make a great mistake if you were to marry him. *Don't do it* I say. Life has not by any means reached its last chapter for you; turn another page and read on!'

Bella Fisher was equally hostile. In June she wrote, 'you will

certainly marry him now if you are beginning to *care for him*, and
you feel self-reliant enough to stand on your own judgement and to
grow together as mutual sympathy developes [*sic*] . . . If your affections
are not engaged and you wish to stop, you must stop soon as you say
– Your relationship as it is *must* give him hopes.' By October Bella
was increasingly concerned; were they to marry 'you would be the
leader at any rate for some time to come – now I rather dread this for
you, for yours is an enthusiastic impressionistic nature and wants
steadying and supporting, rather than stimulating and exciting . . . I
am afraid of your becoming entangled in a web of socialism'. Bella
also warned Beatrice of the social consequences of marrying someone
so beneath her in social class, uncultured and without a 'statesmanlike
mind'.[31] Beatrice was left in no doubt that her old friends saw her
simply grasping at an exit from the despised state of spinsterhood.

Sidney, however, felt encouraged by Beatrice's apparent intimacy
at Box. When they met in London he misread the signals she gave
him; as he put it, 'You had explicitly warned me that your kindness
was only kindness, but you were *so* kind . . .' Emboldened, he made
physical advances to her from which Beatrice recoiled with horror.
The incident seemed to finally shatter his hopes of marriage. Instantly
he wrote begging her forgiveness for that 'comedy changed to tears'
and he promised not to reveal the secrets she had begun to confide to
him: 'I know nothing of your story except your ring and what you
have told me, dearest – it makes no difference to me except for its evil
shadow on your memory.' Stoically he accepted her revulsion from
him as he knew his outward appearance repelled the women he desired.
'I cannot now write about the future – drink the mirage – just at this
moment. I must simply endure my thirst: Dearest, I cannot pretend
not to want you – but I am strong enough to kill that want.'

Beatrice replied with a long and honest letter, saying she had cried
when she received his, but she must tell the truth. 'When you spoke
to me in Glasgow I did not say, as I have said to others, a distinct
"no", because I felt that your character and circumstances offered me
a sphere of usefulness and fellowship which I had no right to refuse
offhand. I felt too how hard it would be for me to lead a lonely life
without becoming hard and nervous and self-willed. On the other
hand, you were personally unattractive to me and I doubted whether
I *could* bring myself to submit to a close relationship. Remember that
I was desperately in love and for six years with another man – and
even now the wound is open . . . I saw that man last summer by
accident and I felt a horrible certainty that I could care for no one else

. . . When I read your letter this morning, though I thought previously our friendship would end in marriage, I had another revulsion of feeling . . . If I were in love it would be different, but I am not in love . . . I cannot and *will* not be engaged to you – never until it is a question of marriage within a few weeks . . . Dear Sidney – I will try to love you – but do not be impatient – I am doing more than I would do for any other man – simply because you are a Socialist and I am a Socialist. That other man I loved but did not believe in, you I believe in but do not love.'[32]

Sidney acknowledged his physical imperfections. 'I know perfectly well how little likely I am to be personally attractive to anyone: and I know also how all one's bad habits and tricks of manner are apt to be positively repellent . . .' Yet still he urged their union, for the service of humanity, although Beatrice's good connections and wealth worried him. Poor and proud, he could anticipate what the world would say if they married.[33] Over the next few weeks he continued to urge Beatrice not to isolate herself from 'the fire of life'. 'You sometimes speak as if you could never be warmed: let me try, and you shall see!' Ardently he assured her, 'Dearest, I have love enough for two – you cannot *help* reflecting back love for me because my heart is so strong. Turn but your face towards me, and love must come – do but give up looking backward.'[34]

Beatrice's connection with Sidney and the Fabians had been of greater psychological benefit than she knew. It had exorcised the phantom of Chamberlain and the anniversary of Chamberlain's marriage in November did not find her melancholy and lacking in vigour, but full of exhilarating confidence. 'Now I am no longer on the bank watching with cold but intense curiosity the surface currents. I am swimming in mid-water with another by my side, and a host to the fore and the rear of me – with the roar of a great ocean of coming humanity.'[35]

But for Sidney a crisis was approaching. In November he became seriously ill with scarlet fever and was forced to stay in bed where, feverish and miserable, he lay thinking of Beatrice and bombarding her with jealous, despairing letters. His illness was prolonged, and isolation in the lonely house affected his spirits. On the last day of the month he wrote to Beatrice, 'You have been good to write to me, but you are always "hard" on me, and you have contrived to make your letters bitter as well as sweet.' His head burned and he was half mad with rage at the doctor and nurse who told him he could not leave his sickroom to keep a tryst with Beatrice for next Friday, because his 'peeling' was taking longer than expected. In a fit of despair he made a bonfire of some of Beatrice's letters in the bedroom fireplace, but the conflagration did little to ease his feelings. Meanwhile, Beatrice teased him for being such a querulous and fretful patient, unable to bear his enforced solitude.

Sidney withered under Beatrice's scorn, feeling he was a whipping boy for the whole male sex. 'Do not attack me as a representative of Man. You have an under-current of anti-male feeling which I simply don't understand.' Bitterly he told her that women said men were brutal, but they should be more frank and less prudish. He brooded over the women's movement, an increasingly topical subject in the press with the furore over the Clitheroe Case, by which a woman finally won the right not to be imprisoned under her husband's roof for the enforcement of his conjugal rights. 'I think the "subjection of women" is bringing as its Nemesis a growing anti-male tension which seems to me . . . bad in its results. It would be an evil thing if women, in any sense, formed a huge trades union . . . against men. I don't want the next great war to be . . . between men and women.'

Beatrice, newly confident, was being cruel to him, or so it seemed to the despondent Sidney. She returned one of his letters, telling him he was a poseur. 'I have a new skin, but not a new heart, and I find no hesitation or doubt as to my Aim in life or my love for you,' he told her with steadfast devotion.[36] But he tossed restlessly on his pillow at night at the news that Beatrice was entertaining R. B. Haldane, the Scottish QC and Liberal MP, a close friend of H. H. Asquith, Sir Edward Grey, and other progressive liberals in the House of Commons. Haldane was putting out feelers in the direction of the Fabians; he was, in Beatrice's words, 'a successful lawyer, tinged with socialism' who had come down to Box to arrange an alliance between his clique and the Fabians. Haldane's fiancée had recently broken off their five-week engagement, which had been a factor in persuading Beatrice that formal engagements were abhorrent to her, and he was back in the marriage market. Sidney had met Haldane at dinner in July at Toynbee Hall, and felt uncomfortably jealous at the rendezvous at Minchinhampton between Beatrice and the eligible barrister.

He need not have worried. Haldane laughed uncomfortably when Beatrice told him she considered matrimony an alternative to suicide. And in her diary she stated her position unequivocally: '*That is exactly it*: marriage is to me another word for suicide. I cannot bring myself to face an act of *felo de se* for a speculation in personal happiness . . . though I am susceptible to the charm of being loved I am not capable of loving. Personal passion has burnt itself out . . .' She was ashamed of having watched outside South Kensington Museum for two days that summer in the hope of catching a glimpse of Chamberlain; only pride prevented her going back a third time. That December Beatrice's overpowering feeling was that her passion for Chamberlain should not be wasted, mingled with self-contempt for 'those moments of womanly weakness when I would throw myself into the arms of any true lover to gain the protecting warmth of a man's love'.

But although Beatrice felt herself incapable of loving, and strong enough to do without a man's love, she could not help a twinge of satisfaction at the attraction she seemed to have for the men who flocked to visit her. 'I am surrounded by men, am constantly meeting others to whom I am more or less attractive,' she wrote, believing she had the gift of intimacy, combined with sex appeal, even in 'middle age' (Beatrice was thirty-two). 'Some women mistake the power of beauty for the result of capacity,' Haldane told her pointedly. So why should she consider Sidney Webb, small, ugly and as devoted as her spaniel?[37]

There seemed no reason. She felt the chain unbearably fretting her. Sidney's assumption that he would be her lover had led to that disgust which revealed her true feelings. The reaction of the Booths and Bella Fisher had made it plain that she could not marry him while her father was still alive, and she could not stand the strain of a secret engagement. It only remained to tell him so. But Sidney saved her the trouble; he had independently come to the same decision. As he sat at home, waiting for his 'peeling' to finish, he wrote that 'with infinite bitterness' he had come to the conclusion that he must abandon his plans to carve out a career in public service. 'I expect to remain all my days a clerk in the Colonial Office.' The next point followed inexorably: 'I see that I must forgo the hope of your one day consenting to marry me.' His self-confidence had never been lower, and he felt that her book on Co-operation was better than anything he was likely to do. Therefore, in all decency, he could not ask her to fly in the face of her family connections and marry him. 'Of course, as you once said, it would be easy if you loved me. But you have let me see only too clearly that you don't.'[38] Sidney's training led him to express his thoughts diagrammatically, and in a final avowal of love he drew a diagram to demonstrate how he and Beatrice together could do so much more than they could apart.

Beatrice delivered the final blow. She told him that it would suit her far better to marry a clerk in the Colonial Office than a leading politician, to whom she would have to sacrifice her own career – something she had already refused to do for Chamberlain. Sidney's socialism and 'moral refinement' had made her try to love him. 'But I do not love you. All the misery of this relationship arises from this . . . there is no change in my feeling except a growing certainty that I cannot love you. To be perfectly frank I did at one time *fancy* I was beginning to care for you – but I was awakened to the truth by your claiming me as your future wife – then I felt – that what I cared for was not *you* but simply the fact of being loved . . . Frankly, I do not believe my nature is capable of love. I came out of that six years' agony . . . like a bit of steel. I was not broken but hardened – the fire must do one or the other. And this being the case – the fact that I do not love you – I cannot, and will never, make the stupendous sacrifice of marriage.'[39]

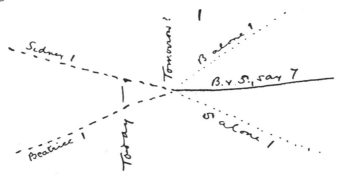

Sidney replied, 'I accept your decision. You will not find that I have ceased to love you, but I will cease to regard you as a marriageable person.'[40] He begged Beatrice to remain friends. Reluctantly she accepted, but on her terms, which were that their future letters must be worded so that they might be read by anybody, that all their previous letters must be returned in a sealed packet, and lastly that Sidney would break off their friendship if it again aroused hopes of marriage in him.

As the year drew to its close, Beatrice took to her bed, ill and out of sorts. Sidney sealed up those of her letters he had not burnt, and sent them to her, assuring her that he did not reproach her, that he knew she felt 'every turn of the screw of my torture'. On the last day of the year Beatrice reflected on her reasons for snapping the tie of intimacy. 'I am alone again,' she wrote. She was an independent woman of thirty-two facing the world, while Chamberlain with his 'smart little wife', as Beatrice contemptuously called her, was sinking into luxury and would soon become a Tory. Meanwhile at his Regent's Park home Sidney made up a new motto: 'Be Patient'. It was based on Beatrice's initials.

XV

THE LONELINESS OF LIFE

'The world will wonder. On the face of it, it seems an
extraordinary end to the once brilliant Beatrice Potter . . . to
marry an ugly little man with no social position and less means,
whose only recommendation, so some may say, is a certain
pushing ability. And I am not "in love", not as I was.'
Beatrice Webb Diary, 20 June 1891

BEATRICE HAD OBEYED HER instincts in rejecting Sidney. She retired quietly to Minchinhampton to work on her book, leaving Sidney weak and humiliated. He had hated The Osborne, the boarding house at Bournemouth where he went to recuperate, where the presence of so many 'consistently idle'[1] people got on his nerves, despite the supportive presence of Graham Wallas. On 3 January 1891 Beatrice allowed Sidney to have dinner with her and Graham in London, where she had come to collect material for her fifth chapter. Sidney was miserable, jealous and excitable, Graham was perplexed by the awkward atmosphere. The two Fabians pressed her to join the Fabian Society, but Beatrice continued to sit on the fence, sending a cheque but not joining formally. Sidney was angry, but told her not to commit herself until she was ready, writing sarcastically, 'I daresay we can manage to keep the Fabian Society alive and undivided until then.'[2]

Beatrice was anxious that no whisper of their relationship should leak out, and railed at Sidney for allowing her most intimate friend, Alice Green, to suspect that he was in love with Beatrice. 'You have . . . laid me open to the reflections of being rather a vulgar coquette,' she told him,[3] and threatened again to withdraw her friendship from him. He defended himself, pleading that Mrs Green had guessed the situation after he broke down in Beatrice's presence one Sunday night after his illness. 'I had no easy task to meet the world,' he told Beatrice pitifully; 'there are limits to anyone's endurance without sign.'

Beatrice accepted his apology. Talk of breaking their friendship was dropped, and gradually the tables began to turn. Between January and Whitsun Beatrice changed her mind about marrying Sidney. At the Co-operative Congress at Lincoln they rediscovered their old 'camaraderie', as Beatrice liked to call it, and the decisive moment came when Beatrice did not withdraw her hand from Sidney's. At the Devonshire House Hotel Beatrice allowed Sidney to kiss her for the first time, and they became secretly engaged.

Several things accounted for this change of heart. Firstly, Sidney created a potent myth for Beatrice of his own indispensability, undermining her confidence in herself as an author, as she struggled in isolation at Box House to structure her first book, her 'slight sketch' as she modestly called it, of the Co-operative Movement.[4] Sidney offered his help with proof-reading in return for the help she had given him with Buxton's Sweating Bill, and Beatrice sent him her first chapter which traced the origin of Robert Owen's socialist ideas. In *The Co-operative Movement* Beatrice wrote as an evolutionary socialist, one among 'those of us who believe in the millennium of a fully developed industrial democracy'.[5] She saw the Co-operative Movement as a state within a state, the kernel of that industrial democracy which might come about, not through violent class struggle, but through progressive taxation and the compulsory acquisition of land from private landlords.

But Beatrice found it difficult to express her ideas at length. Writing a book rather than articles for *Nineteenth Century* was a burden which oppressed her, she told Sidney in February. His criticism of her early chapters undermined her shaky confidence. There was too much matter, and too little concentration of idea, he told her; in addition she changed metaphors too quickly. Beatrice asked him what he meant. He did not mean to imply that her first chapter was *bad*, he explained, damning with faint praise, but 'it would not be honest if I did not own to a disappointment . . . I think, perhaps, that I expected too much from your literary art . . . Shall I be quite candid? Do not take it amiss if I confess to a slight feeling that you have taken too long over it. The book will not be a *very* great work; and you could have written it more quickly . . .'[6] Beatrice sent him no more proofs.

By the end of March, when, after seven months' writing, the book was nearly finished, she decided she had not taken long enough over it, whatever Sidney thought. But he continued to cast doubts as to her ability and stamina. Beatrice was planning to write her next book on Trade Unionism, possibly with Hubert Llewellyn Smith as joint editor, with whom she had worked on the Booth inquiry. Three years was a long time to take over a book, said Sidney grudgingly, and she would have to justify it by the result.

'Your role is to think and inspire: you do not write quickly or easily,' he told her.[7] Perhaps Llewellyn Smith could write up her ideas and leave her just to revise the MS, he suggested, sketching out the role he saw for himself. Beatrice felt like the tortoise to Sidney's hare, as he bombarded her with information on the mass of work he was undertaking. He was 'just now' completing a book called *The London Programme*, he told her casually, setting out his ideas for municipal socialism in the capital and carefully creating a reputation which would help win him a seat in the autumn London County Council elections. His book on the Eight Hours Movement, longer than Beatrice's, was about to appear. In addition he was preparing a reply to Leonard Courtney's attack on Socialism in the *Economic Journal* and undertaking other pot-boiling journalism. When Beatrice remonstrated with him he protested that there were few labourers in the vineyard apart from himself and, in his unhappiness, he felt like using himself right up.[8]

Although Sidney caused Beatrice to doubt her competence, to worry over her productivity and to feel that writing was 'wearisome', her literary ability was greater than his, and her articles had more sparkle than Sidney's factual and thorough but pedestrian output. Touches of humour enlivened her driest work: the world had been waiting two years for the report from the Lords' Committee on Sweating, she wrote, 'Always supposing that such a living thing as a Report should break the shell of chalky indifference and all-round obstruction of a compact body of Whig peers.'[9] There is no reason to doubt that if Beatrice had continued writing on her own, she would not have been able to complete the tasks she set herself. Sidney was not indispensable to Beatrice's work as a social investigator, at which she was something of an expert and he the disciple, when they began writing on Trade Unionism,[10] but he did manage to convince her that she could not easily manage without him.

'You are not fit to write this big book alone,' Sidney told Beatrice in September, as she struggled over the early research for the *History of Trade Unionism*. 'You will never get through it. When I really get to work on it, you will find me ... *the* indispensable help which will turn a good project into a big book.'[11] This conviction of his superior mental and physical powers found an answering chord in Beatrice's own Spencerian belief in female inferiority. Spencer had argued forcibly that sexual difference was a product of women's arrested development at a lower level on the evolutionary scale; women's mental development was inferior to that of men because their energies were channelled into their reproductive systems.[12]

Like other anti-suffragists, Beatrice also believed in women's separate sphere. Upper- and upper-middle-class anti-suffragists clung to the idea that the proper way to bring about political change was indirectly, through manipulating men, as the great political hostesses did, rather than through the vote. As Millicent Fawcett pointed out, one hundred and twenty-eight of those who signed the Anti-Suffrage Appeal of 1889 were titled, and the list included 'a very large preponderance of ladies to whom the lines of life have fallen in pleasant places'.[13] Beatrice, as one of the prominent signatories, was no doubt included in this category. The appeal to which she put her name stated that women's suffrage 'is made impossible either by disabilities of sex, or by strong formation of custom and habit resting ultimately upon physical difference, against which it is useless to contend'.[14] Despite the success which was the fruit of her own ambition, that ambition which had already led her to deviate from the domestic life enjoyed by all her sisters, she was unable to shake off the nagging belief that, in the words of Carlyle, 'The destiny of a woman . . . is to wed a man she can love and esteem, and to lead noiselessly, under his protection, with all the wisdom, grace and heroism that is in her, the life presented in consequence.'[15]

The belief that Sidney was indispensable, because as a man he was mentally superior to her, and that marriage was a woman's destiny, slowly merged into a much greater need: the need for affection and companionship. If Beatrice could not return the love that Sidney offered her – and she could not – she could appreciate that marriage to him would mean the end of loneliness. And loneliness oppressed her, despite Sidney's belief that she had more friends than he had. In December 1890 Beatrice confessed to Sidney that she suffered 'from a new sense of the terrific "loneliness" of life. You say I have friends – but friends are good for bright days – the nearest friends cannot help you in dark times'.[16]

The 'New Woman' journalism and fiction of the early 1890s, until the trial of Oscar Wilde in 1895 brought a changed tone, signalled the early euphoria of the first generation of women to go out to work in any numbers. 'The shrieking sisterhood' of suffragists, as Mrs Lynn Linton called them, and other 'advanced' women trumpeted their revolt against outdated conventions. Yet behind the bravado of the 'new woman' lay the reality of poverty and loneliness for many London working girls in the 1890s. W. T. Stead, who pleaded for Co-operative Homes for the Unmarried in London, remarked in the *Woman's Herald*, a temperance and feminist women's penny paper,

'There are few more pathetic figures in civilisation than the spectacle of the lone woman worker in a great city, earning her daily bread in the midst of a peopled solitude, and then returning at night, as a wild beast to its solitary lair, unnoticed and unloved.'[17] The flood of correspondence which followed Stead's article showed that his words had touched a raw nerve among single working women (and men) among the four million inhabitants of the capital. Stead considered that Residential Women's Clubs, nicknamed 'Spinsterages', were as unhealthy as convents and as unnatural as barracks, and that the sexes should live together in a mixed household. This wholly modern suggestion found favour with readers, who complained that it was impossible to meet a member of the opposite sex in London. Men advertised in the *People* weekly paper for wives, or paid £5 to a matrimonial agency for an introduction, often unsatisfactory. One sad young lady wrote, 'I am 21, domesticated, affectionate disposition, fond of home, and am told I should make a good wife; but as I am keeping home for my father, and have no sisters or brothers, I have no opportunities for meeting anyone.'[18]

Clara Collet, labour correspondent for the Board of Trade and a former fellow-worker of Beatrice's for Charles Booth, summed the situation up by saying that up to the age of thirty women clerks kept cheerful by looking forward to the time when they would get married; until thirty-five, it was 'if I get married', after which their lives were marked by 'dullness and deterioration'.[19] Beatrice herself was thirty-three on 22 January. Loneliness was the lot of many of the women who had left home to become teachers, shop assistants, journalists, or even factory inspectors, and even if Beatrice did not share the problem of poverty which bedevilled the lives of these 'advanced women' whose middle-class occupations were usually poorly paid, she well understood the difficulties of deviating from the well-trodden domestic path, and the strong pull of convention. 'It's jolly hard though! I often think I'd rather be a kitten and cry mew than be a woman trying to earn her living,' was the wry comment of Eleanor Marx.[20]

Sometimes Beatrice felt independent, mistress of herself. 'Men may come and men may go, but I go on for ever,' she wrote that January.[21] But more often she felt like crying mew, especially as her first public lecture loomed nearer. It was not just a fiasco, it was a failure, she confessed to her diary. The need for Sidney became even more apparent when the day before the lecture the editor of *The Times* asked for a press release, which Beatrice had not written. The cunning Mrs Green, with whom Beatrice was staying, suggested asking Sidney round to write it. This he did in a trice, and their old 'camaraderie' was re-established.[22]

At the beginning of the year Beatrice had copied for Sidney the 'device' with which she began her new diary: she sealed a blob of sealing wax with her griffin seal, and encircled it with the words: Love, Faith, Humility, Energy. 'I meant simply to seal myself to keeping these qualities constantly before me,' she explained, fearful that he would laugh at her. By 'love', she meant love of humanity.[23] As the months unfolded it became apparent to Beatrice that alone she was not strong enough to achieve her aims and ideals. And her heart was touched by Sidney's own loneliness and devotion, both to her and their common cause. He was working so hard that he was like a cabhorse who could not be taken out of the shafts for fear he would fall down, he told her, but the secret of life was not to expect too much from it. 'Only children cry for sugar instead. (And I am a child.)'[24]

Although Beatrice and Sidney were drawn together by mutual emotional need, she did not marry him because no other possible husband presented himself. When she went over to Longfords, her sister Mary Playne's house, for a flower show in August, Kate Courtney enquired delicately: 'I wonder whether you will marry?' Demurely Beatrice replied that she thought it highly probable, but that in her case marriage would be subordinate to work. 'That is rather a question for your husband,' protested Kate. 'No: it is the question of the *choice* of my husband,' replied Beatrice. Perplexed, Kate wondered whether it was Haldane or a socialist. Did Beatrice like Sidney Webb better than before after their recent trip to Norway with Graham Wallas? 'I like both these men immensely,' answered Beatrice enigmatically, letting slip that Wallas was coming to stay with her for a week.[25] Haldane had already made indirect advances to Beatrice, and Wallas, son of a clergyman, Shrewsbury and Oxford educated, six feet tall and conventionally handsome, seemed to Kate an altogether more suitable socialist, if Beatrice *had* to marry a socialist, than Webb.

Beatrice was fond of Wallas, whom she described as a 'lovable man'.[26] He became part of a Fabian trio after her marriage to Sidney: 'Your satellite Wallas, and your sun Webb, I being a mere comet,' as Shaw put it.[27] But she would never have married him, for the slouching Wallas lacked ambition. He had intellectual ability but no drive and appeared to others simply as 'a kindly dull fellow'.[28] In Sidney Beatrice found a man whose ambition matched her own, one who had the conceit of Napoleon and equally grandiose aims. It was Sidney whom the other Fabians considered their leader, and in early 1891

Sidney's plans to leave the Colonial Office and seek election to the London County Council in November crystallised. Overcoming the crisis of confidence due to his illness and Beatrice's rejection, he decided to throw himself 'boldly upon the world', earning a living by journalism and using the county council as a springboard for his entrance into Parliament. Beatrice wrote approvingly that there was so much demand for socialist articles that 'Propaganda and Pot-boiling might become identical', and she thought him admirably suited for Parliament for which the county council would be excellent training. She saw that hitching her star to Sidney's, they might rise together; it would be a very different life to the part of 'walking gentlewoman' to the play of Chamberlain which she had earlier rejected.

Beatrice was power-hungry and was now prepared to make the trade-off: sex for power. Her will was indomitable, and she used it to subdue her body, which had so inconveniently demanded sexual satisfaction in the past. Although Sidney was not as grotesquely ugly as H. G. Wells's caricature of a Mongolian figure with a protruding behind and 'reddish swollen-looking eyes over gilt-edged glasses ... [who] talked in an ingratiating undertone, with busy thin lips, and eager lisp and nervous movements of the hand',[29] his disproportionately small body appeared comical beside her tall slender one, and his lisping cockney voice contrasted with her upper-class one, making plain the class difference between them. Sidney wore fusty-smelling black clothes and had an untidy way of eating. He was the Beast to her Beauty, and to the end of her life Beatrice remained painfully aware of this element in their relationship.[30]

If the Fabian leader promised a gateway to political power and influence, he also personified the creed in which Beatrice by 1891 believed. With him she could do the work to which marriage must be subordinate, and which would serve suffering humanity. For Beatrice and Sidney shared a determinist view of history; in 'The Difficulties of Individualism', his reply to Leonard Courtney in the *Economic Journal*, Sidney stressed that social institutions and economic relations were as subject to evolutionary change as any biological organism. 'Thus,' he declared, 'Man becomes the midwife of the great womb of Time.' Inexorably society was moving towards industrial democracy, and in words echoing Beatrice's in *The Co-operative Movement*, he argued that rising death-duties, local rates, graduated income-tax, and the public acquisition of land by the local authorities 'will in due course "collectivise" ' society.[31] When in July Shaw congratulated Sidney on his well-written article, Sidney told Beatrice that this was due to her corrections. Already they were working in tandem.

The parallel lines along which Sidney and Beatrice were thinking were more than ever apparent in Sidney's remarks on the Eight Hours Bill, which had been promoted 'from a fad to a "question"' by the autumn of 1891, as part of Gladstone's election campaign. The miners must submit themselves to the 'collective freedom' of democratic control in the form of the forty-eight-hour week, he wrote.[32] Similarly Beatrice, three years earlier, had demanded that the Factory Acts be extended to the sweating system to produce regulated hours, a minimum wage, and minimum standards of sanitation,[33] a point of view which was directly opposed to the belief of feminists and suffragists in women's right to work, who opposed any restrictions on the labour of married women who worked out of necessity. Were women to be treated like children, or classed with men as adult workers, demanded Caroline Cust, the daughter of a barrister, who believed that the enfranchisement of the male section of the working class only had led male voters, who were women's rivals for jobs, to demand the legal restriction of women's work. If hours of work were to be limited they must be limited to men too, not just women, or else men would be preferred for jobs.[34] To her surprise Beatrice found that being an Anti-Suffragist told against her when she put herself up for election to the London Library, and only got thirteen votes.

By May Sidney's patient courtship was bearing fruit. 'I cannot tell how things will settle themselves,' confessed Beatrice to her diary, 'I think probably in his way. His resolute, patient affection, his constant care for my welfare – helping and correcting me – a growing distrust of a self-absorbed life and the egotism of successful work . . . all these feelings are making for our eventual union.'[35] She added, 'But if I marry, though I shall be drawn to it by affection and gratitude, it will be an act of renunciation of self and not of indulgence of self as it would have been in the other case.'

Sidney was delirious with happiness when Beatrice let him know her decision on the Wednesday after the Lincoln conference. She would consent to marry him on condition their engagement was kept secret while her father lived. The next day Sidney was still in a dream, '*delire, extase, ivresse* . . .' Our souls touch at the highest levels, he told Beatrice. He would be a modern husband: it would not be 'a "chattel" marriage', and she would be freer than she ever had been to do her intellectual work. As to money, everyone told him he could make £1000 or even £2000 a year at journalism – 'do you not suppose that

I would not work myself to the bone before I would allow you to miss any one comfort . . . ?'[36]

Sidney was not blind to Beatrice's steely character. 'I love you all the more for those faults I see – your wilfulness, your natural ambition – indeed they are not in themselves faults at all.' As he pictured her on 'her' common at Minchinhampton, ' "sniffing" the breeze, with dilated nostrils (one of your little habits)', and remembered the beechwoods where on the Sunday of his first visit she 'turned him inside out' as he watched her picking hyacinths, and sat trembling beside her, he felt intense happiness that the fight was at last over. Beatrice and he were two solar systems, he told her, not sun and planet (as Shaw later thought). 'That is why we have fought so long! When two solar systems come together it is a big thing!'

'My own dear Boy,' wrote Beatrice from Box, 'I send you these flowers picked in the early morning while the mist still hangs about the trees and plants.' She also included the wild hyacinths picked on his first visit to Box: 'They have dried up as our love has grown. Always your loving comrade, Beatrice Potter.'[37]

Before Sidney visited Box again, he and Beatrice travelled with Graham Wallas and a prospective girlfriend for Graham called Clara Bridgen to Norway for a three-week holiday among the fiords. There, as Beatrice dreamed away the days in the mountains, and Sidney grew 'brown as a Chilian', she brooded over the new life she was beginning and the nature of her relationship with Sidney. 'His feeling is the passionate love of an emotional man, mine is the growing tenderness of the mother . . . and in the background there is the affectionate *camaraderie*, the "fun" . . . of two young workers in the same cause.'[38] It was more 'fun' than she expected being with Sidney, and for the first time for months Beatrice allowed herself to relax, secure in the knowledge that she was no longer alone, that she had banished loneliness, and found a companion whose aims were her aims.

During the holiday Beatrice told Sidney that the urgent need for him to make money in order to go into politics no longer existed since she would have enough for both of them after her father's death. Despite Richard Potter's speculations, she would be able to count on an unearned income of over £1000 a year which, with frugal living by Potter standards, obviated the need for Sidney to start a new Fabian Review or take on other hack journalism. Sidney was overwhelmed by the news, and gave Beatrice his heartfelt thanks for 'coming to the rescue' over his finances.[39] For the first time in his life the hairdresser's son was released from financial pressures, and became aware of the step up through the class strata he was taking in marrying the daughter of a rich and successful entrepreneur. Beatrice's wealth, which had originally seemed an obstacle to his courtship, had proved his salvation.

A telling argument of Sidney's in persuading Beatrice to marry him had been that 'one and one placed close together in a sufficiently integrated relationship, make not two but eleven',[40] an argument with which Beatrice agreed, finding an echo of her own comment that 'we are both of us second-rate minds, but we are curiously combined – I am the investigator, and he the executor – and we have a wide and varied experience of men and things between us. I have also an unearned salary. This forms our unique circumstances.'[41] It was indeed unique for a couple living on an unearned income to be dedicated to the advancement of socialism and the end of capitalist privilege: but the irony of the situation occurred neither to Beatrice nor to Sidney. Having money was merely a fortunate circumstance which freed them both to dedicate their lives to 'the commonweal'.

While Beatrice discussed tactics with Sidney, urging him to live his life according to a plan with which everything else must fall in, her own secret fear was that domestic life would end her own work. It might have been a mistake to transform the Woman into a Thinker, but if the mistake had been paid for, one should hardly throw away the result. And would married life mean throwing away the fine-tuned instrument she had forged: her analytical mind? It would not, decided Beatrice firmly; she would spend the next year on her trade union book, and she and Sidney would show the world that the marriage of two socialists such as themselves, 'a true marriage of fellow-workers', was one which could be durable and persisting.

Nevertheless it was with her heart in her mouth that Beatrice broke the news of her engagement to Sidney to Mary Booth as Sidney had already made a bad impression on them, and asked her to keep it secret from the family. Beatrice and Sidney had exchanged rings, but although Sidney wore his, it is unlikely that Beatrice did, for she was determined to keep her plans from her father. Her motives were kind, for she knew that the news of Sidney's socialism and lower-class background would be intolerably painful to Richard Potter, if, indeed, he could understand it. But to Mary Booth, who abhorred secrecy of any sort, the request was anathema. 'Is the secrecy really desirable?' she wrote to Beatrice. 'I can't but fear that it will lead to still further irritation on your sisters' part . . . it seems to me that the engagement *must* leak out; and that you would be in a more uncomfortable position if this happened than if you confided in your own family of your own accord.'[42]

Later that day Mary wrote again to Beatrice: 'It is no use to pretend that we are not sorry it is so.' Thanking Mr Webb for his wish that they would not be separated by the engagement, she said, 'It is very good of him, as he knows that we have been to a great extent his enemies.' Although Mary intimated that once they were married she would receive Sidney, Beatrice was deeply hurt, and cried to herself. She was offended too that her cousin had never mentioned Beatrice's book on Co-operation, a copy of which she had sent to Mary. Beatrice comforted herself by saying that Mary had a narrow and conventional mind. In reality Mary was probably jealous of Beatrice's growing reputation; unlike Mary Playne, who enjoyed basking in Beatrice's reflected glory, Mary, who had a high opinion of her own intelligence and who had received no credit for her own patient editorship of her husband's survey, found Beatrice's success irksome. That August Beatrice's photograph appeared in the *Queen*, together with a profile of Sidney which by coincidence came out in the same edition. To congratulate Beatrice on the publication of her first book was more than Mary could stomach.[43]

Marrying Sidney was a courageous act of class rebellion for Beatrice. She feared that snobbery would be added to personal dislike and political prejudice in provoking hostility to their union among the family. Yet Mary Booth had the strength of character to marry a man with a Liverpool accent who never lost the flat 'a' of the Northerner. It was socialism more than snobbery which proved the stumbling block, and eventually Mary Booth took the decision to 'drop' Beatrice. Although Beatrice wrote sadly that 'from Charlie I expected something different: he is too big a mind for that and his feeling for me was warm and strong',[44] she was mistaken. Charles Booth was a cool and self-sufficient personality who had welcomed Beatrice as a valued member of his team, but he had far less need for friends than Beatrice. It was Mary who had been the moving spirit in keeping the close relationship going between the cousins, Mary who, as a lonely young wife in London, had welcomed Beatrice's friendship: it was now Mary who drew it decisively to a close. Although Charles Booth wrote a formal letter of congratulation, he did not offer to see Beatrice; and Mary let Beatrice know that she was not 'at home'.

Beatrice did not confide in her sisters, but R. B. Haldane, like Alice Green, Graham Wallas and Bernard Shaw, was told the 'momentous secret'. Haldane had been manoeuvring closer to the Fabians, despite a bad start over dinner at which Sidney had lectured Haldane insolently on radical reform. Aware that he had behaved abominably, Sidney wrote a letter of apology, and Haldane, who had given Sidney the impression that he was 'not willing to give up his life',[45] began nudging his junta within the advanced Liberal Eighty Club towards Fabianism. Sidney wrote to his new friend with the news, adding that he felt the responsibility not to spoil a life which he regarded as of high value to the world.[46] Haldane, still smarting from his own broken engagement, which had left him with the feeling that black misfortune crowded all around him, warmly assured Sidney that his secret was safe and Haldane would let no trace of it escape him. 'I congratulate you with all my soul on the splendid companionship for life which you have won.'[47]

Determined not to 'fash' herself over the Booths' ostracism, Beatrice threw herself into research on the trade unions, using Herbert Spencer's house as a working base and place of entertainment for trade unionists. She felt the irony of the situation as the portrait of Spencer, prophet of individualism, looked down on the nightly meetings of trade unionists, and socialist talk mingled with clouds of tobacco, aided by whisky. As always, Beatrice was happiest in the company of men, and counted her working-men friends, Benjamin Jones and J. J. Dent, as close as any of her female friends such as Alice Green or Ella Pycroft. The anti-feminine bias she detected among the trade union officials was a challenge to which she rose, and she was exhilarated by working in the Home Office, sitting in solitary glory above Whitehall with the despatch boxes, doing research for her book. Sidney frequently joined her at Avenue Road to work on trade union records, and they developed a mutually rewarding routine of research interrupted by cups of tea, cigarettes, and 'human nature' when they would exchange kisses. 'It is very sweet, this warm companionship in work,' wrote Beatrice.[48]

In August Beatrice returned to Box. The burden of secrecy hung heavy on Sidney, who longed to join Alice Green and Wallas who were already staying there, but when he heard that the Playnes were going to be at home he gave up a promised Sunday visit in order not to arouse suspicion. His father, who had been ill with bronchitis and congestion of the lungs, had died in July, his mother and sister Ada were away on holiday, and everyone was out of town. Sidney longed for Beatrice's letters, reproaching her for not writing every day as he did, although she explained that if a servant was not available she had to trudge into Minchinhampton to post them herself. Sidney divided his days into black or white ones, depending on whether he received a letter from Beatrice, and told her that when he did finally see her, 'I shall be like Don [her dog], ready to devour you.'[49]

That month Sidney sat for his photograph. It was a horrid ordeal: 'Nothing I can do will make a handsome face out of mine, so don't be disappointed if the result is not as you would like,' he told Beatrice. 'Handsome is as handsome does. I could not love you any more if I were perfect in form.'[50] Beatrice was not impressed, and did not mince her words. 'No dear, I do not even look at your photograph. It is too hideous, for anything. Do be done in a gray suit by Elliot and Fry [a fashionable firm] and let me have your head *only* – it is the head only I am marrying!'

During the autumn Beatrice and Sidney were often apart. Beatrice went to the Trades Union Congress at Newcastle, to chase up contacts for her book. Sidney meanwhile formally resigned from the Colonial Office, sending Beatrice the letter of acceptance of his resignation and thanking her again for saving him from worry, anxiety and fear through her financial support. 'I am horribly "bourgeois" by temperament, and the temptation of a fixed income would have been enormous for me.'[51] As Beatrice scurried round the countryside, occasionally meeting Sidney for daringly unconventional rendezvous in hotels, nervous doubts about their union surfaced. She continually worried that marriage would hinder her work, which she loved very much. It was not enough to research written documents on the unions, she should live among the miners and see what place unionism occupied in their lives. It was the approach she had already adopted among the sweaters, which followed naturally from her early deception in Bacup, a method advocated by Charles Booth, who lived for weeks at a time among the inhabitants of the East End. 'How can I combine that with marriage in a year's time?' Beatrice demanded of Sidney. 'Every now and then I feel I have got into a hole out of which I can't struggle. I love you – but I love my work better!' Only by making work the priority could she contemplate marriage: 'We need not love each other the less because with both of us, our work stands first and our union second.'[52]

It was this attitude which alarmed Ella Pycroft when Beatrice at last broke the news of her engagement to her. After the 'thunderclap' of her own broken engagement to Maurice Paul in 1890, Ella determined to be utterly frank with her old colleague: 'I'm just going to tell you the absolute truth Bee – and that is I should be quite genuinely glad if I thought that you cared for him half as much as he does for you – but you know when we were talking about marriage the other day, I felt as if you hadn't the remotest idea of what love meant in my sense of the word . . . You're quite right one wants the intimacy of thought and comradeship, but marriage ought to mean something much more than just that.'[53] Ella hoped she was a goose and utterly wrong: in fact she was right.

Sidney suffered a 'constriction of the heart' when he discovered Beatrice considered him a 'drag' on her. 'My own love, count it *for something* at any rate that I shall be there to help you: the book will not be the worse for me. I can work at it and will.' Beatrice's apprehensions were better founded than he knew; her instinct as a social investigator told her that to live among the miners would add a valuable dimension to her book. But Sidney soothed away her fears, telling her that it would be better not to investigate the effect of Trade Unionism upon the lives of the workers – 'I question whether you ever *could* do that well enough' – and assuring her that they were not going into marriage merely to make things pleasant for themselves. Duty was imperative. Echoing her own thoughts, he told her: 'We could not love each so well, loved we not our work and duty more.'[54]

Sidney was much amused by a conversation over dinner with Massingham, who advised him to marry a woman with £1000 a year. Did he mean Beatrice Potter, asked Sidney. 'No, no, "Potterism" is to be taken with a large grain of salt,' replied Massingham. 'I don't know that you wouldn't find that you had *bitten off more than you could chew.* And I don't think she has much money: she doesn't live like it. No, don't marry a clever woman, they're too much trouble.'[55]

Meanwhile, Beatrice took consolation in a glimpse of Chamberlain and his wife on the Darlington to Durham train. Chamberlain looked complacent and had lost his old ambition, and his wife was a plain little thing, a true example of *la femme complaisante*. Beatrice shuddered at the fate she had escaped.

As autumn deepened into winter Richard Potter continued to linger on although his breathing was poor and his nights sleepless. By November the strain of the six-month secret engagement was telling on Beatrice. Sidney had been booked to give a talk to the Working Men's Club at Thrupp, near her home at Minchinhampton, and Beatrice had seemed to welcome the opportunity to 'rouse the wretched little valley out of its deadening torpor'.[56] But when Mary Playne asked for the visit to be cancelled, Beatrice hinted to Sidney that she would like him to make some excuse not to come; Sidney, anxious not to lose the opportunity of a visit to Box, demurred at telling an untruth. Beatrice boiled over with frustration, writing sharply to Sidney that if he cared for her feelings at all he would cancel, and she was too upset to eat any breakfast. Sidney sent the necessary letter, but not without protest. It was their first quarrel, and Beatrice drew a wise conclusion from it: after Christmas she would tell her sisters the truth. 'Then we can begin the New Year openly – and face everything openly and together.'[57]

Sidney sent Beatrice a copy of Matthew Arnold's poems for Christmas, and Beatrice promised him that it was the last Christmas Day they would spend apart. 'Dear one,' she wrote, 'I will try to repay your love and devotion and to make your home and happiness together – in spite of your "professional" wife. I will try and prove that a woman may be a loving wife and gentle mistress . . . but I shall often stumble and fall – and you must help me up.'[58]

As the year faded Richard Potter's life slipped away. It was the end of months of strain for Beatrice as she nursed her dying father, who struggled for each painful breath, wracked by paroxysms in which he seemed to be drowning. Gradually he slipped into semi-consciousness, watched over by Mrs Thompson, his devoted nurse, and helped on his way by chloroform given by the doctor. On New Year's Day 1892 he died, and Beatrice's vigil was over.

After the funeral her engagement was announced in the *British Weekly*, and she confessed to her sisters, who welcomed Sidney into the family at a formal dinner in London. Beatrice knew she had in turn to make the acquaintance of the lower-middle class, going to stay at Sidney's house, whose ugliness she dreaded, and spending her evenings sitting in front of the gas fire with his mother and sister. Sternly she told herself that her unwished-for dislike of ugly, small surroundings disappeared in the blessedness of love, and she did not mind her step downwards in the social scale if her loss meant Sidney's gain.

Although Beatrice professed not to care, she wanted to gauge the reaction of her sisters as she longed for the approval of the sisterhood and for the approbation of the whole family. Nervously anticipating criticism, she told Lallie Holt, 'Superficially your new brother-in-law will have little to recommend him. He is very small and ugly! he has none of the *savoir-faire* which comes from a leisurely upbringing . . .'[59] Georgina Meinertzhagen, whose own married life was unhappy, either neglected by her husband Daniel or forced to receive his mistresses at country weekends, wrote frigidly, 'Your news certainly surprised us.

I hope that the step you are taking is a wise one and will lead to your ultimate happiness. *You say that we are prejudiced against Mr Sidney Webb but as I have only seen him for half an hour that can hardly be a strong feeling on my part.*' Yet Georgina promised sympathy, telling Beatrice that even if the Meinertzhagens and the Webbs were not 'quite kindred spirits . . . if he makes you happy we shall certainly appreciate him in the end'. Fearful for Beatrice's reputation, she begged her to give up travelling alone with Sidney and Frank Galton, a Fabian ex-student of Sidney's at the Workingmen's College, who was their newly-appointed secretary. Was the 'secretary' meant to be a 'gooseberry', asked Georgina. She would like to be satisfied on that point before she clapped her hands.[60]

Maggie Hobhouse, from whom Beatrice had long drifted apart, professed to be less surprised. She had been sure that 'something was in the wind', although she was astonished by Beatrice's choice of Sidney Webb – 'whom I do not know in the least' – the inference being that Sidney belonged to a social class whose members one did not know. She urged Beatrice not to be afraid to reconsider. 'If you and Mr Webb should find in the next eight months that you are not really suited to each other . . . do let me pray you not to allow any false notions of delicacy . . . to prevent you from breaking off your engagement – *I think marriage at your age and with your very determined character might be fraught with some risk to your happiness and therefore to your husband's.*'[61]

Beatrice was less concerned with Blanche's approval than Mary Playne's, who had supported her in her trials with Rosy, and who was a close neighbour at Box. Unlike the fey Blanche, who wrote with customary vagueness, 'I am ashamed of my ignorance but I don't remember who Mr Sidney Webb is although I feel sure I have heard of him', Mary was well acquainted with Sidney, and had already told Ella Pycroft that she detested him. Her letter reflected this emotion: 'If he thoroughly dislikes and disparages the class to which we belong and the traditions we think have real value, it is not likely there will be much sympathy between us.' She thought Sidney 'uncommonly lucky. He will have as good a wife as a man can have, that there can be no doubt about.'[62]

Bravely Beatrice accepted her sisters' shock and contempt at her misalliance. They were too insulated by prosperity to do more than 'lift their eyebrows and wish me good luck'.[63] Only Rosy, whose husband Dyson Williams was in the last stages of syphilis, did she feel existed on a level which she and Sidney touched. All future relations with her sisters would be 'a relationship of choice', as she told Mary, and the future was in their hands. But Sidney himself did not feel the same sensitivity as Beatrice over his background, and if the sisterhood found him inimical to their class and everything for which it stood, he found they constituted an intellectual vacuum. Their futile little arguments, utterly lacking in logic or acumen, contrasted with Beatrice's trained mind, and as for Mrs Hobhouse's mind, it had atrophied to nothing at all. She seemed unaware, marvelled Sidney to Beatrice, that people existed on less than £5000 a year.

Beatrice had to face one more sad consequence of her engagement: the loss of the position of literary executor to Herbert Spencer. Spencer found himself in a quandary, for he could not contemplate having a known socialist as his executor, but there was no one else available as able as Beatrice and as familiar with Spencer's life and thought. What should he do, he asked Beatrice plaintively, when they met at the Athenaeum. Generously Beatrice suggested a way out of the impasse: Spencer's Life would appear under the name of Howard Collins, Spencer's assistant, of whom Beatrice had a low opinion, and she would give the work the necessary literary gloss.

On 5 March Sidney swept to victory as the Progressive candidate for Deptford in the London County Council elections, and took pardonable pride in the finding that his Elliot and Fry photograph was now offered for sale. Separation became increasingly irksome, as Beatrice continued working in Manchester and Newcastle, attending union meetings, whereas Sidney was isolated in London although content to find himself elected to the four committees he most wanted (which he attributed to the good offices of John Burns), as well as Chairman of the Technical Education Board. 'I feel as if I was separated – not from my love, but from my wife,' he wrote sadly. 'Goodnight dearest.'[64]

As their marriage drew near, Beatrice ordered a light grey dress at a cost of £4. Sidney wrote that he was sure she would look sweet in it – 'even if dark blue silk does suit you better – because you are (I am *so* thankful for this) happy in what you are undertaking. We will go and choose the prettiest little brooch we can find. I am glad you will let me give you this little token. You have so few gifts from me . . .'[65] Beatrice too longed for their separation to be over, although she had one regret: parting with her name. 'I *do* resent that,' she told Sidney.

At 11.45 a.m. on 23 July 1892 Beatrice married Sidney at St Pancras Vestry. Graham Wallas was best man. It was a brief and unromantic affair, 'prosaic, almost sordid', in the words of Kate Courtney, who felt there was something shady about civil marriages. Herbert Spencer pleaded ill health and did not attend. Sidney had doubts about allowing the sisters to come to the ceremony, but in the event the family turned out *en masse* to witness the marriage of the last of the sisterhood to a socialist, and share in the wedding breakfast at the Euston Railway Hotel. 'Bee looked good,' decided Kate. 'Serious and handsome.'[66]

Beatrice's entry in her diary was succinct. 'Exit Beatrice Potter, Enter Beatrice Webb or rather (Mrs) Sidney Webb for I lose alas! both names.'

XVI

WEAVING HER WEBB

*'Certainly persons with brains and independent means may have
a rare good time in the part of permeator or fly on the wheel.'*
Beatrice Webb Diary, Christmas Day 1893

BEATRICE AND SIDNEY SPENT their honeymoon in Ireland. Despite the presence of the Irish, 'a ramshackle race' who lounged in the August sun outside their rude Dublin hovels, it was a joyous time for Beatrice. She and Sidney were 'far too happy to be reasonable', she told Graham.[1] It marked the beginning of a married life which in the early years was very sweet. When away from Sidney Beatrice missed their 'dovecot', the cosy flat in Netherhall Gardens in South Hampstead, and 'my darling old boy – who twists his strong-minded wife round his little finger – by soft sounds and kisses'.[2]

Sidney, too, had every reason to be happy. His dogged courtship had paid off. He had won a wife with beauty, brains, capital and influential friends, something which never ceased to be a source of wonder to him. And by so doing all barriers to his ambition appeared to have fallen. The path by which he might eventually become a Radical minister in a reforming Liberal Cabinet stretched before him: his new role as Chairman of the Technical Education Board, and member of the half a dozen committees which ran the London County Council could be a stepping stone to Parliament and a career beyond local government.

There is little doubt that during their engagement both the Webbs intended Sidney to be 'the politician of the future'.[3] Sidney told the Fabian journalist R. C. K. Ensor that he left the Civil Service in order to cross from the position of clerk to the other side of the desk where, as Minister, he could give orders and further socialism most effectively.[4] Such aspirations came easily to one who had already travelled effortlessly through the examination system to find bureaucratic success, and in consequence had developed an élitist reliance on the 'expert' who would reshape society. Beatrice and Sidney, like Shaw and Wallas, lacked faith in the brutish masses to whom new rights had been extended, but whom they considered too irrational to use them wisely. Like other European intellectuals, their thought had become anti-democratic:[5] 'Reforming society,' declared Beatrice, 'is no light matter, and must be undertaken by experts specially trained for the purpose.'[6] Confident in their own intellectual superiority, the middle- and upper-class Fabians saw themselves as heirs to the Priests of Humanity visualised by Comte, and were sure of their indispensability as the midwives of socialism. It was a dangerous assumption which led them fatally to under-estimate the ability of trade union leaders such as Keir Hardie.

It might have been supposed that an avowedly socialist society would support the formation of a new and separate socialist party, but such was not the Fabian way. It fitted both Fabian élitism and Sidney's personal ambition far better to act as a pressure group upon the existing two-party system which, after the 1886 Liberal split, was fluid and open to infiltration. The 'permeation racket', as Shaw called it,[7] suited both Shaw and Webb, who were not 'front-stairs' politicians by nature, and whose social backgrounds made them both misfits in the existing class system. An Irish Protestant 'downstart' and a cockney 'upstart' together developing a system of capturing the Radical Wing of the Liberal Party had troubled some other Fabians such as Hubert Bland.[8] But Bland's protests were in vain, swept away in the intoxicating 'Fabian boom' of 1888 to 1890 during which Fabian Essays sold by the thousand, Fabian membership soared, and the Progressive party won its surprise victory in the first London County Council election.

Shaw, whose love of sparkling epigrams and his own ego was greater than his concern for historical truth, created the myth of Fabian influence upon the course of politics, which has proved strangely enduring. Shaw's eloquence 'is a devastating example of the historical fraudulence that can be purveyed by scintillating rhetoric'.[9] Shaw claimed that the Fabian Society had 'collared' the *Star* and the *Daily Chronicle* for Fabianism, that under the generalship of Sidney Webb the stage army of Fabians had permeated the Liberal and Radical Associations where 'we pulled all the wires we could lay our hands on with our utmost adroitness and energy ... Such bewildering conjuring tricks with the Liberal thimbles and the Fabian peas'[10] did Webb play that he could take the credit for the 1889 Progressive victory. It is true that the 'L & Rs' welcomed Fabian proposals, but Shaw's claim, by which Webb was also seduced, that the Fabian leader was the originator of municipal socialism, is a myth: the London Programme is not original, but owes the bulk of its ideas to J. F. B.

Firth who founded the London Municipal Reform League in 1881.[11] By 1891 London was crying out for the reforms which had been taking place in provincial cities since the Municipal Corporations Act of 1835, and of which Chamberlain's Birmingham was already a shining example. After Firth's death in 1889 Webb filled his vacant place as Progressive theorist and the London Programme contributed to the 1892 Progressive success, but Sidney was the originator neither of 'gas and water' socialism nor of the Progressive Party.

Shaw's most outrageous claim was that Webb's pamphlet *Wanted a Programme* was the foundation of the Liberals' Newcastle Programme which played a large part in the eighty-two-year-old Gladstone's fourth election victory in August 1892. Its significance lies in the fact that the Webbs and Shaw were taken in by their own myth-making; the belief in permeation became all enveloping and blinded the Webbs to political realities. It led them to make fundamental errors of judgement which fatally affected their future influence and popularity. Like cuckoos, they attempted to lay a collectivist egg in the Liberal nest, but only succeeded in hatching an infertile imperialist hybrid. As a result by 1902 they found themselves outside the mainstream of politics in a Fabian wilderness of their own making.

But in 1892 Sidney was intoxicated with the Progressive success, and eager to take the credit for it. 'It is simply a gorgeous justification of Fabian electioneering and ought to do something to convince the provincials that our game is the right one,' he wrote enthusiastically to Wallas.[12] Beatrice had already interested herself in permeation, telling Sidney to drop 'the bribe and threat argument' in attempting to persuade the Liberals to adopt socialist proposals, and appeal to conviction instead.[13] Once married she abandoned her early scruples about 'wire-pulling' and threw herself heart and soul into following Shaw's suggestion that 'Madame Potter-Webb' should start a socialist salon. 'We must all go into the House in a body next time,' declared Shaw optimistically.[14] As Beatrice recognised, no one was better fitted than herself to pave Sidney's way into Parliament. 'Skill in social intercourse was my special gift,' she wrote candidly, confessing that as an experienced hostess she had never felt a moment's shyness in the company of either sex of whatever status or occupation.[15]

Permeation was not just a technique followed from conviction, it was a game which gave all the Fabian junta intense pleasure, whether in Beatrice's chosen field of the dinner party, in committee where Webb and Wallas 'wire-pulled' gleefully, or in the lecture room or political meeting where Shaw revelled in spinning stories and dreaming dreams. In a typical letter Shaw suggested to Sidney that Beatrice might captivate Asquith, then Home Secretary, in order to persuade him to grant freedom of speech in Trafalgar Square: 'Webb, my bhoy: a wurd wud yuy [sic] . . . I think I once saw Beatrice Potter, in an Indian blanket, fascinating Asquith. Could she get his scalp now, think you?'[16] Beatrice, who confessed that marriage made her feel 'hemmed in' and that she missed flirting with marriageable men, found the prospect a delightful challenge.[17]

Beatrice was less flippant than Shaw but equally determined. She made the decision for her and Sidney to leave their Hampstead flat for 41 Grosvenor Road (now Millbank), within walking distance of Parliament as well as the Council offices at Spring Gardens, where Sidney spent his afternoons. At Hampstead she had worried that she was becoming a recluse, and was slipping into intellectual torpor. Grosvenor Road, by contrast, would serve as the perfect base for entertaining a constant succession of 'professional' friends to dinner or lunch, 'all for some purpose'.[18] So she and Sidney moved into the 'hard little house' so cruelly satirised by H. G. Wells as the home of the Oscar Baileys in *The New Machiavelli*, which they rented for £110 a year. Kate Courtney helped with the choice of wallpaper and paint, and Beatrice agonised over whether she was betraying her socialist principles in spending an extra £100 in buying prettier things than were absolutely necessary. Her sisters announced that they did not see much socialism in Beatrice going to William Morris for wallpapers, and finding 'charming old bits of furniture' in secondhand shops and employing two maids. As Beatrice reminded herself guiltily, efficiency only demanded nourishing food and well-ordered drains.[19]

In fact Beatrice's idea of extravagance produced what was, by other standards, almost a puritanical house. There was a long narrow workroom on the ground floor lined with books and decorated with family portraits; on the half-landing was the office of their secretary Galton, overflowing with boxes of notes. On the first floor was the sitting room with three easy chairs and no sofa, so that as many guests as possible could be accommodated standing. The house's redeeming feature was the view over the Thames where the oared barges and little steamers passed by towards Vauxhall and Lambeth bridges, and on a clear day one could see St Paul's. The house suited Beatrice, who enjoyed walking along the Embankment to see her sister Kate at Chelsea, or to St Paul's to pray.

Beatrice was still determined to live married life according to a plan.

Such a plan 'is a surer basis for a happy marriage than the perpetual shifting desire for self-expression', she had decided at the beginning of her marriage, and she would not deviate from her decision. Individual desires were to be subordinated to the 'partnership'; by such a stratagem Beatrice sought to bury the inconvenient demands of that 'other Ego', Doubt, which had so troubled her adolescence and early womanhood, and thus avoid inner conflict. The basis of the plan was that the Webbs' lives should be divided between active politics and their writing and research. They were scientists, socialists and secularists, declared Beatrice, ignoring her own mystical and artistic needs. While Sidney took the greater part in public life, she would devote herself to writing what she later described as their 'solid but unreadable books',[20] which he would help with when he could spare the time.

Very soon Beatrice began to have second thoughts. She realised that she could not bear to let Sidney go into Parliament, which would take him more than ever away from her, and which she herself could never enter. She could tolerate the London County Council, but 'losing him to the nation' would spoil their 'divine relationship', the pact of marriage which drew them increasingly close.[21] Together she and Sidney had 'love, health, capacity, freedom, friends, all the good things of life in abundant measure', she wrote on Christmas Day 1893.[22] And a seat in Parliament for Sidney would make joint authorship impossible, for increasingly Beatrice was convinced of her intellectual dependence on Sidney. Sometimes she worried that she simply vegetated, watched him working instead of working herself. When she set herself a task, such as writing a lecture on Trade Unionism, a hopeless muddle resulted. 'I was in a devil of a temper,' she confessed,[23] but Sidney's clear head and hand soon recast her meanderings, leaving her feeling something of a parasite.

Aware of his wife's feelings, as early as July 1892 Sidney turned down an offer of the seat at Gateshead, where there was an opening for a Liberal-Labour candidate 'with an advanced programme'.[24] Two years later Beatrice struggled with her guilt at dissuading Sidney from accepting the offers of seats which came in nearly every month: unconvincingly she argued that Sidney, already nicknamed 'Wily Webb' for his habit of collusion with the Moderates [Conservatives] on the Council, would not be a successful wire-puller in the lobbies of Parliament. The real reason, she admitted, was, 'A parliamentary career would destroy our united life; would cut at the root of a good deal of our joint effort. Perhaps that is why I dislike my distrust of his going into Parliament; it would take so much away from me, personally, would add so many ties and inconveniences. Sooner or later I suppose he will have to make the sacrifice – but better later than sooner.'[25] Not until he was an old man did Beatrice allow Sidney to enter the House.

In the meantime there was the fun of permeating the 'common lump' of trade unionists, for whom Beatrice had a snobbish contempt, and enjoyed making dance to the Fabian tune. During 1893 the Webbs drew closer to John Burns, then the general secretary of the embryonic Independent Labour Party formed at Bradford that year by Keir Hardie, whom Burns heartily disliked. Beatrice considered Burns an intellectual, a 'born ruler of barbarians' (his fellow working men), but suspicious and egotistical. There were moments when she thought he could be a useful acquisition to the solidly middle-class Fabian junta, but mostly she used him as a receptacle for Fabian ideas, like Tom Mann, another engineer, and Henry Broadhurst, the stonemasons' leader and MP. Mann 'swallowed the bait' of Sidney's offer to write a Minority Report for the Royal Commission on Labour, and Broadhurst accepted the same offer for the Commission on the Aged Poor. Gleefully Beatrice confided to her diary that she and Sidney had hatched two 'chickens'. 'The truth is that *we want the things done* and we don't much care what persons or which party gets the credit. We are pretty confident that, if it comes to a fight, we know the arts of war as well as our enemies . . .' she wrote. 'The Fabians are still convinced believers in the policy of permeation.'[26]

It was a small victory; yet at the same time Beatrice and Sidney were losing the war over who should lead the labour movement. From their blinkered metropolitan eyrie in Grosvenor Road they opposed and underrated the northern Independent Labour Party, partly because it was provincial and led by trade unionists, partly because they instinctively preferred 'Webbite opportunism',[27] as Shaw called it, to the formation of a separate party, and partly because they disliked Keir Hardie and James Ramsay MacDonald who dominated the Independent Labour Party for the first twelve years of its life. Shaw's note to Webb in August 1892 encapsulates the Fabian leader's opinion of Hardie: 'A Scotchman with alternate intervals of second sight (during which he does not see anything but is suffused with afflatus) and common incapacity.'[28] Beatrice called the Independent Labour Party 'with its lack of money and brains . . . a wrecking party'.

When in January 1895 Hardie, MacDonald and Mann attended an awkward dinner party at Grosvenor Road, it became clear that the clash of personalit s made any alliance impossible. Hardie told the Webbs that they were the worst enemies of the social revolution, to which Beatrice said the Fabians were an educational body, not a party, whose job it was to give everyone the exact dose of collectivism that they could assimilate. Since the main aim of the Independent Labour Party was to get a distinct Labour Party in Parliament, as opposed to the 'Lib-Labs' who sheltered under the Liberal umbrella, and they refused to support Liberal candidates in the coming London County Council election, no *modus vivendi* existed. The Webbs took comfort in the fact that all the Independent Labour Party candidates were defeated, and Hardie lost his seat at West Ham at the general election, ignoring the fact that trade union membership, the party's power base, had grown to one million by 1893. Like the Liberal leaders they remained oblivious of working-class aspirations which would ultimately push the old party of the left into terminal decline.

No episode so well illustrated Webb's and Shaw's misjudgement of the political moment than the broadside they fired against their erstwhile Radical allies in the Liberal Party, 'To Your Tents, O Israel!'[29] The article caused a sensation with its angry taunts at the Liberals for not putting the Newcastle Programme into effect (after only sixteen months in office) and demands that the trade unions set up a parliamentary fund to run fifty independent Labour candidates at the next election. Beatrice had misgivings about this new Fabian manifesto, accepting Wallas's objection that the Fabians were rushed into it for fear of being left behind by the Independent Labour Party. It was, as Henry Massingham, editor of the *Daily Chronicle*, complained, 'a complete and absolute right-about-face' of everything Webb stood for, a trivial and mischievous piece of tomfoolery. He detected, Massingham told Shaw, 'an unchemical combination of you, Webb and Mrs Webb', noting Webb's 'smallness of view and habit of forcing facts to fit his conclusions, and your flippancy'.[30] 'I have been a permeator all my days,' Massingham wrote sadly, submitting his resignation.

Massingham's criticisms were justified, but the harm done to fellow Fabians was little in comparison to that done to Haldane, who considered the manifesto 'a stab in the back', reproaching Sidney for making his job of modifying the Liberal machine immeasurably more difficult.[31] It also harmed Sidney's position with his Radical allies in the London County Council and removed any chance of him becoming 'the London Chamberlain'.[32]

Shaw's facility with the pen came into its own when it came to polishing up Beatrice and Sidney's first joint book *The History of Trade Unionism*. It was the Webbs' habit to spend the summer in the country, and in 1893 Beatrice returned to the Argoed with Sidney. Shaw joined them, wielding his 'pruning-knife' in the mornings on the monumental *History*, and in the afternoons writing *Mrs Warren's Profession*. 'He is an excellent friend,' wrote Beatrice, impressed by the way the Fabians helped each other when necessary. Yet she did not understand Shaw, finding him 'agile, graceful and even virile, but lacking in *weight* . . . a born philanderer',[33] who reminded her a little of the 'Souls', that bright circle of aesthetes and wits she had met at Haldane's. But Beatrice, like the rest of her sex, was not immune to the charm of the tall, lithe, broad-chested vegetarian with laughing blue eyes, whose brilliant conversation made him a delightful companion. She was near the truth when she said that Shaw's vanity was part of the character he imagined himself to be playing in the world's comedy, for Shaw saw himself and Webb as players on a political stage, the mirror image of those actors who performed his drama in the London theatre. To Shaw, the artist, the artifice of Fabian influence created in his imagination *was* the truth, just as his plays encapsulated a poetic truth which was more agreeable than pedestrian reality.

Living with the Webbs was more of a strain for the playwright than Beatrice was aware: 'The frightful sensation of being always on your guard with another man's wife . . . seems to develop itself here to a perfectly devilish intensity,' he told Bertha Newcombe, the artist, who was in love with him. 'Beatrice's nature is so hostile to mine that in spite of all the admiration, esteem, kindly feeling and other dry goods that abound between us, it is only by holding my edge steadily at the most delicately felt angle to her grindstone that I can avoid becoming hateful to her . . . As an Irishman, an irregular artistic person, an anarchist in conduct, and above all, a creator of an atmosphere subtly disintegrative of households, I am antipathetic to her.'[34]

Nevertheless, his affection for Sidney and their common aims held them together. Shaw became part of the 'Bo' family, as Beatrice liked to call herself, Sidney and Graham Wallas, and after the Webbs introduced Shaw to the Irish heiress Charlotte Payne-Townshend in 1896, she too shared the holidays which centred on that new invention, the bicycle. Cycling became a popular form of recreation in the 1890s, needing only a small outlay on a machine and the appropriate costume, and for many Londoners weekend touring in the countryside was 'a tonic better than all the patent medicines in the world'.[35] Beatrice and

Sidney had a 'jolly' time learning to bicycle at Beachy Head in April 1895, and that summer brought three new toys down to the Argoed. 'Bicycling has brought some "fun" or "sport" into my life, an element that was rather lacking in our workaday and somewhat strained existence', decided Beatrice. Five months later she, Sidney and Shaw were attempting their first long ride of forty miles from the Argoed, to Newport and then Cardiff for the Trades Union Congress.

One of Shaw's cycling stories was of the day when he, Webb and Bertrand Russell went cycling together at Chepstow: Shaw was enjoying 'a headlong tearing toboggan' down the hill with his feet on the rests, quite out of control, when Russell, who was ahead of him, jumped off his machine and left it in the road as he stared at a signpost. Shaw was thrown into the air and concussed. Webb suggested brandy, as his friend's lips were violet, but Shaw, after lying down for ten minutes, cycled the fifteen miles to Tintern Abbey and back to the Argoed. 'Nobody but a teetotaller would have faced a bicycle again for six months,' declared Shaw,[36] despite planning to cycle with Beatrice and Sidney back to London from Monmouthshire via Stonehenge and Basingstoke, in time to go to the theatre that evening.

The Webbs' circle of friends was widening, although the loss of the Booths never ceased to be a source of pain to Beatrice. Their home in Grosvenor Road was only a few doors away from that of Hannah and Robert Pearsall Smith, the American Quakers who entertained Beatrice and Sidney after their marriage at their home near Haslemere. Their daughter Mary had married Frank Costelloe, a Fabian friend of Sidney's, who was distraught when Mary ran off with Bernhard Berenson to Italy in 1891. Sidney hurried down to comfort Frank, who he felt was playing 'a very magnanimous game', authorising Mary to sign cheques on his account.[37] Mary's sister, Alys, attracted the attention of the young Bertrand Russell. She was young, beautiful and emancipated, recalled Russell, when he first met her at age seventeen.[38] They married in 1894 and settled in a workman's cottage, The Millhanger, a mile or two from Friday's Hill, where Russell began work on *The Principles of Mathematics*. Serious, philanthropic Alys, who worked with Lady Henry Somerset, the temperance reformer, and ran girls' clubs, appealed to Beatrice, who thought the Russells led idyllic lives. The only thing that marred the Sunday they spent together discussing metaphysics and politics was the absence of children. The six people gathered together were, commented Beatrice, 'all too intellectual or strenuous to bear children.'[39]

* * *

Beatrice needed her moments of relaxation, for she drove herself far harder than she would admit. The chief burden of *The History of Trade Unionism*, and *Industrial Democracy* which followed in 1898, lay on her shoulders. At the same time Sidney was the intellectually dominant member of the partnership, who led her towards an increasing reliance upon facts and documents in their writing. Beatrice revelled in face-to-face interviewing, in disguising her cross-examination as light conversation, in insinuating herself into smoking rooms, offices or conferences, and carrying away confidential information. 'The process of interviewing,' she wrote, 'is a particular form of psychoanalysis. From within the consciousness or subconsciousness of another mind the practitioner has to ferret out memories of past experience . . .'[40] The inside knowledge she gained made her writing original and stimulating to read. But Sidney disliked interviewing trade unionist officials and grumbled when he was sent out to the suburbs of Glasgow to root them out. His preferred method was to choose a particular social institution and try to discover every fact about it, from which, he imagined, would emerge the final hypothesis to which could be applied the last test of verification. Beatrice's passionate desire to find 'a science of society' which led Herbert Spencer to describe her as 'a young woman without a soul, looking upon struggling society as a young surgeon looks on a case as another subject for diagnosis',[41] was incomprehensible to Sidney.

The accumulation of facts about the trade unions became so great that the Webbs developed their own idiosyncratic method of note-taking. Each fact or date was written upon a separate piece of paper and the sheets were then shuffled until new themes or combinations emerged.[42] As Helen Bosanquet remarked tartly, this meant that facts were studied out of context. Yet before the advent of the computer this was probably the only effective way the Webbs had of managing their mass of material.

When Beatrice and Sidney first began the experiment of writing together their ideas sometimes clashed, but generally they 'were struck out in a continuous dualogue in which each was flint to the other's steel'.[43] The actual writing was done by Sidney in his large flowing hand, as Beatrice's handwriting was almost unreadable, and, as Francis Galton said, she disliked the labour. Beatrice's talent lay in the planning rather than the execution, in her ability to use abstract ideas, Sidney's in his phenomenal memory.[44] The disadvantage with this method was that Sidney put the dead stamp of his style upon the books, which sometimes read like the minutes of a committee meeting;

it needed Beatrice to recognise that the first chapter of the *History* 'lacks movement'[45] and to re-draft it.

When their first joint book was finished the Webbs realised that they had written a history, not an analysis of trade unionism. Beatrice fretted that they were becoming enmeshed in facts. 'Shall we have the intellectual grasp to rise superior to our material, or shall we be simply compilers and chroniclers?' she asked.[46] It was a question to which she was often to return. Barbed congratulations like those from Herbert Spencer, which refer to 'a very valuable accumulation of facts',[47] did nothing to allay her fears. Yet Spencer, who was to die in 1903, always failed to appreciate the originality of Beatrice's conception in seeking to chart the development of the trade union movement – something new and topical in the 1890s – or the 'intensity of purpose', which Mary Booth wryly noted, without which Beatrice would not have brought her masterpiece to its conclusion.[48]

Beatrice worried continually that her work was inferior in quality to that which she had done before her marriage, that she found it all a 'mechanical labour'.[49] When she and Sidney set themselves the immeasurably harder task of sociological analysis, moral judgement and even prophecy which make up *Industrial Democracy* she became even more discouraged. 'It is a horrid grind, this analysis – one sentence is exactly like another, the same words, the same construction, no relief in narrative,' she confided to her diary during a hot July in London in 1894, 'I sometimes despair of getting on with the book.'[50] Even when she and Sidney rented Borough Farm, near Godalming, for the summer and autumn, she found deductive thought elusive in the enervating Surrey climate; the dank mist hung over the heathland and woods, and Beatrice had trouble with her bowels. Determined to take her stomach in hand, she put herself on a strict diet, excluding fruit, sugar, alcohol and even most vegetables. 'I feel wonderfully better,' she wrote; it was the beginning of an ascetic regime which was to cause her dramatic weight loss.[51]

It was ironic that although *Industrial Democracy* was intended to be in part a criticism of the trade unions, 'for the good of the unionists!', it was also intended to be a defence of them for the enlightenment of the middle class,[52] yet simultaneously Beatrice and Sidney were becoming ever more estranged from the unionist leaders. Beatrice returned from the Trades Union Congress at Glasgow in 1892 and again at Cardiff in 1895 full of disillusion with the movement, sneering at Lady Dilke, the moving spirit behind the Women's Trade Union League, for entertaining trade union officials on a 'gross scale' to champagne lunches and dinners, and disgusted with the intrigues of John Burns which lay behind the development of the block vote. 'But all said and done, the labour movement has its seamy, I would say its disgusting side . . . and it is this side which is uppermost as a Trades Union Congress', was Beatrice's verdict.[53] It was a lost opportunity for Beatrice, who knew the trade union movement from the inside, and yet who could never succeed in overcoming her inherent class prejudice to see beyond the personal faults of the unionist leaders to their vision and potential.

Disillusion was Beatrice's predominant mood in 1894 to 1895 as she became caught up in election fever as a candidate for the Westminster Vestry elections,[54] turning Galton's study into the campaign headquarters, and was disappointed not to be elected. Only five Progressives were elected out of ninety-six. 'Apparently the slums of Westminster are as completely Tory as the palaces,' commented Beatrice. But the Vestry elections were unimportant compared to the London County Council elections in March 1895, and the issue of a Progressive victory took on an emotional edge for Beatrice as Sidney pitted his wits against Chamberlain, who led the Moderate campaign. 'Chamberlain is a nasty enemy and is going to make it a hot fight for us,' decided Beatrice,[55] irritated beyond measure by Keir Hardie for saying the Progressives were not Socialists, and advising the Independent Labour Party voters to spoil their papers. When a dead heat ensued, which the Progressives interpreted as a defeat after their earlier victories, she could hardly bear the chortling glee of the 'old gang' of anti-collectivist Liberals. Fortunately Sidney had hung on to his seat by a whisker.

Political disillusion mingled with regrets of another sort; Beatrice began to question the decision she had made when she married not to have a child. In 1892 she had felt she was probably too old to become pregnant: 'I had passed the age when it is easy and natural for a woman to become a child-bearer; my physical nature was to some extent dried up at thirty-five after ten years' stress and strain of a purely brain-working and sexless life.' It was a rational choice which, as she said, was made by many intellectual women who decided to forgo motherhood. Now, two years later, when her biological clock had ticked away more years and left her, she felt, without choices, she began to regret the swiftly-made decision. 'If I were again a young woman and had the choice between a brainworking profession or motherhood, I would not hesitate which life to choose (as it is, I sometimes wonder whether I had better not have risked it and taken my chance).'

Fundamental to Beatrice's decision had been her suspicion that her intellect had been honed into an analytical tool which motherhood would prevent her from using. But since marrying Sidney Beatrice had come increasingly to feel that her intellectual stamina was inferior to his, and to question her creative ability, which in reality was superior to his. 'I do not much believe in the productive power of woman's intellect,' she wrote, revealing the enduring legacy of Herbert Spencer's theory of women's arrested development, 'Strain herself as much as she may, the output is small and the ideas thin and wire-drawn from lack of matter and wide experience.'

Unhappy in her unfulfilled maternal instincts, Beatrice now idealised woman's nature and the state of motherhood. 'The woman's plenitude consists of that wonderful combination of tenderness and judgement which is the genius of motherhood, a plenitude springing from the very sources of her nature, not acquired or attained by outward training.' Regrets tumbled from her pen, as she wrote, 'First and foremost I should wish a woman I loved to be a mother . . . from the first I would impress on her the holiness of motherhood, its infinite superiority over any other occupation that a woman may take to.'[56] As Beatrice compared herself to her sisters, all of whom had large families apart from Kate Courtney, and visited her numerous nieces and nephews, it was natural that she felt the pangs of longing for a child. As her relationship with Sidney moved on from the 'showers of kisses'[57] of early married life, it was natural too to want to complete their love with a child. But she was influenced also by the resurgence of 'separate sphere' reasoning by many feminists which grew stronger towards the end of the century, and again claimed a special moral domain for women. Based on the idea and acceptance of sexual difference rather than its denial, the Enlightenment view that environment was responsible for the inequalities in the sexes was discarded; instead of challenging containment within the home as the earlier feminists had done, female Social Purity and Temperance campaigners began to stress the moral *superiority* of their sex.[58] As the century turned motherhood became increasingly romanticised, and the eugenics movement seemed to offer women a vital role as mothers of the race. Yet many eugenicists were often anti-feminists who stressed the maternal role to the exclusion of any other. Like many other socialists, Beatrice was beginning to believe in the mystique of motherhood and to deny, both for herself and the rest of her sex, the intellectual aspirations which she had felt so strongly in the previous decade.

The deep-rooted apprehension that the rigidly intellectual and political life which she had chosen was unsexing her, caused Beatrice to describe motherhood in unrealistic terms. 'To think of the many hours in each day which I idle and mope away simply because I can only work my tiny intellect for two or three hours at the most,' she wrote, with scant regard for truth, 'whereas I could be giving forth tenderness and judgement to my children hour after hour and day after day without effort or strain.'[59]

Beatrice felt a well of unexpressed love for the child she had never borne, and mourned the loss of the faculty of love which was sacrificed with the loss of the function of motherhood. These pensive thoughts led her to ponder 'the woman's question', and to voice her deep doubts at the movement for emancipation. 'We collectivists . . . do not believe that the cry for equal opportunities, a fair field and no favour, will bring woman her goal. If women are to compete with men . . . to vie with men in acquisition of riches, power or learning, then I believe they will harden and narrow themselves . . . And above all, to succeed in the struggle, they must forgo motherhood . . . And what shall we gain? Surely it is enough to have half the human race straining every nerve to outrun their fellows in the race for subsistence or power? Surely we need some human beings who will watch and pray, who will observe and inspire, and, above all, will guard and love all who are weak, unfit or distressed?' This conventional view of woman as passive, but morally and spiritually superior, was in some senses a denial of everything Beatrice had fought for, and illustrated the inner conflict her working life set up within her.[60]

Had Sidney been more than a 'loving comrade' to Beatrice, she might have been less frustrated by unrealised longings, but although she and Sidney had a limited physical relationship,[61] he never touched the springs of passion within her as Chamberlain would have done: a fact which explains why Beatrice continued to build 'castles in the air' about her old admirer, brooding over the charm he retained for 'one of his humbler fellows' every 29 July, the anniversary of the last Sunday they spent together at the Argoed.[62] Kate Courtney noticed approvingly that Beatrice had 'a softness of expression and manner which looks as if her feelings were engaged' when she married Sidney,[63] but it is more significant that Beatrice characterised Sidney's love as 'sublimely restful'[64] – perhaps the antithesis of passion – and in later years claimed that she married him partly out of pity.

Among the 'advanced' socialist and intellectual set of which the Webbs were part, contraception was freely available from doctors such as Elizabeth Garrett Anderson, who succeeded in placing her name on the British Medical Register in 1875. Alys Russell had a 'little penny pamphlet containing pictures and prices of half a dozen varieties of check, all safe and harmless, from one shilling to 2s 6d . . .'[65] But it is likely that Sidney and Beatrice came more and more to rely on abstinence than mechanical 'checks', although in the early days of their marriage there is evidence of Beatrice sitting in Sidney's lap, 'spooning', as she called it. Beatrice, like Alys Russell, saw marriage as an expression of spiritual love and fellowship, and sexual relations as an expression of lower, animal feelings whose purpose was the procreation of children. Although Beatrice would never have agreed with Acton, the influential doctor who claimed that a 'lady' had little sexual feeling, she may have been influenced by the arguments of Josephine Butler, who campaigned against the Contagious Diseases Acts, that birth control was immoral since it made sex available for pleasure alone. Even the 'free love' communities were against birth control and preferred self-restraint, arguing that a woman should have the right to say 'no' to her partner.[66]

If Beatrice could not have a flesh-and-blood child, she could sublimate her feelings in a child of another sort: the fledgling London School of Economics, which was to come into being as a result of the Webbs' vision. In July 1894 'Old Hutch', Henry Hutchinson, a Fabian solicitor, committed suicide, leaving £9000 to the Fabian Society for socialist propaganda; his wife was left only £100 a year, which Sidney arranged to double. When Beatrice and Sidney heard the news at Borough Farm, they quickly dismissed the opportunity to make 'a big political splash' by putting all the Fabian executive up for Parliament. The Independent Labour Party were already rolling the collectivist ball down the hill at a fair pace; what was needed was *hard thinking*, decided Beatrice.[67] And after the first evening by the fireside their plans were made. A new centre for original research should be set up, where Beatrice's dream of 'a science of society' could become a reality.

Sidney's first, characteristic, concern was to keep the bequest quiet. He and Constance Hutchinson were the sole executors and, with Pease, three of the five trustees empowered to administer the trust. Despite Shaw's demands to Beatrice that 'the collectivist flag must be waved' and there should be no pretence about 'pure' or abstract research which would breach the purpose of Hutchinson's bequest,[68] Sidney hid his plans from the rest of the Fabian Society, and used his chairmanship of the Technical Education Board to arrange a grant of £500 a year. When Graham Wallas declined to be the first director,

Sidney invited W. A. S. Hewins, a young don at Pembroke College, Oxford, whom they had met by chance in the Bodleian Library while researching trade unionism. Like the Webbs, Hewins disliked the Manchester School of Economics with its deductive reasoning, and agreed with Beatrice that, 'We are all wandering equally in the labyrinth, searching for the clue of true facts to bring us out on the right side of each particular problem.'[69]

Finding premises for the new London School of Economics and its library caused Webb endless worry, but at last 10 Adelphi Terrace, next door to the Statistical Society, fell vacant at a rent of £360 a year, and the trustees agreed to take it. Charlotte Payne Townshend proved a generous contributor; as Beatrice told Pease, 'She is a good Socialist ... the amount of her cheque showing the degree of her convictions.'[70] Having given £1000 to the Library, and endowed a woman's scholarship, Charlotte then took rooms over the school at Adelphi Terrace, which became the home of the Shaws once the playwright had married the heiress Charlotte Payne-Townshend in 1898. Sidney and Beatrice left no stone unturned in raising money for the library: Beatrice raked up all her old ball partners as contributors, and when Hewins fell ill with exhaustion, Sidney himself spent his mornings with painters and plumbers at the school, interviewing would-be students ready for the opening in October 1896.

Since the 'suicide' of the Independent Labour Party in the 1895 elections, Beatrice saw another important function for the London School of Economics and Political Science: to attract 'clever men from the universities' and permeate them with collectivism. Disenchanted with the 'dense' miners and the lumpen proletariat generally, she let it be known that promising students in economics would have a warm welcome at Grosvenor Road.[71] For the political wind was blowing against Radical Liberalism and an era ended with Gladstone's defeat in 1894. A successful intrigue by Haldane brought the aloof and ineffectual Lord Rosebery into power as his successor, but his short-lived premiership ended in defeat in June 1895, and the election which followed swept Lord Salisbury and the Conservatives back into power. Chamberlain coasted into office as Colonial Secretary, on the back of his little band of Unionists, much to Beatrice's disgust, exacerbated by Chamberlain's hostility to her brother-in-law Leonard Courtney, which deprived him of the chance of the Speakership.

Permeating the Radicals in Parliament and the Progressives in the London County Council, both natural bedfellows of the Fabians, was a policy which could be justified within the existing two-party system.

But, after the bad Progressive showing in the local elections, Beatrice and Sidney had stood aloof from the 1895 general election and kept their options open. Now it was time to re-group. The rout of the Independent Labour Party and the Liberals left them free to build up 'a new party on the basis of collectivism'.[72] 'The atmosphere of politics has to be transformed before the necessary revolution can be achieved,' wrote Sidney in justification of promiscuous permeation.

XVII

DIETS AND DOUBTS

'Are the books we have written together worth (to the community) the babies we might have had? Then again, I dream over the problem of whether one would marry the same man, in order to have babies, that one would select as a joint author?'
Beatrice Webb Diary, 24 April 1901

AT THE BEGINNING OF January 1898, Beatrice permitted herself a glow of pride. The Webbs' 'big book', *Industrial Democracy*, had been published and received a brilliant reception. Shoals of congratulatory letters arrived from their friends. It was time for a holiday after their two years of drudgery and, allowing the 'old Eve' in her to peep out at last, Beatrice decided to have a good 'go' at clothes, revelling in buying silks and satins, gloves, underclothes and furs, for their coming nine months' trip to America, New Zealand and Australia. Delighting in having pretty dresses made for her was 'rather comical in a woman of 40! 40 in all but two weeks – forty, forty, FORTY! – what an age, almost elderly! I don't feel a bit old,' she wrote.[1]

The 'Bo' family came to Euston station to see the Webbs off in March: as Wallas, Shaw, Pease, and Beatrice's sister Kate waved goodbye, Beatrice felt strangely triumphant. The London County Council election that month had resulted in the Moderates being soundly beaten by the Progressives, reversing the 1895 fiasco. The London School of Economics was emerging from an uncertain beginning to become the centre of economic teaching, and their books were, she was sure, the only original work in economics. On the crest of a Fabian wave, Beatrice turned her face to the New World.

It was unfortunate that she brought to her tour of the English-speaking world the prejudices of an upper-middle-class English-woman, and therefore found little to please her in the States. Like many of her compatriots the fact that Americans spoke English – albeit with a 'Yankee drawl' – misled Beatrice into judging her hosts harshly and superficially. In Washington Secretary Gage, the Principal Secretary of the Treasury, had 'that intolerable habit of some Americans of sparing you no word – every sentence being a dull paragraph out of the dullest and most elementary textbook'. He would make, wrote Beatrice, witheringly, 'a fairly good cashier'. Although the Republicans in the House of Representatives were quite respectable, the Democrats were 'heavy slouching men with long hair and big moustaches – a type unknown in England – ci-devant workmen with rough clothes and awkward manners, underdeveloped young men with narrow chests, low foreheads, red ties – what we should call "SDF" youths'. Beatrice often seemed to base her judgements on phrenology, perhaps influenced by Herbert Spencer's interest in the subject.

Yet she liked the wide, tree-lined streets of Washington, the open spaces, green lawns, beautiful public buildings, lack of traffic, the smartly-dressed American women and 'picturesque coloured folk'. Americans impressed her with their lack of that very snobbishness which was one of her own ingrained characteristics. Holding a strap in a crowded street car, you never felt snubbed or ignored, said Beatrice, and she was struck by the absence of brutality or coarseness, and the fresh-eyed, celibate and modest American youth who, unlike the English working class, seldom showed 'raw animalism'. Nevertheless, on balance she found the Americans, 'the most intelligent and the least intellectual of the white races', and America a dully uniform country where 'the tyranny of the stale platitude is maddening'.[2]

The Webbs and their companion, Charles Trevelyan, a Fabian from Cambridge University who was the younger brother of historian G. M. Trevelyan, stopped at Honolulu. Beatrice went surfing with Princess Kaiulani, and for once found it impossible to work among the waving cocoa palms. Sidney was less impressed: 'The island of Skye, with Kew Gardens let loose on the beach and the temperature of a hot house.' The Hawaiians had long since ceased to be Christian, the 'ever-present and urgent lasciviousness' of their nature causing them to break out in heathen orgies and intermarry with the missionaries.[3]

On reaching New Zealand, Beatrice found Auckland delightfully British, the macintoshed women with their swinging gait and general dowdiness reminding her of home. Food was cheap, only 10s 6d a day, but the 'thick common carpets' in the wooden houses with galvanised roofs seemed typical of the English lower-middle class. She and Sidney walked up Ngangataha mountain between the towering Kauri trees and tree ferns, and after visiting Wellington, Dunedin and Christchurch, decided it was delightful to be in a country where there were no millionaires and hardly any slums. 'If I had to bring up a family outside of Great Britain I would choose New Zealand as its home,' was Beatrice's verdict.[4]

By the time the Webbs reached Sydney they were tiring of their journey, finding 'only bad taste and cold indifference' in a city 'seemingly inhabited by a lower-middle-class population suddenly enriched, aggressive in manners and blatant in dress'. It was impossible for Beatrice to escape from her own class background, and to see Australians as other than the servant class, albeit in their own, but unpleasantly hot country. She demonstrated all the qualities of condescension which have made 'Poms' disliked, complaining that the Mayoress of Sydney called lunch 'dinner', dropped her 'H's' and was the quintessence of vulgarity.[5] The nadir of the visit was reached at the Melbourne Cup, where the Webbs mingled with the working men on the Flat before proceeding to the Governor's Box. 'I never saw an uglier crowd,' Beatrice wrote to her sister Mary. The rich women were in 'cheap silks and satins elaborately made: figures like town bred servants and no notion of how to walk or hold themselves'.[6] Yet Beatrice also sympathised with Australian women who, she noted, aged rapidly; the embryonic Women's College in Sydney University was struggling to raise funds, in the face of comments such as 'Let the women keep to the kitchen' from wealthy Australian men. 'The women of Australia are not her finest product,' was her tart conclusion.[7]

As usual, Beatrice preferred the men. In the States she had been impressed by 'the splendid fighting courage' of Theodore Roosevelt, whom she considered the most remarkable man in America.[8] In Sydney she was impressed by the Premier of New South Wales, George Reid, 'a rattling good parliamentary leader' despite his dirty, ill-fitting clothes.

It was with relief that she and Sidney left the colourless gum trees and formless hills of Australia to drift home through the Indian Ocean. Despite examining so many representative assemblies and visiting statesmen in three countries, they were no nearer understanding the white colonies than when they had left.

They returned to a national mood of euphoric imperialism. Beatrice had commented that the crowds were 'drunk' with hysterical loyalty at the time of Victoria's Diamond Jubilee in 1897; Beatrice herself had attended a select Jubilee Dinner organised by Mrs Humphrey Ward at which one hundred distinguished women had entertained one hundred distinguished men, supplying some women factory inspectors to fill up the gaps, as it had proved hard to find enough women who deserved the epithet 'distinguished', while many men who thought themselves to be so had been offended at not being invited. Imperialism had come sharply into focus since the appointment of Chamberlain to the position of Colonial Secretary by Lord Salisbury in June 1895. Chamberlain had long coveted the post, having been refused it by Gladstone with crushing irony – 'Oh! A Secretary of State' – in 1886.[9] Now at last his ambition was fulfilled; even though the Colonial Office was not regarded as a front-ranking Cabinet post, and A. J. Balfour, Salisbury's nephew and leader of the House of Commons, assured Chamberlain that 'the whole field' was open to him,[10] Chamberlain chose to place his hand on the tiller of the Empire which covered one quarter of the world's surface.

Instantly the department was galvanised into movement: 'The sleeping city awakened by a touch,' said one lady journalist. The new chief sat at his desk, a large globe beside him, working with cool efficiency on his papers; as he finished each dispatch he would give the table-bell a ring and announce: 'The machine is ready to take some more.' The previous Minister had been nicknamed 'Peter Woggy' but Chamberlain showed at once where his sympathies lay. 'I believe that the British race is the greatest of governing races that the world has ever seen,' he declared. Yet the imperial dream needed sustaining and cherishing: 'That empire . . . hangs together by a thread so slender that it may well seem that even a breath would sever it . . .' he said of the Durban to Johannesburg railway link, which was part of Cecil Rhodes's vision of a Cape to Cairo railway which would enable trade to follow the flag. There was fresh paint on the Ministry walls and electric light in place of candles, to symbolise the new aggression with which imperial interests would be pursued.[11]

Beatrice had always suspected that Chamberlain was an unprincipled opportunist, and the Jameson Raid at last proved her correct. Cecil Rhodes, Governor of Cape Colony since 1890 and the founder of Rhodesia, was determined to wrest the gold-rich Transvaal from its president, Paul Kruger, and bring it under the Union Jack. In the Transvaal the Uitlanders were demanding civil rights, which Kruger denied them as he was determined to maintain Afrikaaner independence. The threatened Uitlander rising tempted Rhodes to make a premature strike into the Transvaal, but the raid, launched by his friend Dr Jameson on 31 December 1895, proved a dismal failure. Rhodes was forced to resign and it was soon whispered that Chamberlain was implicated in the conspiracy.

Beatrice's first reaction to Chamberlain's handling of the South Africa crisis was uncritical admiration. 'The occasion has found the man. Joe Chamberlain is today the National Hero,' she enthused, praising his swiftness, courage and strong will which gave the nation confidence.[12] When the Inquiry into the raid opened in July 1896 political ruin stared 'Joseph Africanus' in the face. 'I don't care a twopenny damn for the whole lot of them; but if they put me with my back to the wall, they'll see some splinters,' Chamberlain growled defiantly.[13] But at the Inquiry – called the 'Lying in State' – Rhodes was whitewashed although he was forced to resign as Cape Premier and Chairman of the Chartered Company. Chamberlain was exonerated from any complicity in the affair, although the 'missing telegrams' from Rhodes's agent in London were evidence that the Colonial Secretary was guilty of at least some collusion.[14] Sidney and Leonard Courtney blamed Chamberlain, but Beatrice shyed away from condemning him, although she acknowledged that he showed the same coarse indifference to Boer feelings which he had once shown to her own. She marvelled at the adroit charm and quick wit with which he wriggled off the hook, calling Rhodes, who had so lamentably failed to 'fix it' for him, a 'fine fellow'. A scapegoat was found, Sir Graham Bower, Imperial Secretary at the Cape who had handled the negotiations with the plotters, and who agreed to be sacrificed.[15]

Further patriotic feeling rallied behind Jameson and Chamberlain when the Kaiser, Queen Victoria's grandson Willy, sent a congratulatory telegram to Kruger. As Oom Paul, seventy-year-old veteran of the Great Trek, re-armed, ordering thirty-seven thousand Mausers from Krupp's, Sir Alfred Milner, Balliol scholar, ex-suitor of Margot Tennant and an advocate of 'race patriotism', arrived in the Cape as the High Commissioner and Governor. It was soon apparent to Milner, as to Chamberlain, that he who controlled the Transvaal, the richest and most populous state, controlled South Africa; and the struggle for South Africa was part of a much larger struggle for world supremacy. If the Anglo-Saxon race were to rule the world – and this was Britain's imperial mission in the eyes of Chamberlain and Milner – then Kruger, that 'ignorant, dirty, cunning' old man who had united the volk against the *rooineks* [rednecks or English], must be crushed.[16]

By 9 October 1899 the Boers had been manoeuvred into issuing an ultimatum, and British public opinion had been supposedly 'softened up' by Milner and Chamberlain. Imperialism was eagerly embraced by the upper classes[17] and had its counterpart in music-hall jingoism, which brought colour and a sense of significance into the drab lives of ordinary Victorian people. The idea of empire was explained in simple terms in newspapers such as the *Daily Mail*, 'We send out a boy here and a boy there, and the boy takes hold of the savages of the part he comes to, and teaches them to march and shoot as he tells them, to obey him and believe in him and die for him and the Queen. A plain, stupid uninspired people, they call us, and yet we are doing this with every kind of savage man there is.'[18]

'Joe's War', as it was popularly called, divided society. Chamberlain's name was on every lip and in every newspaper; 'Empire-builder-in-Chief' Henry Asquith called him, while at the Colonial Office he was 'the Master'. Beatrice, unwilling to believe her hero had feet of clay, yet unhappily conscious that his provocative talk had caused the war, was 'a prey to an involved combination of bias and counter-bias'. She imagined the life she might have had as Chamberlain's wife: 'I should have hardened and coarsened if I had been subject to the strain of a big flashy social position. The sweet little thing he has chosen is far better suited to be his wife . . .'[19] Her protests were unconvincing.

If the war had at first seemed a laughably unequal struggle between a great empire and a small, primitive nation, the success of the Boer commandos against the lumbering British troops soon corrected this impression. The war was 'a mad mistake', wrote Beatrice to her sister Mary during 'Black Week' in December 1899. 'What a ghastly business it is – what a fiasco of ignorance. Of course we have got to beat them, but I imagine we shall be feeling sick of it before we have finished . . . It is rather humiliating for the Empire to be engaged in fighting a population not larger than Brighton! Everybody in London is very sick – even the newsboys have lost their lungs for crying "British Reverses" – and stand mournfully silent. Personally I think it folly in ever allowing the Boers to arm so thoroughly . . .'[20]

By the end of January the war was a 'nightmare' to Beatrice. 'The Boers are, man for man, our superiors in dignity, devotion and capacity – yes, in *capacity*.' Could we take a beating and benefit from it, she wondered. Britain was wealthy, the middle class materialistic, the working class stupid and the intelligentsia sceptical. But if it won the war, would it learn any lessons, or would English gentlemen soon be boasting that they had 'muddled through'?[21]

Despite Beatrice's admiration for the Boers, family and class loyalty exerted a stronger pull. Mary Playne's son Bill was soon to embark for the Cape, and Beatrice passed on all the political gossip: people were saying that Wolseley had 'incipient softening of the brain' and forgot vital information; that he and Lansdowne were not on speaking terms; that Milner had sent in his resignation unless Sir Redvers Buller, the bumbling Commander in Chief of the British forces, was recalled; that Chamberlain had threatened to resign unless the government supported Milner . . .'[22] Mary meanwhile was supporting the Gloucestershire Yeomanry who embarked from Liverpool in February, after recovering from influenza which had run through both men and horses. The gentlemen behaved excellently, Mary told Beatrice, and even the tradesmen 'who hate fighting' had contributed generously.[23] But while Mary planned a summer garden party for the relations of the Gloucester yeomen, Lallie was 'ashamed of England'.

The war did not only disrupt the Potter sisterhood, it split the Fabians and divided the Liberal party into fragments. In 1900 Ramsay MacDonald, who, like other Independent Labour Party socialists, agreed with J. A. Hobson that the war was a capitalist intrigue, left the Fabian Society in disgust.[24] Already irritated that the Webbs did not consider that he had done enough original work to lecture at the London School of Economics, he accused them of being traitors to the socialist cause.[25] Although the Webbs were seeing much of the Courtneys, who were socially ostracised because of Leonard's pro-Boer stance (indeed Sidney himself was pro-Boer), at this point they made an error of judgement which was to have profound consequences: they became Richard Haldane's puppets, following him into the political grouping known as the 'Limps' or Liberal Imperialists, and abandoning the pro- Boer Radical group of Campbell-Bannerman, Harcourt and Morley.[26]

Haldane's affable exterior and 'pawky humour' hid an inner loneliness after he was jilted by Valerie Munro-Ferguson, and he remained a confirmed bachelor. Cheated of family life, he spent his talents in manipulating his friends, exhibiting what Beatrice called 'a dilettante desire to be in every set'.[27] It amused Haldane to bring the Webbs and the Limps together at the moment Sidney lost his awkward, slightly insolent aggression and became more socially adept. His improved manner was due to happiness, 'To the blessed fact of loving and being loved with a love without flaw or blemish,' as Beatrice put it.[28] By 1899 Sidney and Beatrice were ready to leave behind the intellectual proletariat and 'drift upwards' in society.

On the night of the debate on the Jameson Raid, at which Chamberlain 'hissed like a snake' at his victim Courtney,[29] Haldane gave a dinner party for, among others, Lord Curzon, the Asquiths, John Morley, and Lady Rothschild whose husband, Nathan, had become treasurer of the London School of Economics. Beatrice was so pleased to be asked that she copied the table plan into her diary.[30] It was only the beginning. In the spring of 1900 Haldane again asked the Webbs to dinner to meet Arthur Philip Primrose, 5th Earl of Rosebery, and his fellow Limps. Beatrice was seated next to the ex-premier, who did his best to change the seating, to no avail. Beatrice put herself out to be pleasant, although she objected to Rosebery's egotism. He looked better than when he was premier, having lost 'that drugged look, heavy eyes and morbid flesh', and by the end of dinner Beatrice had made another conquest. 'Don't tell the world of this new intrigue of Haldane's,' Rosebery called out to Sir Edward Grey as he hurried off to court, and winked at Beatrice. For it *was* a new intrigue, as Beatrice realised: Haldane was putting together an anti-little-England group which crossed party lines.[31]

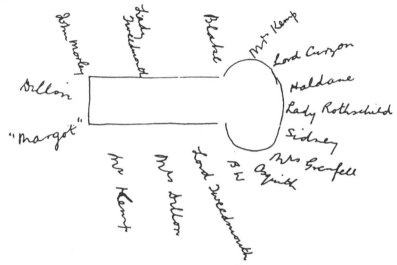

'England is governed by cliques of friends and acquaintances,' wrote Beatrice, justifying her behaviour. 'If you are inside the clique you help to rule: if you are outside you cry in the wilderness.'[32] She was reverting to the social milieu of her youth. Unwisely dismissing Campbell-Bannerman, whom she also met in 1900, as a 'quite stupid person',[33] Beatrice did nothing to prevent Sidney attending a Limp dinner held after the October 1900 'Khaki' election in which the Conservatives had increased their majority. Pressed hard by Haldane to go, Sidney was on the horns of a dilemma. He loathed the war, now in its 'guerrilla' phase in which Kitchener was herding the Boers into concentration camps, was afraid of becoming unpopular with the Radicals, but was loyal to his friend. 'It is not my show,' he told Beatrice miserably, for the Webbs had no expertise in foreign affairs. Thinking, foolishly, that his going or not did not much matter, Sidney went – and lost his reputation.[34]

* * *

The Webbs and Haldane were subject to a mutual delusion: firstly that Rosebery would prove an effective leader of the Limps, and secondly that he could be persuaded to accept Fabian ideas. No one was more convinced that the earl was a fit subject for socialist permeation than Shaw. 'Our policy is clearly to back him for all we are worth,' he told Beatrice,[35] urging Sidney to write a magazine article about it. 'I would do it myself if my reputation were of a nature to help Rosebery. But it isn't; and Webb's is.' When Sidney hesitated Shaw told him he was talking 'middle-aged dry rot' and, unlike Shaw, with his 'accursed talent for pure literature', was 'the free-est man in England', the only one with the singleness of purpose to write the article. If Beatrice had not walked out of Ibsen's play (she had recently taken Mrs Green to *Peer Gynt*) because she disliked the playwright's views on the emancipation of women, she would have learnt that the pillars of society were only the tools of society. 'Rosebery, being a peer and a political pillar, is necessarily a political tool. He is at present screaming for somebody to come and handle him, exactly like the madman in *Peer Gynt* who thinks he is a pen and implores people to write with him . . . Your strength has always lain in your willingness and your capacity to be the tool wielder . . . You are married to the only woman in England who dare ask Rosebery to dinner and ask him whether he will take beer or whiskey. That is a tremendously strong position . . .'[36]

If Sidney would only put his fingers to the keyboard, pleaded Shaw, Rosebery would become the Pied Piper which the children (meaning the British public) would follow, for now the time was ripe for Rosebery to reconstruct the Liberal Party on the basis of Collectivism. By such flattery Shaw persuaded Sidney to become the tool-wielder, and Sidney who, as Beatrice knew, disliked the personal struggle for leadership, and took the line of least resistance for the cause he believed in at whatever cost to his own reputation and advancement, agreed.[37] But at this point Shaw was even more out of touch with political reality than the Webbs, for while they were in the States his foot had swelled up to the size of Beatrice's 'largest cat . . . All the anguish would have been averted if you had stayed home to take care of your family',[38] he told her reproachfully. In her absence he had to deliver himself over to the knife and the ether bag in the shape of a surgeon who diagnosed bone necrosis. When Charlotte returned from Rome, where she had gone in a huff because Shaw had not proposed, she 'was the inevitable and predestined agent appointed by Destiny'. Shaw found his objection to marriage had vanished with his objection to his own death, and he hopped down to the Registrar who married him to Charlotte on one leg.[39] But when Charlotte took a house at Hindhead for Shaw's convalescence, he fell downstairs on his crutches and broke his arm, which Charlotte splinted with butter pats until the doctor came. Further operations followed, and Shaw proved a bad patient. As Charlotte said, 'It is a trying thing to be married to a Sprite, but a Sprite with necrosis is the devil.'[40]

Nevertheless, Sidney did the Sprite's bidding, writing a provocative call to arms to Rosebery, entitled 'Lord Rosebery's Escape from Houndsditch'. Ghosted by Shaw from Studland Rectory, where he was dallying with Charlotte, it compared the Liberals to worn-out tailors, claiming that Campbell-Bannerman was still 'piecing together Gladstonian rags and remnants, with Sir William Harcourt wielding the scissors and Mr John Morley unctuously waxing the thread . . . Lord Rosebery is the only person who had turned his back on Houndsditch [the centre of the tailoring trade] and called for a complete new outfit'. As the Fabians knew, the socialist boom of 1885 to 1892 had collapsed to be succeeded by an imperialist boom, but, pleaded Sidney, what was the use of Empire if at its core was the submerged fifth, that stunted, demoralised mass, of eight million people living on less than £1 a week, who were unfit to breed the imperial race? Our horses were better housed, washed, and watered than our poor, he thundered, and unless every manual worker had a minimum standard of education, sanitation, leisure and wages, England could not raise an efficient army. Three rooms and a scullery was 'the minimum necessary for breeding an even moderately imperial race'.[41] The explicit link made by Sidney between imperialism and social reform was not new, but not until the 1906 Liberal landslide was it to result in policy changes.

Rosebery sent smooth congratulations to Beatrice, joking, 'I hope you will keep Webb out of London or have him protected by the police. For his life can hardly be safe since the publication of his article . . .'[42] Kate Courtney poured cold water over Beatrice and Sidney's 'Cobwebbery', writing that Leonard did not think 'you will catch that bird effectively at all . . . I think you will want a more inspiring and inspired personality than Lord Rosebery to draw them [the imperialists] into your net'. It was not a simple world, cautioned Kate, 'Rosebery's vanity is considerable and he will not be cajoled into being your Prime Minister.'[43]

The sensation made by 'Lord Rosebery's Escape' made it all the more vital for Beatrice to at last allow Sidney to enter Parliament, urged Haldane. 'Sidney and you would bring in a new expert element . . . Think this over seriously please.'[44] But Beatrice, even though she kept tucked in her diary an article from the *New Age* entitled 'Men Who Ought to Be in Parliament: Sidney Webb', refused point blank. Reluctantly Haldane accepted her decision '*for the present*', protesting that Sidney must come in soon to direct his own programme of efficiency at the Local Government Board or in the Education Office.

Never had Beatrice felt less able to spare Sidney for public office, for during 1900 and 1901 she was experiencing severe depression. Nine years of marriage to Sidney produced a mental crisis in which frustrated sexual longings and guilt mingled to produce psychosomatic physical symptoms; she fantasised constantly, unable to work on the book on local government which she had started with high hopes in 1899. 'The one subject my mind revolts at is local government,' she confessed in 1901.[45] Beatrice was depressed by the death of her friends Cary Darling and Mandell Creighton, Bishop of London, and the falling away of old friendships in middle age. When she and Sidney had suggested cycling over from Leicester to see the Booths at Gracedieu, 'I was peremptorily put off, I think with some incivility, for they knew we were in lodgings for over a fortnight in broiling hot weather a few miles from their gates and they did not ask us even to lunch!'[46] Beatrice was unaware of the impression she and Sidney made on other people: 'Very clever, very conceited, very full of energy and life. Altogether a good spurring cold-water bath,' was how her sister Maggie put it, complaining that the Webbs made her feel inferior.[47] Perhaps Audrey Wallas and Charlotte Shaw shared this impression: Beatrice was conscious that neither of them liked her very much.

Beatrice's career flourished, although she was putting less effort into it than ever before. Still opposed to the 'screeching sisterhood', she was also writing a book on factory legislation as a counterblast to the Women's Rights Movement, lecturing at the London School of Economics (which now had university status after the Webbs had 'packed' the University Commission), as well as at Oxford and Birmingham universities, and was ruthlessly interviewing local government officials who were much easier to manipulate without Sidney quibbling at her tricks of the trade. As a 'religious agnostic' she had stood up for her principles at the meetings of the National Union of Women Workers, of which Louise Creighton was president, and demanded that there should be no Anglican prayers before meetings in deference to the feelings of agnostics, Catholics and Jews.

Yet her busy life was no protection against feelings which threatened to overwhelm her. As early as June 1899 she was feeling depressed after smoking her evening cigarette, 'castle-building' about the past, until she felt she was losing self-control. By May 1900 'foolish day-dreams based on self-consciousness and personal vanity' were preventing her working. It was no accident that these feelings coincided with the onset of the Boer War. 'I have been struggling with a terrible depression. It may be that I am not physically well,' she wrote in her diary in October 1900.

The event which triggered the downward spiral was a disturbing meeting with Chamberlain that summer on the terrace of the House of Commons, her first for thirteen years. As Beatrice stood with Haldane awaiting the last of his guests, the Colonial Minister strolled on to the terrace; their eyes met, and Beatrice stepped quickly forward and introduced Sidney. 'I think you were in MY office,' remarked Chamberlain with kind condescension. 'That is hardly quite correct: when I was there YOU were not,' replied Sidney quickly. It sounded gauche, even rude, although Sidney meant to say that he had not the honour of serving under Chamberlain.

After five minutes' conversation, during which Haldane and his guests watched Beatrice's every move, they separated to dine. But as Haldane's party sat out again on the terrace afterwards, Chamberlain noiselessly joined them and sat beside Beatrice in the summer twilight. For an hour they talked – America, Birmingham, even economics. 'He looked wan and tired: he was uncertain of himself and obviously anxious to be gentle and kind towards me,' recorded Beatrice. At last the strain of making conversation under the gaze of so many watchful eyes became too much, and she rose to leave. 'Mrs Webb is terminating the interview,' remarked a female guest to Sidney, and Chamberlain grasped Beatrice's hand and hurried away.[48]

Beatrice's old phantoms came back to haunt her, and she found it impossible to bury her feelings for the man 'I loved, loved but could not follow'. In October Massingham let drop a rumour that Chamberlain's wife had left him, and was travelling alone on the Continent. 'How very terrible,' said Beatrice. 'I thought they were so fond of each other.' From that moment her depression was intensified; she was disabled by the thought of Chamberlain's misery, although she knew she had her own life to lead. 'But oh! the pity of it! . . . And to think that I am over forty, and he is over sixty! What an absurdity!'[49]

Beatrice's 'cursed imagination' led her to fear that Chamberlain was being brutal to his wife; alternatively, that people were blaming her for his separation from his wife. All November she anxiously scanned the newspapers, feeling remorse for keeping in touch with Chamberlain's sister, Clara Ryland, and his daughter, Beatrice. Saddened by the news that Leonard had lost his seat in Parliament for standing out against the imperialist tide of sentiment sweeping the country, she went down to Margate to nurse her brother-in-law, Alfred Cripps, the 'little jewel of an advocate', as Richard Potter used to call him. Alfred was 'running on to the shoals of a degenerate melancholia',[50] as he explained to Beatrice, feeling more than ever the loss of Theresa, who had died of diphtheria in 1893, and was mortified not to have been appointed Solicitor-General. Beatrice was fond of Alfred, with whom she had spent many Christmases at Parmoor, although she considered him 'a hypochondriacal wreck'. Alfred too was attached to Beatrice, thanking his 'dear mental physician' for being 'so sweet';[51] clearly he enjoyed her visits more than Georgie's, and begged Beatrice to keep her promise to see him again if he stayed out his month in Margate. Alfred was just one among the many men who found Beatrice an attractive and amusing woman, and with whom she enjoyed flirtatious banter; this was especially so when she found herself the only woman at a masculine dinner, as she did again in February when she sat beside Rosebery at an intimate 'Limp' dinner, surrounded by Haldane, Asquith, Hewins, and 'we talked, laughed, "showed off" '.[52]

Moving upwards in society made Beatrice more than ever conscious of her sex appeal, while it intensified the guilty pleasure she felt at rubbing shoulders with the great. Her inner conflicts became inescapable. Early in 1901 again she raked over the embers of her old desire for Chamberlain, those days when she was young and 'ripe for love' but so dogmatic an individualist that she could not appreciate his passionate desire for reform; 'I was left bleeding and wounded while he departed to seek more attractive metal.' Perhaps she owed him a debt, she mused, for he absorbed the whole of her sexual feelings, although she saw him at rare intervals and loved him through the imagination. Thus the affair had left her free to develop her career until at last she met Sidney. From the first meeting she had realised he would fall in love with her. That he stimulated neither her physical passion nor her social ambition had seemed a plus, and so she had married him, partly from pity because his love seemed so overpowering, partly because they shared a moral aim, and partly as a cold-blooded investment for the sake of the community. And it had been a good decision . . . yet still Beatrice wondered 'whether I have been dutiful to the community in shirking motherhood, whether in point of fact I have not lost at once a safety valve for feeling and a valuable experience'.[53]

That Easter Beatrice and Sidney took a thatched cottage at West Lulworth in Dorset, spending their mornings on 'the book' and their afternoons on a regulation two-hour walk. Sidney read twenty-six books, while Beatrice brooded. At last the weather turned hot, and while Sidney was in London Beatrice abandoned herself to sensation; the sea was 'sapphire, amethyst, emerald, moonstone – the white chalk cliff rising out of it in mysterious lines of white, pink, grey'. She lay in the sun, listening to the suck of the waves, the sound of the gulls: 'The music of that slow withdrawing of the ocean swell from the pebbled beach, a sound of infinite sweetness and sadness, like the inevitable withdrawal of a lover from a mistress he loves; the bubbling and gurgling of the tide in the caves of the rocks beneath me, the spirit of children not yet born to life . . .'[54]

The truth was that although Beatrice frequently asserted that life with 'her boy' was like a honeymoon, the contrast between him and Chamberlain was becoming increasingly painful; Sidney did not excite her sexually, nor was he a leader, in contrast to the still handsome and harshly dynamic Colonial Secretary who was the man of the hour after the Conservative victory in the Khaki election. Beatrice mooned away the summer at Friday's Hill with the Bertrand Russells, full of admiration for the mathematician's 'fine chopping logic' and the puritanical routine of work, lunch, croquet and work, which so well accorded with the Webbs' own chosen way of life. 'They sleep and dress in the same room,' she noted with interest, 'and they have no children.'[55] She found this latter fact a comfort.

By October Beatrice's depression was breaking out into physical symptoms of constant tiredness, nausea and a total incapacity to concentrate or control her feelings. She began to be obsessed by a presentiment of her own death, crying herself to sleep. She was convinced that she had a fatal illness, and was troubled by acute eczema all over her body and particularly her ears. But help of a sort was at hand: at Bradford Beatrice met Dr Andrea Rabagliati, a believer in alternative medicine and author of *Air, Food and Exercise*. Enthusiastically he described how cancer, influenza, pneumonia and almost all modern diseases could be cured by diet. 'How much ought a woman to eat who is over forty years of age, weighs 8 stone 11 lbs, height 5 ft 6 ins, and who is a brainworker?' enquired Beatrice. Three-quarters of a pound or at most one pound in twenty-four hours, taken twice a day, the doctor told her.[56]

Eagerly Beatrice began the experiment, eating four ounces at 8 a.m., six ounces at 1.30 p.m. and six at 7.30 dinner. She drank a small cup of tea without milk or sugar at 7 a.m., another at 4.30 p.m., and a cup of black coffee at night. With meals she took hot water. After breakfast she ate no other starchy food, substituting meat, green vegetables and fruit. 'If only I can have a steadfast mind in a healthy body my life will approach the ideal,' she wrote. 'Abstinence and prayer may prove to be the narrow way to salvation in this world – at least for me.'

Every Monday morning Beatrice went to Charing Cross station to weigh herself, and by November found her weight was dropping. Although she was less troubled by flatulence and indigestion, she was sleeping badly, still bothered by eczema and was feeling muddle-headed. She wrote to Andrea Rabagliati, who assured her that English people could add fifteen years to their lives by following his diet. 'I believe people think I am crazy,' he told Beatrice, but 'I have revolutionised my own health.' Beatrice could cure her 'old enemy' eczema by a few weeks of a diet of milk and soup. In the meantime he prescribed some mercury ointment, which Beatrice soon complained made her mouth, gums and teeth sore. Rabagliati warned his patient that even when she got on the right food-lines, she would still have an attack or two of her old maladies. 'Nature is eliminating the waste matters with which the blood is loaded . . . the eliminating process is a very trying one.'[57]

By November Beatrice was 'an emaciated white creature, unfit for play or work', with a very sore mouth.[58] She was overcome with apathy, worrying that her urine was 'muddy', which she supposed meant the waste products were still not eliminated. 'I do not want you getting too thin; as perhaps you will if you diminish the starch too much,' wrote Rabagliati with concern, urging her to take two ounces of rice, sago or tapioca pudding during the day. Yet since he told her that it was excess starch which caused her eczema, it is hardly surprising that Beatrice was reducing it from her diet.[59] By mid-November her weight had dropped to just over eight stone. Unable to work, Beatrice had been staying with the Playnes, first at Freshwater in the Isle of Wight, then at Longfords where she found Mary's cheerful commonsense restful. But although her eczema was improved, her monthly period was late and she felt weak and insomniac.

Eczema is a stress disorder which in Beatrice's case had worsened because she was denying the physical feelings which rose unbidden to the surface under the stimulus of meeting Chamberlain face to face.

Controlling her diet became a means of controlling unwelcome urges. 'Until I took to the rigid diet, the sensual side of my nature seemed to be growing at the expense of the intellectual,' she wrote in December 1901. Sensuality was intensified by 'a real or imaginary increased personal attractiveness typified by the admiration which I thought I had or had actually excited in the minds of some prominent personages . . .' Beatrice kept this 'ridiculous business' secret from Sidney, but her senses were heightened by the attentions of an admirer or admirers. There are references to an unspecified episode which upset her. Earlier Beatrice had referred to the 'magnetic effect' she had on men,[60] but the consciousness of being 'grizzled, wrinkled and over forty' led her to view her feelings as ridiculous.

Anorexia was Beatrice's response to temptation. By starving her body she gained 'complete control over my thoughts and feelings'.[61] Anorexia was also a cry for attention, but Sidney did not respond. He neither noticed Beatrice's flirtations with other men, nor her depression. Intensely involved in the building up of the London School of Economics, no detail of which escaped him from the number of student lockers to the inventory of library furniture, supremo in the University Senate and Technical Education Board, Sidney was in an intoxicatingly powerful position. 'No one can resist him,' wrote Beatrice. 'He knows every rope and has quick and immediate access to every person of influence.'[62] Again and again she wondered whether this 'wire-pulling' was quite wholesome, complaining that she would rather win by hard work than through 'these capricious gusts of fancy in great folk. I feel that I am skating on rotten ice which might suddenly give way.'[63] Spasms of guilt seized her, but, like Sidney, she enjoyed wire-pulling too much to give it up.

By 1902 Beatrice had adopted an ascetic eating regime which left her 'cool and sensible'. She had conquered sensuality. 'I am far too thin (only 8 stone),' she wrote, her eczema lingered on and she felt weak; but she continued for the rest of her life to eat little.[64] In the summer she decided her eczema was due to drinking coffee, which was 'rank poison', and began to try to omit it, together with tea and tobacco. By the end of 1903 she informed her sister Georgie, who had sent her some pheasants, that she was 'a rigid anti-flesh-fish-egg-alco-hol-coffee-and-sugar eater', and had never been in better health.[65] Sidney, somewhat unwillingly, also became a vegetarian.

Although Beatrice emerged from her mid-life crisis to find new equanimity with Sidney, she confessed on their tenth wedding anniversary to a sense of permanent melancholy which lay in the background of their unique comradeship.[66] She was Sidney's 'devoted wifsey', but after 1902 she showed more tolerance and understanding to her family in their own misfortune. Beatrice had been particularly censorious towards Rosy, who after the death of Dyson Williams had appeared to Mary and Beatrice to be leading an immoral life. Fearing that Rosy might be pregnant, and would shame the family with an illegitimate baby, Beatrice went to visit her and found Rosy 'in one of her naughty humours'. Although the matron assured Beatrice that Rosy was not pregnant, 'I should not be in the least surprised if she were,' Beatrice told Mary. 'She is not likely to "keep straight" if she does not get married. I am not sure that *sanity and celibacy* are both within her capacity.' Grimly she told Rosy that 'the family would drop her if she behaved improperly and that she would find life unendurable if she was cut by every responsible person'. Innocently Rosy assured Beatrice that she was 'the best and purest of women'. After Rosy married George Dobbs in February 1899, Beatrice still considered her mad or bad or both, until her own depression softened her arrogance and left her with a sense of humiliation. After 1901 Beatrice's relations with Rosy improved.

In 1905 Beatrice's sister Blanche committed suicide. For months Blanche had struggled with suicidal thoughts, and had tried once to strangle herself, after her husband Willie fell in love with an Italian singer, Julia Ravogli. Blanche had long been unstable, finding consolation in painting huge canvases, several at a time being set about in their Argyllshire garden. In June she hanged herself from the shower.

Depression was not the monopoly of the Potters; during 1902 no one needed Beatrice more than Alys Russell, whose ideal marriage, as it had seemed to Beatrice, began to disintegrate. Bertrand Russell, who confessed in a passage he later deleted from his *Autobiography*, that 'it is not in my nature to remain physically fond of any woman for more than seven or eight years',[67] had fallen under the spell of Evelyn Whitehead, the friend of a colleague. He went out bicycling one afternoon, and suddenly realised he no longer loved Alys; on his return he bluntly told her so. Alys fell into a state of nervous collapse. Beatrice, always good, if overpowering, to her friends, suspected the marriage was in difficulties and suggested a holiday in Switzerland. At first Alys was reluctant to be closeted with Beatrice for three weeks with nothing to do but talk about food and the novels of H. G. Wells (the Webbs' and Wallas's new protégé) but in July the pair left for Monte Generosa. Beatrice was keen to instil 'useful mental hygiene'[68] into Alys, but her companion, who constantly broke down in tears, did not confide in her and was conscious that Beatrice was homesick for Sidney. It was not a happy holiday.[69]

Beatrice returned to find the Webbs' enemies gathering. Although early in 1902 she had recorded that 'we are at present very thick with the "Limps" ',[70] she was becoming disillusioned with the clique's 'limpness': Rosebery remained an enigma, 'Pretty Fanny' Asquith was wooden and spent all his energy on his law cases, Grey was just a stick for someone else to use; and their wives were no better. Margot Asquith was only interested in hunting and society, Lady Grey, like the Munro-Fergusons, merely a pleasant aristocrat. Why were they in this galley, wondered Beatrice. The answer was unpalatable, but obvious: because they preferred the company of the Limps to the 'hardworking little "cads" ' among the Progressives, and because their policies and those of the Radicals had deviated so that no common ground existed. But as the Conservative government drifted towards the end of its life in the early years of the twentieth century, Beatrice and Sidney began cultivating the 'Divine Arthur', Lord Salisbury's nephew A. J. Balfour, who had succeeded his uncle as Prime Minister in July 1902.

Beatrice was first struck by Balfour's urbane charm in the autumn of 1902, when she was introduced to him by Lady Elcho, a member of 'The Souls'. At dinner at Mrs Horner's, the set's 'high priestess', a further social triumph awaited Beatrice. 'I took the Prime Minister in to dinner!' she exclaimed to her diary. Balfour fascinated Beatrice, who found him 'a man of extraordinary "grace" of mind and body',[71] although a strange paradox as Prime Minister, since he avoided social and economic questions, delighting instead in parrying epigrams with Beatrice on music, literature and philosophy. The social merry-go-round whirled faster and faster, as Beatrice gave a 'thrilling' dinner for Lady Elcho, deftly mixing guests from different social strata: John Burns injected an element of social realism into a party which included Shaw and Asquith. In August 1902 Edward VII had been crowned, and society dedicated itself to pleasure with a new singlemindedness made possible by cheap servants, royal example, and the frenzy of a class whose way of life was soon to vanish for ever. Beatrice gave three dinner parties and two evening parties in eight days at Grosvenor Road, with only two living-in servants, hiring extra waitresses when necessary.

Never had Beatrice's social skills been more necessary, or more purposeful, for Sidney was in the thick of a dogged battle to revolutionise the educational system. Aligned against him was his old enemy, Ramsay MacDonald, who had begun a whispering campaign against Sidney on the London County Council, to which MacDonald had been elected in 1902. Sidney worked closely with R. L. Morant who was responsible for drafting the 1902 Education Act, the Minister for Education, the Duke of Devonshire, being preoccupied with horse-racing and often in bed till noon. Altruistically concerned to advance the cause of education, rather than himself, Sidney was determined to raise British educational standards, particularly in science and technology, to those of the Germans,[72] and create a unified three-tier system with a scholarship ladder for poor, bright children like himself. The only practical way of achieving this objective seemed to the Webbs to be to agree to 'Rome on the rates', the financing of denominational schools by ratepayers. 'Webb's Act' as the 1902 Act was called, although it was Balfour, won over to Sidney's way of thinking, who proposed it in the Commons, abolished board schools and handed them over to the new Local Educational Authorities.

Inevitably this antagonised the Radicals, many of whom were Nonconformist, and in control of the school boards. To the Radicals the Webbs seemed to have abandoned both their friends and their principles. A sour MacDonald spread the rumour that Sidney was making 'a good thing' out of lecturing at the London School of Economics. Indignantly Sidney repudiated these accusations,[73] but at times his courage failed. 'I am not a big man,' he told Beatrice plaintively. In October 1902 Beatrice noted that their Radical friends were so 'bitter or sullen' that if he had political ambitions his educational policy would have been suicidal. By March 1903 the 'slump in the Webbs' was serious as Sidney wire-pulled frantically to push through the 1903 Act which abolished the great London School Board; he lost his chairmanship of the Technical Education Board. Graham Wallas, who was a member of the Board, could not understand how Sidney, himself an agnostic, could countenance religious teaching on the rates,[74] and in 1904 resigned from the Fabian Society.

Beatrice was conscious of being regarded as 'both a spy and a traitor' by many different camps. 'They say that you have hitherto led us by the nose, Webb,' remarked the Progressive Whip on the London County Council with venom. 'Now it is your turn to follow.'[75] Virulent unpopularity on all sides was the price Sidney and Beatrice paid for their blatant manipulation of almost every London clique for, although their intentions were honourable, their methods were Machiavellian.

As H. G. Wells frankly told Beatrice, Sidney gave a 'foxy' impression, and together they were regarded as a 'combination' to be feared; while Beatrice alone was seen as a reactionary who influenced Sidney in the wrong direction. Unhappily Beatrice decided, too late, that in future she would stifle her inclinations 'to run the show'.[76]

If the education issue spelt political suicide for the Webbs, it was also the death knell of the Conservative government; combined with Chamberlain's Tariff Reform campaign, by which he split the Conservative party as fatally as he had split the Liberals in 1886, it caused the Nonconformists to rally to the Liberal party and led to the Liberal landslide of 1906. For Beatrice and Sidney it was another nail in the coffin of their Radical pretensions. By 1906 they had lost credibility and were in a political cul-de-sac of their own making.

XVIII

AN EAGLE IN A GALE

'Altiora Bailey . . . was a tall commanding figure, splendid but a
little untidy in black silk and red beads, with dark eyes that had
no depths, with a clear hard voice that had an almost visible
prominence, aquiline features and straight black hair that was
apt to go astray, that was now astray like the head feathers of
an eagle in a gale . . . Her soul was bony, and at the base of her
was a vanity gaunt and greedy!'
H. G. Wells, *The New Machiavelli* 1911

As EDWARDIAN SOCIETY flickered like a moth around a dying candle as World War I approached, a new clamour arose that something should be done for the poor. Social Darwinism, the belief that among nations only the fittest would survive, took on a fresh and frightening relevance as writers such as H. G. Wells prophesied total war, fought by aircraft and tanks.[1] Let us cut 'through all this mud and slush of make believe – these busy people chattering, eating and drinking in a kind of nightmare progress of aimless gossip and entertainment. Above all let's not relax our eagerness to do something for the poor; *all the world's agin the poor!'* cried Charles Masterman, author of *The Condition of England*.[2]

The Committee on Physical Deterioration reported in 1904 on the poor physique of British soldiers. The spectre of race degeneracy rose before the ruling classes, and a stubbornly high infant mortality rate coupled with a declining birth rate led to accusations that 'inefficient' working-class mothers threatened the future of the Anglo-Saxon race.[3] Succouring the submerged tenth became politically as well as altruistically desirable, and led 'Prince Arthur' Balfour to appoint a Royal Commission on the Poor Law and Relief of Distress; one of his last acts as Prime Minister was to appoint Beatrice to the Commission.

At last Beatrice was offered the opportunity to step into the limelight, and she seized it eagerly. Psychosomatic diseases vanished overnight as she revelled in the role reversal which left Sidney mouldering quietly at the London County Council headquarters at Spring Gardens, which most of his former Progressive enemies had left for the House of Commons, while she at last sampled the aphrodisiac quality of power. On the Royal Commission Beatrice demonstrated strength, energy, aggression and intransigence, leading her to show contempt for her adversaries and, even worse, to lie in order to gain her own ends. Yet underneath her fierce defiance lay a high ideal, namely the desire to rescue the poor from that misery which her experiences in the East End had indelibly printed on her mind, and to create a national minimum of civilised life beneath which no one would fall. Beatrice anticipated the Welfare State in its fullest flowering, and clung to her dream that the 'Samurai', the Wellsian élite, could bring order, wealth and happiness into the lives of the forgotten 'residuum' at the base of the social pyramid.

Beatrice and Sidney had met H. G. Wells in 1902 after reading *Anticipations of the Reaction of Mechanical Progress Upon Human Life and Thought* and sensed that his utopian speculations would be useful to 'gradgrinds' like themselves. Wells, son of a lady's maid and professional cricketer who ran an unsuccessful china business in Bromley, had himself escaped from an apprenticeship at the Southsea Drapery Emporium to become a writer and journalist, and was flattered to be taken up by the Webbs. In January the squeaky-voiced prophet with the protuberant eyes, and his second wife, Jane, entertained the Webbs at Spade House, Sandgate, an encounter which left Wells 'awfully afraid of Mrs Webb'.[4]

In November that year Beatrice invited Wells to join the Co-Efficients Dining Club – a name she had conjured up herself – which she hoped would be the think-tank behind a new party of national efficiency. The club, which Wells later satirised in *The New Machiavelli* as the Pentagram Circle, was composed of 'experts' sympathetic to imperialism. There was Haldane, Grey, H. J. Mackinder, Hewins, the director of the London School of Economics, Bertrand Russell, W. Pember Reeves, the agent general in London for New Zealand, whose daughter was soon to fall hopelessly in love with Wells, L. S. Amery from *The Times*, 'Lunatic' Leo Maxse, editor of the *National Review*, and later Shaw, Milner, Henry Newbolt the poet-editor, and J. L. Garvin, another journalist.[5] The chattering classes enjoyed many a convivial dinner with the politicians in the Ship Tavern in Whitehall, but by 1908 the club had petered out, split by Chamberlain's Tariff Reform campaign. The Webbs had backed the wrong horse. While they chased the will-o'-the-wisp of a new Limp party, Sir Henry Campbell-Bannerman had regrouped with solid competence, and in the 1906 election the Liberal Party swept to victory with four hundred seats. Had Rosebery been Prime Minister instead of Campbell-Bannerman Sidney might well have become President of the Local Government Board instead of his old ally who was soon to become a ferocious enemy, John Burns, and the course of history might have been changed.

Despite its collapse, the ideas behind the club remained in vogue. 'Most of the land worth having on this planet . . . is British,' wrote Arnold White with pride, '[but] when efficiency goes out at the door, it is inevitable that Empire will fly out at the window.'[6] It was too late to save the present doomed generation of the unfit, but what of babies now being born, the soldiers of the future? Beatrice went to see Shaw's *Man and Superman* with its echoes of Nietzschean selective breeding, and *Major Barbara* in which Shaw thundered that poverty was a crime which poisons us all morally and physically, that the poor did not want Salvation Army bread and treacle and dreams of heaven, but thirty shillings a week and good drainage;[7] she found it 'hell tossed on the stage'.[8] But audiences flocked to Shaw, now feted by society, for he expressed the new mood of doubt and fear troubling the upper classes.

It was this mood which helped the Liberals win the election, and Beatrice put on a brave face at the result. 'Our friends the Limps have romped in,' she wrote: Grey was at the Foreign Office, Haldane at the War Office, John Burns, the first working-class Minister, looking after the unemployed at the Local Government Board. Proudly he came to call on Beatrice, and paced her drawing room for an hour rehearsing a firm, 'This is my decision, gentlemen', to his civil servants. As Beatrice mockingly recorded, the story went that when Campbell-Bannerman offered him a seat in the Cabinet, Burns 'clasped the Premier by the hand. "I congratulate you, Sir Henry: it will be the most popular appointment that you have made." '[9] Unnoticed by Beatrice was one significant result of the Liberal landslide, born of the Lib-Lab pact between Herbert Gladstone, the Liberal Chief Whip, and Ramsay MacDonald: the arrival of twenty-nine Labour MPs at the House.

Beatrice's confidence in the Limps was misplaced: although they did not know it, the Webbs in 1906 were on the periphery of events, isolated by their rejection of the Left in the past and their subsequent unpopularity. Their great store of knowledge seemed about to run to waste.[10] The new stars who were soon to burn brightly in cabinet were Lloyd George and Winston Churchill, intuitive politicians able to empathise with the people in a way increasingly foreign to Beatrice as she came under Sidney's influence. And Haldane and Grey, no longer concerned with domestic policy, drifted away from the Webb orbit.

But Beatrice was not depressed. Her 'little teacup of a Royal

Commission' had had its first meeting under the chairmanship of Lord George Hamilton, a Conservative, and it was evident from the first moment that there would be fireworks. The combustible elements were the widely antipathetic Commissioners, who included Beatrice's old enemies from the Charity Organisation Society, Octavia Hill, Helen Bosanquet, and C. S. Loch, who were strongly opposed to 'doles' to the poor and believed the family should help itself.[11] Set against them were the Socialists, Beatrice, her old mentor Charles Booth, George Lansbury, a Labour Poor Law guardian from Poplar, William Chandler, woodworker and trade unionist, and the Very Rev Dr Henry Wakefield, Rector of St Mary's in Bryanston Square, who was an ardent Radical rather than a Socialist. The remaining members of the seventeen-person Royal Commission included four Local Government Board principals, two from England, among them Sir Samuel Butler Provis, and one each from Scotland and Ireland. There were also three Charity Organisation Society members of whom Lancelot Phelps, Fellow of Oriel, was the most positive personality, and Dr Downes, Senior Medical Inspector of the English Poor Law.[12] Octavia Hill was sixty-seven, Helen Bosanquet forty-five; both women's views were as unmovable as Beatrice's.

When Beatrice took Arthur Balfour to the matinée of *Major Barbara* and he asked her to serve on the Commission, she suspected that his brother Gerald, President of the Local Government Board before the advent of Burns, was the instigator of the Commission. After a nostalgic visit to Gracedieu to see Charles Booth, she concluded that the Commission was to be spoon-fed evidence which would lead it to recommend a return to the deterrent Poor Law of 1834: once again the workhouse was to be made less attractive to the pauper than the most degraded form of work.[13]

At the first meeting in December 1905 the battle-lines were drawn up: Booth and Beatrice wanted to investigate the causes of pauperism. So elastic were the terms of reference of the Commission, so unbusinesslike Lord George's procedure, without even an agenda at the first meeting, that anything seemed possible. Fearing that as a woman her 'rights' would be pooh-poohed, Beatrice set off on the wrong foot, firing salvoes from all her guns at once. Her manner was aggressive. 'I was not over pleased with my tone this afternoon and must try to do better. Beware of showing off superior knowledge,' she wrote contritely. But the damage had been done; Helen Bosanquet became alarmed that Beatrice would dominate the Commission, especially when she heard her enemy had already complained both to the chairman and secretary. 'I don't want to make myself disagreeable,' Beatrice told Lord George. 'It is extraordinarily unpleasant for a woman to do so on a commission of men.'[14] But no one doubted that she was prepared to do so.

By a swift flanking movement Beatrice outwitted her opponents, requesting a private interview with Lord George who, though approaching sixty, was still vulnerable to Beatrice's persuasive charm and quick mind. She used her preferred method of attack: the dinner party. By mid-February she had entertained Lord George and his wife to a carefully selected dinner at Grosvenor Road, together with Benjamin Rowntree, the investigator of poverty in York, the Barnetts, and Henry Hobhouse. 'We are all rather awed by our *grand seigneur* chairman,' fluttered Beatrice to Lord George, congratulating herself that she had made friends with him.[15] Helen Bosanquet sharply declined a similar invitation, having no wish to be caught in the coils of the 'webspinners', as Virginia Woolf nicknamed Sidney and Beatrice.[16]

'The COS are far more suspicious of me than I am of them,' noted Beatrice as the Commission began meeting regularly. She demanded to see all documents relevant to the cross-examination of witnesses, which irritated Sir Samuel Provis. Beatrice and he had 'a little tiff across the table', and she won her point. Determined that there would be no aristocratic 'muddling through', Beatrice called on Sidney to help her draw up a memo on methods of inquiry.[17] This formidably clear document bore the stamp of Sidney's bureaucratic mind, but was also the product of the Webbs' own experience in researching local government. The indefatigable work they had done on the history of the parish and the Poor Law made them impatient with those less well informed; unfortunately Beatrice showed it. 'It is extraordinarily unpleasant when one has to force people's hands and make them attend to one by sheer ugly persistency at the cost, of course, of getting back a certain insolence of attitude on the part of hostile men,' she wrote in her diary.[18] Sir Samuel proved a hard nut to crack, and Beatrice, used to getting her own way with men she set out to charm, provoked him into losing his temper and shouting that 'he would not have a picking enquiry into LGB policy'. Beatrice kept her temper and refrained from shouting back, but afterwards Charles Booth ticked her off for antagonising the Local Government Board officials. Beatrice took no notice; Booth, she decided, was losing his intellectual grip, and would not be much use to her. By February 1906 she had made up her mind that, 'If one begins by being disagreeable, one may come in the end to a better bargain.'[19]

By early March Sir Samuel's teeth had been drawn at a carefully selected dinner party, but Beatrice was finding it tiring combining the Commission work with her own local government research, which was 'dragging on painfully'. In truth Beatrice was not as temperamentally suited to this laborious sifting through local records as Sidney was, which led her often to compare herself unfavourably with him, complaining that he could do four times more work than she, despite all her efforts with her diet. She sparkled far more in the company of other people, even enemies. But at the Commission she seemed about to meet her Waterloo. 'I was defeated . . . I was beaten . . .' she recorded dismally,[20] as she fought to get particulars of each union made available, and to launch a historical survey of the Poor Law. The majority was against her. 'The PLC is turning out a rather heavy and unpleasant business,' complained Beatrice to her sister Mary. 'The LGB officials are dead set at thwarting all investigation that does not directly point to their own conclusions. Whether I shall get them to do anything that is worth doing in the way of ascertaining the facts, I rather doubt.'[21]

'We are spending about £12,000 a year,' wrote Beatrice, outraged by the Commission's extravagance: 'I would undertake to get more information and better verified information for £1200.'[22] The problem was that Beatrice already considered herself an expert, and the rest of the Commission, with its chaotic ways, as amateurs. Impatience led her to interrupt when she should have kept silent: 'You did not behave nicely yesterday,' said Lord George . . . 'So I thanked him warmly for the hint, and promised to be "seen and not heard" in future . . . Ah! How hard it is for the quick-witted and somewhat vain woman to be discreet and accurate,' confessed Beatrice to her diary.[23]

She did not keep her promise. Only a week later Loch was white with rage as Beatrice, skilled at cross-examination and interviewing, led a weak witness up a collectivist garden path of her own devising. Open war was avoided only when Beatrice decided to strike out on her own, since Lord George was eager to limit the inquiry, and she to widen the terms of reference to include old-age pensions, the condition of the children on outdoor relief, and the Poor Law infirmaries which overlapped with existing hospitals. Charlotte Shaw came to the rescue with the offer of funds and Beatrice began hiring research assistants: Mrs Amy Spencer to look into Poor Law administration, Dr Louisa Woodcock to examine medical relief, Marion Phillips to begin an inquiry into public health provision, Miss Longman – 'a clever Girton girl' – to study central policy. It had flashed across Beatrice's mind that instead of limiting medical treatment to paupers, as the Charity Organisation Society commissioners wanted, medicine should be *preventive*, with compulsory medical inspection and treatment of the poor. Beatrice was anxious to impose order and uniformity upon the overlapping services in the treatment of disease, finding it ridiculous that in London infectious disease hospitals were part of the Poor Law organisation but were open to all, so that both rich and poor were financed by the poor rate, but in the provinces such hospitals came under the Public Health Act, were financed on the borough rate, and often refused paupers.[24] The confusion between the sphere of operation of the two rival authorities seemed to cry out for change, and Beatrice sent six hundred Medical Officers of Health a letter asking for their views.

'I just take my own line,' wrote Beatrice gamely, but the burden of work worried her over Whitsun as she struggled to finish the section on the City of London in the Webbs' joint study of municipal government, write the memo on the central policy of the Poor Law authority, and sift through the records of Norwich. 'Keep your hair on, missus,' was Sidney's advice – 'reminiscent of the London street boy,' remarked Beatrice. Meditation helped Beatrice, and she would lie on her sofa or bed just letting her mind go blank; she was certain that this trick of complete relaxation, coupled with abstinence in indulging her 'appetites' for food, alcohol or sex, gave her the power of rapid and intense thought when necessary. For Beatrice believed with John Stuart Mill that the exercise of intellect – perhaps suffused with love – brought the highest human happiness.[25]

Beatrice revelled in socialising with the aristocracy, especially 'The Souls', but with the result that she felt horribly guilty, torn between the longing to 'show off' in public, conscious that she looked attractive in her new 'pictuer' dress, but chided by Sidney for accepting. When invitations came for three evening parties, Sidney's line was that he and Beatrice might know the society hostesses privately, but not go to their soirées. 'If you do,' he told her with brutal frankness, 'it will be said of us as it is of Sir Gilbert Parker – in the dead silence of the night you hear a distant but monotonous sound – Sir Gilbert Parker climbing, climbing, climbing.' 'And I recognised the better voice and tore up the cards,' wrote Beatrice.[26]

This was one of the few occasions when Sidney won. Generally he acquiesced in Beatrice's compulsive entertaining – to have thirty people a week to lunch or dinner was not unusual – and particularly in her delight in the company of 'Prince Arthur' Balfour. Beatrice rationalised

Balfour's attraction for her by arguing that his power justified it: he was one of those men with the 'power to alter things'. To him she owed her seat on the Commission. But this was only half the story. AJB, as Beatrice referred to him in her diaries, had blue blood, irresistible charm and striking good looks, and he brought the 'fun' into her life for which part of nature craved. When he walked into the dullest party, often late from the House, her boredom evaporated. He took her in his fastest motor for a 'veritable whirl through the country' when Beatrice and Sidney went to stay with the Balfour family at Whittinghame House, East Lothian. In this unattractive mansion, cold in a Scottish September, with echoing passages and formal rooms, she felt too conscious of being 'Arthur's latest friend' to be quite at ease. 'The party each night became a watched *tête-à-tête* between the two of us,' she wrote,[27] conscious that tongues were wagging about the relationship, some suspecting that Beatrice was the successor to Lady Elcho, the 'beautiful soul' who was previously Balfour's mistress.

'Philanderer, refined and consummate, is Prince Arthur . . . How many women has he inspired with a discontent with their life and life companion, haunted with the perpetual refrain "if only it had been so",' Beatrice wrote in her diary. With Balfour Sidney could hardly compete; more pertinently, Balfour was prepared to talk about topics which Sidney found a waste of time, particularly the great questions of life and death to which Beatrice so often returned. As Beatrice remarked, Sidney would rather study a statistical abstract than consider man's relation to the universe; but she, like her sister Mary to whom she became increasingly close in this period, was drawn to prayer and religious ritual. Beatrice often walked to St Paul's to take Communion, and agonised over her agnosticism, regretting that she could not find the peace she sought in the forms of the Anglican Church.

Like Wordsworth, Beatrice had a mystical relationship with nature; as she cycled past the fields of red clover and sweet-smelling hay of the Meon valley during the summer of 1906, when she was staying near Georgina at Brockwood Park, she wondered, not for the first time, if 'there is a spiritual force towards which we humans are tending, or whether we are mere animals . . . which are to-day and to-morrow are not – like the leaves of a tree or the blades of the grass'. In another era Beatrice would have made a great abbess; few understood her as did Leonard Woolf when he wrote: 'Beneath the metallic façade and the surface of polished certainty, there was a neurotic turmoil of doubt and discontent, suppressed or controlled, an ego tortured in the old-fashioned religious way almost universal among the good and the wise in the nineteenth century.'[28] Reason would not allow Beatrice to 'swallow religious dogma, or accept the existence of God; yet she fervently believed in religious teaching in schools – to the annoyance of H. G. Wells and Leonard Woolf – and the efficacy of prayer.

Balfour captivated Beatrice because his mind soared to metaphysical heights undreamt of by the more prosaic Sidney, although when she tried to draw him on social and economic questions he remained at a loss. 'By the way, what exactly is a trade union?' enquired the puzzled aristocrat of his hostess: a startling query, as the journalist Charles Masterman remarked, when the working class was up in arms at the Osborne Judgement which made trade unions liable for damages caused by their members.[29]

Balfour, a bachelor although 'star' of 'The Souls', was lonely, as Beatrice realised, and therefore sought her company: guilt returned as she spent evenings at the Asquiths where Margot Asquith's indiscreet disjointed sayings sparkled against the bejewelled *décolleté* of the Souls' womenfolk, and the garish electric light lit up the groaning table and the flunkeys waiting on their betters. Weekends at Stanway, the home of Lady Elcho, and Taplow Court where Lady Desborough was hostess were equally mannered, in contrast to Deal Castle, home of Lord George Hamilton, where Beatrice was impressed by the dowdy and unpretentious simplicity of her chairman and his wife; she reserved her contempt for the 'stupid, commonplace' Duke of Northumberland who gave her nothing to eat but peas and apricot tart at Alnwick, and the Duke of Westminster and his wife, 'Little White People' scorned by H. G. Wells. The goddess of gold seemed to Beatrice the idol worshipped by Edwardian society when she dined with the millionaire Julius Wernher, and 'wealth – wealth – wealth – was screamed aloud wherever one turned'.[30]

And so the merry-go-round continued and, like a painted Harlequin and Columbine, Beatrice and Sidney smiled behind their masks at the audience who had come to spectate at the political circus. And the game of politics excited its own powerful fascination upon its players, so that Beatrice, even while she debated the ethics of the game, became dazzled by the excitement of game-playing and failed to notice the inherent falsehood of her position. But among the aristocrats she made a new and valued friend: Lady Betty Balfour, wife of Gerald Balfour and sister of Lord Lytton, was a very different woman from the superficial 'Souls' womenfolk. She was largely responsible for changing Beatrice's mind about women's suffrage. Beatrice was flattered when Lady Betty confided that, 'Arthur told Frances on the links that there was no house in London at which he more enjoyed a dinner than at your house . . . As for me, I feel greedy for more of your company and hope we may meet often again.'[31]

As the militant suffragette movement attracted criticism in the press after Christabel Pankhurst and Annie Kenney demanded 'Votes for Women' and were arrested for spitting, a technical assault, at a political meeting in Manchester, Beatrice contacted Millicent Fawcett to say she had recanted: 'As the women suffragists were being battered about rather badly, and coarse-grained men were saying coarse-grained things, I thought I might as well give a friendly pull to get the thing out of the mud, even at the risk of getting a little spattered myself,' she wrote. Her letter, which was printed in *The Times*, together with Louisa Creighton's change of heart, spoke of the 'personal suffering and masculine ridicule'[32] of women forced to commit a breach of the peace. Lady Betty wrote to Beatrice about her sister, Lady Constance Lytton, who went on hunger-strike in prison, that 'Con's bodily frailty is the only thing I dread', when she heard she was to be put in an ordinary cell, although 'she looked quite charming in her prison clothes'.[33] Her fears were well founded, for when Constance disguised herself as 'Jane Wharton' and was force-fed, her ordeal led to life-long paralysis.

The fashion for the Fabian which led Shaw, the Webbs, and H. G. Wells to be taken up by the smart set, had also an unlooked-for consequence. There was a boom in Fabian membership, partly a product of the Zeitgeist, partly due to the high profile Wells was giving to the society, which he had joined in 1903. 'Do not underestimate Wells,' Shaw warned Webb. 'You do not appreciate the effect his writing produces on the imagination of the movement.'[34] Wells's advocacy of free love in his new novel *In the Days of the Comet* excited the younger membership of the society and brought to a head the latent antagonism between himself and the Webbs. Wells's early admiration for Beatrice had given way to disillusion by 1904: she was a 'faceted' person, he told her sharply, whose 'large main facet towards social and political enquiry' was flawed by her worldliness. 'You got on my mind . . . I have already devoted large lumps of my *Modern Utopia* to a careful analysis of the difference between kinetic people (you) and poistic people (me) . . . I shall do a whole book about you exclusively. I shall call it The Anatomy of Sidney Webb.'[35]

Wells's obsession with the Webbs 'broke out' in a new form: a palace revolt against the supremacy of the 'Old Gang', whom by 1906 he believed to be authoritarian and stultifying. His friendship with the promiscuous Hubert Bland and his wife Edith Nesbit, whose daughter, Rosamund, Wells tried to seduce, expressed his growing conviction that sex was the mainspring of human behaviour.[36] Wells believed that Beatrice considered sexual passion as hardly more legitimate than homicidal mania, and although she and Sidney loved 'in an intellectual way . . . and a fond way',[37] they were strangers to beauty and physical sensation. He guessed that she had 'forgotten' sex in marrying Sidney, 'the gnome', as Wells mischievously called him, and found a substitute in string-pulling. He might have been surprised to find Beatrice admitting that she often thought about sexual promiscuity, and believed, 'You do not, as a matter of fact, get to know any man thoroughly except as his beloved and his lover – if you could have been the beloved of the dozen ablest men you have known, it would have greatly extended your knowledge of human nature and human affairs.' She concluded, regretfully, that women would be left without any brain to think with from such an increase in sexual emotion – 'and that way madness lies?' The question mark is significant.[38]

Wells's attack got off to a flying start with two outrageous lectures, 'This Misery of Boots' and 'Faults of the Fabian'; and a committee was set up to consider how the society might be reformed. Although Beatrice considered Wells all puff and bluster, Shaw was more alarmed. 'The day of our family jokes will be at an end,' he complained querulously to Sidney, accusing him of putting up the backs of the revolutionaries, Bland, Ensor and Pease. 'I sometimes ask myself what would become of you if I were to die, and leave you without any point of contact with the real world,' said the egotistical playwright. 'The truth is that we are getting old and reckless and testy . . . You . . . are becoming like an old colonel with a bad liver.'[39]

Bad liver or no, Sidney, like Beatrice, was anxious to placate Wells and prevent him becoming a literary J. R. MacDonald. In July the Webbs went down to Sandgate to visit Wells and his wife Jane; with shock Beatrice realised that Wells considered 'Sidney is weak and I am bad, and we are partially deceiving the world and ourselves as to our motives and methods'.[40] In October Wells dropped a further bombshell in an address to the Fabian Society on 'Socialism and the Middle Classes' in which he seemed to Beatrice to attack the family in calling for free love and the public Endowment of Motherhood which would liberate women from their dependence on men. These ideas found an audience among the New Women of the time who were eager to burst their chains and win sexual freedom as well as political rights. 'I will not be slave to the thought of any man, slave to the customs of any time. Confound this slavery of sex!' cries Ann Veronica, Wells's heroine in his novel of that name. 'I am a man!'[41] The stimulus of Wells was a potent factor in the formation of the Fabian Women's Group, which was founded in Maud Pember Reeves's drawing room in 1908 by Charlotte Wilson, the anarchist and early Fabian member. The 'ardent suffragists' among the Fabian women wanted greater recognition of their struggle than the mere change of the Fabian basis to acknowledge equal rights for women. Newly blooded from 'rushing' the House of Commons, marching in 'mud' processions, breaking windows with toffee-hammers they carried in their handbags, and attacking government ministers with dog-whips, they were ready to answer Wells's call for change.[42]

But his challenge proved abortive; when it came down to it the Fabians were not prepared to turn out the old Executive, nor abandon permeation in favour of becoming a new Socialist Party. Shaw declined to serve up Sidney Webb's head on a platter, and finally trampled on Wells in a virtuoso lecture which annihilated his enemy; it had been, decided Beatrice, 'an altogether horrid business'. By December 1907 the Old Gang were triumphant, and the next year Wells resigned from the society. But the Wells–Webb clash took a new and scandalous twist when Wells put free love into practice in a passionate love affair with Amber Reeves, the gifted daughter of two Fabians. 'He seduced Amber within the very walls of Newnham,' wrote Beatrice in horror. Since she was a 'little heathen' and he a sensualist, and they both 'let themselves go', Amber was soon pregnant, although not before achieving a double first in Moral Science. At first the lovers were defiant; Wells rented a cottage in which he installed Amber, but when another Fabian, Rivers Blanco White, offered to marry her, Amber wavered. 'You will have to choose – and that shortly – between a happy marriage and continuing your friendship with H. G. Wells,' wrote Beatrice to Amber. '*That is the essential fact in the present situation.*' She offered to come and talk to Amber, because, 'I have a *real* liking for you and a respect for Blanco. I have even a quite genuine desire to see HGW saved from a big smash.'[43] At heart Beatrice blamed herself for introducing Wells to the Elcho–Balfour–Desborough set where, among the flattery of duchesses and countesses, he abandoned bourgeois morality and became 'a Goethe-like libertine'.

Although Amber allowed herself to be married to Blanco, she refused to have him near her; he lived in chambers in London while his wife continued to consort with Wells. 'The real difficulty is that

Amber brags of the exploit,' Shaw told Beatrice. Yet he thought that the situation could still be saved. 'Nobody knows who pays for the cottage; nor would it greatly matter if they did. Why should not W, who, if not seventy, is old enough to be Amber's father, pay for a young couple's cottage?' Warning Beatrice not to be an accomplice in 'a questionable social experiment', he hoped that Wells and Amber would recognise that they had behaved badly and part; 'But as they finally and certainly won't, I am not going to waste my time . . . giving advice that won't be taken . . . What will occur, then, is that W will stand by Amber until the "ripping child" (who, alas! may not be a ripping child) is born. That much is certain. After that we shall see . . . In the course of nature he will go back to Jane, and she will press on to fresh adventures.'[44]

It was an accurate forecast. In August 1909 Wells threatened Beatrice for allegedly spreading tales about him: 'Practically you are leaving Amber and myself no alternative but a public smash to clear up this untraceable soaking nastiness against us. We've made pretty big sacrifices to avoid that and it's bound to hurt Blanco White, and Reeves, and my wife very dreadfully.'[45] 'You and Sidney have the knack of estranging people and I think you have to count me among the estranged,' he told her in another vitriolic letter.[46] But as Amber's pregnancy progressed Wells abandoned her; the thinly-veiled tale of their love affair reached beyond the inner Fabian circle through the publication of *Ann Veronica*, to be met with damning reviews. Wells became intent on salvaging his reputation and Amber settled down to motherhood with her young husband.

While the Wells débâcle rumbled in the background, Beatrice struggled against the growing hostility of her enemies on the Royal Commission on the Poor Law. It had become 'a regular scramble', she told her sister Mary. 'I look upon myself as solicitor, barrister, judge and jury all in one – but others take themselves very seriously and sit scheming day after day', becoming horribly irritated and angry with her when she advised witnesses. Only '*the very stupid ones* really try to take in everyone's view and everyone's facts without partiality and end up being completely paralysed'.[47] 'You are a splendid fighter', a weary Lord George told Beatrice, beset with complaints about her on all sides. 'One man actually asserted that I had hypnotised the witness!' joked Beatrice grimly.

In fact she was deadly serious. Lord George curtly demanded that Beatrice give up investigating on her own account, because she was trespassing on Helen Bosanquet's inquiry into children on outdoor relief; fortunately she defied him, for her research has left for future historians a comprehensive picture of the poverty of women and children before 1914. From April 1907 it struck Beatrice that the Poor Law should be gradually broken up, and its functions handed over to the appropriate government departments. Unlike her enemies, she foresaw the need for specialisation in the treatment of the needy rather than punishing them as paupers. 'Take the stuff out drop by drop – the sick first, and place them under the sanitary authority; then the children, placed under the education authority; then the aged . . .'[48] It seemed so simple, so logical, and would end the stigma of pauperism. In July she and Sidney borrowed the Shaws' weekend cottage at Ayot St Lawrence to work, setting up their own mini-commission with their three research assistants and many young Fabians. Beatrice's investigation into Poor Law children had been taken over by the Royal Commission, placed under the supervision of Dr Ethel Williams, and extended to twelve more unions beyond the original two, Derby and Paddington, and her two assistants were paid by the Commission. The Webbs continued to work at high speed on the memoranda on central policy and medical provision.

Fundamental to Beatrice's vision was her scheme for a national health service formed from the existing twin Poor Law and Public Health medical services, and she was encouraged by the support of many of the Medical Officers of Health canvassed. 'My paper on Poor Law Medical Relief . . . has started a ball rolling and it promises, I think, to be a snowball,' she wrote confidently.[49] But the Charity Organisation Service would have to learn 'a little lesson' from the Commission: widespread destitution was the problem which needed solving. It was not mere maladministration which caused pauperism.

Beatrice no longer cared that the majority of her colleagues disliked her and unwisely she began lobbying her old allies among the bishops and politicians to 'make an atmosphere' favourable to her scheme for reform that would influence both the chairman and witnesses. She wondered fleetingly if she was becoming masculine in her treatment of her enemies. Could it be said of her as of Ann Veronica, 'I'm not a good specimen of a woman. I've got a streak of male. Things happen to women – proper women – and all they have to do is to take them well. They've just got to keep white. But I'm always trying to make things happen. And I get myself dirty.'[50] If winning meant getting dirty, Beatrice was prepared to accept the challenge. Helen Bosanquet demanded that she produce her private correspondence with the

Medical Officers as evidence. ' "I shall be charmed . . ." I said cheerily.'
That evening Beatrice carefully selected favourable replies (although
the majority of the Medical Officers were against change), mixing in
a few hostile ones to give the appearance of balance, and handed them
over. Afterwards she was seized with paroxysms of guilt, just as she
had been when she gave inaccurate evidence to the House of Lords
Select Committee. Exhausted and in a state of nervous collapse she
retired to a hotel at Beachy Head with 'a bad nervous breakdown' for
ten days' complete rest. When Helen Bosanquet asked for all the letters
to be printed, Sidney refused. Beatrice was furious at 'this mean little
tricky attempt to trip me up' but she had lost credibility in the eyes of
her colleagues and her duplicity had increased their antagonism.[51]

Sidney was so worried over Beatrice's condition that he sent her to
Dr Henry Huxley to be overhauled. 'He says I am completely sound,'
Beatrice told Mary. 'Every organ in a perfectly healthy condition –
until I recover my weight, as I had run down to 8 stone 5 lbs. I think
considering the strain of the last two years I am a real credit to my
regimen. It is something to be perfectly healthy in one's 50th year after
the sustained work I have done! This is an egotistical letter . . .'[52]
Beatrice had reason to be pleased at her own good health, for during
1907 she had worried constantly over Mary, her 'dearest sister', who
had breast cancer, from which she recovered. Beatrice's conviction that
early diagnosis saved Mary from premature death encouraged her to
campaign for preventive medicine. Only the year before Lallie had
died, estranged from her husband Robert Holt, and sped on her way
by cocaine.

Beatrice's concern for the sick, widows and children, and the aged,
who made up the 'non able-bodied' category within the Poor Law,
did not prevent her turning her attention to the 'disease of unemployment'. The solution she proposed was for a Ministry of Labour and
a network of labour exchanges. In early 1908 she visited Hollesley
Bay Colony in Suffolk, a 'wild weird place' where three hundred
unhappy-looking unemployed men were supposed to be training for
emigration or agricultural work but in fact longed for their wives,
children or the Public House in the familiar London slums.[53] More
impressive was the Salvation Army colony at Hadleigh Farm, where
Beatrice likened the officers to Wells's 'Samurai' caste, who live by
self-denial, neither smoking nor drinking, and confining sex to 'a
straight and clean desire for a clean and straight fellow-creature'. 'The
chapters on the Samurai will pander to all your worst instincts,' Wells
had laughingly told Beatrice,[54] knowing that she would see herself

among the élite of experts whose task was to reconstruct society. Like the Samurai Beatrice was prepared to sacrifice herself, spending February trudging round the workhouses and labour yards of Lancashire despite the cold and damp. She loathed it 'more than I used to in the old days, but it has to be done', she told Mary. 'It is a great comfort, as one gets elderly, to feel how completely one has oneself and one's faculties under control ... I often think this complete self-control is the one great additional happiness of elderly existence.'[55]

Never had Beatrice needed her iron will and self-control as she did in the test which lay ahead, and never again would she so clearly see that she was both hated and loved. It was now apparent that there could be no unanimity on the Commission. 'It will be amusing to see how much "Webb" this Commission will stand – what exactly will be saturation point?'[56] Beatrice had written at the turn of 1907: by December C. S. Loch, the chief Charity Organisation Society spokesman, and his allies had rejected the draft scheme for Poor Law reform which she presented, and the way lay open for Beatrice to write her own Minority Report. Again she and Sidney went to ground, having prepared the way, or so they thought, by circulating the scheme, in strict confidence, to Asquith, Lloyd George, Haldane, Winston Churchill, McKenna, and John Burns among the Liberals, and the Balfours and other allies on the Conservative side.

The Webbs lived a peripatetic life, moving from the Playnes to London, and then to a cottage in the grounds of Sir Julius Wernher's estate near Luton where, surrounded by fifty-four gardeners and thirty indoor servants, listening to the whirr of the pheasants fattening for the autumn slaughter, they composed their collectivist document. Beatrice lived 'on the most rigorous hygienic basis – up at 6.30, cold bath and quick walk or ride, work from 7.30 to 1 o'clock, bread and cheese lunch, short rest, another walk, then tea and work until 6 or 6.30'. She felt in danger of breaking down again from 'brain excitement'. Early in the morning she prayed for a solution to the unemployment problem; in the daylight hours it was grind, grind, grind at their task. By 1 January 1909 the report was finished. ' "You have declared war," wrote one of the inspectors of the Local Government Board, "and war this will be." '[57]

The Minority Report was a revolutionary document, as Balfour discovered. 'No doubt the change you propose may seem revolutionary; but nothing less than a revolutionary change is necessary if we are to re-mould the whole of our poor law system,' he told Beatrice.[58] Sidney too recognised the significance of the undertaking, explaining to Graham Wallas, 'We are wrestling with the biggest thing we have yet tackled, namely a complete survey and reform of the Poor Law, for that is what Beatrice's Minority Report will be.'[59]

Beatrice's aim was nothing less than to cleanse the base of society, to eradicate destitution. She realised that the two-parent family was the basis of society, and that when the breadwinner was absent through death, desertion, illness, unemployment or a prison sentence, then the bargain which the community made with the woman on her marriage, that the man should maintain the home, was broken. When this happened Beatrice believed the state should step in, helping mother and children to remain together. 'It is suicidal for the nation to drive the mother to earn money in industry, at the expense of so neglecting the children that they grow up, if they grow up at all, stunted, weak, untrained,' she argued.[60] The evidence of the Women's Industrial Council, a pressure group founded in 1894, indicated that seasonal work patterns led to hardship in the mills, just as it did among the cigar makers, dressmakers, milliners and shirtmakers in London, where in the factories working-class mothers toiled making jam, paper, matches, or in sweaters' dens pulling fur, making cardboard boxes or sorting seeds. Starvation wages of 6s to 8s a week for unskilled work was the only option for working-class mothers, and without a male breadwinner the children sickened and died. Yet Beatrice's concern had a punitive and a coercive side too, for she believed that if a mother went out to work her children should be taken from her.[61]

That poverty had a female face was evident from the tragic evidence collected by Mrs Harlow. Ninety-five per cent of Outdoor Relief was given to 'able-bodied' women, sixty thousand in all, who had young dependent children and yet were forced to work. If the mother died, argued Beatrice, the cost to the state was great: a foster-mother cost 4s to 5s a week, while Poor Law schools or Cottage Homes for orphans cost 12s to 21s a week. Therefore the state must give the mother adequate assistance.[62] The most pitiful tales of human suffering were of those families refused relief because of 'bad character': the single mother visited in January living in one room with five children, her one-month-old baby wasting away, dependent on her neighbours for a half-pennyworth of cow's milk or the occasional tin of condensed milk; by March the baby was dead, the mother evicted; or the old lady whom the Charity Organisation Society called 'a vile woman – too vile to be called a woman at all', because she was alcoholic. When Mrs Harlow urged one woman who had not eaten for three days to go into the workhouse hospital, she refused, saying, 'I won't give up my bit of a home.'[63] It was obvious to Beatrice that the deterrent policy was a failure; the working class hated the 'Bastilles' as they called the workhouse, and the Poor Law system perpetuated the cycle of deprivation. How ridiculous were the rules that insisted a nine-year-old epileptic girl could not be treated in the Workhouse Infirmary unless her 'able-bodied' father also came into the 'House';[64] that allowed adults and children, vagrants, the mentally defective, and the aged sick to all be herded together in the General Mixed Workhouse; and resulted in forty per cent of babies born in some workhouses dying within a year.[65]

Underlying Beatrice's concern for the working-class mother and her environment lay a eugenic desire to improve the race. The Webbs believed that the existing Poor Law was 'anti-eugenic' because it encouraged the procreation of the mentally handicapped and 'morally degenerate', allowing thousands of 'unfit' mothers to treat the local workhouse and infirmary simply as a free maternity hospital. Beatrice, confident that middle-class standards should be imposed on the poor, criticised the ignorant working-class mothers who 'may nurse their children themselves, or may use the most insanitary bottles; they may feed their infants properly, or give them potatoes or red herrings; they may lock them up in a deserted room all day . . . or they may leave them (with dummy teats and "comforters") with the most careless neighbour; they may even insure their little lives with one of the Industrial Insurance Companies, and so use some of the Guardians' Outdoor Relief money thus hideously to speculate in death . . .'[66] Like Sir John Simon, Chief Medical Officer of the LGB, Beatrice believed that the high infant mortality rate was evidence of the poor environment in which the babies were reared. Unlike many eugenists, she did not accept that the 'fit' survived and the 'unfit' died in the slums. As Sidney told the Eugenic Society, the state must bring about social change by eradicating slums, disease, starvation, and crime which bred the delinquent of the future. To the Webbs, as to Karl Pearson, the problem seemed urgent because the middle classes were using birth-control while the idle and drunken working class were increasing and multiplying.[67]

The aim of the Minority Report, claimed Sidney, was, 'To deliberately alter the social environment to render impossible the present prolific life below the National Minimum or the continuance at large of persons of either sex who are unable or unwilling to come up to the Minimum Standard of Life'. Medical inspection would discover the 'unfit', who would then be segregated. These ideas were also popularised by Shaw, but they represented an attack upon individual liberty which many people who might have sympathised with the Minority Report found hard to stomach. 'I do not believe in the compulsory principle,' wrote Hugh Elliot, Herbert Spencer's biographer, to Beatrice;[68] 'I believe that voluntary co-operation will do infinitely more . . .' Even Shaw was alarmed, telling Beatrice of 'the enormous weight of the Benthamite-Whig objection to your scheme as destructive of liberty . . . The Minority Report assumes a bureaucracy of Webbs; and Webbs do not grow on gooseberry bushes . . . This is the repulsive side of the report'.[69]

It was not the only objection to Beatrice's grand scheme to 'tumble down Humpty Dumpty so he will never get set on the wall again'.[70] When she went to see her friend Reginald McKenna at the Board of Education to discuss handing over the pauper children to the education authority, he said: 'The worst of all your proposals, Mrs Webb, is that though each one seems excellent, they are all more expenditure. And where are we to get the money?'[71] Expensive, too radical for its time, compulsory, and confusing, was the verdict of the public on the Minority Report. Few realised its prophetic quality or saw it as the blueprint for a future welfare state. 'You don't by any means make the quality of your differences from the Majority Report plain, nor are you in the slightest degree convincing . . . I am left wondering just what it is you think you are up to,' complained a truculent Wells.[72]

Beatrice had anticipated a grand splash for her Minority Report; it was therefore with much chagrin that she saw the Majority, ably written by Helen Bosanquet and Professor Smart, get a rousing reception. To its readers it appeared quite radical enough, with its proposals to abolish the Guardians and the deterrent principle, even though the Poor Law was to be retained. By February 1909 Beatrice was deeply depressed. She could not but be aware that Haldane and Asquith disliked the Minority scheme, and wished to bury it. Worse still, she and Sidney had lost their chance to influence the Radicals, Lloyd George and Winston Churchill, by fatally antagonising the 'Goat', as the Chancellor was nicknamed, over breakfast at 11 Downing Street.

Winston Churchill, who had married Clementine Hozier in September 1908, a match of which Beatrice approved because the bride was 'not rich', was an old ally of the Webbs. They had met in 1903, when Beatrice found him an egotistical, bumptious and shallow-minded Tory; the next summer she still condemned him for drinking too much, talking too much, and doing no thinking worthy of the name.[73] But Winston had faith in his own star; as he told Violet Bonham Carter: 'We are all worms. But I do believe that I am a glow-worm.'[74] By 1908 his readiness to listen to the Webbs' proposals had caused Beatrice to change her mind. In July he assured Sidney that he hoped that labour exchanges might be brought within the scope of his department. 'Now let me say that you will always find the door of my room open whenever you care to come, and I hope you will feed me generously from your store of information and ideas,' he told him.[75] Churchill adopted the Webbs' principle of the National Minimum in the Trade Boards Act 1909, which prevented the worst exploitation of the sweatshops, one of the few examples of Webbian proposals directly translated into law. Therefore when Lloyd George returned from Germany impressed with German social insurance in 1908, he and Churchill asked the Webbs to breakfast in October to discuss it.

Unfortunately when George explained his scheme, 'Mr and Mrs Webb, singly and in pairs, leapt down his throat: "That's absurd; that will never do," they told the Chancellor. "It's criminal to take poor people's money and use it to insure them; you should give it to the public health authority to prevent their being ill again." '[76] Sidney was too excited to eat his breakfast, and Lloyd George, who had just read Wells's *The New Machiavelli* with its caricature of the Webbs, was highly amused. Later Sidney apologised for his 'unpardonable truculence', but the damage was done. Henceforth Lloyd George ignored the Webbs, and from that moment was as determined as John Burns to 'dish' them. Beatrice's fundamental objection to social insurance was that any payment should be conditional on good conduct, a hangover from her own Charity Organisation Society days. She could not accept the new principle of benefits being paid as of right in return for weekly contributions, and was therefore vehemently opposed to what was a practical and inspired improvisation which began to raise the standard of living of the submerged tenth.[77]

Beatrice knew she was a 'well-hated person'. She had also antagonised John Burns, whom she considered 'a monstrosity', vain and complacent and not up to his job. Burns by 1908 had come to dislike George, Churchill and especially the Webbs for their habit of trying to slip their protégés such as Morant into key departmental positions. 'Ah, I've smashed 'em, and there's more behind them than George and Churchill . . . 41 Grosvenor Road,' he gloated to Charles Masterman. But by 1909 Asquith had to admit that he and Churchill were like 'a pair of nurses running the child JB' who complained, 'I've 'ad a 'ard job of it, Charles', as Beatrice made her last, supreme effort to finally destroy the Poor Law.[78] The genius of Lloyd George was to understand that by side-stepping Burns he could outwit the Webbs and capture the public imagination with his 'Ninepence for Fourpence' Act.

'Perhaps there will be another call. I must be strong enough to answer: "Yes, we will come and do it",' Beatrice wrote after her Minority Report was published. Soon she heard the call: to take the word into the furthest corner of the country, to launch a great crusade which would 'clean up the whole bad business of a class of chronically destitute persons. Sooner or later the wealthy have to pay for a demoralised and degraded slave population', she wrote, in words reminiscent of Chamberlain's. In May 1909 Beatrice and Sidney set up the National Committee for the Promotion of the Break-Up of the Poor Law, a cumbersome title later simplified to the National Committee for the Prevention of Destitution. In order to go 'on the stump', Beatrice took lessons in voice production between 6.30 a.m. and 8 a.m. every morning on the beach, orating to the waves at Bryntirion, near the Fabian summer school in Wales. 'It is rather funny to start a new profession at 50!' she told her sister Georgina, whose daughter, another Beatrice or Bobo, was helping in the campaign.[79]

For Beatrice the life of the evangelist answered a deep-felt need in her nature; at last the latter-day Theresa had found her cause, and a more honest way of bringing about socialism than wire-pulling or the knife-and-fork. She brought a sense of spiritual service to her war against poverty which can be compared to the sense of sacrifice shared by the militant suffragettes and their leaders, for whom the struggle for the vote was akin to a religion; and the same outpouring of repressed female energy activated Beatrice. Her crusade was both a radical break with and the culmination of her career, just as the suffragette movement was a radical break with and the culmination of the Victorian women's movement. Boldly challenging cabinet ministers and civil servants, the received wisdom of male officialdom, invading male space on the public platform, Beatrice was determined that nothing would stand in the way of her fight for a living wage and decent living standards for the dregs of society. It was said of Constance Lytton's sacrifice: 'Con was seized and used. She was both flame and burnt offering.'[80] Beatrice too was prepared to give the last drop of blood in the service of high ideals.

The reaction of polite society was predictable. 'We have been quite strangely dropped by the more distinguished of our acquaintances and by the Liberal Ministers in particular. I have never had so few invitations as this season . . .' remarked a puzzled Beatrice, particularly hurt by being cut by Asquith at an evening party.[81] Even loyal Lady Betty Balfour wondered if Beatrice's campaign did not accentuate the difference between the two reports, whereas if the difference could have been bridged over the Liberals might have been able to deal with it.[82] Haldane's sister Elizabeth remarked that after 'that wonderful Budget . . . [the People's Budget] I am not sure that your plan of knife to knife opposition is the wisest thing . . .'[83]

But Beatrice was deaf to remonstrances. 'Oh, these revolutionary wild oats! Why don't you sow them at the proper age, like me?' asked Shaw.[84] Instead she took an office at Clements Inn, hired a paid staff of five, with ten volunteers, and began enrolling thousands of young Fabians in the campaign. Soon £1500 had been raised, and a newspaper founded, the *Crusade*, as the organ of her war against poverty. Taking her 'raging, tearing propaganda' all over the country on punishing lecture tours excited Beatrice who, speaking in her 'sweet clear voice, with great ease and fluency',[84] revelled in the role of preacher. The gypsy splendour, of which Wells spoke, the tall graceful yet authoritative presence, the theatrical gifts as yet unused, now came into their own. 'I enjoy it because I have the gift of personal intercourse . . . I genuinely *like* my fellow mortals . . . Also, I enjoy leadership,' she wrote frankly. Perhaps it became clear how much more she, rather than Sidney, would have excelled as an MP, in those heady moments in front of the crowd.[85]

Victory was not to be hers, however. The campaign was a brave but ultimately unsuccessful gesture. Lord George launched his own movement, the National Poor Law Reform Association, which had official support, and by claiming to deal with the family as a whole rather than assign the different areas of care, such as medicine and health to different authorities, seemed to pose a simpler solution. Public opinion became diverted into the great constitutional crisis precipitated by the Budget, and the Peers versus the People elections which followed. By 1910 Beatrice was so exhausted that she was in danger of fainting during a big lecture, although that year the Bill prepared by her National Committee was debated in the House. Dislike of the Webbs was so great that it led the Conservative rank and file to support Lloyd George's Insurance Bills in order to keep the bogey of socialism at bay. Beatrice continued to oppose Lloyd George: 'These reforms are not socialism,' she wrote angrily to Lady Betty, furious that George proposed to 'give away' £20 million in 'doles'. '*Moreover I loathe his arguments*.'[86] But the Goat had won, and the Webbs were well and truly 'dished'. 'We have spiked your guns, eh?' sneered Charles Masterman triumphantly to George Lansbury.[87] In 1911 the exhausted Webbs wound up their campaign, Sidney resigned from the London County Council and they left on a journey round the world.

XIX

AND THEN THEY WERE RADICAL CHIC

*'The Labour Party exists and we have to work with it. A poor
thing, but our own.'*
Beatrice Webb Diary, Christmas 1912

*'Quelle vie! Quelle femme! Quelle livre! . . . It is all alive – and
alive with you.'*
Charles Mostyn Lloyd to Beatrice Webb, 22 February 1926

As THEIR SHIP ROLLED across the Pacific Beatrice forgot her 'deep down
tiredness', and began to revive. She and Sidney took a small dose of
neat brandy and whisky before each meal against seasickness,[1] and
tried to learn Japanese. Canada had been 'splendidly wholesome', and
Beatrice was impressed by the English pioneers who lived on the
north-west prairie, but it was 'the active, neat, clean little Japanese
men and women'[2] whom she preferred when they landed at Yoko-
hama. The Webbs were warned that they would receive lavish
hospitality 'in the hope that you will defend the Japanese government
. . . among your Socialist friends. I do not think it is likely that you
will be deceived, but the Japanese are very clever in producing a good
impression', wrote Robert Young of the *Japan Chronicle*.[3] Living
exclusively with the Japanese in the north-east provinces did indeed
lead Beatrice to write glowingly of the schools, where there were no
'dirty heads', the untiring efficiency of industry, the postal service and
the police, and to conclude that the Japanese 'are the most executive
race in the world'.[4] To the Webbs 'gallant little Japan', who had
already smashed the Russian bear in the 1902 war, embodied the
Fabian traits of the 'Samurai' élite extolled by Wells.

It was relief to reach India after a narrow escape from Peking. The
city was on the eve of revolution as Beatrice and Sidney fled in the last
train out of the city, found a seat by the conductor who was an
Independent Labour Party member. Beatrice had heartily disliked both
the Chinese and the Koreans, but she fell in love with India. It left one
gasping at its squalor and beauty, piety and vice, starvation and
magnificence which presented a baffling contrast, she told Clifford
Sharp.[5] Beatrice was not a racist, and criticised the Collector at Benares

who was 'vastly amused and scoffed at giving "the natives" any better education – they were much better left alone'. A more hopeful experiment seemed to be Annie Besant's Hindu Central College where one thousand students worshipped their Theosophist principal.

The Webbs tried to be thorough in their tours of each country, even though they brought with them preconceptions which affected their view of the different races. It was typical of their approach to go into camp with a Collector like Mr Hope Simpson, who worked near Gorakpur in the United Provinces. 'The day is brilliantly fine with a cool, even wind, and this great plain of wheat and sugar cane, of blue flowered linseed and yellow flowered dhal, broken into lines by mango groves, mud walled villages and pagoda temples, stretches right to the distant Himalayas,' recorded Beatrice.[6] She made herself a riding habit from a few yards of holland, and rode out with Simpson to visit a neighbouring village. The village elders, dressed in white, bowed and salaamed to the sahib, and Beatrice and Simpson inspected the local school. 'What splendid material these village boys would make for the Boy Scouts,' exclaimed their English visitor, as she watched a gymnastic display. Yet she was struck by the poverty of the villagers, their homes built near stagnant pools alive with mosquitoes, and she took her quinine every day.

They moved on to Chhatapur on the edge of the Nepalese border, where for five days they rode elephants, swishing through the tiger grass and dense woods, and sleeping at night in overcoats because of the deadly cold. At Bhopal Beatrice was shocked by the temples when she looked closely at the 'hideously and brutally coarse' sculpture: 'In England it would be locked up with the unexpurgated edition of Burton's Arabian Nights,' she commented. It was all part of the 'fascinating nightmare' which was India, the heat of the sun, the 'incontinence' of the religion, and the caste system which led her to pity the sixty million Untouchables who had to cry out when they approached so that their shadow should not fall on a Brahmin.

Beatrice became more and more conscious that the Indians, like the Burmese, felt themselves a subject race, excluded by 'the white man with his Polo and his sports and his military band playing English airs – seeming to belong to a new and hostile world'.[7] What right did the British have to give themselves airs, she wondered, as she gazed on the Taj Mahal, built over two hundred years before, 'when we could build nothing better than the Banqueting Hall at Whitehall . . . One feels rather ashamed of the sneers of the young English officer at "the Niggers" with whom he refuses to associate'.[8] The Hindu quest 'to find emancipation from the Wheel of Human Desire' appealed to the ascetic in Beatrice, and she found the Hindus delightful intellectual companions, preferable to the more blimpish of her fellow compatriots. She especially admired the Begum of Bhopal, the only woman ruler in India, who looked like George Eliot, and told Beatrice that a woman ruler was a mother to her people. The Begum took Beatrice to the Purdah Club where, in cotton leggings and a knitted shawl, looking like 'a dear old working woman', she lectured her audience of elegant Mohammedan ladies in satin and gauzy veils.[9] As the Webbs sailed home they did not feel optimistic for the future of India under British rule.

Before leaving for the East Beatrice had become increasingly convinced that the time was ripe for a 'genuine socialist party with a completely worked-out philosophy',[10] which would be energised by the enthusiasm of the clever young men and women in the Fabian nursery,[11] the Cambridge Fabians like Hugh Dalton, James Strachey, and Rupert Brooke, who flocked to the Fabian summer schools, and were often trained in economics and Webbian collectivism at the London School of Economics. She returned from India more radical than when she left, and was determined to take the Fabian Society more seriously.[12]

Unfortunately just as Beatrice decided to give the Fabians a decisive lead, the clever young men and women declined to follow it. At first events went her way. Determined to pull the society together after a period in the doldrums, she refused to follow Shaw's suggestion that 'we must all go together, with the limelight on, and full band accompaniment'.[13] Let Bland and Shaw leave the Executive: she would sit on it for the first time and, in a significant leftwards move, join the Independent Labour Party too. 'I have joined the ILP: don't leave it, just as I am coming in!' Beatrice begged George Lansbury, who had just lost his seat in Parliament in November 1912.[14] She briskly wound up the National Committee for the Prevention of Destitution and launched a new 'War Against Poverty' to agitate for the National Minimum, run by the Fabians and the Independent Labour Party together. Knocking on the head the would-be reformers in the Fabian Society who, led by Henry Schloesser,[15] had tried to usurp the 'Old Gang' by capturing the society for the Labour Party, Beatrice set up the Fabian research department as a haven for the 'angry young men'.

But while the Webbs had been on their travels the urgent militancy of the trade unions, which spilled over into the miners', dockers' and railwaymen's strikes of 1910 and 1911 and was to lead to the Triple

Alliance, had been growing. Their inspiration was the doctrine of George Sorel, Syndicalism, which preached the power of the general strike and of workers' control of industry. The 'solid stupid folk', as Beatrice called the trade union delegates,[16] were not the only people to be influenced by Sorel's justification of violence: those very university alumni from whom Beatrice hoped for so much were infected by their own brand of the disease – Guild Socialism. Beatrice had guessed as much while she was away: were all her campaign workers 'busy with striking or smashing windows', she enquired of Sharp.[17] Once home she found a 'Pleasant Sunday Afternoon' at Clifton spoilt by the Syndicalists. Syndicalism had taken the place of Marxism on the far left, and 'the angry youth, with bad complexion, frowning brow and weedy figure', like the 'glib young workman', together mouthed the phrases of Syndicalism at her.[18] It was the antithesis of the Webbs' bureaucratic socialism with its faith in the expert; the Guild Syndicalists, led by G. D. H. Cole, put their faith in the producer or workman, believing nostalgically that through re-created guilds in which brotherhood and craftsmanship reigned, workers could control industry while the state owned it.[19]

To Cole, an intense and rebellious Fabian from Oxford University who was, Beatrice felt, the ablest newcomer since Wells, it seemed as if the Webbs had put their stamp on the Fabians and the whole Labour movement for far too long. As Margaret Postgate, Cole's wife and another clever young university Fabian, explained, people resented being pushed around by the Webbs, and particularly by Beatrice. 'People,' Beatrice said, 'are really quite simple':[20] but they did not like to be so regarded. They did not appreciate Beatrice and Sidney interrupting and taking charge of the conversation, one beginning speaking as the other finished, so that their opponents were steam-rollered into submission. They did not like particularly the Webbs' assumption that they were always right. The perfect intellectual accord in which Sidney and Beatrice existed, the high-minded, puritanical exterior which gave no hint of the private agonies of which Beatrice's diary was the only confidant, was both frightening and irritating to the young intelligentsia.

Margaret Postgate, or 'Mopps' as she was nicknamed for her mop of dark hair, had a sharp nose and chin, defiant eyes, and smoked a pipe. Probably she was as much a puzzle to the childless Beatrice as the 'Oxford boys' who caused her so much trouble at a Fabian conference where they refused to obey the rules and go to bed at eleven o'clock. Beatrice quelled the rebellion by telling them she would sit up with them every night 'for as many hours as they had the heart to keep a poor old woman out of her bed'.[21] It was an effective threat: the 'boys' went sullenly to bed, but they sat separately from the 'Old Gang', drinking copiously the beer they had especially ordered, hoisting the Red Flag and singing revolutionary songs so loudly that the police were called in.

Cole failed, like MacDonald and Wells, in his takeover bid for the Fabian Society. At a stormy meeting in 1915 when he tried to restrict the work of the society to research only, the vote went against him and he lost his temper. When called to order he sprang to his feet: 'I withdraw the word fools, I say "bloody fools".' White with rage, he marched out of the room.[22] It was the end of another abortive rebellion, but Cole did succeed in commandeering the Fabian research department, which had been busily investigating the control of industry and the working of the insurance bill. From now on it was no longer Beatrice's to direct. In 1917 Cole was still fulminating at Beatrice when she reminded him that the research department depended on the Fabian Society for money; 'I do not like being regarded as a Fabian or having anything I do mixed up with the Fabian Society . . . which to be candid, I detest . . . I believe this is a rude letter.'[23] But Cole was more bark than bite, and eventually he and Margaret became heirs to the 'Old Gang'.

In another venture Beatrice was more successful: the launching of the *New Statesman* in 1913. After the death of the *Crusade* there was no Fabian mouthpiece in the newspaper world, and Beatrice was determined to start on this 'mad adventure' in journalism. Shaw was pessimistic. 'We are too old,' he told her (he was fifty-six on 26 July 1912). 'The art of pleasing in literature takes more out of you than you think . . . My bolt is shot . . . The Harlequin must be content to play the heavy father and it is too late for Sidney to step into his spangles.'[24] But generous as ever the playwright offered to contribute £1000 and so with the tiny capital of £5000 the paper was launched into competition with the *Daily Herald*, edited by Lansbury, the *Spectator* and the *Nation*. Two thousand Fabians took out subscriptions, and the 'young and jolly' Clifford Sharp became editor. Beatrice saw no reason why the new weekly should not become as solvent as the London School of Economics which, from a shaky start, had become independent.

Problems appeared when Shaw refused to sign his articles. 'We have the disadvantage of his eccentric and iconoclastic stuff without the advantage of his name,' wrote Beatrice unhappily. 'He is spoilt – spoilt by intense vanity and intellectual egotism.'[25] But jeers from their rivals at the *Nation* stiffened her backbone: 'Sidney and I are not quite so one-sided as we look . . . Sidney has an encyclopaedic knowledge and we have seen a few things,' she wrote defiantly. The Webbs wrote regularly for the new weekly, and the series of supplements they and Shaw produced were very popular despite her foreboding; in fact the rebellious Fabian research department contributed to them. Under its next editor, Kingsley Martin, the infant weekly 'ate up' three of its weekly competitors.[26]

Shaw's egotism was understandable: he was in love again, this time with 'Mrs Pat', the actress Stella Campbell. 'You ask me, do I love her,' he wrote in 1912. 'The answer is "yes, yes, yes, yes, yes, yes".'[27] She starred as Eliza in *Pygmalion*, which Shaw wrote for her, and their collaboration fanned the flames of his desire. In July 1913, when the relationship was at its height, Beatrice visited Shaw's wife, Charlotte. Although she had felt for some time that Charlotte did not like her, and she did not really care for Charlotte, Beatrice was sympathetic to the wronged wife, who lay, gentle and dignified, on the sofa. Beatrice recalled Shaw repeating to her Mrs Pat's sneering remarks about Charlotte's large waist. He was the fly to Mrs Pat's spider, concluded Beatrice, sad that the playwright had reverted to the cruel philandering of his youth.[28] By September however, the playwright and the actress had parted, and the Shaws were together again.

Loyalty to old friends was one of Beatrice's best traits. She hated to lose a single one, and often made lists in her diary on the state of her relationships. In June 1911 Alys Russell had written to tell Beatrice that she and Bertie were finally separating after nine unhappy years and she was going to live with her brother Logan.[29] She wrote again, saying that although she knew how busy Beatrice was, she made no apology for troubling her: 'I long ago found that your work never interferes with your loyal friendships.'[30] Bravely trying to 'get the victory over my selfishness' she asked Beatrice to call on Bertie.

Beatrice, who categorised people as either 'A's' – Artist, Anarchist and Aristocrat – or 'B's' – Benevolent, Bourgeois and Bureaucratic (she put herself into the last category and Bertie into the first) – was loyal to Alys. When Bertie remonstrated that she was not 'at home' when he called on her, she wrote: 'Now don't be angry with me, if I ask you to put yourself in my place. Supposing . . . you became aware that Sidney had repudiated me, and that I was living in a state of dark despair. Would you not . . . feel rather sore with Sidney?'[31] Bertie, who was involved with Lady Ottoline Morrell, had to admit the truth of her remarks. 'I wish you were here to talk things over. I very much need your advice . . . there's no one else understands as you do,' wrote Arthur Colegate, a young Fabian in trouble with his engagement, to Beatrice when she was abroad.[32]

Nineteen-thirteen was the year in which Beatrice felt most keenly the pain of being 'more disliked, by a larger body of persons, than ever before'. To the Syndicalists the Webbs were out-of-date state socialists; to the propertied class they were dangerous revolutionaries. Their one comfort was that both sides could not be right: but Beatrice's other comfort was more tangible and more enduring: her husband. In her fifties Beatrice's relationship with Sidney settled into a mellow love, untroubled by sex. As she told Georgina, 'I have come to the conclusion that one only becomes thoroughly "adaptable" after fifty – before that age one is terribly handicapped by one's body . . . Certain it is that one's body becomes less and less of an incubus as the years roll on.'[33] The socialist ideal they shared bound them tightly together; when she wrote 'he is the most perfect of lovers, by night and by day, in work and in play, in health and in sickness!'[34] she meant that Sidney was a loving comrade. The companionship of late middle age was sweet, now that she no longer yearned for sex or a child of her own.

Never was Beatrice to need Sidney's support more than during the nightmare of war which swept over Europe in August 1914; Britain had to stand by Belgium, Beatrice was sure, but she dreaded the overpowering efficiency of the German army, especially after Haldane confided that Kitchener said the Germans would slice through the French army like butter. Pacifists John Burns and Ramsay MacDonald resigned, and Arthur Henderson, an ironmoulder, became the new leader of the Labour Party in parliament. It was a significant development, for Henderson, formerly a Liberal MP, had joined the Fabians in 1912, and used Sidney as his tame 'expert'. In this way the influence of the Fabians on the Labour Party, with whom the Webbs had found it impossible to work under Ramsay MacDonald, increased and superseded that of the Independent Labour Party, and it was Sidney who drafted the 1918 Nottingham Constitution of the Labour Party.[35]

Beatrice, however, had little to do but worry. She saw very clearly the causes of war, that Germany was determined to push her claims by the sword, that Britain fortified her empire, and the French armed for revenge for their defeat in the Franco-Prussian war. 'When and where will arise the spirit of love?' she cried.[36] Socialists everywhere had believed that the brotherhood of workers could prevent war, that class loyalty would be stronger than national loyalty. They were mistaken, and to Beatrice the hell taking place in the trenches was the proof of the moral bankruptcy of Western civilisation. 'I am gloomy, desperately gloomy, about the results of the war,' she wrote to Lady Betty Balfour. 'I see the fine energy and cheerful self-sacrifice, the eager self-effacement of our recruits ... but it is a tragedy that these splendid qualities should be insolubly connected with all the vulgar impulses of national domination, delight in the loss and suffering of other races, and in many cases with the horrors of lust to kill and injure individually. It is after all a return to barbarism – to animal pugnacity; and the heroism of the trenches has its likeness in the heroism of the wild animal ...'[37]

Soon the conflict began to touch her personally. Paul Hobhouse, Maggie's youngest son, joined the Somerset Light Infantry, and Beatrice feared for his life. 'My dear people,' the young officer wrote to his family, 'I am afraid one of our brigades has had a hot time and we have lost a good many men and officers.'[38] Within a month he was 'safely' wounded in the left shoulder, but his mother's rejoicing was premature. Although Maggie believed fervently that as the seventh child of a seventh child he had a charmed life, by Christmas 1917 Paul had lost his early idealism and felt a new revulsion against the war which had claimed so many comrades; in April 1918 Captain Hobhouse fell near St Quentin as the Germans made their final push against the Fifth Army before relief came from the Americans. Only three weeks before the Armistice the dead body of Noel Williams, Rosy's son, was also found. Paul and Noel were Beatrice's favourite nephews – 'clean-living gallant youths' – and she mourned with her sisters for these dead soldiers, substitutes for the sons she never had.

The plight of the young Fabians affected her too; 'I suppose before many months are past we shall have some big pushes – and a good many of us won't come home any more,' wrote C. M. Lloyd to Beatrice.[39] He was lucky enough to be knocked out on the first day of the 'show', the British offensive on the Somme in July 1916. His right arm was broken, and he wrote Beatrice a stoical left-handed letter from the 4th London General Hospital. It was 'pretty hellish (despite the rhapsodies of the newspaper men)' in the trenches; the Colonel's wife had been in to tell him that the battalion was 'badly cut up ... 9 officers killed and 9 wounded (18 casualties out of 20), and only 140 men left out of 775 ... I am betting on the war still being on next year,' he told her bravely.[40] 'I cannot bear to look at the fresh young faces in each week's "Roll of Honour",' wrote Beatrice, horrorstruck by the mounting toll of killed and maimed young men.[41] She felt no sympathy for the conscientious objectors among whom, after conscription was brought in in January, were Cole and his guild socialist accomplices. It was amusing to watch these young intellectuals squirming like worms on a hook as they, who were so quick to preach violence to working men, now claimed to abhor its use in defence of their country. They were not true conscientious objectors, merely professional rebels, in Beatrice's opinion, and she was scornful of Cole's wiles in getting 'badged' as a member of the Amalgamated Society of Engineers to avoid the call-up.

Nor did Beatrice feel there was any justification for the stand taken by another nephew, Stephen Hobhouse, Maggie's eldest son. 'I don't believe in non-resistance . . . there is no morality in watching a child being murdered,' she wrote.[42] Stephen was a Quaker who gave up his inheritance apart from a small allowance of £350 from his father, but his lugubrious manner and long, doleful face did not appeal to Beatrice; nor did she approve of his wife, Rosa Waugh, daughter of the founder of the Society for the Prevention of Cruelty to Children, who was also an ardent pacifist. Stephen was determined to be a martyr, wrote Beatrice tartly, although he could have been exempt either on religious or medical grounds as he had a weak heart. Instead 'all the effort of the war office to prevent the scandal of 'Hard Labour' for a saint [was] . . . of no avail',[43] and he found himself in Wormwood Scrubs. Indeed, Stephen courted even severer penalties by deliberately breaking prison rules until his mother in 1917 wrote a vigorous plea for the conscientious objectors, *I appeal unto Caesar*, which resulted in his release.[44]

Beatrice bought the newspapers and pored over the obituaries, marvelling at the way ordinary working men squared their shoulders and 'died game', with no thought of being heroes, and young intellectuals too accepted discipline and sacrifice with equanimity. She sank into deepening depression, exacerbated by her sense of being surplus to requirements, while Sidney sat on the Labour Party executive and was busy. A split in her friendship with Lady Betty Balfour depressed her further; she had told Lady Betty that it was 'rubbish' to say that motor cars could not be used in Flanders because of the mud and was angry that Lady Betty seemed to demand of the working class sacrifices that her own class were not prepared to make. The workers, most vocal on the Clyde, resented the war-time ban on strikes and the imposition of conscription, and Beatrice warned her old friend that 'we are confronted with a class war far more bitter than anything we have yet experienced'.[45] The newly radicalised

Beatrice declared in her diary, 'There can be no real friendship between persons inspired by radically different social ideals and whose daily life is rooted in altogether different traditions and circumstances.'[46] She accepted that the centre of Lady Betty's life was her famous brother-in-law, and as soon as he ceased to be interested in the Webbs, so would she. Two painful meetings in St James's Park finalised the breach, as Beatrice became aware of the expression of acute boredom on the face of the 'divine Arthur' when she accosted him to talk about the mismanagement of the Prince of Wales relief fund. Since causes bored him, and the person pressing them also did, they no longer had anything to say to each other; once again, Beatrice had been 'dropped', and by two people who had exercised a potent fascination over her.

By the summer of 1916 Beatrice was not sleeping, feeling constantly tired and was losing weight. Her dizziness, long restless nights, and frequent pain convinced her that she had cancer, that she needed an operation to remove the growth, and that she would die under the anaesthetic. Even the imperturbable Sidney became infected by her anxiety and, fearing the worst, took her to see a specialist. There was no organic trouble, he told her firmly, counselling her to eat more and take a sleeping draught. Beatrice felt humiliated, both at her obsession and her cowardice in the face of death. She realised her neurasthenia, as she called it, was psychosomatic, caused by her reaction to the decimation of the young generation, by her feeling of uselessness and by the consciousness of unpopularity. The profound pessimism occasioned by these feelings led her to prophesy the apocalypse: 'I am haunted by the fear that all my struggles may be in vain, that disease and death are the ends towards which the individual, the race and the whole conceivable universe are moving with relentless certainty. If so my own life is not happy enough to justify human existence and that long agony of individuals and races.'[47]

Within a few years Beatrice lost three sisters from cancer. The first to die was Georgina, from cancer of the liver in November 1914. Bobo (Kate) and Bardie (Barbara), Georgina's daughters, blamed themselves for encouraging their mother to have her gall-bladder removed, which they afterwards feared shortened her life.[48] Although, as Beatrice told Mary, she was never intimate with Georgie, the loss was a great blow to her equanimity: 'Some of my sisters will have to outlast the others, but we shall accumulate sadness in doing so.'[49] Georgie's death stirred up a greater fear, the fear that one day she and Sidney must be parted. 'I am haunted by the dread of that parting . . .' she wrote apprehensively.

Another chapter in Beatrice's life ended with the death of Joseph Chamberlain in 1914; it was an event to which she did not refer in her diary.

Her sister Maggie was the next to become ill. In adolescence they had been close, and in old age they had grown close again. Beatrice was, as Henry Hobhouse told her, his wife's 'dearest and most intimate sister'. Maggie had lung cancer, and the doctors gave her only a few months to live. 'The sporting chance has always appealed to me,' she wrote bravely to Beatrice, allowing herself to be given a course of copper inoculations on the advice of a well-known specialist.[50] 'You would be horrified by the doctors prescribing sugar as the finest heart stimulant and nourisher going,' Maggie told her ascetic sister, 'I fancy you must mend your ways and fatten in old age. You want more nourishment.'[51] Trying a diet cure, Maggie ordered in a stock of dried and fresh fruit. 'I shall vary it with occasional oysters, milk and cream, with the bananas as bread . . . Coffee is my standby at breakfast and tea puts a new face on the world and in the early hours of the morning and at four in the afternoon. Like tobacco, if they are poisons, well they are slow ones.'[52]

Two months later Maggie needed all her courage: Beatrice walked daily across the park to Airlie Gardens to sit with her as she slowly weakened. 'I wish I could do more for you, old chum,' said Beatrice, as Maggie gasped for breath, 'but all my love cannot sweep away the loneliness of death. Paul may help you but I cannot.' 'Paul, Theresa and Mother,' whispered Maggie. 'After Sidney you are the person I love most dear one,' answered Beatrice. They kissed for the last time and held hands, 'close up to the blank wall of death'.[53]

All elderly folk lived in terror of cancer, decided Beatrice, and she pondered the pros and cons of taking an overdose. Maggie had thought at the beginning of her illness that she would do so, and had provided herself with the means; 'but in the last days when she was actually dying she clung to life.'

The next to go was Mary, and although, as she watched her sister fight breast cancer, Beatrice hated the weary, painful process of dying, she feared that hopeless invalids would be expected to depart of their own accord by relations and friends anxious to be rid of them if euthanasia were a possibility, and decided nature should not be tampered with.[54] In Mary's case death was welcome as she had developed Alzheimer's Disease and had become little more than an automaton. Talking to her was like pressing the button of a speaking doll, thought Beatrice, as poor Mary endlessly repeated questions to

Beatrice, jumping restlessly from one occupation to another and smoking incessantly. When Beatrice came to take the place of Mary's companion, Bice, she could not have borne the strain without a private sitting room to escape from her sister's chatter.

Beatrice suffered a breakdown so acute that she stopped working for six months. The 'panics' to which she was subject, which she called her 'Mr Hyde', lasted for the next two years, although her outward behaviour betrayed little discomfort. Sidney's calm – *'he is always sane'*, she wrote[55] – helped to soothe her. The war, he announced matter-of-factly, 'is a sag back, but presently there will be a sag forward ... Let us do our own work like the French peasant cultivates his fields close to the fighting line'.[56] When a Zeppelin came over, its cigar-shaped body gliding above the Strand in the night sky, faintly lit by searchlights, Sidney was as excited as a schoolboy. Shaw, too, took out his motor car to inspect the burning vessel, but Beatrice watched the shrapnel falling in the river and thought of women and children dying.

In January 1917 Beatrice had bought a cheap typewriter and began making a 'Book of My Life' from her diaries. It was no more tiring than reading or trying to knit soldiers' socks, and she was enjoying her childhood memories when a new call came on her time. In February she was asked to sit on the Reconstruction Committee first set up by Asquith in March 1916 to examine post-war problems, and now chaired by the new Prime Minister, Lloyd George. The 'little Welsh conjuror's' Coalition government had fatally split the Liberal party, whose 'strange death' had been approaching through the troubled Edwardian years,[57] and Beatrice marvelled to see Labour leaders in alliance with Tory chiefs. The Coalition was the work of the great press lords, she concluded, particularly Lord Northcliffe, whose *Daily Mail* and *The Times* had discredited Asquith and Grey.

Soon Beatrice learnt from Tom Jones, an economics lecturer and Webbian Fabian also on the Reconstruction Committee, together with Marion Phillips, how she had been chosen. Given a list of names which included the Webbs, the Prime Minister had pondered and said, 'Yes, we will have one of the Webbs ... Mrs Webb I think ... Webb will be angry, Mrs Webb won't.'[58] Beatrice was pleased to have a more enthralling task to fill than sitting on the Pensions Committee, which she had been attending in a perfunctory way. Considering the relation of the State to industry was the sort of work she and Sidney were skilled in. Vaughan Nash, a civil servant, was Secretary of the

Reconstruction Committee, which Beatrice felt was full of young and vigorous people, including Edwin Montagu, an ex-Cabinet Minister, and the acting chairman. But by June she was as critical of her colleagues as she had been on the Royal Commission on the Poor Law: Montagu was a 'dead failure' who simply sat smoking a large cigar, Vaughan Nash 'woolly-headed', weak, suspicious and secretive, Leslie Scott too busy coining money at the Bar to give them more than the leavings of a lawyer's brain, Jack Hills 'a big baby', Lord Salisbury too talkative, and as for the Labour members, they never turned up. Marion Phillips turned out to be shrewd and capable, but contentious: 'She tries to oppose everything I propose, out of some vague desire not to be considered a Webb disciple,' recorded Beatrice.[59]

Beatrice was soon sitting on a plethora of committees. In November the Webbs asked Leonard and Virginia Woolf to lunch, since Leonard, having retired from the civil service after eight years in Ceylon and married Virginia, had been writing a Fabian memorandum on international relations. 'One of the worst Webb meals to which we have been,' recalled Leonard, who was accustomed to a 'bleak plate of roast mutton' in the dark dining room at Grosvenor Road. Beatrice 'talked incessantly and every tenth word was "committee". She has apparently succeeded in inventing a committee for babies, a committee for lunatics, a committee for the sick, a committee for the disabled, and a committee for the dead; but the scheme or the Cosmos is not complete because she has so far failed to invent a committee for the Able-bodied and unemployed . . . Immediately after lunch we fled.'[60]

Beatrice, Haldane, Montagu and Morant were investigating the 'swollen world of Whitehall', which had grown enormously during the war creating a new Leviathan of government departments, bureaux and ad hoc committees.[61] The Machinery of Government committee, chaired by Haldane, explored the functions of government with a view to seeing how the different Ministries should be re-grouped after the war. In an important memorandum Beatrice suggested a new Ministry of Health not dominated by the British Medical Association, which came into being in 1919 in place of the old Local Government Board.[62] Virginia Woolf recorded after a weekend with Beatrice that her hostess looked like 'a moulting eagle, with a bald neck and a bloodstained beak',[63] but despite her incessant talking and sparse dinners, Beatrice had not completely lost her ability to influence people. It suited her to make up with Lord George Hamilton when a new committee on Poor Law reform was mooted. They had an affecting interview in his house, and then he walked all the way to Hyde Park corner with Beatrice:

'You want me to serve on this Committee, Mrs Webb? Very well, I will.' Beatrice breathed a sigh of relief. Lord George's mind had been converted to the break-up of the Poor Law by his service on the Venereal Disease Commission. In the battle in committee Lord George backed Beatrice up nobly in her duel with the wily Local Government Board representative, Symonds, who did not want the Poor Law abolished.[64]

Setting up the Local Government Committee and pressing through a 'unanimous report written in three months embodying all the conclusions of the Minority Report of the Poor Law Commission was, I think, my masterpiece', Beatrice wrote triumphantly in her diary.[65] Using Sir Samuel Provis, whom she had won round on the Pensions Committee, she approached the representatives of the Majority, Minority, and the Local Government Board, pointing out that the new departments springing up controlled services to millions of persons in the spheres of health, labour and pensions through the local authorities, and were excluded from the jurisdiction of the Local Government Board: in fact it was throttled by its connection with an obsolete and emasculated Poor Law. The needs of war were willy-nilly bringing about the changes for which Beatrice had fiercely fought as creeping collectivism came in by the back door and the principles of state interference and equality were accepted in, for example, rationing and conscription for all, regardless of class.[66]

Seizing on the joint desire for the abolition of the Poor Law guardians, she again made her plea for an end to the stigma of pauperism, so detested by the working class. Children must be classified according to the needs of the child, for it was not they who were 'destitute' but their parents or guardians; 'It is most important to treat the children themselves as normal,' Beatrice wrote, as she begged for an end to special Poor Law schools, and the overlapping and the inefficiency which followed from having, for example, five separate authorities to look after the mentally ill. This time Beatrice was not aggressive; she had, she acknowledged, at last learnt committee manners. Norman MacLean, the chairman, agreed with her that services which could be clearly differentiated such as education, housing and health should be dealt with by a separate department.[67] It was the death-knell for the Local Government Board, and the climax of her six-year struggle; the establishment at last accepted Beatrice's argument that a department should be based on its category of service. 'The social questions which a congested population generates cannot be satisfactorily solved by amateurs,' asserted Lord George, as if he had stumbled on a new idea, summarily dismissing *laissez-faire* and arguing for the Fabian expert.[68]

The war had strengthened the Labour Party with its new experience of office; it also stiffened its backbone after Lloyd George dismissed Arthur Henderson from the Cabinet. Henderson's resultant hatred for the Welshman made him determined to make Labour an independent political party capable of becoming His Majesty's Government. Sidney became the 'mind' of the Labour Party, writing the new constitution adopted at Nottingham, and two important pamphlets, *War Aims* and *Labour and the New Social Order*. Sidney was, realised Beatrice, making the reputation of the Labour Party just as formerly he made the reputation of the Progressive Party on the London County Council.

It was hard to believe that the divided Labour Party in its ramshackle office at 1 Victoria Street could ever play a part in the reconstruction of Britain after the war. It was a mixture of Independent Labour Party socialists under Snowden, an 'official' Labour Party under Henderson, who was at odds with his treasurer Ramsay MacDonald, idealist intellectuals gathered around G. D. H. Cole, and trade unionists. But at last Beatrice admitted that a trade unionist, J. H. Thomas, the general secretary of the railwaymen, who had sat on the Reconstruction Committee with her, could be able, even statesmanlike. And when Mrs Asquith, whom she had not seen for twelve years, extended an effusive invitation to Beatrice to call, mimicking Henderson's self-important manner and repeating her daughter's witticisms about his 'sheep walk and sleep walk', Beatrice finally knew, in her sixtieth year, where her loyalties lay.[68] The Asquiths were touting for Sidney's support for a Liberal–Labour coalition, but it was obvious to Beatrice that the Liberal leaders only took the Webbs up when they were in opposition and dropped them when they were in office. 'The policy of permeation is played out and labour and socialism must either be in control or in whole-hearted opposition,' declared Beatrice. When Lloyd George too came round offering to 'do a deal' Beatrice was indignant. 'All his ways are crooked and he is obsessed by the craving for power,' she wrote angrily, aware that he too sought a coalition with Labour.[69]

'Sidney has not the remotest wish to go into Parliament,' Beatrice had believed in the autumn of 1917;[70] it was wishful thinking. Sidney was eager to stand for the University of London seat in the 'Hang the Kaiser' election of December 1918 in which for the first time six million women over 30 voted. 'Trinity, Oxford and Cambridge are exceptionally snobbish, and require a special air of patronising the Labour Party instead of belonging to it,' Shaw advised Sidney,[71] telling him to treat the Labour candidate as a new departure necessitated by the spirit of the age. Shaw had sensed the *Zeitgeist* correctly, for although Sidney lost at the University the Liberal Party were slaughtered. It was the big surprise of the election. 'I put the Labour members at 60 and they came back 59; but I never thought they would become HM Opposition. It means a revolution in British political life and one wonders whether the Labour Party is quite ready for the role,' wrote Beatrice.[72]

At last the Webbs were Radical chic. Labour had come of age, polling one fourth of the votes, and the Liberals were consigned to the history books, mere 'garlanded prisoners', in the words of Cole,[73] of the Conservatives, led by Bonar Law. The desire of so many after the war to make the world a better place found an outlet in the new Labour Party. Full of hope, Beatrice said, 'Never again will the manual workers accept the position of outcasts from all that makes for civilisation; never again will they agree to a position of social servility; never again will they trust the representatives of the ruling class . . . Their leaders will fall into all sorts of traps, but the great multitude behind will press forward, stumbling slowly over innumerable obstacles to a world based on social equality . . .'[74]

Once again the political spotlight was focused on Sidney, and Beatrice was consigned to the shadows. He had a 'rollicking good time' when Lloyd George appointed him to the Sankey Commission to deal with the demands of the miners for higher pay and shorter hours.[75] This led to a request by the mining constituency of Seaham in Durham in 1920 for him to become their parliamentary candidate. Sidney was at first reluctant, but Beatrice persuaded him to accept. Seaham appealed to her because it was virgin soil upon which sympathetic intellectuals like the Webbs could make an impression, and she pitied the short, pale miners' wives, forever struggling against the coal dust, and the 'bookish miners' looking for a lead. Besides, the climate was invigorating, and she soon found a pleasant little hotel with a private sitting room at 7s 6d a day. By December Beatrice and Sidney were embarking on a punishing lecture tour round the mining villages. It was 'pretty hard work for an old lady nearing sixty-three years of age', complained Beatrice, speaking in eleven freezing halls in the teeth of a piercing wind straight from the North Sea, even though they used motor cars to take them from venue to venue.[76]

Beatrice felt too old and ill to enjoy the 1922 election campaign, wistfully longing for the old life of 'learned leisure' with Sidney. He by contrast was like a boy going to his first term at public school after the triumphant count at Seaham on 17 November. At the age of sixty-three he entered Parliament for the first time, and was asked by Ramsay MacDonald, the new leader of the party, to sit on the opposition front bench. But euphoria turned to disillusion when the Tories began to bully him, for Sidney was not a natural speaker like Shaw and his voice was too weak to carry above the hubbub of the Commons. Writing to Beatrice, who was alone in the country, Sidney said, 'I did quite well, I think, in a quiet way.' He had not been interrupted by Tory jeers when he welcomed Neville Chamberlain as Minister of Health.[77] But Sidney's Whip, Robertson, an outspoken Scottish miner, had to take him aside for a few tips. 'Speak out; and speak more slowly,' he told the Fabian. 'You are too accustomed to talk to small classes of persons who *want* to listen to you.'[78] When Beatrice sat in the Ladies' Gallery to hear Sidney speak she was humiliated by the continuous hum kept up by the Tories, who resented Labour members they considered class traitors like Sidney and Patrick Hastings KC, and, fresh from convivial dinners, shouted 'Sit down, Nannie', referring to his goatee beard, when he rose to correct a statement. So loud was the 'row' that Sidney could not complete his speech.

'Does not your husband mind?' Hastings asked Beatrice, when he came to dinner. 'No, I don't think he bothers,' she answered. 'You see, he has his career behind him – it lies in his books.' Although Sidney was not a success as a parliamentarian, Beatrice took comfort in the fact that the rank and file of the party were genuinely appreciative of him, but his lack of vigour probably had a physical cause. In the winter of 1922 Sidney seemed to have a slight stroke, falling unconscious and having difficulty walking for some weeks afterwards.[79] Although he recovered, Beatrice noted that he looked much older afterwards. She too often complained that she did not feel strong enough for the life she had to lead, disliking the noise of the constant motor traffic past their house and the strain of seeing people, and her thoughts turned to a weekend cottage in the country. An advertisement in the *New Statesman* for a house with pretty views away from 'cocks or dogs' produced Passfield Corner, near Liphook, with eight acres, which the Webbs bought for £1750 in 1923.

That spring Beatrice and Sidney travelled to Germany where Beatrice saw the results of the 'infamous peace' of Versailles which had left a heavy burden of reparations among the Germans. At the Socialist Congress in Hamburg she felt a sense of foreboding at the dark brooding silence of a defeated race, saw the little children looking already old in their pale-faced apathy, felt the suppressed anger in the faces of the Germans as they stared, then walked silently round the uncomfortable Webbs. At the railway station an official, mistaking Sidney for a Yankee, asked, 'Pardon me, Sir, but can you show me an American dollar?'[80] His voice betrayed the German reverence for the mighty dollar, the standard by which the mark had fallen a thousand-fold during the last few months.

The 'black fever of unemployment' was creeping over Britain, leading Prime Minister Stanley Baldwin to adopt Protection as cure-all for the effects of the post-war slump. Beatrice forecast, accurately enough, that he would be conclusively beaten in the election in which he appealed to the country: she herself was too worried about Europe to feel much concern about the outcome. 'With Germany slowly drowning and those damned French knocking her on the head when she tries to save herself, what does it matter? . . . It is too late for Great Britain to save Europe from chaos and another war.'[81] In any case, she was too busy moving into Passfield Corner with her maid Jessie, apart from being glad that Sidney was 'on velvet' at Seaham.

The result of the January 1924 election was historic: with one hundred and ninety-one seats Labour formed its first minority government with Ramsay MacDonald as Premier. Conscious of the irony of the occasion, 'Altiora and Oscar Bailey' entertained the victorious Labour Party at Grosvenor Road. Wells, with whom Beatrice was again on cordial terms (although she still felt he was 'an unclean beast'), should have been there to describe the Webbs' moment of triumph, laughed Beatrice. They were no longer out in the cold but respected confidants of MacDonald, their former enemy, and the Labour inner circle.

If the previous year had been Sidney's first term at public school, in 1924 he was looking forward to being a prefect. On Wednesday 23 January twenty Labour Cabinet Ministers were sworn in at Buckingham Palace; everyone laughed, said Beatrice, to see Wheatley, the revolutionary, actually going down on his knees to kiss the King's hand. Sidney managed to fit into the frock coat he had bought from Japan, and not looked at since 1912. 'Would you take the Ministry of Labour and shoulder the unemployment difficulties . . . If you consent, please say nothing to a living soul – not even Miss B [Margaret Bondfield],' MacDonald had written anxiously to Sidney. 'I pray of you to consent.'[82] In the event MacDonald upgraded his offer to President of the Board of Trade, and so, by strange coincidence, Sidney entered the Cabinet in the post held by Joseph Chamberlain when Beatrice first knew him.

Beatrice's role as Minister's wife was less fulfilling, and she was often lonely in the dank cold and all-enveloping silence of Passfield Corner while Sidney struggled ineffectually with his red boxes. Aware that the wives of Labour MPs sometimes felt isolated in London, Beatrice had founded the Half-Circle Club in 1920 to prepare them for the time when their husbands might take office: now that victory had come, Beatrice's telephone never stopped ringing. The number, Victoria 7413, had been ex-directory since the telephone was put in in 1920, but was leaked all over London. As doyenne of the Ministers' wives Beatrice was constantly asked to settle the two chief questions: clothes and curtseys, by the Labour wives. 'A sort of underground communication is going on between Grosvenor Road and Buckingham Palace which is at once comic and tiresome,' wrote Beatrice, busy fixing up Mrs Clynes at 11 Downing Street with a housekeeper, cook and butler. Her latest task was soothing the feelings of Ethel Snowden, wife of Philip Snowden, who was deeply offended at being excluded from the usual residence of the Chancellor of the Exchequer, in favour of the Leader of the House. 'But the whole of the Labour world would have revolted at the bare idea of Ethel established in the official residence. She is a climber of the worst description . . .' wrote Beatrice. 'Hence every class conscious Labour man or woman listens for the echoes of Ethel – climbing, climbing, climbing, night and day! Out of the Labour world into that of plutocrats and aristocrats.'[83]

Beatrice was amused but not taken in by the sudden, effusive resurrection of old acquaintances who had dropped them in Poor Law days. People she had not seen for twenty years sent braces of pheasants with their cards, followed by pressing invitations to dine. Lady Elcho, now the Countess of Wemyss, also 'resumed' Beatrice, as did Mildred Buxton, who had become a Viscountess. But one letter of congratulation got short shrift from Beatrice: 'May I send my love to Mrs Webb?' enquired Betty Balfour of Sidney. 'She cannot send what she has not got,' replied Beatrice tartly. 'You had better leave me out of the picture.'[84] And she ignored the shoals of cards which arrived daily.

Beatrice was adamant that she did not want the Labour Party to become the 'plaything' of London Society, for she remembered her own 'lapses' when her head was turned by the glitter of the great houses. In March she refused to go to Buckingham Palace to be presented, as some of the other wives had done. 'I cut the knot by refusing in the curiously ungracious accepted formula, "Mrs Sidney

Webb is unavoidably prevented from obeying Their Majesties' command to, etc, etc" – to take the first step into the charmed circle.' She was alarmed that MacDonald was taking his daughter Ishbel, of whom she approved in her pretty new frock, with her simple, direct ways, into the vortex of luxurious living. 'It is impossible for Ishbel to do her duty to the Party,' said Beatrice. '*We had better go out in the summer*. If we don't go out this year we shall go rotten.'[85]

Her efforts failed, for Labour found London Society no less fascinating in the 1920s than Beatrice had done in the 1880s, and the wives resented any hint of patronage from Beatrice, even though she found a fine clubhouse for the Half-Circle Club. It was all very well for Beatrice to say 'We have all done it in our day . . . "Good Society" is stale stuff.'[86] To MacDonald it was a novelty with which abstemious receptions at Grosvenor Road could not compete. Soon he was outdoing Beatrice in her heyday as a webspinner: 'MacDonald is more adept at intrigue and word twisting and word spinning than even Lloyd George himself,' complained George Lansbury to Beatrice.[87] Beatrice recognised that deep in his heart MacDonald preferred the company of Tory aristocrats and Liberal capitalists to that of trade union officials and Liberal capitalists. 'It may be human nature but it is not good comradeship; it is not even successful politics,' she wrote. But she did not accuse him of treachery, since she thought he had never been a socialist, either of the revolutionary type like Lansbury or the administrative type like the Webbs. What stuck in her throat was that MacDonald was a poser, a man who *posed* as a socialist, and was therefore more Machiavellian than the Webbs. 'For after all, *We are and have always been Socialists*.'[88]

So distinguished did MacDonald look in his gold-braided court dress that his new aristocratic friends found it hard to believe that he was the illegitimate son of a Scottish serving girl. 'He is no Labour man, he is one of us,' Milly, Duchess of Sutherland told Beatrice: perhaps the illegitimate son of the Duke of Argyll; 'No,' said another grande dame, 'he is the son of the Duke of Richmond.'[89] In 1930 his relationship with Lady Londonderry, who called him 'Hamish the Hart', scandalised the Labour world still further, as the Premier paid court to his hostess in 'the Ark', the Londonderrys' magnificent home in Park Lane.[90] It led to the charge that his corruption by the aristocracy lay behind his treacherous decision to abandon his party to lead the National Government in 1931.

Beatrice was meanwhile busy nursing Sidney's constituency, writing monthly letters to the Women's Section giving them the news from

Westminster, and together the Webbs wrote *The Miners of Seaham*; Beatrice had become genuinely fond of the miners and their wives, who reminded her of the simple Bacup community in which she had felt at home. Otherwise the Webbs were more separate than at any other period in their life together: when Sidney returned from Westminster 'we love each other', wrote Beatrice. 'But he has interests about which I know little and I am absorbed in creative writing in which he has no part.'[91] In 1926 her autobiography *My Apprenticeship* was published: it was, as Beatrice admitted, an autobiography with the love affairs left out.

'*Quelle vie! Quelle femme! Quelle livre!*' wrote Charles Mostyn Lloyd when he read the book; and Beatrice, who had been nervous about its reception, was relieved. 'It is all alive – and alive with you,' he told her. 'And it is extraordinarily stimulating to me, as you yourself always have been in real life.'[92] Harold Laski, by now a lecturer at the London School of Economics, opined that 'if you hadn't married you would have been an abbess of a sisterhood', but castigated her for her absence of intellectual discipline. 'You flew about life and didn't know how to plan it. That (I whisper) is where SW was not unhelpful.'[93]

Sister Kate mused over Beatrice's relationship with Chamberlain. 'I think that year or two was a bit inflating, and perhaps a little arrogance on your part excited him – don't you think? I remember thinking you swaggered a little when you first became head of Father's household and dispenser of his wealth and no wonder for it was a big position for a handsome clever girl.'[94] Shaw teased her for her Victorian reserve about her love affairs. 'It even suggests that they were affairs instead of states of mind,' he wrote perceptively, asking how her sociological work was 'saved from staleness' by her sexual and romantic trains of thought. 'How long did each hero last; and did they overlap; had you an intellectual hero, and a romantic hero, and a lump of a fleshly hero simultaneously?' he asked.[95] Shaw understood Beatrice far better than she realised; she had been a literary inspiration to him, as he confessed, complaining that she had not put him in any of *her* books.

Beatrice's powerful imagination, fired by romantic desire, gave her early writing a brilliance which fell away as Sidney broke her into a dual harness; their later work has a curious flatness. It was, said Beatrice, a 'grind' and she feared their books were unreadable. Although she in fact enjoyed working on the utopian *A Constitution for the Socialist Commonwealth of Great Britain* the style was all

Sidney's, and presented a huge contrast to Beatrice's vivid diaries with their sharp comments on personalities and political events. Most marked is the Webbs' obstinate faith in 'the inevitability of gradualness', rooted in the Victorian belief in evolutionary progress,[96] which contrasts with Beatrice's constant fear, expressed in the diaries, that another European war must follow the brutal Peace of Versailles. Yet although the Webbs' proposal for two Parliaments was unworkable, a 'constant preoccupation' of their Social Parliament would have been to protect the environment, to stop factory owners polluting streams, and mine-owners building slag heaps.[97]

When the first Labour government fell over the McVitie biscuit scandal and the Zinoviev letter in October 1924, Beatrice was relieved, but in 1929 she again had to sacrifice the ageing and increasingly ineffectual Sidney to office in MacDonald's second government. The premier asked Sidney to take the Colonial Office and a peerage. Although Sidney was delighted to be Minister in the very office where once he was clerk, the request posed a problem for Beatrice, who refused to adopt the title 'Lady Passfield'. 'A title ignored is an honour deflated,' she announced, determined to set an example to other Labour wives.[98] But when Ethel Snowden passed on the message that the King and Queen were 'hurt', she resigned herself to attending a garden party. Slipping quietly through the crowd, she was not available when the Queen asked to talk to her, and was shocked by Mrs Baldwin shouting ' "Lady Passfield" we shall call you whether you like it or not.' At seventy, Beatrice had done her duty to Society. It was time to return home to Passfield Corner, to plan her garden with Oliver the gardener, and to walk her terrier, Sandy.

After the 1929 Wall Street Crash panicked MacDonald into forming the National Government, Sidney was at last released. The Labour Party spat out MacDonald, the man they hated; Sidney remained true to his principles, siding with Henderson and Lansbury.[99] It seemed that at last the aged Webbs might be turned out to grass.

XX

THE LAND OF MILK AND HONEY

*'A pilgrimage to the mecca of the equalitarian state led by a few
Fabians, all well over seventy years of age, will bring about the
world's salvation!'*
Beatrice Webb Diary, 4 January 1932

*'Come my dear,
"'Tis not too late to seek a newer world.
Push off, and sitting well in order, smite
The sounding furrows: for my purpose holds
To sail beyond the sunset; and the baths
Of all the western stars,
Until I die." '*
Sidney to Beatrice, suggested by John A. Kingsbury, New York,
24 December 1937, in a letter to Beatrice Webb

SICK AT HEART AT the private luxury of the rich, and the new Labour
arrivistes, who amused themselves shopping in Bond Street and going
to the races while babies went without milk and men without jobs,
Beatrice felt relieved at the fall of the Labour Government in 1931.
Sidney's disgust was more personal, as he had been one of Mac-
Donald's few friends, one with whom the lonely, autocratic Prime
Minister shared a glass of milk and a biscuit in lieu of lunch at the
Labour Party Conference in Liverpool in 1925.[1] Despite Sidney's
failure to solve the Palestine problem – 'People will say your husband
has not been a success,' he told Beatrice sadly[2] – MacDonald had
written him a friendly letter congratulating him on his seventieth
birthday: in it he made an enigmatic remark concerning the lack of
heavyweights in the Cabinet: 'We have not the material in our party
that we ought to have. The solution will have to come, I am afraid,
by moves which will surprise all of you.'[3]

When MacDonald returned from Buckingham Palace at noon on
Monday, 24 August 1931, to announce to his startled ministers that
he had jettisoned most of his Cabinet and accepted the King's plea to
form a National Government, Sidney was convinced that MacDonald
had been hatching a plot, although Beatrice did not agree. In January

1932 Sidney published an article in the *Political Quarterly* in which he accused MacDonald of plotting for two months beforehand to betray the Labour Party. 'Why did Mr Ramsay MacDonald, after thirty years of building up the British Labour Party, decide to do his best to smash it?' demanded Sidney.[4]

In vain did Malcolm, MacDonald's son, protest that he had kept a diary of his conversations with his father, which showed that he wanted the Labour cabinet 'to stick together to carry the country through the [unemployment] crisis'. There was nothing in the story that his father had secretly planned a National Government, pleaded Malcolm: for such an act 'would have amounted to an act of treachery to his colleagues'.[5] 'I do not feel able to discuss with you – and you cannot discuss with me – the propriety of your father's conduct. We must all have our own views,' replied Sidney.[6] It is probable that MacDonald was not as guilty as Sidney thought. Although J. L. Garvin, editor of the *Observer*, had floated the idea of a National Government as the financial crisis deepened, and the increasingly stressed and isolated MacDonald considered the idea in his diary, there is no proof that he plotted a coup.[7] But the 'gross betrayal' of the British Labour Party[8] by MacDonald had implanted itself into the minds of the Webbs and was a catalyst in the development of their Communist sympathies. Further proof came for Beatrice when Britain went off the Gold Standard on 21 September – the very event the new government had been formed to prevent – and the pound failed to collapse. 'Thomas and Mac had slobbered over the agony of "going off gold",' complained Beatrice. Now the 'consummate trickery' of capitalist financiers lay revealed.[9]

At the Labour Party conference in October Beatrice sensed a new, dour determination 'never again to undertake the government of the country *as the caretaker of the existing order of society*'.[10] She was impatient to slough off the capitalist skin which had grown over the Labour movement and led MacDonald to abandon even a pretence at socialism. His betrayal, the greatest in history in Beatrice's eyes, was for her simply a final symptom of disease, the proof that capitalism was rotten to the core. The ineffectuality of two Labour governments had led her to question her earlier belief that a gradual transition could be made from capitalism to Fabian socialism. As early as 1923 she and Sidney had written a trenchant critique of capitalism, which Beatrice doubted could ever recover from World War I. Was reformism dead? In 1926 she had confessed to Maynard Keynes: 'For a long time I have felt that the particular line of research which we in the Fabian

Society started in the 1890s – the working out of a national minimum of civilised life, so far as regulation and public services can secure it – is now exhausted as a discovery though not yet applied, and that the new inventiveness must necessarily concern itself with the control of capitalist enterprise and landlordism at the top . . .'[11] In February 1931 she wrote, 'What I am beginning to doubt is the inevitability of gradualness . . . Anyway, no leader in our country has thought out *how* to make the *transition* without upsetting the apple-cart. Sidney says "it will make itself" . . . We shall slip into the equalitarian state as we did into political democracy.'[12] As so often before, taking the initiative in ideas if not in their execution, Beatrice put her views forcibly to Sidney.[13]

The belief in gradualism was an inherent part of Fabianism; the stained-glass window designed by Caroline Townshend, 'Fabians at the Forge', shows Sidney and Shaw as patient smiths, hammering the world into a new shape, and bears the motto, 'Remould it nearer to the heart's desire . . . Pray devoutedly hammer stoutly'.[14] But the metal was proving obdurate, and time running out for the patient Fabians. Beatrice, for one, was no longer content to 'hasten slowly', and had begun to cast her eyes across the sea to where a new experiment in socialist utopias was taking shape: Soviet Russia. It was to prove a watershed in her life as significant for Webbian collectivism as the abandonment of Spencerian individualism had been.

Beatrice's ideas crystallised in the months after MacDonald's 'betrayal'. She was surer than ever that 'the game was up with profit-making enterprise'.[15] Both Tory and Labour governments had proved helpless in the face of rocketing unemployment, and as the World Depression tightened its wintry grip upon Europe, the bombast of the Fascist leaders found an answer in the desperation of their audiences. As early as 1931 Beatrice saw western civilisation hurtling headlong towards another war. But it was not merely economic problems capitalism seemed powerless to solve: with the breakdown of Christian taboos on immorality it seemed to Beatrice that there was no 'notion that the sexual act is sinful . . . or that the sexual impulse differs from the appetite for food in the rightfulness of its satisfaction'.[16] She was shocked by the illicit relationship between William Beveridge, director of the London School of Economics, and Mrs Mair, his assistant, who later became Lady Beveridge. Malcolm Muggeridge, married to Beatrice's niece, Kitty, daughter of Rosy Dobbs, added fuel to the flames of Beatrice's Victorian disgust. 'Dear Aunt Bo,' he wrote, 'Sex is becoming exaggerated just because it is almost the only easily accessible creative activity that is left for the ordinary man. His work has . . . lost its joy, his religion has collapsed, there is no longer any direct naked contact with the earth for him . . . and the phallus alone is able to stand up against such an environment.' By rights education should have corrected the situation, argued Muggeridge, but 'in my school – a Government Secondary School – boys used to masturbate in class even as a relief for preparing for matriculation'.[17]

Shaw, who had been criticising Muggeridge's play *The Three Flats*, disagreed. 'Sport and Art . . . are the safety valves of sexual pressure,' he wrote in a disapproving note over Muggeridge's letter, 'and they are far more accessible than under Victoria. What has really changed is the licence to discuss it and to confess one's sexual life . . . The play would have been as impossible then as this letter from a young man to his wife's aunt.' Muggeridge was not impressed. 'He doesn't see beneath the blazers and flannel trousers and tennis frock: and doesn't see that these only hide what Lawrence calls – The Dirty Little Secret,' Muggeridge wrote to his Aunt Bo. Work was the only catharsis – 'otherwise they will just be blazers wrapping up a revolting corpse'.[18]

For Beatrice, living largely alone at Passfield Corner, sexual immorality was more than a preoccupation: it became an obsession. Eschewing evening entertainments, cut off from active political life, and relying on the wireless and weekend visitors for information, she became increasingly puritanical and bigoted in her views. 'Mrs W. is far less ornamental than of old,' wrote Virginia Woolf, whose honeyed letters to Beatrice contrast with her hostile diary entries, 'wispy, untidy, drab with a stain on her skirt and a key on her watchchain; as if she had cleared the decks and rolled her sleeves and was waiting for the end, but working.'[19] Insomniac, muzzy-headed, with 'whizzing' in her ears, 'talking, talking' as she tramped over the common with her guests, Beatrice was an easy subject for caricature, especially by those who did not share her sense of socialist purpose. Yet in eccentricity she retained a charm which still captivated, despite the exhaustion experienced by guests such as Kingsley Martin at the 'long meaty conversation' which was the main fare at Passfield Corner.

Convinced that her fellow countrymen were living on the 'breaking crust' of a rotten civilisation, Beatrice forecast a doom-laden scenario in which Russian Communism and American Capitalism would clash in a final battle of the Titans, just as Islam and Christianity had done in the twelfth to sixteenth centuries. Which culture would win? Beatrice heard the voices of the future calling her from Russia,[20] a country where there was none of the 'repulsive mixing-up of sexual, sadist and mystical emotions, all associated with blood and abandonment to physical impulse and the dominance of the lower organs of the body over the brain', characteristic of D. H. Lawrence. 'I prefer the hard hygienic view of sex and the conscious subordination of sexuality to the task of "building up socialism" characteristic of Soviet Russia . . .'[21]

It had not always been so. Although Beatrice had welcomed news of the Russian Revolution in February 1917, which she at first saw as a victory for democracy, she was horrified by the 'hot terror' which followed the Bolshevik victory. After the return of a Labour delegation to Russia in May 1920 Beatrice realised that a dictatorship or 'creed autocracy . . . a servile state run by fanatics who refuse any compromise with the "bourgeois fetish" of personal freedom' had been established.[22] Wells might poke fun at Sidney by calling Lenin 'a power-hungry beast . . . a Russian Sidney Webb, a rotten little incessant egotistical intriguer';[23] but the truth was that not until after the failure of two Labour governments did Beatrice turn away from gradualism to an authoritarian regime, which answered her mystical need for a creed and a faith in which to believe.

Beatrice's response to Russia was primarily emotional, which partly explained why she was able to suspend her critical judgement when the long-awaited visit came about. In 1929 she had been unimpressed by meeting Trotsky, but she was not alone among the intelligentsia in putting her faith in central planning and Collectivism during the 'Red Decade' of the 1930s.[24] The tide was running towards Russia in those hopeful days before the horrors of Stalin's purges filtered through to the West. Communism was as fashionable as Syndicalism had been before World War I, and Grigory Sokolnikov, Russian Ambassador in Britain from 1929 to 1932, found eager ears to listen as he talked persuasively in broken English and French of the first Five Year Plan.

The Webbs met the Sokolnikovs in February 1930, when Beatrice had them to dinner in her little flat in Artillery Mansions, Victoria. As a 'veritable puritan', an unpretentious tee-total non-smoker, the ambassador impressed her favourably. In August the Sokolnikovs came to stay at Passfield Corner; sitting in the loggia after lunch they painted a rosy picture to Philip Snowden, Chancellor of the Exchequer, of Communist workers gladly accepting low wages for the good of the state. 'I sometimes despair about the working class,' confessed Snowden to the Ambassador. 'They want more wages, shorter hours . . .' 'Ah, Mr Snowden,' said Beatrice, 'you will never get the British workman to work harder on less wages when he sees the employing class enjoying leisure . . .'[25] In November, at lunch at the Soviet Embassy in Kensington Palace Gardens, Sokolnikov planted the idea in Beatrice's mind of going to Russia: it was not expensive, he told her.[26] 'How I should revel (if I were thirty years younger) in a year spent in the USA and also in Russia,' Beatrice wrote wistfully in her diary.[27]

A fact-finding exodus of left-wing intellectuals to Russia began. One of the earliest to go had been Bertrand Russell with his wife Dora, who in 1920 received the red-carpet treatment reserved for prominent foreigners, staying in a 'sumptuous' palace where all the luxury of the ancien régime had been preserved, and enjoying hearty breakfasts and cigars at dinner. But he shuddered at the sight of Russian mathematicians in Petrograd living like tramps, was overwhelmed with horror at the cruelty, poverty, suspicion, and persecution which formed the very air he breathed. For Russell everything he valued in human life was being destroyed by a 'glib and narrow philosophy'. 'Imagine yourself governed by a mixture of Sidney Webb and Rufus Isaacs,' he told Lady Ottoline Morrell, 'you will have a picture of modern Russia. I went hoping to find the promised land . . .'[28] Instead he found a tyrannical bureaucracy. Walter Citrine, General Secretary of the Trades Union Congress, was depressed by the sense of despondency he encountered in 1925, the bare-footed eighteen-year-old girls doing manual labour on the railways, the pestering beggars in Sebastopol, and found himself snapping at the comrades that 'Lenin wasn't Jesus Christ', at which a pall of silence fell over the conversation, and Citrine realised he had 'outraged the deity'.[29]

The most potent influence however upon Beatrice was that 'blarneying Irish liar' Shaw, who trumpeted from Leningrad his verdict, 'If the future is with Lenin we can all smile, if the world follows the old path the future will be a melancholy one.'[30] Admitting to herself that Shaw's whirlwind tour of Russia in 1931 with Lady Astor was simply 'ten days inspection of show institutions', remembering that only three years ago he had been just as enthusiastic about Mussolini, Beatrice still listened with biased ear to his declaration: 'It *must* be right! . . . The Russian Revolution was pure Fabianism – Lenin and Stalin had recognised the "inevitability of gradualness"!'[31] It was a theme echoed by George Lansbury, who told Sidney, 'In 1920 I advised Lenin to send for you two because they were only applying good sound Fabian principles, and that as you were two of the originators you were just the people they needed to show them how to do it . . . I am pretty sure you will both come back convinced Bolsheviks.'[32] That Soviet Communism was no more than the final flowing of Fabianism was too flattering an idea to ignore: and what could be easier to believe for two elderly Socialists who were still prophets without honour in their own country?

By the summer of 1931 Beatrice was reporting that the Russian embassy was the only one in which she felt 'at home'. 'Without doubt we are on the side of Russia,' she wrote.[33] A month later the government fell, leaving them free to make the longed-for visit to the Soviet Republic. Excitement mounted, as Beatrice gathered kindred spirits around her at Passfield, and shut out dissenting voices. In 1932 Margaret Cole and her colleagues in the new Fabian research bureau, including Kingsley Martin and Hugh Dalton, also visited Russia. 'It is like a dream come true . . . One has come home . . . It's as simple as becoming a Socialist,' reported a euphoric Margaret to her husband Douglas on her arrival in Moscow.[34] Although she failed to master 'the bloody language', she approved of the way Russian women worked alongside the men, and praised the 'elasticity of this so-called "rigid system"' to Beatrice on her return.[35] The Muggeridges came to stay before they too departed for Russia, 'very confident of its success', as Rosy told Beatrice.[36] By September Malcolm was reporting that 'I feel happier than I ever have in my life before', in a little wooden house outside Moscow.[37]

On 22 May 1932 the Shaws waved goodbye to the Webbs as their Russian steamer *Smolny* drew slowly away from the quayside. It was not a comfortable journey. There were no chamber pots on board, complained the seventy-four-year-old Beatrice, and 'no hot water unless you go and fetch it from the kitchen for your hot water bottle . . . I am already regretting that I discarded one box of biscuits and an extra hot water bottle as likely to be unnecessary'. Nevertheless she took a keen interest in the ship and its workings, noting with approval the 'Lenin corner' in the dining room, where photos of Marx and Engels and a bronze statuette of Lenin were lit by a red electric light. The Captain explained to her that when the Bolsheviks first took over, each ship was managed by the unions and the Captain had to obey orders: such a system soon proved unworkable, and by 1922 the skipper was back in command. Despite this volte-face, the ship did not meet Beatrice's western standards and she wrote a very lengthy memo for the Chief Steward who passed it on to the Captain. There was nothing to vomit into, no water, no baths, 'great slabs of pork' served to the Jewish passengers, and the handles of the doors were 'hard for delicate hands'. The Captain accepted her criticisms graciously and was 'very grateful'.[38]

The Webbs stepped ashore at Leningrad to a royal welcome: for the Russian Communist Party they had, as Margaret Cole remembered, an almost mystical prestige as the authors of the *History of Trade Unionism*, which had been translated by Lenin himself. They were no less than the father and mother of the Revolution.[39] And so began a love affair which was to last the rest of the Webbs' lives, for they fell 'hopelessly in love'[40] with Russia and, like most lovers, remained blind to the faults of the object of their affections. Before leaving for Russia the Webbs had finished *Methods of Social Study*, in which they sum up their empirical method: the investigator should approach his work as free from bias as possible, they warned, and must leave no stone unturned to ascertain the facts before drawing his conclusions. Yet in their infatuation with Russia, Sidney and Beatrice did just the opposite, abandoning the painstaking, inferential method in which Booth had trained his young cousin, and attempted to force the facts to fit a hypothesis already formed before they left England. In January Beatrice had concluded exultantly that the constitution of the Soviet Union exactly corresponded to that of their earlier book *A Constitution for the Socialist Commonwealth*. It had just the same three-fold structure they had suggested, with the trade unions in a desirably subordinate position. 'There is no d—d nonsense about Guild Socialism!' she wrote happily.[41]

But it was the soul of Russia for which Beatrice hungered. 'Being a mystic and a moralist,' as she acknowledged, 'I always hankered after a spiritual power, always felt instinctively that there *must* be some such force if salvation were to be found.' Before arriving in Russia Beatrice had convinced herself that the Communist Party was akin to a religious order, that it obeyed rules of poverty, obedience and near-chastity. It was the Communist Party which breathed life into a dead constitution, Communism which was – so Beatrice reasoned by some imaginative intellectual leap-frogging – Comtism, the religion of humanity preached by Auguste Comte which had so strong a hold over her as a young woman. Sidney did not share Beatrice's ardent quest for a spiritual creed but he, too, was disenchanted with capitalism and willing to believe it terminally ill. Where she led, he followed; and thus the two pilgrims began their search for the holy grail, as credulous as any medieval couple who made their pilgrimage to worship the true cross or watch blood liquefy in the age of faith.

In Moscow Beatrice and Sidney stayed in the former palace of a millionaire in the grounds of the Foreign Office. It was a huge villa with palatial bedrooms, and the Webbs had their own sitting room and a convenient bathroom. Beatrice was impressed by the grand staircase, fine crockery, silver and linen marked with the imperial crest, but one problem still remained: the 'universal absence of chamber pots . . . and the plumbing of the lavatories and bathrooms is indescribably bad'. However she soon made friends with her interpreter, Mrs Tobinson, a 'charming little lady'. A Jewess from Warsaw, Mrs Tobinson had returned to Russia when the Revolution broke out; her husband, as she confided to Beatrice, was thrown into prison. Mrs Tobinson's skills as a trained nurse were soon to prove invaluable.

Beatrice and Sidney showed energy and intellectual curiosity remarkable in two such elderly people, but once in Russia they were in the hands of their guides. Unable to speak the language, unable to stray from the beaten track, hampered by tiredness and illness, they were forced to rely on tours of show institutions for their information, and printed material supplied by the Russians, which they accepted with child-like trust. Beatrice could not fail to realise that the large elementary school she was shown in Moscow was 'evidently a show place'. But so carried away was she at the sight of the well-clothed, clean and sturdy children that she made an impromptu speech, urging them 'to make the Russian socialist state a success so that we might imitate them, whereupon they all cheered enthusiastically'.[42]

A whirlwind tour followed. Beatrice was impressed by the tractor plant she was shown at Stalingrad, although she and Sidney had to admit that the Autostroy motor plant was a failure. Steaming down the Volga tired her immensely, and a packed programme which took them to Verblude and Gigante in the North Caucasus, where Beatrice had to stay in farm lodgings on the collectives, was her undoing. In Rostov she collapsed with 'stomach fever', as the Russian doctor called it, and was confined to bed. Sidney travelled on alone to the Ukraine with his own interpreter, Rakov, while Beatrice was sent to convalesce at Kislovodsk in the Caucasus. She submitted to a rigorous treatment of fasting and castor oil from her 'attractive' Russian doctors, and when her temperature dropped was able to take some rice water and sour milk.

The Webbs' gullibility was most in evidence in their admiring attitude to the state farms, the product of Stalin's crash collectivisation programme begun in April 1929.[43] These farms were, reported Beatrice, 'a marvel', and the development of mechanised agriculture was 'one of the wonders of Soviet Russia'. Knowing little of agricultural techniques, they were easily deceived. Grim was the picture painted by Andrew Cairns, an agricultural expert from the new Fabian research bureau, of the Ukraine, Crimea and North Caucasus in the very same summer as when the Webbs were there, of spindly crops choked with weeds, acres of land uncultivated, of soaring prices in the bazaars and ragged hungry peasants begging for bread. In Kiev lay 'scores of men and children with badly swollen tummies, in rags, asleep on the ground (while flies by the thousand crawled over them), or begging or picking up scraps of vegetables and fish scales to eat'. In the street Cairns watched men and women die of starvation in front of him. Unlike the Webbs, he understood that the October Revolution Commune to which he was taken was a showplace for tourists, whose names filled the visitors' book. Able to speak some Russian, he understood the women who sucked in their cheeks and told him bitterly there was nothing to eat, nothing at all, and, pointing at the crowd fighting for bread, said 'there is the Five Year Plan for you'.[44]

Beatrice reserved her greatest enthusiasm for the Comsomols and Pioneers of the Communist Youth. The note of 'hygienic self-control' at the Comsomol conference in Moscow exactly tallied with her own ideas that 'you must not waste time and strength on sex . . . Certainly there is singularly little spooning in the Parks of Rest and Culture', she recorded in her sparse notes on the Russian trip. 'European dancing is taboo, it being held, by the faithful, that its promiscuous embraces are an unwholesome manifestation of the erotic impulse.' The Russians told Beatrice what she wanted to hear – that promiscuity was punished by expulsion from the Party. Naively she recorded the story of a badly-behaved Party member to whom Stalin was reported to have said: 'If there is any more nonsense about women, you go to a place where there are no women.' Had the Webbs met Stalin, which they did not, they might have better understood the nature of the threat. Instead Beatrice rhapsodised about the physical exercise in sunshine and wind, cold water inside and outside the body, open windows when asleep and awake, alcohol, tobacco and gambling all 'bad form', which made up a puritan's paradise.

Beatrice was not totally impervious to the 'dark side' of Russian society. She admitted that she and Sidney had little opportunity to observe it, but she was not unaware of the sudden 'trap-door' disappearance of unwanted persons, which the Russians openly defended as a necessary 'war measure'.[45] She sensed the atmosphere of suspicion and fear which permeated academic circles but, convinced that the Soviet system had solved the economic problems of production and consumption which overwhelmed the West, allowed herself to believe that terrorism was no more than the 'growing pains' of a new civilisation.[46]

Tired but triumphant Beatrice and Sidney returned home to Passfield in July, and immediately plunged into the daunting task of writing up their conclusions. 'What does it matter what two "over-seventies" think, say or do, so long as they do not whine about getting old and go merrily on, hand in hand, to the end of the road?' Beatrice had written in one of her insomniac diary entries in the small hours.[47] In fact it mattered very much: the Webbs' conversion to Soviet Communism was a coup for the Russians and a source of sadness to their friends as news of the treason trials filtered home, and some early enthusiasts like Harold Laski began to change their mind about the Soviet Union.

One of the first to do so was Malcolm Muggeridge, the *Manchester Guardian* correspondent in Moscow, who wrote to Beatrice in February 1933 that he had seen that 'the thing is bad and that it is based on the most evil and cruel elements in human nature'. Horrified at the Webbs' public advocacy of the Soviet Union, he begged Beatrice to think again: 'But the horror of it! The Humbug! Why should Uncle Sidney say in Edinburgh: "I indignantly repudiate the slander that there is forced labour in the Soviet Union" when every single person in Russia knows that there is forced labour?' His despairing plea summed up what many were saying about the Webbs: 'I know your premises are wrong. I know you've been deliberately misled. Your own intellectual integrity and courage have been the means of deceiving you, and through you, others. Can you imagine, Aunt Bo, a government taking by force from millions of peasants every scrap of grain they produced, leaving them without any food at all, and then announcing that the standard of life of the workers and peasants has risen?'[48] The editor of the *Catholic Herald* was even more brusque: as the *Daily Express* ran a series of articles on the Terror, he asked Sidney why 'Lady Passfield and yourself spent so much time in Russia and came back and had nothing to say about these ... terrible happenings?'[49]

Blind and deaf to such entreaties, Beatrice struggled with exhaustion and cystitis on her return. She had an exploratory operation for 'carbuncles' on the bladder at Hastings Hospital in October 1933. The death of Graham Wallas in August 1932, the first of the Fabian 'old gang' to go, was an intimation of her own mortality. The five Fabian founders and their wives, Edward Pease, Shaw, Webb, Olivier and Wallas, had never quarrelled in fifty years and, thought Beatrice with satisfaction, they had all 'made good': two peers and a millionaire, and four out of five in *Who's Who*. It was a record to be proud of. And in the recent years of their old age she and Sidney had found a new task to occupy and divert their daily lives – their 'biggest baby', as she called it – which brought them a fresh circle of acquaintances. Later, Beatrice was often conscious that although the Webbs' output had always been heavy going, 'tasteless fare, not to say indigestible',[50] especially when compared to Shaw's sparkling prose. *Soviet Communism: A New Civilisation?* (the question mark was dropped in the second edition) was more indigestible than most since it was largely written by Sidney. In the preface Beatrice explains why 'two aged mortals, both nearing their ninth decade', undertook a work of such magnitude.[51]

'We had a world to gain,' she wrote, 'and we had nothing to lose by the venture – not even our reputation.'[52] It was the Webbs' tragedy that they believed this to be so. Unable to separate propaganda from fact, they relied heavily on research material from the USA, accepted statistics on the success of the Five Year Plan printed in *Pravda* and other 'leading journals', and English language documents supplied by the Communist Party. Believing as they did, along with Karl Marx, that 'the philosophers have only interpreted the world; our business is to change it',[53] they in turn became Communist propagandists. Blithely dismissing the 1931 to 1932 Russian famine as a 'partial crop failure', they painted a rosy picture of life on a Russian collective, whitewashed the 1933 purge as a necessary 'cleansing' of the Party, and naively explained that Stalin was not 'the sort of person to claim or desire such a position' as that of dictator.[54] Beatrice, who had been speaking on the BBC since 1929, was as usual led to the microphone by an announcer in evening dress to give a talk on Russia in her assured and musical voice.

The Webbs saw no ulterior motive in the warm friendship forged with them by Ivan Maisky, the Soviet ambassador from 1932, and his wife Agnes. Maisky took a 'broad' view of Communism, explaining plausibly to Beatrice that repression in Russia was only temporary, and she stifled her doubts as fresh news trickled in of bad harvests, heresy hunts and purges in Russia.[55] Even a heartfelt plea for help from Professor Paul Haensel, a Russian refugee in Illinois, who was sending food parcels and money to his relatives to save them from starvation, did not prick the bubble of the Webbs' complacency. 'One wife wrote to me,' he told Sidney, ' "I have broken off my tooth bridge and brought it to the Bank for sale. I received four dollars for it.' It was not easy to chew, 'but at any rate we had something to eat.'[56]

Old friends felt forced to remonstrate with the Webbs. Betty Balfour wrote to tell Beatrice that women and children were starving and homeless in the streets of Moscow.[57] Kitty Muggeridge, home from Moscow, came to Passfield, but Beatrice dismissed Muggeridge's reports of famine in the North Caucasus and Ukraine as 'arrogant', convincing herself that the press knew nothing of Russia as they spent their time drinking in Intourist hotels.[58] Her strength was failing and she felt frequently dizzy with 'whizzing' in her ears; only able to stumble after Sidney as he wrote mechanically, she leaned more and more heavily on the Maiskys for reassurance. Was there some fire behind Malcolm's smoke, she wondered, but soothingly Maisky told her that the spring sowing was already bringing good results. 'An experiment that fails is often as illuminating as one that succeeds. When all is said and done, we still believe in its ultimate success,' Beatrice wrote in her diary;[59] no such doubts appeared in the finished text of their 'illegitimate' book.

Soviet Communism: A New Civilisation? was a bombshell for former disciples of the Webbs like Harold Laski, who did not mince his words: 'I see no evidence to support your view that Stalin was a "necessary" hero,' he wrote, 'and the degree to which he has built up a personal "machine" ... goes far beyond anything you indicate.'[60] William Beveridge protested in anguish, '*Do not make light of hateful things* ... It hurts me to think of ... any persons for whom I care being associated with the kind of brutality represented by the present Russian regime, or appearing in any way to condone or make light of it.' Mortality in the villages was thirty per cent, he told Beatrice, and no foreign correspondents were allowed in the stricken areas. 'Turn your backs on Russia ... Please forgive me,' the letter ended.[61]

It is possible that if Shaw had changed his mind about the Soviet utopia, Beatrice and Sidney might have done the same. But while Shaw kept faith with the Soviet Union, so did the Webbs, finding comfort in being still united if embattled. The finger of Divine Providence had guided them towards Russia, Shaw told Beatrice. 'No one else could possibly have done it.'[62] 'A country of wild beasts,' muttered William Beveridge, over lunch at the London School of Economics. Content in her obsession, Beatrice danced wildly to the strains of the 'Internationale' booming over the radio from the Red Square, to

Arthur Henderson's amusement, and listened nostalgically to the ringing of the Kremlin bells. Passfield Corner became a shrine to Stalin, whose portrait dominated the staircase of the cottage.

Even the news of the Moscow show trials of Zinoviev and other Bolsheviks in 1936 did not shake her conviction. 'Is Christianity a sham because brutal deeds have been done by the Christian churches?' she asked Margaret Cole. With scant regard for historical accuracy, Beatrice compared the trial of her old friend Sokolnikov to that of the murderers of Lord Frederick Cavendish in 1883, and cited the evidence of an English KC, Pritt, who was sure that the trials were 'conducted fairly'.[63] Shaw too shrugged off the trials as 'a Popish Plot without a Titus Oates', although he wondered 'why should Sokolnikov lend himself to such insanity even if Trotsky were mad enough for it?'[64]

'This child is our last begotten,' mused Beatrice about the book as she watched Sidney work, passing her days in a three- or four-mile walk with her West Highland terrier, Sandy, listening to the concerts on the wireless and sorting material for Sidney. Weekend visitors were still taken for a Sunday afternoon walk, Beatrice taking the lady and Sidney the gentleman. Sidney, once out of sight of the house and his wife's watchful eye, was liable to sink into a haystack for an afternoon snooze, making sure that the return journey was strenuous enough to work up a light sweat; in this way Beatrice's suspicions were not aroused.[65] Maurice Hankey remembered his 'long tramps' with the Webbs, who had no breakfast, and told Hankey that 'after the age of sixty, if one wanted to get fit, one had to make up one's mind to give up a good deal in gradual stages'.[66] This was Beatrice's prescription for good health rather than Sidney's, for when Bertrand Russell stayed in a hotel in Normandy with the Webbs, Beatrice remained upstairs rather than bear the painful spectacle of the party breakfasting; Sidney would come down for rolls and coffee. Beatrice sent a message by the maid, 'We do not have butter for Sidney's breakfast.'[67] It was but one example of her habitual use of the royal 'we' when referring to the 'partnership'. Sidney's abstinence, like his vegetarianism, was paper-thin, for after Beatrice's death he swiftly reverted to a bacon-and-egg breakfast.

Problems with her kidneys continued to trouble Beatrice, and at the age of seventy-six she had her right kidney removed. It was a brave decision to take. 'I have done the work I intended to do and lived the life I preferred,' she wrote in her diary just before the operation. 'Today we see the promised land . . .' 'Courage old lady, courage; count your blessings!' she exhorted herself during a painful convalescence.[68] Slowly she recovered at Passfield, unable to accompany Sidney to Russia for a second visit in September 1934, just before the Kirov murder. Her niece Bardie (Barbara Drake) went instead, excited at 'seeing Russia from the front row of the stalls'.[69] 'See, see, it works, it works,' Sidney would whisper to her during the second stage-managed tour.[70]

Happily reunited with Sidney, Beatrice returned to sifting through her old diaries to write *Our Partnership*,[71] the story of the marriage of two 'second-rate minds', as she had described them at the time of her engagement, to form one of the most remarkable intellectual combinations in history. 'One and indivisible', as Beatrice described herself and Sidney, or, in the words of Bernard Russell, 'the most completely married couple I knew',[72] they were 'happy ghosts' living in shadowland, content with each other's company. The painting of the Webbs by William Nicholson captures the essence of Beatrice, stretching out her tapering fingers to the fireside, a small, utilitarian fire set in a red-brick chimneypiece. She is daydreaming, her eyes gazing towards the vision of a new social order. Sidney, by contrast, stands with his neat goatee beard and pince-nez, papers in hand, his eyes resting affectionately on his wife, who dominates the portrait.[73] Beatrice at eighty, recorded Alexei Tolstoy, 'as she sat on a low seat before the fire, looked elegant and young with her brilliance of mind and freshness of ideas'.[74]

Irritable in his old age, Sandy mauled Beatrice and had to be put down. 'I doubt whether I shall get another dog,' she wrote, saddened at the parting. But the family party for her eightieth birthday held in the summer of 1938 in the garden at Passfield was a cause for pleasure, as 'Aunt Bo' proudly entertained over one hundred R.P.s, descendants of Richard and Lawrencina Potter. How delighted her father would have been, thought Beatrice, to see her sisters' children, grandchildren and great-grandchildren talking and laughing together. In later life Beatrice took a great interest in their doings, following the career of Stafford Cripps through regular letters to his wife Isobel and Stafford himself. She was closest to Bardie, with whom she stayed in Sheffield Terrace, Kensington, on her rare visits to London, and who took her to visit the ninety-three-year-old Mary Booth.

At the beginning of 1938, just after Beatrice's birthday, a blow fell irrevocably altering the Partnership. Sidney, who had been suffering from shortness of breath and poor circulation, collapsed with a stroke. 'If only we could talk together,' lamented Beatrice, as Sidney lay in bed with a day and night nurse in attendance. But she kissed him and petted him, telling him the news and talking about the past. 'We have written the book,' said Beatrice, and Sidney would smile. For Beatrice there was a sense of *déjà vu*; she remembered her father's stroke over fifty years ago and the loneliness which followed. But patiently she listened as Sidney struggled to recover his speech, walking round the landing with him, and reading aloud, and by May he was able to speak a little. 'In old age and infirmity we love each other more tenderly than we did in the prime of life,' she declared.[75]

By now even Beatrice was increasingly troubled by the show trials and executions in the Soviet Union. Hardly a day passed without news of the sudden disappearance of a Russian ambassador; but publicly she continued to explain away these incidents, although secretly she found them harder and harder to accept. When she sent Maynard Keynes and Lydia Lopokova, the Russian ballerina with whom he lived, a copy of her latest pamphlet on Soviet Russia, Lydia refused to read it. 'I, too, do not know what to say,' wrote Keynes. 'There seems to be almost a defence, or if not a defence an excuse, or, if not an excuse an explanation, of the reign of blood and liquidation by official murder of the old Communist Party.'[76]

Why did Beatrice and Sidney not change their minds? Bertrand Russell believed the Webbs to be fundamentally undemocratic and élitist: they considered it the function of government to bamboozle or terrorise the populace.[77] As a member of the governing class Beatrice was always attracted to the notion of an élite corps, whether Samurai or Communists, who would do the thinking for the untutored masses. Also, both the Webbs had a strangely inhuman quality which led them to ignore individual suffering in favour of the needs of the State. 'Sidney tends to ignore personalities and I study them as specimens. Our main end and preoccupation has been to discover how to change society in order to increase the well-being, energy and dignity of the human race,' admitted Beatrice.[78] It was now psychologically impossible for them to renege on their belief in the social system which they felt was the logical culmination of their life's work, and the only hope of the world as capitalism convulsed in its final death throes.[79]

But Beatrice's hopes were shattered by the news of the anti-aggression pact signed by the Soviet Union and Germany. 'Even Sidney is dazed and I am, for a time at least, knocked almost senseless!' It was a negation of all that they had stood for.[80] In September 1939 Prime Minister Neville Chamberlain, younger son of Joseph Chamberlain, declared war after the invasion of Poland, and within a few days the first air-raid alarm came. Beatrice, who had continual difficulties with the servants in old age, walked into Sidney's room to find him sitting up with his gas mask on. When she told him to take it off, Mrs Grant, the housekeeper, turned on her, ' "*You have no right* to tell Mr Webb to take his off," she said in a menacing voice. "Pardon me," I said. "I am his wife and the mistress of this house. Keep yours on if you like. It is damned nonsense putting on gas masks out in the country." '[81] And Sidney dispensed with his mask.

'Why have we lived so long? One war was enough,' enquired a weary Shaw of Beatrice.[82] 'As you say, we are too old to live in such tragic times – but we should miss each other!' replied Beatrice.[83] Her spirits sank further after the invasion of Poland, when Russia invaded Finland. 'I can't help being very glad that you do not approve the aggressive attack by huge Russia on little Finland,' wrote Lady Betty who had picked up her friendship with Beatrice again. Nevertheless the Fabian quartet of the Webbs and Shaws refused to be panicked by the war. 'I slept through the raid, what would have been the use of getting up – No point unless you have Anderson shelters . . . which I haven't. Anyhow we have had our day so what does it matter?' enquired Shaw philosophically.[84] In August Beatrice was having her bath when the bombers swept overhead, and explosions shook the walls. 'I must not be found naked,' was her first thought, as she hurriedly dressed.[85] Mrs Grant and Annie prepared breakfast as usual. From Woking Lady Betty wrote that no amount of bombs would get her and Gerald out of bed at night.[86]

By good fortune the Shaws were out of London when a bomb fell on County Hall, opposite their flat in Whitehall Court. It was impossible to sleep at night Blanche Patch, Shaw's secretary, told Beatrice. 'We can hear London firing and see the flashes from the guns and there is a dump about a mile off where they bring the unexploded bombs and let them off during the day, and we all leap in the air when that happens. If GBS is in his shelter he puts his ear plugs in, the result being that he never hears the bell ringing to summon him to his lunch.'[87] In Liphook it was mercifully quiet, while London took the full force of Hitler's attack, and Beatrice worried for Alys Russell in Chelsea, and Bardie. She began to long for release from life, as sleeplessness, and chronic cystitis made pain a nightly bedfellow.

As the Battle of Britain raged came the news that Virginia Woolf had drowned herself in the river Ouse. Ten years earlier, after a Sunday with the Webbs, Virginia had written to Beatrice: 'I wanted to tell you, but was too shy, how much I was pleased by your views upon the possible justification for suicide. Having made the attempt myself, from the best of motives as I thought – not to be a burden on my husband – the conventional accusations of cowardice and sin have always rather rankled. So I was glad of what you said.'[88] Beatrice was depressed that Virginia had yielded to the passion for death. 'I think she may have been profoundly and most courageously right,' wrote Lady Betty, 'but I wish she had done her deed in a way less agonisingly painful for those who found her.'[89] By May 1942 Lady Betty too was dead, and it seemed to Beatrice that a light had gone out of her world. 'Do you wish to go on living?' Beatrice asked Sidney, as they sat in the garden. 'No,' he replied.[90]

To Beatrice's immense joy Anthony Eden had announced in June 1941 that Britain and Russia were allies since the German invasion of Russia. The swing of the political pendulum towards the Soviet Union was reflected in a flood of requests to Beatrice for talks and messages in favour of Russia. She was featured as 'the thinker' in *Picture Post*, *Reynolds* and *Tatler*, was interviewed by the BBC as a contemporary 'great woman', and was begged to remain as President of the Fabian Society because of her 'Red' sympathies. Showing the remarkable vitality at eighty-three upon which journalists remarked, Beatrice published a final pamphlet, *The Truth About Soviet Russia*, in which she again denied that Stalin was a dictator. 'Russia has lit a flame in the heart of our own people which neither inertia nor power nor complacency can conquer,' wrote Laski, who like other intellectuals had now changed his mind about the Soviet system. 'The October Revolution sets the intellectual framework of the next age.'[91]

Vindication of another sort came with the publication of the Beveridge Report, which at last proposed that the State should provide every individual with the minimum of civilised life which Beatrice and Sidney had long advocated. It was, as Beveridge said, a revolution, although Beatrice feared that unemployment benefit would increase the number of work-shy.

As the war bit deeper domestic troubles crowded on Beatrice as her servants fell ill. 'If only I had been brought up to know how to cook and clean,' she wrote despairingly.[92] Visits from her sister Rosy Dobbs, who had become an eccentric old lady, were a trial to Sidney. Rosy was liable to turn an electric fire upon its back to cook over it, and had to be banished eventually to a local hotel.[93]

In January 1943 Beatrice celebrated her eighty-fifth birthday. Her remaining kidney was failing, and the pain was hard to bear. As she lay awake in the grey dawn, hot water bottle in the small of her back, she pondered whether a Temple of Anaesthesia should not be established to allow an honourable and voluntary withdrawal from life. She did not believe in the 'myth' of life after death, 'this false hope of personal immortality', which she considered debased Christianity, but her deeply religious nature had always longed for a life of personal holiness and in old age she found comfort in an animistic belief in God in nature. 'Just a few more years, Mother Nature, and I will testify to your beneficence,' she had written at seventy-six. Now, as melancholy overwhelmed her in the final months of her life, only Sidney's love and dependence prevented her following Virginia Woolf's example of suicide, or VWL – voluntary withdrawal from life – as Beatrice called it.

Beatrice wrote that she was content that she and Sidney had lived the life they wished, and they had been proved right about Soviet Communism, and with this thought she comforted herself. In reality hers had been a life of both triumph and tragedy: for Beatrice marriage had been both a unique intellectual partnership and a form of *felo de se*, the wastepaper basket into which she had thrown the most passionate and creative side of her personality. In suppressing this side of her personality she paid a high price, for in gaining power and influence she lost warmth and tolerance; in 'discovering' a socialist utopia in Soviet Russia she developed a bigoted and blinkered mind. Yet it was, as she foresaw when she married Sidney, an epic life in which she proved how much can be accomplished by unwavering will. The little group of Fabians had indeed remoulded the world nearer their hearts' desire, bringing a peculiarly British form of socialism into flower in Attlee's coming to power in 1945, and in the birth of the Welfare State which Beatrice had anticipated as far back as 1909.

In the last entry in her three-million-word diary Beatrice expressed the final letting-go of the spirit as she felt herself merging with infinity: 'Suddenly I ceased to exist . . . We shall all disappear . . . The garden will disappear . . . the earth and the sun and the moon. God wills the destruction of all living things, man, woman and even a child. We shall not be frozen or hurt, but merely not exist.'

She died eleven days later, on 30 April 1943. For some time Sidney kept her ashes on the mantelpiece. 'That's Beatrice, you know,' he would say to visitors, gesticulating at the urn. After his death in 1947, their ashes were buried together in a spot she had chosen in the garden at Passfield. Shaw attempted to raise a subscription for a statue of

Beatrice and Sidney Webb to stand upon the Embankment, so that they might gaze in death as in life over the Thames. When this failed he wrote to *The Times* asking that their ashes be transferred to Westminster Abbey, where they now lie, the only married couple to be so honoured.

THE POTTER SISTERS'
ANCESTRY

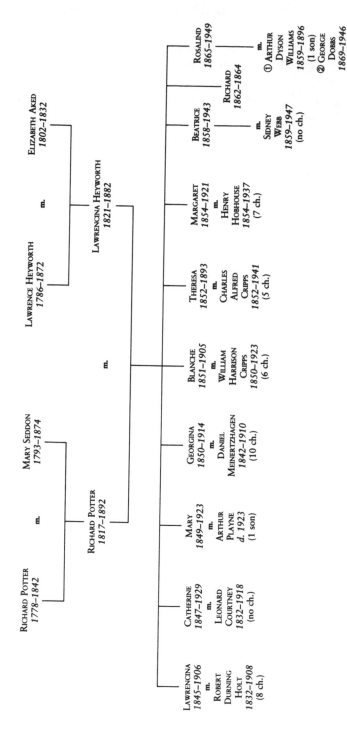

Based, by kind permission of Lord Methuen, on a genealogy
prepared for private circulation to the descendants of Richard Potter.

NOTES

CHAPTER I

1. Beatrice Webb, *My Apprenticeship*, Cambridge, 1979, p. 10.
2. Lawrencina Potter, unpublished journal, in the possession of Jonathan King.
3. BW, op. cit., 13.
4. Heyworth Family Tree, Royal College of Arms. I am indebted to Nicholas Meinertzhagen for this information. He has also traced the incidence of manic-depression in the Richard Potter descendants.
5. Georgina Meinertzhagen, *From Ploughshare to Parliament*, 1908, p. 191.
6. Richard Potter to Elizabeth Potter, 23 July 1817, Box IIIA, Richard Potter Papers, BLPES. It is probable that Mary Seddon developed a puerperal psychosis consequent upon post-natal depression, of which paranoid delusions were a symptom. Nicholas Meinertzhagen, grandson of Georgina, says research shows that there is no foundation for the belief Mary Seddon was Jewish; her father was baptised a Christian.
7. BW, op. cit., p. 25, cites H. Taine, *Notes on England*, 1972, p. 93.
8. Ibid., p. 4.
9. Ibid., note, pp. 4–5.
10. Ibid., p. 8.
11. Barbara Caine, *Destined to be Wives*, Clarendon Press, Oxford, 1986, pp. 18–19. Stephen Hobhouse, *Margaret Hobhouse and Her Family*, Rochester, 1934, pp. 16–17.
12. Ibid., p. 8.
13. Ibid., p. 10. Conversation with Kitty Muggeridge 8.10.87, who remembers her mother telling her that her grandparents were unhappy together.
14. Richard Potter to Beatrice Potter, 21 July 1874. Passfield Papers, BLPES.
15. Lawrencina Potter journal.
16. BW, *My Apprenticeship*, p. 11.
17. BW, *My Apprenticeship*, p. 18.
18. B. Potter to Lawrencina Potter, 12 June 1862 PP.
19. B. Potter to Kate Potter, 1862 PP.
20. L. Potter journal.
21. Rosalind Dobbs Autobiography, Courtney Collection vol. XXXIX, BLPES.
22. BW, *My Apprenticeship*, p. 58.
23. Ralph Dutton, *The Victorian Home*, London, 1954, p. 65.
24. BW, *My Apprenticeship*, p. 40.
25. Ibid., p. 11.

26. Ibid., pp. 59, 60.
27. Ibid., p. 43.
28. B. Potter to Fanny, undated PP.
29. BW, *My Apprenticeship*, p. 11.
30. Ibid., p. 13.
31. BW, *My Apprenticeship*, p. 16.
32. Mary Playne to Beatrice Potter, 16 Oct. 1883 PP.
33. L. Potter journal.
34. BW, *My Apprenticeship*, p. 45.
35. Ibid., Introduction, p. xliii.

CHAPTER II

1. Charles Darwin, *The Descent of Man*, 1871, in Julia Swindells, *The Roar on the Other Side of Silence: Working Women and Writing in the Nineteenth Century*, p. 13.
2. R. Meinertzhagen, *Diary of a Black Sheep*, 1948, p. 63.
3. Virginia Woolf.
4. Tennyson, 'The Princess, in Christ', op. cit.
5. Swindells, op. cit., p. 20.
6. E. Sigsworth and T. Wyke, 'A Study of Victorian Prostitution and Venereal Disease', in M. Vicinus, Ed., *Suffer and Be Still: Women in the Victorian Age*, Methuen, 1972, p. 83.
7. Cecil Woodham-Smith, *Florence Nightingale*, London, 1950, p. 94.
8. Harriet Martineau, *Autobiography* vol. 1, Virago, 1983, p. 94.
9. Elizabeth Longford, *Eminent Victorian Women*, Weidenfeld and Nicolson, 1981, p. 88.
10. After her marriage Barbara Leigh Smith was known as Barbara Bodichon.
11. Candida Lacey, Ed., *Barbara Bodichon*, 1987, Introduction.
12. Strachey, op. cit., p. 92.
13. E. Lynn Linton in the *Saturday Review*, 1868, in Crow, p. 196.
14. Longford, op. cit., p. 9.
15. Caine, *Destined to be Wives*, p. 70.
16. L. Potter to B. Potter, early 1870.
17. B. Potter to L. Potter, 1870 PP.
18. L. Potter to B. Potter, 13 May 1878 PP.
19. BW, *My Apprenticeship*, p. 29.
20. Herbert Spencer, *Autobiography*, 1904, vol. 1, pp. 260–261, quoted in Webb, op. cit., p. 22.
21. Ibid., p. 22.
22. Ibid., p. 25.
23. Ibid., pp. 24–25.
24. Ibid., p. 61.
25. Ibid., p. 25.
26. B. Potter to L. Potter, after 1867 PP.
27. BW, *My Apprenticeship*, p. 26.
28. Herbert Spencer, *Autobiography*, 1904, in David Wiltshire, *The Social and Political Thought of Herbert Spencer*, Oxford, 1978, p. 7.
29. Wiltshire, op. cit., p. 5.
30. E. M. Elliott, The Political Economy of English Dissent, quoted in Wiltshire, op. cit., p. 14.

31. BW, *My Apprenticeship*, p. 15.
32. Kitty Muggeridge and Ruth Adam, *Beatrice Webb*, p. 39.
33. Ibid., p. 42.
34. BWD, 12 Sept. 1881.
35. BW, *My Apprenticship*, p. 59.

CHAPTER III

1. B. Potter to Lawrencina Potter (no. 142), 30 July ?1865 PP.
2. B. Potter to Lawrencina Potter (nos 152, 153), Summer 1870 PP.
3. BWD, not dated, 1868.
4. K. Potter to B. Potter (no. 67), 1873 PP.
5. BWD, 23 Dec. 1872.
6. BWD, 23 Dec. 1872.
7. F. K. Prochaska, *Women and Philanthropy in 19th Century England*, Clarendon Press, Oxford, 1980, pp. 119–122.
8. Florence Nightingale, *Cassandra*, privately printed 1852, appendix to Ray Strachey, *The Cause*, 1928, Virago edn, 1978, p. 404.
9. Cecil Woodham-Smith, *Florence Nightingale*, pp. 60–61, 67, 76.
10. George Eliot, *Middlemarch*, p. 30. Deborah Epstein Nord, *The Apprenticeship of Beatrice Webb*, MacMillan 1985, p. 62, discusses St Theresa as a model for women who sought to triumph over vanity and achieve greatness, and points out similar traits, e.g. daydreaming, sense of sin, in Victorian hagiography.
11. Eliot, op. cit.
12. BWD, Dec. 1873, B. Webb, *My Apprenticeship*, p. 72.
13. BWD, 13 Sept. 1873, B. Webb, *My Apprenticeship*, p. 65.
14. BWD, 25 Sept. 1873.
15. BWD, 7 Oct. 1873, B. Webb, *My Apprenticeship*, p. 66.
16. Letter from Margaret Potter, Dobb Papers, Sept. 1872, Kitty Muggeridge, *Beatrice Webb*, p. 47.
17. BW, *My Apprenticeship*, p. 9.
18. BWD, San Francisco, 24 Oct. 1873, B. Webb, *My Apprenticeship*, p. 67.
19. BWD, Salt Lake City, 1 Nov. 1873, B. Webb, *My Apprenticeship*, pp. 68–70.
20. Maggie Potter to B. Potter, 25 Nov. 1873 PP.
21. BWD, Dec. 1873, B. Webb, *My Apprenticeship*, p. 72.

CHAPTER IV

1. BWD, 13 March 1874.
2. BWD, 18 Jan. 1874.
3. BWD, 6 March 1874.
4. BWD, 24 March 1874.
5. BWD, 13 March 1874.
6. BW, *My Apprenticeship*, p. 46.
7. Margot Asquith, *Autobiography*, p. 92.
8. Mary Soames, *Clementine Churchill*, Cassell, 1979, p. 65.
9. R. Dutton, *The Victorian Home*, 1954, 1984, p. 104.
10. Leonore Davidoff, *The Best Circles*, Croom Helm, 1973, pp. 24–25.
11. Ibid., p. 43.
12. BW, *My Apprenticeship*, p. 51.
13. Dutton, op. cit., p. 124.

14. BW, op. cit., p. 48.
15. M. Asquith, op. cit., pp. 49–51.
16. BWD, 3 Aug. 1874.
17. K. Potter to B. Potter, May 1873.
18. BWD, 3 Aug. 1874.
19. BW, op. cit., p. 52.
20. The *Queen*, 11 July 1885.
21. Ibid.
22. BWD, 3 Aug. 1874.

CHAPTER V

1. Sir Francis Galton, *Memories of My Life*, Methuen, 1908, p. 287, and D. W. Forrest, *Francis Galton: The Life and Work of a Victorian Genius*, London 1974, p. 84.
2. BW, *My Apprenticeship*, pp. 55, 57.
3. Galton, op. cit., p. 323. Galton published 'Hereditary Genius' in 1869 and was the father of fingerprinting. He developed the science of 'race improvement' in the 1880s.
4. BW, op. cit., p. 57.
5. BWD, 24 Sept. 1874.
6. Galton, op. cit., p. 315.
7. Richard Meinertzhagen, *Diary of a Black Sheep*, p. 61.
8. Galton, op. cit., p. 317.
9. Maggie Potter to Beatrice Potter, 1874 (no. 129) PP.
10. Maggie Potter to Lawrencina Potter, October 1874 PP, and S. Hobhouse, *Margaret Hobhouse and Her Family*, Rochester, 1934, p. 49.
11. BWD, 11 Dec. 1874.
12. Carol Dyhouse, *Girls Growing up in late Victorian and Edwardian England*, 1981, pp. 46–47.
13. Lawrencina Potter to Beatrice Potter, Jan. 1875 PP.
14. BWD, 3 Oct. 1875.
15. BWD, 19 Sept. 1875.
16. BWD, 16 Aug. 1876.
17. BW, *My Apprenticeship*, p. 82.
18. Maggie Potter to B. Potter, 23 Dec. 1876 PP (Hobhouse, p. 82).
19. Maggie Potter to B. Potter, Toronto 1874 (no. 129) PP.
20. Maggie Potter to B. Potter, Liverpool Jan. 1879 (no. 134) PP.
21. Maggie Potter to Richard Potter (no. 136) 1879 PP.
22. Kate to B. Potter (no. 71) 7 Gt College St, ?1873 ?1875.
23. Maggie Potter to B. Potter (no. 137) 1879 PP.
24. BWD, 8 Nov. 1879.
25. BWD, 13 Sept. 1877, Webb, op. cit., p. 89.
26. BW, op. cit., p. 90.
27. BWD, 15 July 1878.
28. BWD, 30 Sept. 1889.
29. Maggie Potter to B. Potter, Nov. 1878 (no. 131) PP.
30. BWD, 9 Nov. 1878 Wiesbaden.
31. BWD, 30 March 1879.
32. Theresa Potter to B. Potter (no. 122) 1879.
33. Theresa Potter to B. Potter (no. 121) 1879.

CHAPTER VI

1. Maggie Potter to B. Potter, 25 Nov. 1873 (no. 128) PP.
2. Maggie Potter to B. Potter, 23 Dec. 1879 (no. 137) PP.
3. Stephen Hobhouse, *Forty Years and An Epilogue: An Autobiography 1881–1951*, pp. 11–15.
4. Mottisfont Abbey was given to the National Trust in 1857 by Mrs Gilbert Russell, who with her husband created the present-day garden. The Abbey is famous for its collection of historic roses in the Walled Garden.
5. BWD, 28 Nov. 1880, Florence.
6. BWD, 22 Jan. 1881, Rome.
7. BWD, 28 April 1881, San Remo.
8. BWD, 2 June 1905.
9. Blanche Cripps to B. Potter, July 1877 (no. 99) PP.
10. BWD, 8 Sept. 1881.
11. Rosalind Dobbs Autobiography, vol. XXXIX Courtney Collection, BLPES, p. 16.
12. BW, *My Apprenticeship*, pp. 16–17.
13. B. Potter to Lawrencina Potter, mid-October 1880 PP.
14. B. Potter to Lawrencina Potter, 5 Nov. 1880 (no. 167) PP.
15. B. Potter to Lawrencina Potter, 21 Nov. 1880 PP.
16. Lawrencina Potter to B. Potter, Nov. 1880 (no. 60) PP.
17. Ibid.
18. BW, op. cit., p. 16.
19. Lawrencina Potter to B. Potter, 3 Jan. 1881 (no. 63) PP.
20. Mary Playne to B. Potter, Feb. 1881 PP.
21. Lawrencina Potter to B. Potter, n.d. 1881 (no. 62) PP.
22. BWD, undated note, Mother's Last Illness. (Lawrencina died on 13 April 1882.)
23. BWD, 23 April 1882.
24. BWD, 27 Aug. 1882.
25. Ibid.
26. BW, op. cit., p. 113.
27. BWD, 23 April 1882, BW, *My Apprenticeship*, p. 114.
28. Ibid.
29. BWD, 3 Dec. 1882.
30. BW, op. cit., pp. 107–108.
31. Mary Playne to B. Potter, 11 Nov. 1882 (no. 86) PP.
32. Ibid.
33. Mary Playne to B. Potter, 16 Oct. 1883 PP.
34. BW, op. cit., p. 107.
35. BWD, 17 April 1882, BW, *My Apprenticeship*, p. 107.
36. Mary Playne to B. Potter, 16 Oct. 1883.
37. Maggie Harkness to B. Potter, 1878 (no. 46) PP.
38. BWD, 2 Jan. 1883 (MS Diary, PP only).
39. BWD, 10 Sept. 1882 (MS Diary, PP only).
40. BW, *My Apprenticeship*, p. 105.
41. Ibid., p. 132.
42. BWD, 24 March 1883.
43. Extract from Herbert Spencer, *First Principles*, BWD, 2 Jan. 1883 (MS Diary, PP).

44. BW, op. cit., p. 134.
45. BWD, 22 Feb. 1883.
46. BWD, 26 Feb. 1883.
47. BW, op. cit., p. 121.
48. BWD, 24 April 1883.

CHAPTER VII

1. F. K. Prochaska, *Women and Philanthropy in Nineteenth Century England*, OUP 1980, p. 205.
2. Gareth Stedman Jones, *Outcast London*, Peregrine 1976 ch.
3. Arnold Toynbee, Lecture Jan. 1833, Progress and Poverty, St Andrew's Hall, London.
4. Henrietta Barnett, *Canon Barnett*, vol. 1, 1918, p. 69.
5. K. Woodroofe, *From Charity to Social Work*, 1966, p. 50.
6. Hannah More, Coelebs, quoted E. Yeo, unpublished essay, 'Women, Social Science and Social Work in Britain, 1789–1914'.
7. Frances Power Cobbe, quoted Prochaska, p. 8.
8. W. R. Greg, quoted in *Independent Women, Work and Community for Single Women*, 1850–1920, M. Vicinus, Ed., p. 2.
9. Ibid.
10. Vicinus, p. 39.
11. Florence Nightingale, quoted Julia Swindells, *The Roar on the Other Side of Silence: Working Women and Writing in the Nineteenth Century*, Polity Press, 1985, p. 79.
12. Prochaska, *Women and Philanthropy*, p. 11.
13. BWD, 8 Sept. 1884, BW, *My Apprenticeship*, p. 149.
14. Edward R. Pease, *History of the Fabian Society*, 1926, p. 18.
15. BW, *My Apprenticeship*, pp. 146–148.
16. Ibid., p. 149.
17. BWD, 15 March 1889, BW, *My Apprenticeship*, p. 149.
18. *Merrie England*, quoted in Martin J. Wiener, *English Culture and the Decline of the Industrial Spirit*, 1850–1980, CUP 1981, p. 119.
19. Hollingshead, *Ragged London*, 1861, p. 61.
20. G. Stedman Jones, *Outcast London*, Peregrine edition, 1976, p. 167.
21. David Owen, *English Philanthropy 1660–1901*, Harvard UP, 1966, p. 373.
22. Henry George, *Progress and Poverty*, p. 200.
23. *G. B. Shaw: An Autobiography*, Stanley Weintraub, Ed., 1969, p. 132.
24. Henry Mayers Hyndman, *Record of an Adventurous Life*.
25. Annie Besant, *Our Corner*.
26. Rev. Andrew Mearns, *The Bitter Cry of Outcast London*, 1883, p. 55.
27. Anthony S. Wohl, intro. to *Bitter Cry*, p. 16.
28. G. R. Sims, *How the Poor Live and Horrible London*, 1889, p. 21.
29. G. B. Shaw, *Fabian Essays*, p. 22.
30. Courtney Papers, LSE, *Diaries of Kate Courtney*, 1875, vol. XXI.
31. Owen, *English Philanthropy*, pp. 375–387.
32. Canon Barnett, vol. 2, p. 28.
33. Kate Courtney Diary, Courtney Papers, vol. XXI.
34. Barnett, p. 106.
35. BWD, 17 March 1883, Virago edn, p. 77.
36. Kitty Muggeridge and Ruth Adam, *Beatrice Webb: A Life*, 1967, pp. 74, 75.

37. *The Autobiography of Margot Asquith*, Mark Bonham Carter, Ed., 1962, p. 37.
38. Prochaska, p. 113, quoting Guides to Visitors, C. S. Loch.
39. Octavia Hill, *Nineteenth Century*, 'A Few Words to Fresh Workers', July–December 1889, no. 26.
40. Ibid.
41. BW, *My Apprenticeship*, p. 195.
42. K. Woodroofe, *From Charity to Social Work in England and the United States*, 1966, p. 26.
43. Barnett, vol. 1, p. 107.
44. Owen, *English Philanthropy*, p. 387.
45. BWD, 18 May 1883.
46. Octavia Hill, *Nineteenth Century*, 'A Few Words to Fresh Workers', July–December 1889, no. 26.
47. Woodroofe, p. 41.
48. BWD, 20 May 1883.
49. BWD, 20 May 1883.
50. BWD, 7 July 1883.
51. BW, *My Apprenticeship*, p. 208.
52. Barnett, vol. 1, p. 115.
53. Ibid., p. 191.
54. BW, *My Apprenticeship*, p. 201.
55. Ann Summers, 'A Home from Home: Women's Philanthropic Work in the Nineteenth Century', in *Fit Work for Women*, S. Burman, Ed., p. 54.
56. Helen Bosanquet, *Social Work in London*, p. 279.
57. BW, *My Apprenticeship*, pp. 203, 198.
58. Ibid.
59. Stefan Collini, *Liberalism and Sociology*, CUP, 1979, p. 34.
60. BWD, 3 June 1883 (Virago, p. 88).

CHAPTER VIII

1. BW, *My Apprenticeship*, Cambridge University Press, 1979, p. 172.
2. R. Norman-Butler, *Victorian Aspirations: The Life and Labour of Charles and Mary Booth*, London 1972, p. 62.
3. BWD, 16 March 1884.
4. BWD, 22, 24 July 1882.
5. Letter from J. F. Main to B. Potter, 23 July 1882 PP.
6. BWD, 11 March 1885.
7. BWD, 9 Nov. 1878.
8. Cary Darling to B. Potter, May 1884 PP.
9. Theresa Cripps to B. Potter PP.
10. BWD, 5 May 1883.
11. BWD, 27 June 1883.
12. BWD, 24 May 1883.
13. B. Potter to Mary Playne, July 1883 PP.
14. Rosalind Dobbs Autobiography, Courtney Collection vol. XXXIX; K. Muggeridge and R. Adam, *Beatrice Webb: A Life*, London, 1967, p. 72.
15. Ibid., p. 72.
16. BWD, 1 Feb. 1883.
17. BWD, 15 July 1883.

18. J. L. Garvin, *The Life of Joseph Chamberlain*, vol. 1, MacMillan, 1933, p. 43.
19. Ibid., p. 56.
20. Richard Jay, *Joseph Chamberlain: A Political Study*, Clarendon Press, 1981, p. 18.
21. Ibid., p. 25.
22. BWD, 27 Aug. 1883.
23. BWD, 26 Sept. 1883.
24. Ibid.
25. Kate Courtney Diary, vol. 21, Courtney Collection, LSE.
26. Ibid., p. 108.
27. BWD, 5 Nov., The Argoed.
28. BW, *My Apprenticeship*, pp. 154, 155.
29. B. Potter to R. Potter in op. cit., p. 155.
30. Ibid., p. 161.
31. BW to Mary Playne, Oct. 1883 PP.
32. BWD, 11, 19 Oct. 1883 PP.
33. Joseph Chamberlain to B. Potter, 16 Dec. 1883 PP.
34. BWD, 7 Dec. 1883.
35. BWD, New Year's Eve, 1883.

CHAPTER IX

1. BWD, 12 Jan. 1884, Passfield Papers.
2. Magnus, *Gladstone*, p. 218.
3. BWD, 12 Jan. 1884.
4. Ibid.
5. J. L. Garvin, *The Life of Joseph Chamberlain*, 1935, vol. 1, p. 206.
6. Elletson, p. 39.
7. BWD, 16 March 1884.
8. BWD, 8 April 1884.
9. BWD, 22 April 1884.
10. BWD, 9 May 1884.
11. Elizabeth Wolstenholme Elmy in Sheila Jeffreys, *The Spinster and her Enemies* (Pandora Press, 1985), p. 44.
12. BWD, 28 July 1884.
13. Passfield Papers, II, 1 (ii).
14. Passfield Papers, II, 1 (ii).
15. BWD, 15 Oct. 1884.
16. BWD, 24 Oct. 1884.
17. BWD, 6 Nov. 1884.
18. BWD, 26 Nov. 1884.

CHAPTER X

1. Octavia Hill in 'A Few Words to Fresh Workers', *Nineteenth Century*, no. 26, 1889.
2. D. Owen, *English Philanthropy 1660–1960*, p. 387.
3. BW, *My Apprenticeship*, p. 260.
4. Ibid., p. 261.
5. Ibid., p. 262.
6. Ibid., p. 263.

7. H. Barnett, *Canon Barnett*, vol. 1, p. 138.

8. Ibid., p. 139.

9. BWD, 16 Jan. 1885.

10. BWD, 8 March 1885.

11. Ibid.

12. E. Denison, Letters, Baldwyn Leighton, Ed. (1872) 3 Sept. 1867.

13. William Booth, *In Darkest England and the Way Out*, 1890, p. 13.

14. BWD, 4 June 1885.

15. BWD, 12 April 1885.

16. BWD, 4 June 1885.

17. J. L. Garvin, *Life of Joseph Chamberlain*, vol. 1, p. 549.

18. Ibid., p. 556.

19. BWD, vol. IV, 29 Jan. 1885, Passfield Papers only.

20. BWD, 29 Jan. 1885.

21. BWD, 1 Feb. 1885.

22. PP only, BWD, 13 March 1885.

23. PP only, BWD, 4 Jan. 1885.

24. Peter Fraser, *Joseph Chamberlain: Radicalism and Empire, 1868–1914* (1966), p. 65.

25. BWD, 22 May 1885.

26. Passfield Papers, B. Potter to Mary Playne, July 1885.

27. Courtney Collection, vol. 21, Kate Courtney Diary, pp. 140–141.

28. PP, B. Potter to Mary Playne, July 1885.

29. PP, in BWD: Letter from Kate Courtney to B. Potter, 23 July 1885.

30. PP, Mary Booth to B. Potter, 25 July 1885.

31. PP, Leonard Courtney to B. Potter, 28 July 1885.

32. PP, B. Potter to Mary Playne, August 1885.

33. BWD, 15 Sept. 1885.

34. BW, *My Apprenticeship*, p. 273, MS Diary, 12 Nov. 1885.

35. O. Hill, 'A Few Words to Fresh Workers', *Nineteenth Century*, vol. 26.

36. See E. Yeo, unpublished essay, 'Women, Social Science and Social Work in Britain, 1789–1914, Dress Rehearsal of an Argument'.

37. PP, Ella Pycroft to B. Potter, 9 Feb. 1886.

38. BW, *My Apprenticeship*, pp. 267–268, MS Diary, 13 Aug. 1885.

39. General Booth, *In Darkest England and the Way Out*, pp. 48, 49.

40. PP, B. Potter to Richard Potter, August 1885.

41. PP, Ella Pycroft to B. Potter, 19 Feb. 1886.

42. PP, Ella Pycroft to B. Potter, 26 Feb. 1886.

43. PP, B. Potter to R. Potter, August 1885.

44. General Booth, *In Darkest England and the Way Out*, pp. 50–52.

45. PP, Ella Pycroft to B. Potter, 9 Feb. 1886.

46. BW, *My Apprenticeship*, p. 269, BWD, 15 Sept. 1885.

47. PP, B. Potter to R. Potter, Aug. 1885.

48. PP, B. Potter to R. Potter, Sept. 1885.

49. Norman MacKenzie, note in Virago edn, BWD, vol. 1, p. 143.

50. PP, B. Potter to R. Potter, Nov. 1885.

51. PP, B. Potter to Mary Playne, 20 Nov. 1885.

52. PP, Mary Playne to B. Potter, Feb. 1885.

53. Courtney Collection, vol. XXXIX, Diary of Rosalind Dobbs, ch. 2, p. 19.

54. PP, B. Potter to Mary Playne, Nov. 1885.

55. BW, *My Apprenticeship*, p. 273, MS Diary, 8 Nov. 1885.
56. BWD, 6 Oct. 1885.
57. BW, *My Apprenticeship*, p. 272, BWD, 23 Oct. 1885.
58. PP, B. Potter to R. Potter, Nov. 1885 (not in *My Apprenticeship*).
59. PP, B. Potter to R. Potter, Nov. 1885 (*My Apprenticeship*, p. 275).
60. BWD, May 1886, *My Apprenticeship*, p. 279.
61. PP, Ella Pycroft to B. Potter, 9 Feb. 1886.
62. BWD, May 1886.
63. HJ Laski, Fabian Socialists, in Annan (ed) *Ideas and Beliefs of the Victorians*, 1949, p. 82.
64. BW, *My Apprenticeship*, p. 267, BWD, 8 Nov. 1886.
65. PP, Ella Pycroft to B. Potter, 15 July 1886.
66. PP, B. Potter to R. Potter, 8 Nov. 1885, BW, *My Apprenticeship*, p. 276.
67. BWD, 19 Dec. 1885.
68. PP, B. Potter to M. Playne, Dec. 1885.
69. BWD, 19 Dec. 1885.
70. BW, *My Apprenticeship*, p. 282.
71. BWD, Jan. 1886.
72. BWD, 11 Feb. 1886.
73. Julia Swindells, *The Roar on the Other Side of Silence: Working Women and Writing in the Nineteenth Century*, CUP, p. 147.
74. BW, *My Apprenticeship*, p. 284.

CHAPTER XI

1. Gareth Stedman-Jones, *Outcast London*, p. 290.
2. Joseph Burgess, *John Burns: The Rise and Progress of a Right Honourable*, 1911, p. 46.
3. H. M. Hyndman, *Record of an Adventurous Life*, 1911, pp. 400–420.
4. Michael Rose, *The Relief of Poverty 1834–1914*, 1972.
5. MacKenzie, *The First Fabians*, p. 88.
6. B. Potter, 'A Lady's View of the Unemployed', *Pall Mall Gazette*, 18 Feb. 1886.
7. BWD, 6 March 1886.
8. Joseph Chamberlain to B. Potter, 25 Feb. 1886 (Passfield Papers).
9. Ella Pycroft to BW, 19 Feb. 1886 PP.
10. Samuel Barnett to B. Potter, 26 Feb. and 4 March 1886. PP.
11. Joseph Chamberlain to B. Potter, 28 Feb. 1886 PP (Fraser, p. 122).
12. Michael Rose, *Relief of Poverty*, pp. 16–17.
13. Pat Thane, 'Women and the Poor Law in Victorian and Edwardian England', *History Workshop Journal*.
14. Labour Exchange suggestion bore fruit: see Joan S. Clarke, 'The Break Up of the Poor Law', in *The Webbs and their Work*, 1949.
15. Joseph Chamberlain to B. Potter, 28 Feb. 1886 PP.
16. Ella Pycroft to B. Potter, 26 Feb. 1886.
17. Samuel Barnett to B. Potter, 3 March 1886.
18. B. Potter to Joseph Chamberlain, 4 March 1886 (Fraser, pp. 123–124).
19. Joseph Chamberlain to B. Potter, 5 March 1886.
20. BWD, 6 March 1886.
21. BWD, 15 March 1886.
22. Belinda Norman-Butler, *Victorian Aspirations: The Life and Labour of Charles and Mary Booth* (G. Allen and Unwin, 1972), p. 53.

23. Ibid., pp. 23–29.
24. Mary Booth to B. Potter, 13 March 1886 (Passfield Papers).
25. Ella Pycroft to B. Potter, 25 June 1886 PP.
26. BWD, 9 June 1887.
27. D. H. Elletson, *The Chamberlains*, 1966, p. 66.

CHAPTER XII

1. B. Norman-Butler, *Victorian Aspirations*, p. 75.
2. Mary Booth to B. Potter, 6 June 1886 PP.
3. Mary Booth to B. Potter, 30 Sept. 1886 PP.
4. BWD, 10 Dec. 1886.
5. BWD, August 1886.
6. T. S. Simey and M. B. Simey, *Charles Booth: Social Scientist* (OUP 1960), pp. 98–99.
7. BW, *My Apprenticeship*, p. 221.
8. Charles Booth to B. Potter, 31 July 1886 PP.
9. BWD, 30 March 1887.
10. BW, *My Apprenticeship*, p. 236.
11. Ibid., p. 300 (MS Diary, May 1887).
12. B. Potter, 'The Dock Life of East London', in *Nineteenth Century*, vol. XXII, Oct. 1887.
13. BWD, 12 May 1887.
14. BWD, 13 May 1887.
15. Ibid., and BW, *My Apprenticeship*, p. 303.
16. BWD, 30 Sept. 1887.
17. BW, *My Apprenticeship*, p. 307 (BWD, 1 Dec. 1887).
18. Simey, *Charles Booth*, p. 101.
19. B. Potter, 'Pages from a Work Girl's Diary', *Nineteenth Century*, Sept. 1888.
20. BW, *My Apprenticeship*, p. 321.
21. Anthony Wohl, 'Sex and the Single Room: Incest Among the Victorian Working Classes', in *The Victorian Family*, p. 206 (see Hansard, Third Series, CLXI (1861) 1070–1071).
22. Ibid., p. 199.
23. Ibid., p. 10.
24. B. Potter, 'Pages from a Work Girl's Diary', *Nineteenth Century*.
25. B. Potter, 'The Tailoring Trade', in *Nineteenth Century*, August 1888.
26. B. Potter, Ibid.
27. Ibid.
28. H. M. Hyndman, *Record of an Adventurous Life* (MacMillan, 1911), p. 331.
29. Samuel Barnett, 'A Scheme for the Unemployed', quoted by Gareth Stedman Jones, *Outcast London*, p. 304.
30. Charles Booth, quoted by BW, *My Apprenticeship*, p. 254.
31. Stedman Jones, *Outcast London*, p. 309.
32. BW, *My Apprenticeship* p. 343.
33. BWD, 27 Nov. 1887.
34. BWD, May 1887, BW, *My Apprenticeship*, p. 304.
35. BWD, 9 April 1888.
36. BWD, 1 Nov. 1887.
37. D. H. Elletson, *The Chamberlains* (John Murray, 1966), p. 71.
38. J. L. Garvin, *Joseph Chamberlain*, vol. 2, p. 332.

39. Ibid., p. 338.
40. Ibid., p. 337.
41. Ibid., p. 370.
42. BWD, 26 April 1888.
43. Elletson, *Chamberlain*, p. 82.
44. BWD, 14 Nov. 1888.
45. BWD, 18 Nov. 1888.
46. BWD, 3 Sept. 1888.
47. Ella Pycroft to B. Potter, 21 Sept. 1888 PP.
48. BWD, 30 Sept. 1889.
49. M. Vicinus, *Independent Women: Work and Community for Single Women, 1850–1920* (Virago, 1985), p. 14.
50. BWD, 14 Sept. 1889.
51. BWD, 8 March 1889, BW, *My Apprenticeship*, p. 353.
52. Frederic Harrison to B. Potter, 7 July 1889 PP.
53. BWD, 7 June 1889.
54. BWD, 28 May 1886.
55. Prof. Francis Edgeworth to B. Potter, June 1889 PP.
56. BWD, 4 June 1889.
57. Ibid.

CHAPTER XIII

1. Extract from sonnet to 'W.D.F.' by SW, 4 May 1883 PP.
2. 'Reminiscences' by SW and BW, *St. Martin's Review*, Dec. 1928 (quoted by M. A. Hamilton, *Sidney and Beatrice Webb*, Sampson & Co., 1933, p. 18).
3. G. B. Shaw, *Sixteen Self-Sketches* (Constable & Co.) 1949, p. 56.
4. Pease, Edward, *The History of the Fabian Society*, 1918 (3rd edition, 1963), p. 17.
5. G. B. Shaw, op. cit., p. 56.
6. Ibid., p. 44.
7. Ibid., p. 65.
8. Fabian Tract 1, W. L. Phillips, 'Why Are The Many Poor?', 1884.
9. Fabian Tract 41, G. B. Shaw, 'The Fabian Society: Its Early History', 1892.
10. MacKenzie, *The First Fabians* (Weidenfeld and Nicolson), 1977, pp. 58, 63.
11. Kay Daniels, 'Emma Brooke: Fabian, Feminist and Writer', unpublished essay, quotes SW. See Fabian Society Papers, Nuffield College, Oxford.
12. Ibid.
13. Florence Boos, Ed., 'William Morris's Socialist Diary', *History Workshop Journal*, Spring 1982, p. 5, quotes Thomson, Robert, *Letters of William Morris*, 1 Jan. 1885.
14. Jan Marsh, *Jane and May Morris: A Biographical Story 1839–1938*, p. 183.
15. G. B. Shaw, Tract No. 41.
16. BWD, 1 Feb. 1890.
17. Boos, 'William Morris's Socialist Diary'.
18. BWD, 18 March 1889.
19. M. Cole, *Beatrice Webb* (Longmans) 1945, p. 33.
20. BWD, 26 Nov. 1889 and BW, *My Apprenticeship*, pp. 400–401.
21. BW, *My Apprenticeship*, p. 405.
22. BWD, 25 May 1888.
23. BW, *My Apprenticeship*, p. 407.

24. BWD, 16 Nov. 1888 (MacKenzie, p. 266).
25. SW to G. Wallas, 25 May 1885 PP.
26. SW to G. Wallas, 2 July 1885 PP.
27. SW to G. Wallas, 26 July 1885 PP. See also MacKenzie, *The First Fabians*, p. 66.
28. SW to G. Wallas, 7 Aug. 1885 PP.
29. SW to G. Wallas, 8 Dec. 1885 PP.
30. SW to G. Wallas, 17 Sept. 1887 PP.
31. SW to Margery Davidson, 13 Dec. 1888 PP.
32. Bella Fisher to B. Potter, 21 Feb. 1889 PP.
33. BWD, March 1889.
34. BWD, 13 March 1889.
35. Annie Besant, 'White Slavery in London', in *The Link*, 1888. See Olivia Bennett, *Annie Besant*, Hamish Hamilton, 1988.
36. BWD, 29 Aug. 1889.
37. BWD, 1 Feb. 1890.
38. BWD, 14 Feb. 1890.
39. B. Potter to SW, 2 May 1890 PP.

CHAPTER XIV

1. See Linda H. Peterson, *Victorian Autobiography: The Tradition of Self-Interpretation*, Peterson defines hermeneutic or spiritual autobiography in the Bunyan tradition as that in which the author seeks to interpret his or her life and illumine a way for others to follow.
2. BWD, 15 Feb. 1890.
3. BWD, 26 April 1890.
4. BWD, 5 May 1890, BWD, 5 May 1890.
5. BWD, 23 May 1890.
6. SW to B. Potter, 24 May 1890 PP, SW to B. Potter, 24 May 1890 PP.
7. B. Potter to SW, ?29 May 1890.
8. SW to B. Potter, 30 May 1890.
9. B. Potter to SW, 31 May 1890.
10. B. Potter to SW, 11 June 1890 (Austria).
11. BWD, 1 June 1890 (Cologne).
12. BWD, 20 July 1890.
13. B. Potter to SW, 11 June 1890.
14. SW to B. Potter, 29 July 1890.
15. B. Potter to SW, 29 July 1890.
16. SW to B. Potter, 11 Aug. 1890.
17. SW to B. Potter, 2 Aug. 1890.
18. B. Potter to SW, ?14 Aug. 1890.
19. SW to B. Potter, 13 Aug. 1890.
20. B. Potter to SW, 11 Aug. 1890.
21. B. Potter to SW, ? Sept. 1890.
22. B. Potter to SW, 11 June 1890.
23. SW to B. Potter, ?13 Aug. 1890.
24. SW to B. Potter, 30 May 1890.
25. David Rubenstein, *Before the Suffragettes: Women's Emancipation in the 1890s* (Harvester, 1986), p. 14. Ch. 1 *passim* gives a useful survey of 'New Woman' fiction.

26. SW to B. Potter, 26 Aug. 1890.
27. SW's 'Commonplace' Book, 17 Sept. 1890.
28. BWD, 2 Oct. 1890.
29. G. B. Shaw to B. Potter, 6 Oct. 1890 PP.
30. Mary Booth to B. Potter, 15 Oct. 1890.
31. Bella Fisher to B. Potter, June, Oct. 1890.
32. B. Potter to SW, ?8 Oct. 1890.
33. SW to B. Potter, 9 Oct. 1890.
34. SW to B. Potter, 12 Oct. 1890.
35. BWD, 6 Nov. 1890.
36. SW to B. Potter, 30 Nov. 1890.
37. BWD, 1 Dec. 1890.
38. SW to B. Potter, 4 Dec. 1890.
39. B. Potter to SW, ?7 Dec. 1890.
40. SW to B. Potter, 5 Dec. 1890.

CHAPTER XV

1. SW to B. Potter, 14 Dec. 1890 PP.
2. SW to B. Potter, 19 Jan. 1891 PP, p. 247 MacKenzie.
3. B. Potter to SW, ?21 Jan. 1891 PP.
4. B. Potter, *The Co-operative Movement in Great Britain*, 1891, Swan Sonnen-schein, p. 224.
5. William Morris, *The Dream of John Ball*, 1888, quoted in *The Co-operative Movement*, p. 232.
6. SW to B. Potter, 14 March 1891 PP.
7. SW to B. Potter, 6 April 1891 PP.
8. SW to B. Potter, 6 April 1891 PP.
9. B. Potter, 'The Lords and the Sweating System', *The Nineteenth Century*, vol. XXVII, June 1890, pp. 885–905.
10. T. H. Marshall, Introduction to 1975 edition, SW and BW, *Methods of Social Study*, 1932.
11. BW, *My Apprenticeship*, p. 413.
12. Jane Lewis, *Women in England 1870–1950: Sexual Divisions and Social Change*, Wheatsheaf Books, Brighton, 1984, pp. 83–84. See also J. Lewis, 'Re-reading Beatrice Webb's Diary', in *History Workshop Journal*, Issue 16, Autumn 1983.
13. Quoted in Brian Harrison, *Separate Spheres: the Opposition to Women's Suffrage in Britain*, Croom Helm, 1978, p. 116.
14. Ibid., p. 116.
15. Ibid., p. 56.
16. B. Potter to G. B. Shaw, ?9 Dec. 1890 PP. Unfortunately Beatrice's letters for this period are missing, and their sense can only be surmised from Sidney's replies.
17. W. T. Stead, 'Co-operative Homes for the Unmarried', *The Woman's Herald*, 13 April 1893.
18. Reader's letter, *The Woman's Herald*, 27 April 1893.
19. Quoted by David Rubenstein, p. 70, Clara Collet, 'Prospects of Marriage for Women', *The Nineteenth Century*, vol. XXXI, p. 542.
20. Quoted by David Rubenstein, p. 87, Olga Meier, Ed., *The Daughters of Karl Marx, Family Correspondence 1866–1898*, Deutsch, 1982, p. 210.
21. BWD, 22 Jan. 1891.

22. BW, *My Apprenticeship*, p. 411.

23. B. Potter to SW, undated letter, ?Jan. 1891 PP.

24. SW to B. Potter, 14 March 1891 PP.

25. B. Potter to SW, 20 Aug. 1891 PP.

26. BW, *Our Partnership*, first published 1948, 1975 edition, p. 38. See also Martin J. Wiener, *Between Two Worlds: The Political Thought of Graham Wallas*, Clarendon Press, Oxford, 1971, ch. 1.

27. G. B. Shaw to BW, 20 July 1894, in Dan H. Lawrence, Ed., *Bernard Shaw: Collected Letters*, 1965, p. 452.

28. BW, *Our Partnership*, pp. 37–38.

29. H. G. Wells, *The New Machiavelli*, London, 1913, p. 205.

30. Conversation with Lady Theresa Rothschild, gt. niece of BW, 26 April 1989. Lady Rothschild remembers that when she was a Bedales schoolgirl and spent Sunday lunches with the Webbs at Passfield Corner, Liphook, Sidney's vowels were still shaky and he had a pronounced lisp. Belinda Norman-Butler, granddaughter of Charles and Mary Booth, remembers the fusty smell of Sidney's shiny black suits and his bad table manners. See *Victorian Aspirations* for the story of Sidney gulping food behind a display of chrysanthemums at Gracedieu which hid from Beatrice the fact that he was eating meat, which she did not allow.

31. SW, 'The Difficulties of Individualism', *Economic Journal*, 1891 PP.

32. SW, 'The Eight Hours Bill', *The Speaker*, 19 Sept. 1891, and 'The Miners Eight Hours Bill', *The Speaker*, 1 Nov. 1891.

33. B. Potter, 'East London Labour', in *The Nineteenth Century*, 1888, pp. 166–183.

34. Caroline Cust, 'A Review of Labour Legislation', *The Women's Herald*, 25 May 1893.

35. BWD, 22 May 1891.

36. SW to B. Potter, ?21 May, 25 May 1891 PP.

37. Undated, ? Summer 1891.

38. BWD, 20 June 1891 (MacKenzie, p. 358).

39. SW to B. Potter, 14 July 1891.

40. BW, *My Apprenticeship*, p. 411.

41. BWD, 7 July 1891.

42. Mary Booth to B. Potter, 15 July 1891.

43. Mrs Norman-Butler believes Mary was jealous of Beatrice, whose photo came out in the *Queen* on 28 Aug. Charles Booth retained his Liverpool accent to the end of his life.

44. BWD, 15 July 1891.

45. SW to B. Potter, 27 Jan. 1891 PP.

46. SW to R. B. Haldane, 25 July 1891.

47. R. B. Haldane to SW, 27 July 1891.

48. BWD, 11 Aug. 1891.

49. SW to B. Potter, 27 Aug. 1891.

50. SW to B. Potter, 31 Aug. 1891.

51. SW to B. Potter, 9 Sept. 1891.

52. B. Potter to SW, ?12 Sept. 1891.

53. Ella Pycroft to SW, 10 Jan. 1892.

54. SW to B. Potter, 14 Sept. 1891 (2 letters).

55. SW to B. Potter, 15 Sept. 1891.

56. B. Potter to SW, ?15 Nov. 1891.
57. B. Potter to SW, 21/22 Nov. 1891.
58. B. Potter to SW, Christmas Day 1891.
59. B. Potter to Lallie Holt, Jan. 1892 PP. See also Jeanne MacKenzie, *A Victorian Courtship: The Story of Beatrice Potter and Sidney Webb*, 1979, p. 131.
60. Georgina Meinertzhagen to B. Potter, Jan. 1892.
61. Maggie Hobhouse to B. Potter, Jan. 1892.
62. Mary Playne to B. Potter, Jan. 1892.
63. BWD, 27 Dec. 1891.
64. SW to B. Potter, 3 May 1892.
65. SW to B. Potter, 6 July 1892.
66. Kate Courtney MS Diary BLPES.

CHAPTER XVI

1. SW and BW to G. Wallas, 29 July 1892 PP.
2. BW to SW, Sept. 1892 PP.
3. BWD, 14 Sept. 1891.
4. R. C. K. Ensor, 'Permeation' in M. Cole, Ed., *The Webbs and Their Work*, 1949, p. 60.
5. For a discussion of this point see Martin J. Wiener, *Between Two Worlds: The Political Thought of Graham Wallas*, pp. 32–37.
6. BWD, 21 Sept. 1894.
7. G. B. Shaw to SW, 12 Aug. 1892 PP.
8. Hubert Bland, essay 'The Outlook' in *Fabian Essays*; see R. C. K. Ensor, op. cit., and E. J. Hobsbawm, *Labouring Men: Studies in the History of Labour*, pp. 250–258.
9. Paul Thompson, *Socialists, Liberals and Labour: The Struggle for London 1885–1914*, p. 140.
10. G. B. Shaw, Tract 41, 'The Fabian Society: Its Early History', 1892.
11. See A. M. McBriar, *Fabian Socialism and English Politics 1884–1918*, pp. 187–197.
12. SW to G. Wallas, 6 March 1892 PP.
13. B. Potter to SW, ?23 or 24 Aug. 1891 PP.
14. G. B. Shaw to SW, 12 Aug. 1892 PP.
15. BW, *Our Partnership*, CUP, 1948, 1975 edition, p. 12.
16. G. B. Shaw to SW, 12 Aug. 1892 PP.
17. BWD, 10 March.
18. BWD, Christmas Day 1893.
19. BWD, ?Oct. 1893.
20. BW, *Our Partnership*, p. 15.
21. BWD, 21 June 1893.
22. BWD, Christmas Day 1893.
23. BWD, 19 Sept. 1893.
24. Frank Drummond to SW, 24 July 1892 PP.
25. BWD, 10 July 1894.
26. BWD, 1 Dec. 1894.
27. Quoted by P. Thompson, op. cit., p. 146; for reasons behind the formation of the ILP see Henry Pelling, *Popular Politics and Society in Late Victorian Britain*, pp. 106–123.
28. G. B. Shaw to SW, 12 Aug. 1892 PP.

29. By the Fabian Society, 'To Your Tents, O Israel!', *Fortnightly Review*, CCCXXIII, 1 Nov. 1893, p. 568.

30. Henry Massingham to SW, ?Oct. 1893, and Henry Massingham to G. B. Shaw, 20 Oct. 1893 PP.

31. R. B. Haldane to SW, 2 Nov. 1893 PP.

32. R. C. K. Ensor, op. cit., p. 65. A comparison of the tone and style of 'To Your Tents O Israel!' with Webb's earlier article, of which he was the sole author, 'What Mr. Gladstone Ought to Do', in the *Fortnightly Review* CCCXIII, 1 Jan. 1893, demonstrates that Webb writing alone showed a greater appreciation of the practicalities of politics and Gladstone's overriding obsession with Home Rule: 'Social legislation of any extensive kind may therefore well prove to be impossible.'

33. BWD, 17 Sept. 1893.

34. G. B. Shaw to Janet Achurch, 31 Aug. 1895, Dan H. Laurence, Ed., *Bernard Shaw: Collected Letters 1874–1897*, 1965, p. 555.

35. Elizabeth Robins Pennell in *Young Woman*, April 1893.

36. G. B. Shaw to Janet Achurch, 16 Sept. 1895, Laurence, op. cit., p. 557.

37. SW to B. Potter, 14 Sept. 1891.

38. Bertrand Russell, *Autobiography*, vol. 1., quoted in Strachey, op. cit., p. 156.

39. BWD, 20 July 1896.

40. SW and BW, *Methods of Social Study*, 1932, p. 138.

41. BW, *My Apprenticeship*, pp. 190, 399.

42. T. H. Marshall, introduction to Webb, *Methods of Social Study*, p. XXIV, and 'Note-Taking' in ibid., p. 162. This method was described by Langlois and Seignoboy in 1898.

43. R. H. Tawnay, quoted by T. H. Marshall, in introduction to *Methods*, p. XI.

44. F. Galton, 'Investigating With the Webbs', in M. Cole, Ed., *The Webbs and Their Work*, pp. 32, 33.

45. BWD, 30 Dec. 1892.

46. BWD, 23 May 1900.

47. Herbert Spencer to BW, 1 May 1894 PP.

48. Mary Booth to BW, May 1894 (undated) PP.

49. BWD, 30 July 1893.

50. BWD, 10 July 1894.

51. BWD, 21 Sept. 1894.

52. BWD, 10 Aug. 1894, BW, *Our Partnership*, p. 45.

53. BWD, 17 Sept. 1892.

54. The vestry was the basic unit of local government in London, based on parish boundaries.

55. BWD, 12 Jan. 1895.

56. BWD, 25 July 1894.

57. BWD, 18 Jan. 1897, BW, *Our Partnership*, p. 51.

58. See Olive Banks, *Faces of Feminism*, Martin Robertson, 1981, Basil Blackwell 1986 edition, pp. 88–102, and Philippa Levine, *Victorian Feminism 1850–1900*, Hutchinson Education, 1987, pp. 148–156; also Brian Harrison, *Separate Spheres: The Opposition to Women's Suffrage in Britain*, p. 56.

59. BWD, 25 July 1894.

60. Barbara Caine, 'Beatrice Webb and the Woman Question' in *History Workshop Journal*, issue 14, Autumn 1982.

61. On Beatrice and Sidney's physical relationship, Belinda Norman-Butler is convinced that the Webbs slept together in early married life. Kitty Muggeridge

says that later they were sleeping in separate bedrooms, as far from each other as possible. Beatrice's excuse was, 'Sidney snores'.

62. BWD, 30 July 1893.
63. BW, *Our Partnership*, p. 27, Kate Courtney MS Diary.
64. BWD, 28 Feb. 1892.
65. Mary Costelloe to Bernhard Berenson, in B. Strachey, *Remarkable Relations*, p. 151.
66. Olive Banks, op. cit., pp. 74–77, cites Acton, *Functions and Disorders of the Reproductive Organs*.
67. BWD, 21 Sept. 1894.
68. G. B. Shaw to BW, 1 July 1895 PP.
69. BWD, 8 May 1875.
70. BW to E. Pease, 18 Feb. 1896 PP.
71. BWD, Nov. and Christmas 1895.
72. BWD, 16 July 1895.

CHAPTER XVII

1. BWD, 11 Jan. 1898.
2. *Our First Journey Round the World*, BWD, vol. 17, 29 March 1898 PP. See also David A. Shannon, Ed., *Beatrice Webb's American Diary 1898*, University of Wisconsin Press, 1963.
3. Ibid., pp. 157–158.
4. *Our First Journey* PP.
5. A. G. Austin, Ed., *The Webbs' Australian Diary 1898*, Pitman, Melbourne, 1965, p. 23.
6. BW to Mary Playne, 7 Nov. 1896 PP.
7. *Australian Diary*, p. 49.
8. Ibid., p. 14.
9. J. L. Garvin, *Joseph Chamberlain*, vol. 3, 1934, p. 9.
10. Ibid., p. 5.
11. Flora Shaw, *The Times* Correspondent on colonial affairs, quoted Garvin, p. 11.
12. BWD, 5 Jan. 1896.
13. Garvin, p. 125.
14. D. Judd, *Radical Joe: A Life of Joseph Chamberlain*, 1977, pp. 195–201. Garvin's belief in Chamberlain's innocence does not convince modern biographers.
15. Thomas Pakenham, *The Boer War*, 1979, p. 31.
16. Ibid., pp. 19–20 and 38–39, and Judd, pp. 214–215.
17. Henry Pelling, *Popular Politics and Society in late Victorian Britain*, 1968, p. 89. Pelling points out that the majority of recruits in the early stages of the war were upper or middle class, and quotes J. A. Hobson's remarks on the 'credulity displayed by the educated classes'. Psychology of Jingoism, p. 21.
18. G. W. Stevens, *Daily Mail*, 23 June 1897, quoted by Judd, op. cit., p. 111.
19. BWD, 10 Oct. 1899.
20. BW to Mary Playne, mid-Dec. 1899 PP.
21. BWD, 31 Jan. 1900.
22. BW to Mary Playne, 28 June 1900.
23. Mary Playne to BW, 26 Feb. 1900.
24. Austen Morgan, *J. Ramsay MacDonald*, Manchester Univ. Press, 1987, p. 26.
25. BWD, 19 July 1900.

26. H. H. Asquith, *Memories and Reflections*, 1928, p. 151.
27. BWD, 29 July 1897.
28. BWD, Christmas 1895.
29. H. H. Asquith, op. cit., p. 163, quotes Kate Courtney, *Life of Lord Courtney*, p. 348.
30. Table plan, BWD, 29 July 1897.
31. BWD, 16 March 1900.
32. BWD, New Year's Day 1901.
33. BWD, 15 Dec. 1900.
34. BWD, 9 July 1901.
35. G. B. Shaw to BW, 24 July 1901 PP.
36. G. B. Shaw to SW, 26 July 1901 PP.
37. BWD, 16 May 1899.
38. G. B. Shaw to SW and BW, 7 May 1898 PP.
39. G. B. Shaw to SW and BW, 21 June 1898 PP.
40. G. B. Shaw to SW and BW, 18 Oct. 1898 PP.
41. SW, 'Lord Rosebery's Escape from Houndsditch', *Nineteenth Century*, vols XIX–XX, p. 366, Sept. 1901.
42. Lord Rosebery to BW, 3 Sept. 1901 PP.
43. Kate Courtney to BW, 12 Sept. 1901.
44. Haldane to BW, 15 Sept. 1901.
45. BWD, 2 Jan. 1901.
46. BWD, 9 Dec. 1900.
47. Maggie Hobhouse to Rachel Hobhouse, quoted by MacKenzie, BWD, vol. 2 (Virago), p. 194.
48. BWD, 4 July 1900.
49. BWD, 19 Oct. 1900.
50. Alfred Cripps to BW, 16 Nov. 1900 PP.
51. Alfred Cripps to BW, 20, 22 Nov. 1900 PP.
52. BWD, 9 Feb. 1901.
53. BWD, New Year's Day 1901.
54. BWD, 24 April 1901.
55. BWD, 1 July 1901.
56. BWD, 1 Oct. 1901. Andrea Carlo Francisco Rabagliati was a food reformer whom some thought a crank. *Air, Food and Exercise* was published in 1897.
57. A. Rabagliati to BW, 17 Oct. 1901 PP.
58. BWD, 1 Nov. 1901.
59. A. Rabagliati to BW, 18 Oct. 1901.
60. BWD, 8 March 1901.
61. BWD, 21 Oct. 1901.
62. BWD, 13 Oct. 1901.
63. BWD, 9 Feb. 1901.
64. BWD, 30 Jan. 1902.
65. BW to Georgina Meinertzhagen, 7 Dec. 1903 PP.
66. Nicholas Meinertzhagen, son of Luke and Sheila Meinertzhagen and gt grandson of Georgina, has plotted the incidence of 'melancholia' and mental instability in the descendants of Richard and Lawrencina Potter. It is his opinion that a manic-depressive strain exists in the family. Fritz Meinertzhagen (son of Georgie) also committed suicide 1962, and Jenny, Georgie's granddaughter, in 1960. He notes a number of Potter descendants who have had 'breakdowns'. It

is alleged that Lallie (d. 1906) became addicted to cocaine before her death. See also B. Caine, *Destined to be Wives: The Sisters of Beatrice Webb*, Oxford 1986, p. 198.

67. Bertrand Russell, quoted by Barbara Strachey, *Remarkable Relations*, 1981, p. 216.

68. BW to SW, ?4 July 1902 PP.

69. Strachey, op. cit., p. 219.

70. BWD, 28 Feb. 1902.

71. BWD, 23 July 1903.

72. Sidney wanted the University of London to have a college of science and technology comparable to the Charlottenburg Institute in Berlin.

73. SW to Dr Archibald Robertson, Vice-Chancellor of University of London, 3 Jan. 1903. N. MacKenzie, Ed., *The Letters of Sidney and Beatrice Webb*, vol. II, p. 176.

74. M. Wiener, *Between Two Worlds: The Political Thought of Graham Wallas*, Oxford 1971, pp. 53–56.

75. BWD, 6 Dec. 1902.

76. BWD, 19 April 1904.

CHAPTER XVIII

1. H. G. Wells, *Anticipations*, 1902, quoted in W. Warren Wegar, Ed., *H. G. Wells: Journalism and Prophecy 1893–1946*, Bodley Head, 1965, pp. 24–42.

2. Lucy Masterman, *C. F. G. Masterman*, 1939, p. 115?

3. See Anna Davin, 'Imperialism and Motherhood' in *History Workshop Journal*, no. 5, and Jane Lewis, *The Politics of Motherhood*, pp. 13–57.

4. MacKenzie, Ed., *Letters of Sidney and Beatrice Webb*, vol. 2, 1892–1912, H. G. Wells to Edward Pease, 13 Jan. 1902, p. 145.

5. Bernard Semmel, *Imperialism and Social Reform*, 1960, pp. 133–134.

6. Arnold White, *Efficiency and Empire*, Harvester 1973, first pub. 1901, pp. 23–24.

7. Arnold Silver, *Bernard Shaw, The Darker Side*, Stanford Univ. Press, 1982, p. 157, and G. B. Shaw, *Major Barbara*, 1905.

8. BWD, 29 Nov. 1905.

9. BW, *Our Partnership*, p. 325.

10. R. C. K. Ensor, 'Permeation', in M. Cole, Ed., *The Webbs and Their Work*, p. 70.

11. Helen Bosanquet, *The Family*, 1923.

12. For a full exposition of the reasons behind the setting up of the RCPL see A. M. McBriar, *An Edwardian Mixed Doubles: The Bosanquets versus the Webbs – A Study in British Social Policy 1890–1929*, Clarendon Press, Oxford, 1987, pp. 175–195.

13. BW, *Our Partnership*, p. 322, BWD, 2 Dec. 1905.

14. Ibid., p. 324, BWD, 15 Dec. 1905.

15. Ibid., p. 327, BWD, 15 Dec. 1905.

16. Anne Olivier Bell, Ed., *The Diary of Virginia Woolf, vol. 1, 1915–1919*, Hogarth, 1971, Penguin edition, 1979, p. 26.

17. MacKenzie, Ed., *Letters*, vol. 2, pp. 224–228.

18. BW, *Our Partnership*, p. 328, BWD, 9 Jan. 1906.

19. Ibid., p. 331, BWD, 12 Feb. 1906.

20. Ibid., p. 336.

21. BW to Mary Playne, 21 Jan. 1906 PP.
22. BW to Mary Playne, 29 July 1906 PP.
23. BW, *Our Partnership*, p. 341.
24. BW, Lecture to Medical Officers of Health, December 1906 PP.
25. BW, *Our Partnership*, p. 344, BWD, 15 June 1906.
26. Ibid., p. 294, BWD, 20 June 1905.
27. Ibid., p. 353, 16 Sept. 1906.
28. Leonard Woolf, *Sowing, 1880–1904*, 1960, OUP paperback 1980, pp. 28–29.
29. Lucy Masterman, *CFG Masterman*, p. 60.
30. BW, *Our Partnership*, p. 347.
31. Lady Betty Balfour to B. Webb, Sept. 1906 PP.
32. Letter to Millicent Fawcett, *The Times*, 5 Nov. 1906, BWD, 5 Nov. 1906.
33. Lady Betty Balfour to BW, 28 March ?1910.
34. G. B. Shaw to SW, 25 Nov. 1906.
35. H. G. Wells to BW, 19 Oct. 1904.
36. See Roslynn D. Haynes, *H. G. Wells, Discoverer of the Future*, Macmillan, 1980, pp. 188–192.
37. H. G. Wells, *The New Machiavelli*, 1911, Penguin, 1946, pp. 172–173.
38. BWD, 18 Oct. 1906.
39. G. B. Shaw to SW, 19 Jan. 1907.
40. BWD, 15 July 1906.
41. H. G. Wells, *Ann Veronica*, 1909, Virago, 1980, p. 184.
42. Nuffield College Oxford. See also Sally Alexander's introduction to Maud Pember Reeves, *Round About A Pound A Week*, Members of the FWG helped Beatrice in her research, e.g. Marion Phillips, and Beatrice was a member of the group.
43. BW to Amber Blanco White, 11 Sept. 1909 PP.
44. G. B. Shaw to BW, 30 Sept. 1909 PP.
45. H. G. Wells to BW, August 1909 PP.
46. H. G. Wells to BW, August 1909 (2).
47. BW to Mary Playne, 19 Jan. 1907 PP.
48. BWD, April 1907.
49. BWD, 18 Jan. 1907.
50. H. G. Wells, *Ann Veronica*, p. 202.
51. A. M. McBriar, op. cit., pp. 231–236. Beatrice kept back one third of the letters she received of which the majority were against change. Of the letters tabled 23 were in favour, 47 against, 30 don't know. See *Our Partnership*, pp. 392–393, and BWD, 29 Oct. 1907.
52. BW to Mary Playne, 20 Nov. 1908.
53. BW to Mary Playne, 1 Jan. 1908.
54. N. and J. MacKenzie, *H. G. Wells, The Time Traveller*, 1987, Hogarth Press, pp. 190–191.
55. BW to Mary Playne, 22 Feb. 1908.
56. BW, *Our Partnership*, p. 396.
57. Ibid., p. 421.
58. A. J. Balfour to BW, 13 April 1908.
59. SW to G. Wallas, undated 1908.
60. SW and BW, *Minority Report of the Poor Law Commission*, vol. 2, p. 278.
61. Ibid., p. 322.
62. Ibid., p. 20.

63. RCPL Harlow Report, Appx XXI, vol. LII. Report on an Inquiry in Certain Unions into Cases of Refusal of Outdoor Relief. See also MA Dissertation, C. Bigland, Sussex University 1988.

64. RCPL Report by Dr John McVail.

65. *Minority Report*, pp. 96–106. The Report was signed by George Lansbury, Francis Chandler, Russell Wakefield and Beatrice Webb.

66. Ibid., pp. 87–88.

67. SW, 'Eugenics and the Poor Law', Lecture to Eugenics Society, 15 Dec. 1909.

68. Hugh Elliot, biographer of Herbert Spencer, to BW, 8 June 1909.

69. G. B. Shaw to BW, 26 June 1909.

70. BWD, 8 Oct. 1907.

71. BW, *Our Partnership*, p. 379.

72. H. G. Wells to BW, 22 Feb. 1909.

73. BWD, 8 July 1903, 10 June 1904.

74. Violet Bonham Carter, *Winston Churchill As I Knew Him*, 1965, p. 16.

75. Winston Churchill to SW, 6 July 1908. This proposal, originally the idea of William Beveridge (see W. Beveridge, *Unemployment, The Problem of Industry*, 1909) became law by the 1909 Labour Exchanges Act. Churchill embodied the Webbs' idea of the National Minimum in his Trades Boards Act 1909.

76. W. J. Braithwaite, *Lloyd George's Ambulance Wagon: Being the Memoirs of William J. Braithwaite, 1911–1912*, 1957, p. 116.

77. See R. Titmuss, *Commentary on Braithwaite*, p. 44.

78. Lucy Masterman, *Masterman*, p. 123.

79. BW to Georgina Meinertzhagen, 8 Aug. 1909.

80. Quoted in M. Vicinus, *Independent Women: Work and Community for Single Women 1850–1920*, pp. 250–251.

81. BWD, p. 428.

82. Lady Betty Balfour to BW, 4 Dec. 1909.

83. Elizabeth Haldane to BW, end 1909.

84. G. B. Shaw to BW, 9 Dec. 1910.

85. Interview with Mrs S. Webb, *The Young Woman*, 3 Feb. 1895.

86. BWD, New Year's Eve 1909, Southsea.

87. BW to Lady Betty Balfour, 22 Dec. 1910.

CHAPTER XIX

1. BW to Kate Courtney, Aug. 1911 PP.

2. BW to ?Clifford Sharp, 18 Oct. 1911.

3. R. Young to the Webbs, 2 Oct. 1911.

4. BWD, 16 April 1911.

5. BW to Clifford Sharp, 15 Jan. 1912 (Sharp was editor of *The Crusade*).

6. BW to Mildred E. Buckley, 24 Jan. 1912.

7. BW to Clifford Sharp, 8 Nov. 1911 (from Mandalay).

8. BW to Clifford Sharp, 28 Feb. 1912.

9. BW to Clifford Sharp, 14 Feb. 1912.

10. BWD, 7 March 1911.

11. The Fabian Nursery, a group of young Fabians, was set up in 1908. Amber Reeves was a member.

12. M. Cole, *Beatrice Webb*, 1945, p. 117.

13. G. B. Shaw to SW, 5 March 1911.

14. BW to G. Lansbury, ?Nov. 1912, MacKenzie, Ed., Webb letters, vol. 3, p. 10.

15. Henry Schloesser was chairman of the Fabian Reform Committee, later Lord Slesser.
16. BWD, 5 Sept. 1912. *Reflections on Violence* by George Sorel made an impact on the universities and filtered down to trade unionists such as Tom Mann, who published the *Industrial Syndicalist*. The 1914 Triple Alliance of miners, railwaymen and transport workers was frustrated by the war.
17. BW to Clifford Sharp, 7 April 1912 (Bombay).
18. BWD, 1 Dec. 1912.
19. G. D. H. Cole (1889–1959), S. G. Hobson and A. R. Orage (editor of the *New Age* weekly) were associated in the Oxford Union and developed the ideas of Guild Syndicalism. They believed that industry could be owned by the State and run by modern-day Guilds, in the medievalist tradition of William Morris.
20. M. Cole, op. cit., p. 123. Margaret Postgate, daughter of Professor Postgate, a classicist, married G. D. H. Cole in August 1918.
21. BWD, 21 July 1914.
22. BWD, 15 May 1915.
23. G. D. H. Cole to BW, March 1917.
24. G. B. Shaw to BW, 10 July 1912.
25. BWD, 5 July 1913.
26. M. Cole, op. cit., p. 125.
27. Alan Dent, Ed., *Bernard Shaw and Mrs. Patrick Campbell: Their Correspondence*, Victor Gollancz, 1952, p. 96.
28. BWD, 13 July 1913.
29. Alys Russell to BW, 3 June 1911 PP.
30. Alys Russell to BW, 9 Oct. 1912.
31. BW to Bertrand Russell, 11 Oct. 1912, MacKenzie letters, vol. 3, 1912–1947.
32. William Colegate to BW, 18 Aug. 1911.
33. BW to Georgina Meinertzhagen, 8 Aug. 1909.
34. BWD, 8 March 1911.
35. A. M. McBriar, *Fabian Socialism and English Politics 1884–1918*, CUP, 1966, pp. 340–343. Sidney also drafted the Report, *Labour and the New Social Order*.
36. BWD, 12 Aug. 1914.
37. BW to Lady Betty Balfour, 8 Dec. 1914.
38. Paul E. Hobhouse to Family, 31 July 1915. See also Stephen Hobhouse, *Margaret Hobhouse and Her Family*, 1934, pp. 221–245.
39. C. M. Lloyd to BW, ?May 1916.
40. C. M. Lloyd to BW, 11 July 1916.
41. BWD, 18 April 1915.
42. BWD, 28 Aug. 1914.
43. BWD, note, 18 Aug. PP.
44. Stephen Hobhouse, op. cit., pp. 233–239. In January 1916 the Military Service Act called up unmarried men aged 18–41.
45. BW to Lady Balfour, 28 Oct. 1915.
46. BWD, 26 April 1915.
47. BWD, 14 Nov. 1915.
48. BW to Mary Playne, 21 Oct. 1914.
49. BW to Mary Playne, 2 Nov. 1914.
50. Maggie Hobhouse to BW, mid Dec. 1920.
51. Maggie Hobhouse to BW, early 1920.
52. Maggie Hobhouse to BW, mid Dec. 1920.

53. BWD, 9 Feb. 1921.

54. BWD, 22 Sept. 1923 PP only.

55. BWD, 24 June 1916.

56. BWD, 25 Sept., 12 Oct. 1916.

57. Graham Dangerfield, *The Strange Death of Liberal England*, Constable, 1936.

58. BWD, 22 Feb. ?1917. Leslie Scott was a Conservative MP, later Solicitor General.

59. BWD, 3 June 1917. Marion Phillips, an Australian Jewess, graduated from Melbourne University. Scholarship to LSE. Assistant PL Commissioner. Quarrelled with her chief Dr Ethel Williams, whose housemate and friend Dr Ethel Bentham she carried off in triumph to live with her in London. Joined Fabian Soc. and in 1911–1913 was involved in revolt v. the Old Gang. Wrested the Secretaryship of the Women's Labour League from Margaret Bondfield.

60. Note by Leonard Woolf in Ann Oliver Bell, Ed., *The Diary of Virginia Woolf*, vol. 1, 1915–1919, p. 74.

61. Charles Loch Mowat, *Britain Between the Wars 1918–1945*, 1955, CUP paperback, p. 15.

62. Memorandum on Functions of Government Departments, Reconstruction Papers, vol. 2, 1916–1918, July 1917 PP.

63. MacKenzie, note in BWD, vol. 3, p. 259.

64. Note added by BW to diary entry, 11 Dec. 1917 PP.

65. Ibid.

66. Mowat, op. cit., pp. 16–17.

67. Norman MacLean to BW, 7 Jan. 1918, Reconstruction Papers PP.

68. Lord George Hamilton to BW, 3 Jan. 1918.

69. BWD, 1 March 1918.

70. BWD, 31 Oct. 1917. During the Coupon Election sitting members who supported the Coalition were endorsed by a letter signed by Lloyd George and Andrew Bonar Law, Coalition leaders. This letter Asquith termed the 'coupon'. Although Henderson and MacDonald lost their seats, Labour polled 2,374,000 votes, a huge increase from 400,000. Asquith was defeated and the Asquith Liberals won only 26 seats; the Coalition won 484, of whom 338 were Conservatives.

71. G. B. Shaw to SW and BW, 26 Sept. 1918.

72. BW to Mary Playne, ?Jan. 1919.

73. G. D. H. Cole used this phrase.

74. The Labour Party under its new constitution became a national party for the first time with local branches, instead of a loose alliance of trade unionists and Socialist Societies.

75. BWD, 23 June 1919. Coal Mines Act 1919 limited the miners' day to 7 hours, but the government did not accept the majority verdict of the Sankey Commission to nationalise mines, to the miners' disgust. BW wrote *The Story of the Seaham Miners* for SW's constituents.

76. BW to Mary Playne, 2 Jan. 1921.

77. SW to BW, 9 March 1923.

78. BWD, 11 May 1923 PP.

79. BWD, 9 Aug. 1922.

80. BWD, 11 May 1923 PP.

81. BWD, 19 Nov. 1923. The Conservatives won 258 seats, but Labour (191) and Liberal (158) combined outnumbered them.

82. Margaret Bondfield was suggested as SW's PPS by Ramsay MacDonald, letter to SW received 1 Jan. 1924. SW's colleagues protested that the Minister of Labour was not a first grade post, so MacDonald offered him President of the Board of Trade, an almost equally lowly cabinet position. Haldane became Lord Chancellor, Alfred Cripps Lord Parmoor and Leader of the House of Lords, Henderson Home Secretary and J. R. Clynes (1869–1949) who was on the Reconstruction Committee with Beatrice became Leader of the Commons.
83. BWD, 23 Jan. 1924 PP.
84. BWD, 7 July 1923.
85. BWD, 3 March 1924 PP.
86. BWD, 26 July 1923. BW had 130 Labour MPs to her Wednesday lunches and to dinner during the 1923 session.
87. George Lansbury to BW, Feb. 1924. Lansbury was General Manager of the *Daily Herald*.
88. BWD, 15 March 1924 PP.
89. 4 Sept. 1915 *John Bull* published the birth certificate showing MacDonald was illegitimate and his true surname was Ramsay.
90. Austen Morgan, *J. Ramsay MacDonald*, Manchester Univ. Press, 1987, p. 225. Lord Londonderry built Seaham Harbour as an outlet for coal, so when MacDonald was given Sidney's safe seat of Seaham, his relationship with Lady Londonderry was even more open to criticism. He made Lord Londonderry Minister for Air in 1931.
91. BWD, 28 June 1924.
92. C. M. Lloyd to BW, 22 Feb. 1926 PP.
93. Harold Laski to BW, 24 Feb. 1926 PP.
94. Kate Courtney to BW, 26 Sept. 1926.
95. GBS to BW, 14 April 1926 PP.
96. Samuel H. Beer, Introduction to S. and B. Webb, *A Socialist Commonwealth of Great Britain*, CUP, 1975, pp. XXX–XXXI.
97. Ibid., pp. 322–323.
98. BWD, 20 June 1929.
99. Snowden and Thomas also remained in MacDonald's National Government.

CHAPTER XX

1. SW to BW, 28 Sept. 1925 (MacKenzie letters, vol. 3, p. 248).
2. BWD, 14 Dec. 1930. MacDonald blamed Sidney for antagonising Carl Weizmann and other Jews who were holding the British government to its 'fatuous' promise of a Palestine Jewish Home enshrined in the Balfour Declaration. The Webbs had moved from their earlier Zionist viewpoint to sympathise with the Arabs whom they felt should be protected.
3. J. R. MacDonald to SW, 14 July 1931 PP.
4. SW, 'What Really Happened in 1931: A Record'. *Political Quarterly*, Jan.–March 1932. Reprinted in Fabian Tract 237. Ramsay MacDonald's motives remain controversial. Without doubt the idea of a National Government had been mooted for some months, especially by J. L. Garvin, Lloyd George and Sir Arthur Balfour, the steel magnate, and had been mulled over by MacDonald in his diary. MacDonald believed that Arthur Henderson was trying to usurp his position. Mowat, pp. 396–399.
5. Malcolm MacDonald to SW, 6 Jan. 1932 PP.
6. SW to Malcolm MacDonald, 1st draft of letter sent 9 Feb. 1932 PP.

7. D. Marquand, *Ramsay MacDonald*, sees the Labour leader as a 'prisoner of circumstance' rather than a conspirator. From the evidence of his diary MacDonald believed he was sacrificing himself for the good of his party, but his isolation from his ministers prevented them putting this interpretation on his actions.

8. SW, *Political Quarterly*, op. cit. In July 1931 there was a drain in gold. The Bank of England borrowed £50m from foreign bankers. In August the Bank told the government that a new loan of £80m was necessary, and foreign bankers demanded that the Budget be balanced and unemployment benefit be cut. Sidney voted *for* the unemployment cuts, but with the resignation of eight ministers MacDonald's government was no longer viable. Instead of resigning, however, he accepted the King's invitation to lead the National Government.

9. BWD, 23 Sept. 1931.

10. BWD, 10 Oct. 1931.

11. BW to Maynard Keynes, 22 Feb. 1926. S. and B. Webb, *The Decay of Capitalist Civilisation*, Longmans 1923.

12. BWD, 4 Feb. 1931 (MacKenzie Letters, vol. 3, p. 237).

13. BW to SW, 9 Feb. 1931.

14. The original of this window, created in the early 1900s by Caroline Townshend, is in the USA. John Parker, President of the Fabian Society, has described how the window disappeared from Beatrice Webb House, Dorking, previously owned by the Fabian Society. An American antique dealer offered the window to the Fabian Society, which could not afford to buy it.

15. BWD, 4 Jan. 1932. Unemployment was 2.7m in Feb. 1931.

16. BWD, 24 June 1931 PP only.

17. Malcolm Muggeridge to BW, 20 Dec. 1929. Muggeridge was working as a civil servant in Egypt.

18. Malcolm Muggeridge to BW, 9 Feb. 1930. BW went to see *The Three Flats*, which was produced by The Stage Society in February 1931. She sent Sidney the review in the *Times*: 'very favourable – and not shocked at all (!), which shows how aged we are'. BW to SW, 17 Feb. 1931.

19. Virginia Woolf Diary, vol. 2. See note in MacKenzie, BWD, vol. 4, p. 112. During this visit Virginia had a raging argument with Beatrice over religious education.

20. BWD, 5 April 1930.

21. BWD, 5 Oct. 1932.

22. BWD, 1 July 1928.

23. H. G. Wells to Upton Sinclair, ?date 1918 PP (MacKenzie, p. 311).

24. L. P. Carpenter, *GDH Cole: An Intellectual Biography*, OUP, 1973, p. 154. Ben Pimlott, *Labour and the Left in the 1930s*, CUP, 1977, Allen and Unwin edition 1986, p. 9.

25. BWD, 3 Aug. 1930.

26. BWD, 12 Nov. 1930.

27. BWD, 19 Nov. 1930.

28. Bertrand Russell, *Autobiography*, vol. 2, pp. 102–103, 122. Russell's relationship with Lady Ottoline Morrell followed his break with Alys, his first wife. Sir Rufus Isaacs was Attorney General in the Liberal government before WW1 and was involved with the Marconi scandal.

29. Citrine Papers, BLPES, compiled by Dr Angela Raspin 1978.

30. *Manchester Guardian* report, 28 June 1931.

31. BWD, 8 Aug. 1931.

32. George Lansbury to SW, 18 April 1932.

33. BWD, 19 Sept. 1931.

34. Betty D. Vernon, *Margaret Cole 1893–1980: A Political Biography*, Croom Helm, 1986, p. 86. Dalton was a Fabian and Chancellor of the Exchequer in the Labour 1945 government.

35. Margaret Cole to BW, 11 Sept. 1932 PP. The New Fabian Research Bureau was founded by G. D. H. Cole and approved by the Webbs, Arthur Henderson and Prof. Harold Laski in 1931. On her return Margaret Cole edited *Twelve Studies in Soviet Russia*, 1933.

36. Rosy Dobbs to BW, 17 Aug. 1932.

37. Malcolm Muggeridge to BW, 28 Sept. 1932.

38. 'Russian Tour', Appendix to BWD, vol. 46, 1932 PP.

39. Margaret Cole, *Beatrice Webb*, p. 169.

40. Vernon, op. cit., p. 119.

41. BWD, 4 Jan. 1932.

42. 'Russian Tour' PP. May 1932.

43. Robert Conquest, *The Great Terror: Stalin's Purge*, MacMillan, 1968, p. 18.

44. Andrew Cairns, *Description of a Tour in the Ukraine, Crimea and North Caucasus, June–July 1932*, Lloyd Papers 4/32 BLPES.

45. 'Russian Tour' PP.

46. BW and SW, *The Truth About Soviet Russia*, Longmans, 1942, p. 48.

47. BWD, 14 May 1932.

48. Malcolm Muggeridge to BW, 8 Feb. 1933, and Muggeridge, *Chronicles of Wasted Time, vol. 1, The Green Stick*, 1972, pp. 256–259.

49. Editor *Catholic Herald* to SW, 15 Nov. 1932.

50. BWD, 22 Sept. 1932.

51. SW and BW, Preface to *Soviet Communism: A New Civilisation?*, Sept. 1935, Longmans WEA edition, p. xii.

52. Ibid. BW wrote 4 Jan. 1933, 'This little book will not be a work of original research; our material will be practically secondhand.'

53. Ibid., vol. 2, p. 1.

54. Ibid., vol. 1, p. 432.

55. Robert A. Conquest, *The Great Terror: Stalin's Purge*, 1968, p. 277. Lenin's 'hot terror' was not part of a big planned operation from above; by contrast Stalin, in cold blood, began a deliberate, unprovoked 'cold terror' 1936–1938.

56. Prof. Paul Haensel, NW Univ., Illinois, to SW, ?June 1932. Haensel asked for help for his old friend Dr Ivan Ozezov, thrown into prison during the 'terrible years of wholesale persecution of Russian scholars 1930–1931'.

57. Lady Betty Balfour to BW, 20 Oct. 1934.

58. BWD, 27 Jan., 29 March 1933.

59. BWD, 13 April 1933.

60. Harold Laski to BW, 9 March 1935.

61. William Beveridge to BW, March 1935.

62. G. B. Shaw, Preface to *The Truth About Soviet Russia*, and also letter G. B. Shaw to BW, 20 April 1935.

63. BW to Mme Halévy, 1 Sept. 1936.

64. G. B. Shaw to BW, 4 Sept. 1936.

65. Conversation with Malcolm Muggeridge, Oct. 1988.

66. Maurice Hankey to BW, 28 Oct. 1937.

67. Bertrand Russell, *Portraits From Memory: Sidney and Beatrice Webb*, 24 July

1952, BBC Sound Archives T17971.

68. BWD, 7 Jan., 25 Jan. 1933.

69. Bardie Drake to BW, 18 Oct. 1934.

70. Margaret Cole, 'The Webbs and Soviet Communism' in Cole, Ed., *The Webbs and Their Work*, 1949, p. 227.

71. *Our Partnership*, the second vol. of B's autobiography, was unfinished at her death and was edited by Margaret Cole. She was the first person to read Beatrice's diaries, which even Sidney had not been allowed to see.

72. Bertrand Russell, Sound Archives.

73. Sir William Nicholson's portrait of the Webbs 1928 hangs now in the Shaw Library at the LSE.

74. Interview with Alexei Tolstoy, *Pravda*, 13 April 1937.

75. BWD, 13 Aug. 1938.

76. J. M. Keynes to BW, 23 Dec. 1937.

77. Bertrand Russell, Sound Archives.

78. BWD, 13 Aug. 1938.

79. John Strachey, *The Intellectuals and the Labour Movement: The Webbs*, 14 July 1960, BBC Sound Archives, LP26835.

80. BWD, 25 Aug. 1939.

81. BWD, 7 Sept. 1939.

82. G. B. Shaw to BW, 17 Sept. 1939.

83. BW to G. B. Shaw, 29 Sept. 1939.

84. G. B. Shaw to BW, 27 June 1940.

85. BWD, 14 Aug. 1940.

86. Lady Betty Balfour to BW, 14 Aug. 1940.

87. Blanche Patch to BW, 9 Oct. 1940.

88. Virginia Woolf to BW, 8 April 1931.

89. Lady Betty Balfour to BW, 7 April 1941.

90. BWD, 6 Oct. 1941.

91. Harold Laski to BW, 11 Nov. 1941.

92. BWD, 24 Feb. 1942.

93. Malcolm Muggeridge, *Chronicles of Wasted Time*, vol. 2, *The Infernal Grove*, 1973, pp. 265–268.

PRIMARY SOURCES

British Library of Political and Economic Science, London School of Economics: Passfield Papers, including: MS diaries of Beatrice Webb, letters of Richard Potter family, letters of Beatrice and Sidney Webb, Our First Journey Round the World, reconstruction papers.

Booth papers, Shaw Collection; Courtney Collection, Lloyd papers, Citrine papers, Pease papers; Nuffield College, Oxford, Fabian Society papers, including material on the Fabian women's group; Burns papers, British Library; Poor Law records, Public Record Office, Kew; Royal Commission of the Poor Law reports on microfiche, Minority Report on the Poor Law, Fabian Society tracts and pamphlets, unpublished Ph.D. theses on the Webbs through inter-library loans, MA dissertation on the Langham Place Group, nineteenth-century press, Sussex University library; Suffragette papers and memorabilia, Josephine Butler Collection; nineteenth-century women's magazines, Fawcett Library; Suffragette collection and memorabilia, Museum of London.

Family Papers:

Unpublished journal of Lawrencina Potter in the possession of Jonathan King.

'One Family of Ten' by Beatrice Mayor, in the possession of Lady Rothschild.

Memoir of Theresa Cripps by Alfred Cripps, in the possession of Seddon Cripps.

Descendants of Richard Potter (1817–1892) and Lawrencina Heyworth (1821–1882) compiled by Lord Methuen, copy in possession of Seddon Cripps. Potter and Heyworth genealogy researched by Nicholas Meinertzhagen.

BBC Sound Archives: Memories of the Webbs by Bertrand Russell and John Strachey.

Newspapers and periodicals consulted: *Industrial Syndicalist, Justice, Link, Our Corner, Pall Mall Gazette, Punch,* The *Queen,* The *Lady's Newspaper, Manchester Guardian, New Statesman, Nineteenth Century, Political Quarterly, Crusade, Daily Mail, Edinburgh Review,* The *Times, Vanity Fair, Woman's Herald.*

Articles and tracts of particular relevance:

Besant, Annie. 'White Slavery in London', *Link*, 1888.

Cracanthorpe, B. 'The Revolt of the Daughters', *Nineteenth Century*, 1894.

By the Fabian Society. 'To Your Tents O Israel!', *Fortnightly Review*, Nov. 1893.

Hill, Octavia. 'Our Dealings with the Poor', *Nineteenth Century*, July–Dec. 1887.

Hill, Octavia. 'A Few Words to Fresh Workers', *Nineteenth Century*, July–Dec. 1889.

Potter, Beatrice. 'A Lady's View of the Unemployed', *Pall Mall Gazette*, 18 Feb. 1886.

Potter, B. 'Pages from a Work-Girl's Diary', *Nineteenth Century*, Sept. 1888.

Potter, B. 'The Dock Life of East London', *Nineteenth Century*, Oct. 1887.

Potter, B. 'The Tailoring Trade', *Nineteenth Century*, Aug. 1888.

Potter, B. 'Women and the Factory Acts', Fabian Tract 67, 1896.

Potter, B. 'A Crusade Against Destitution', 1909.

Potter, B. 'Socialism and the National Minimum', 1910.

Potter, B. 'The Minority Report in its relation to Public Health and the Medical Profession', 1910.

Potter, B. 'Complete National Provision for Sickness: How to Amend the Insurance Act', 1912.

Potter, B. 'The Wages of Men and Women: Should They Be Equal?', 1919.

Shaw, G. B. 'The Fabian Society, Its Early History', Tract 41, 1892.

Interview with Mrs S. Webb. *The Young Woman*, 3 Feb. 1895.

Stead, W. T. 'Co-operative Homes for the Unmarried', *Woman's Herald*, 13 Apr. 1893.

Webb, S. 'Lord Rosebery's Escape from Houndsditch', *Nineteenth Century*, Sept. 1901.

Webb, S. 'What Mr Gladstone Ought to Do', *Fortnightly Review*, Jan. 1893.

Webb, S. 'The Difficulties of Individualism', Fabian Tract 69, 1896.

Webb, S. 'The Eight Hours Bill', *Speaker*, 19 Sept. 1911.

SECONDARY SOURCES

Alexander, Sally. Introduction to Pember Reeves, M., 'Round About A Pound A Week', Fabian women's group pamphlet.

Boos, Florence, Ed. 'William Morris's Socialist Diary', *History Workshop Journal*, Spring 1982.

Caine, Barbara. 'Beatrice Webb and the Woman Question', *History Workshop Journal*, no. 14, 1982.

Davin, Anna. *Imperialism and Motherhood*.

Daniels, Kay. 'Emma Brooke: Fabian, Feminist and Writer', 1984, courtesy of Anna Davin.

Lewis, Jane. 'The Politics of Motherhood', *History Workshop Journal*, no. 5.

Lewis, Jane. 'Re-reading Beatrice Webb's Diary', *History Workshop Journal*, no. 16, Autumn 1983.

Lewis, Jane. Lecture, 'Social Facts, Social Theory and Social Change: The Ideas of Booth in relation to those of Beatrice Webb, Octavia Hill and Helen Bosanquet', Charles Booth Day Conference, OU Milton Keynes, 15 Apr. 1989.

Thane, Pat. 'Women and the Poor Law in Victorian and Edwardian England', *History Workshop Journal*.

Yeo, Eileen. Unpublished essay, 'Women, Social Science and Social Work in Britain 1789–1914', 1987.

BIBLIOGRAPHY

This bibliography is not comprehensive, but it includes the books I found most useful and which are generally available.

Annan, N. Ed. *Ideas and Beliefs of the Victorians: An Historic Revaluation of the Victorian Age,* 1949.

Asquith, Herbert. *Memories and Reflections,* Cassell, 1928.

Asquith, Margot. *Autobiography,* Bodley Head, 1920.

Austin, A. G. Ed. *The Webbs' Australian Diary,* Sir Isaac Pitman and Sons, Melbourne, 1965.

Banks, Olive. *Faces of Feminism,* Martin Robertson, 1981.

Barnett, H. *Canon S. Barnett,* John Murray, 1918.

Bell, E. A. C. Moberley, *Octavia Hill,* Constable, 1942.

Bernstein, George L. *Liberalism and Liberal Politics in Edwardian England,* Allen and Unwin, 1986.

Bevington, M. M. *The Saturday Review.*

Bonham Carter, Violet. *Winston Churchill As I Knew Him,* 1965.

Booth, C. *Life and Labour of the People in London,* vols 1–4. London, 1889.

Booth, C. *A Memoir, by his Wife,* MacMillan, 1918.

Booth, W. *In Darkest England and the Way Out,* 1890.

Bosanquet, H. *Social Work in London.*

Braithwaite, W. J. *Lloyd George's Ambulance Wagon: Being the Memoirs of William J. Braithwaite, 1911–1917,* 1957.

Brock, M. & E. Eds. H. H. Asquith, *Letters to Venetia Stanley,* OUP, 1982.

Burgess, Joseph. *John Burns: The Rise and Progress of a Right Honourable,* 1911.

Butler, J. *Personal Reminiscences of a Great Crusade,* 1896.

Burton, Hector. *Barbara Bodichon,* 1949.

Caine, B. *Destined to be Wives: The Sisters of Beatrice Webb,* Clarendon Press, 1986.

Carpenter, L. P. *G. D. H. Cole: An Intellectual Biography,* OUP, 1973.

Collini, Stefan. *Liberalism and Sociology: L. T. Hobhouse and Political Argument in England 1880–1914,* CUP, 1979.

Cole, Margaret I. *Beatrice Webb,* Longman, 1945.

Cole, M. I. Ed. *Twelve Studies in Soviet Russia,* 1933.

Cole, M. I. Ed. *The Webbs and their Work,* Frederick Muller, 1949.

Cole, M. I. *Growing Up Into Revolution,* Longmans Green, 1945.

Cole, M. I. *The Story of Fabian Socialism,* Heinemann, 1961.

Cole, M. I. *The Life of G. D. H. Cole,* MacMillan, 1971.

Conquest, Robert. *The Great Terror: Stalin's Purge*, MacMillan, 1968.

Courtney, Kate. *Life of Lord Courtney.*

Dangerfield, George. *The Strange Death of Liberal England 1910–1914*, London, 1935.

Davidoff, Leonore. *The Best Circles: Society, Etiquette and the Season*, Croom Helm, 1973.

Denison, F. *Letters*, Ed. Baldwyn Leighton, 1872.

Dent, Ed. *Bernard Shaw and Mrs. Patrick Campbell: Their Correspondence*, Gollancz, 1952.

Dyhouse, C. *Girls Growing Up in Late Victorian and Early Edwardian England*, Routledge, 1981.

Dutton, R. *The Victorian Home*, Batsford, 1954.

Elletson, D. H. *The Chamberlains*, 1966.

Eliot, George. *Middlemarch*, 1871.

Fabian Society. *Fabian Essays*, 1889.

Forrest, D. W. *Francis Galton, The Life and Work of a Victorian Genius*, 1974.

Forster, Margaret. *Significant Sisters: The Grassroots of Active Feminism 1839–1939*, Secker and Warburg, 1984.

Fraser, P. *Joseph Chamberlain: Radicalism to Empire 1868–1914*, Cambridge, 1974.

Fried, A. & Elman, R. Eds. *Charles Booth's London*, London, 1971.

Galton, Francis. *Memories of My Life*, 1908.

Garvin, J. L. *The Life of Joseph Chamberlain*, 3 vols, MacMillan, 1933, and Amery, Julian, vol. 4, 1951.

Haldane, Richard Burton. *An Autobiography*, Hodder and Stoughton, 1929.

Hamilton, Mary Agnes. *Sidney and Beatrice Webb*, Marston, 1933.

Harrison, Brian. *Separate Spheres: The Opposition to Women's Suffrage in Britain*, Croom Helm, 1978.

Harrison, Royden. *Before the Socialists: Studies in Labour and Politics 1861–1881*, London, 1965.

Haynes, Rosalind D. *H. G. Wells, Discoverer of the Future*, MacMillan, 1980.

Hobhouse, Stephen. *Margaret Hobhouse and Her Family*, Stanhope Press, 1934.

Hobhouse, S. *Forty Years and An Epilogue: An Autobiography 1881–1951.*

Hobsbawm, E. J. *Labouring Men: Studies in the History of Labour*, 1964.

Hobson, J. A. *Imperialism*, 1902.

Hollingshead, *Ragged London*, 1861.

Hyndman, H. M. *The Record of an Adventurous Life*, London, 1911.

Jay, R. *Joseph Chamberlain: A Political Study*, Clarendon Press, 1981.

Jeffreys, S. *The Spinster and Her Enemies*, Pandora, 1985.

Jenkins, Roy. *Mr Balfour's Poodle: An Account of the Struggle Between the House of Lords and the Government of Mr Asquith*, New York, Chilmark, 1954.

Jenkins, Roy. *Sir Charles Dilke*, 1958.

Jenkins, Roy. *H. H. Asquith.*

Judd, D. *Radical Joe*, Hamish Hamilton, 1977.

Lacey, Candida A. Ed. *Barbara Leigh Smith Bodichon and the Langham Place Group*, 1987.

Laurence, D. *Bernard Shaw: Collected Letters*, 2 vols, OUP, 1965.

Levine, P. *Victorian Feminism 1850–1900*, Hutchinson, 1987.

Lewis, Jane. *Women in England 1870–1950: Sexual Divisions and Social Change*, Wheatsheaf Books, Brighton, 1984.

Longford, Elizabeth. *Eminent Victorian Women*, London, 1981.
Masterman, Lucy. *C. F. G. Masterman*, 1939.
McBriar, A. M. *Fabian Socialism and English Politics 1884–1918*, CUP, 1960.
McBriar, A. M. *An Edwardian Mixed Doubles: The Bosanquets versus the Webbs – A Study in British Social Policy 1890–1929*, Clarendon Press, 1987.
MacKenzie, Norman and Jeanne, Eds. *The Diaries of Beatrice Webb*, 4 vols, Virago Press, 1982.
MacKenzie, N. Ed. *The Letters of Sidney and Beatrice Webb*, 3 vols, Weidenfeld and Nicolson, 1978.
MacKenzie, N. & J. *The First Fabians*, Weidenfeld and Nicolson, 1977.
MacKenzie, N. & J. *The Time Traveller: The Life of H. G. Wells*, Simon and Schuster, 1973.
MacKenzie, J. *A Victorian Courtship*, Weidenfeld and Nicolson, 1979.
Marquand, D. *Ramsay MacDonald*, Cape, 1977.
Marsh, Jan. *Jane and May Morris: A Biographical Story 1839–1938*, Pandora, 1986.
Martineau, H. *Autobiography*, vol. 1, first published 1877, Virago, 1983.
Mearns, Andrew. *The Bitter Cry of Outcast London*, 1883.
Meier, Olga, Ed. *The Daughters of Karl Marx, Family Correspondence 1866–1898*, Deutsch, 1982.
Meinertzhagen, G. *From Ploughshare to Parliament: A Short Memoir of the Potters of Tadcaster*, John Murray, 1908.
Meinertzhagen, R. *Diary of a Black Sheep*, Oliver and Boyd, 1964.
Mitchell, H. *The Hard Way Up.*
Morgan, Austen. *J. Ramsay MacDonald*, Manchester UP, 1987.
Morris, William. *The Dream of John Ball*, 1888.
Mowat, Charles Loch. *The Charity Organisation Society, 1869–1913.*
Mowat, C. L. *Britain Between the Wars, 1918–1940*, Methuen, 1955.
Muggeridge, K. & Adam, R. *Beatrice Webb: A Life*, Secker and Warburg, 1967.
Muggeridge, M. *Chronicles of Wasted Time*, 2 vols, 1973.
Muggeridge, M. *The Thirties, 1930–1940 in Great Britain*, Hamish Hamilton, 1940.
Newton, Ryan & Walkowitz, Eds. *Sex and Class in Women's History*, 1983.
Nord, D. Epstein, *The Apprenticeship of Beatrice Webb*, MacMillan, 1985.
Norman-Butler, B. *Victorian Aspirations, The Life and Labour of Charles and Mary Booth*, Allen and Unwin, 1972.
Owen, David. *English Philanthropy 1660–1901*, Harvard UP, 1966.
Pakenham, Thomas. *The Boer War*, Weidenfeld and Nicolson, 1979.
Pearson, Hesketh. *Labby: The Life of Henry Labouchere*, Hamish Hamilton, 1936.
Pease, E. *History of the Fabian Society*, 1918.
Peterson, Linda H. *Victorian Autobiography: The Tradition of Self-Interpretation.*
Pearson, Hesketh. *Bernard Shaw*, Methuen, 1961.
Pelling, H. *Popular Politics and Society in Late Victorian Britain.*
Pelling, H. *Origins of the Labour Party, 1880–1900*, OUP, 1965.
Pemberton Reeves, M. *Round About a Pound a Week.*
Peterson, L. *Victorian Autobiography.*
Pimlott, Ben. *Labour and the Left in the 1930s*, CUP, 1977.
Pinchbeck, Ivy. *Women Workers and the Industrial Revolution 1750–1850*, Virago, 1981.

Pugh, P. *Educate, Agitate, Organize: 100 Years of Fabian Socialism*, Methuen, 1984.

Prochaska, F. K. *Women and Philanthropy in the Nineteenth Century*, Clarendon Press, 1980.

Rabagliati, Anrea Carlo Francisco. *Air, Food and Exercise*, 1897.

Radice, Lisanne. *Beatrice and Sidney Webb: Fabian Socialists*, MacMillan, 1984.

Roberts, Elizabeth. *A Woman's Place: An Oral History of Working-Class Women 1890–1940*, Basil Blackwell, 1984.

Rose, A. *Rise Up Women!*, London, 1974.

Rose, Michael. *The Relief of Poverty 1834–1914*, 1972.

Rosenberg, C. E. *Healing and History, Essays for George Rosen.*

Rubenstein, David. *Before the Suffragettes: Women's Emancipation in the 1890s*, Harvester Press, 1986.

Russell, Bertrand. *Autobiography.*

Semmel, B. *Imperialism and Social Reform*, 1960.

Shannon, D. A. Ed. *Beatrice Webb's American Diary*, University of Wisconsin Press, 1963.

Shaw, George Bernard. *Sixteen Self Sketches*, Constable and Co, 1949.

Shaw, George Bernard. Major Barbara, 1907.

Shaw, George Bernard. Man and Superman, 1903.

Shaw, George Bernard. *The Intelligent Woman's Guide to Socialism and Capitalism*, Constable, 1928.

Shaw, George Bernard. *Everybody's Political What's What*, 1944.

Shaw, George Bernard. *Letters to Ellen Terry*, Reinhardt and Evans, 1949.

Silver. *Bernard Shaw, The Darker Side.*

Simey, T. S. *Charles Booth*, London, 1960.

Sims, G. R. *How the Poor Live and Horrible London*, 1889.

Spencer, Herbert. *Autobiography*, Williams and Norgate, 1904.

Spencer, Herbert. *First Principles*, Williams and Norgate, 1904.

Spencer, Herbert. *The Man and the State.*

Stedman Jones, G. *Outcast London*, Oxford, 1971.

Strachey, Barbara. *Remarkable Relations: The History of the Pearsall Smith Family.*

Strachey, R. *The Cause*, G. Bell and Son, 1928; Virago, 1978, including appendix 1, Cassandra, from vol. 2 of Florence Nightingale's unpublished *Suggestions for Thought to Searchers after Religious Truth*, written 1852 and privately printed 1859.

Summers, Anne. 'A Home from Home – Women's Philanthropic Work in the Nineteenth Century', in *Fit Work for Women*, Ed. Burman, 1979.

Swindells, J. *The Roar on the Other Side of Silence: Working Women and Writing in the Nineteenth Century*, Polity Press, 1985.

Thompson, J. A. *Herbert Spencer*, 1906.

Thompson, Paul. *Socialists, Liberals and Labour: The Struggle for London 1885–1914*, London, 1967.

Turco, A. *Shaw's Moral Vision: The Self and Salvation*, Cornell UP, 1976.

Vernon, Betty D. *Margaret Cole 1893–1980: A Political Biography*, Croom Helm, 1986.

Vicinus, M. *Independent Women: Work and Community for Single Women 1850–1920.*

Young, A. F. & Ashton, E. T. *British Social Work in the Nineteenth Century*, 1956.

Walkowitz, J. R. *Prostitution and Victorian Society.*

Wallas, G. *Human Nature in Politics*, 1908.

Webb, B. *The Co-operative Movement in Great Britain*, Sonnenschein, 1891.

Webb, B. *My Apprenticeship*, Longman, 1926.

Webb, B. *Our Apprenticeship*, M. I. Cole and B. Drake, Eds, Longman, 1948.

Webb, B. *The Prevention of Destitution*, London, 1911.

Webb, B. *The Story of the Seaham Miners*, 1919.

Webb, S. and B. *The History of Trade Unionism*, London, 1894.

Webb, S. and B. *Industrial Democracy*, London, 1897.

Webb, S. and B. *The Minority Report of the Poor Law Commission*, 1909.

Webb, S. and B. *English Local Government*, London, 1906–29, ten volumes.

Webb, S. and B. *A Constitution for the Socialist Commonwealth of Great Britain*, London, 1920.

Webb, S. and B. *The Consumers' Co-operative Movement*, London, 1920.

Webb, S. and B. *The Decay of Capitalist Civilization*, London, 1923.

Webb, S. and B. *Methods of Social Study*, London, 1932.

Webb, S. and B. *Soviet Communism: A New Civilization?*, London, 1935.

Webb, S. and B. *The Truth About Soviet Russia*, Green and Co, 1942.

Weintraub, Stanley, Ed. *G. B. Shaw: An Autobiography*, 1969.

Wells, H. G. *Anticipations of the Reaction of Mechanical Progress Upon Human Life and Thought*, Chapman and Hall, 1916.

Wells, H. G. 'This Misery of Boots', Fabian Society, 1905.

Wells, H. G. *Ann Veronica*, T. Fisher Unwin, 1909.

Wells, H. G. *The New Machiavelli*, Bodley Head, 1911.

Wiener, Martin. *Between Two Worlds: The Political Thought of Graham Wallas*, Oxford, 1971.

Wiener, Martin. *English Culture and the Decline of the Industrial Spirit 1850–1980*, CUP, 1981.

White, A. *Efficiency and Empire*, Harvester, 1973, first pub 1901.

Woolf, Leonard. *An Autobiography 1880–1911*, OUP, 1980.

Woolf, Virgina. *The Diary of Virginia Woolf*, vol 1, Penguin, 1979.

Wiltshire, D. *The Social and Political Thought of Herbert Spencer*, Oxford, 1978.

Woodroofe, K. *From Charity to Social Work in England and the United States*, 1962.

Woodham-Smith, Cecil. *Florence Nightingale*, Constable, 1950.

Wohl, A. S. *The Eternal Slum*, Arnold, 1977.

Wohl, A. S. *Endangered Lives: Public Health in Victorian Britain*, Dent, 1987.

Wohl, A. S. *The Victorian Family*, Croom Helm, 1978.

INDEX

Hobhouse 1880 54–6; takes Beatrice on honeymoon in Italy 57–8; and Positivism 69–70, 219; dies 292
Hobhouse, Paul 289
Hobhouse, Stephen 290
Hobson, J. A. 245
Holt, Lallie, née Potter 2, 7, 19, 218, 273
Holt, Robert Durning 19
House of Lords Select Committee on Sweating 159
Hutchinson, Henry 236
Huxley, Henry 273
Huxley, Thomas 21, 25, 64
Hyndman, Henry Mayers, author of *England for All* 72; founder of Marxist Social Democratic Federation 136, 161

incest 158
Independent Labour Party 280
individualism, and Herbert Spencer 84, 160; *The Difficulties of Individualism*, by S. Webb 210

Jackson, Martha ('Dada'), Mrs Mills 1, 6, 7, 29, 96
Jameson Raid 242–5
'Jones, Miss', Beatrice's alias 96–7
Jones, Benjamin, of Co-operative Wholesale Society 167, 215

Katherine Buildings 114–18, 128, 130–3
Kenney, Annie 268
Kenrick, Harriet, Joseph Chamberlain's first wife, mother of Austen 89, 104
Kenrick, Florence, Joseph Chamberlain's second wife, mother of Neville 89
Keynes, Maynard 305, 319
Kingsley, Charles 47
Kitchener 246, 288

Knowles, Sir James, editor of *Nineteenth Century* 167, 195
Kropotkin, Prince 174, 183
Kruger, Paul, Boer leader 242–3

Ladies' National Association for the Diffusion of Sanitary Knowledge 18, 114
Ladislaw, Will, husband of Dorothea in *Middlemarch* 32
Langham Place Group, early Women's Movement 17
Laura Gay, by Lawrencina Potter 12
Langtry, Lily 38
Lansbury, George 262, 281, 286, 301, 303, 309
Laski, Harold 302, 314, 316, 321
Law, Bonar 297
Lawrence, D. H. 307–8
Leigh Smith, Barbara, *see* Bodichon
Leigh Smith, Benjamin, MP for Norwich 17
Lenin, Vladimir 308–311
'LIMPS', Liberal Imperialists 245–8
Llewellyn Smith, Hubert 162, 205
Lloyds, Charles Mostyn 289, 302
Lloyd George, David 261–4, 271, 274, 277–9, 293–6
Loch, C. S., Secretary of the Charity Organisation Society 67, aims to reduce pauperism 77–85, 147, 262, 274
London County Council 222, 233
London School of Economics 236, 237–9, 249, 254
Londonderry, Lady 301
Lopokova, Lydia 319
Lynn Linton 18, 207
Lytton, Lady Constance 268, 279

Macaulay, Charles, brother of historian Thomas Babington Macaulay 4, 86, 145
Macaulay, Mary, *see* Booth
MacLean, Norman 295

syndicalism *285*

Tariff Reform Campaign, the *260*
Tennant, Margot *see* Asquith
The New Machiavelli, by H. G.
  Wells *ix*
Tillett, Ben *183*
Trevelyan, Charles *240*
Trotsky, Leon *308, 317*
Twining, Louisa *18*
Tyndall, John *21, 25*

Unitarianism, and individualism
  24; and Joseph Chamberlain *93*

Vanderbilt, Consuelo *38*
Victoria Press *18*
Victoria, Queen, opponent of
  women's rights *19*; and London
  Society *39, 40, 73, 101–2, 241,
  243*
Vincey, Rosamund, anti-heroine in
  Middlemarch 32

Wakefield, Dr Henry *262*
Wallas, Graham, one of the 'Old
  Gang' of Webb, Shaw, and
  Olivier, of the Fabian Society;
  LSE lecturer *179, 196–7, 204,
  209, 212–15, 220–2, 228–9,
  237–9, 314–15*
Wales, Edward, Prince of *38*; and
  the Marlborough Club *40*; friend
  to Margot Tennant *40*
Wales, Alexandra, Princess of *38*
Ward, Mrs Humphrey *167, 195,
  241*
Warren, Sir Charles *152*
Webb, Ada *215*
Webb, Beatrice, née Potter, birth *1,
  2*; childhood: relationship with
  parents *6–9*, with servants *10*,
  homesickness *11*, ego conflict
  12–13, education *14–16*, and
  women's rights *19*, and Spencer
  20–5; adolescence, inspired by

Dorothea Brooke in George
Eliot's *Middlemarch* to seek an
epic life as a 'later-born Theresa'
27–32; accompanies Richard
Potter to the USA *33–5*;
self-education *36, 37*; enters
London Society *37–43*; and
Christianity *44–6*; at Stirling
House *46–8*; presented at Court
1876 *48*; and Maggie *49–51*;
religious quest *51–2*; meets Cary
Darling *52*; *Weltschmerz 53*; in
Italy *54–6*; Lawrencina's death
57–60; runs father's household
60–3; 'multiple personality'
63–6; and *Zeitgeist 67*;
positivism *69–70*; and housing
problem *74*; joins Charity
Organisation Society *76–84*;
meets Joseph Chamberlain *85*;
Professor Main *86*; and Cary
Darling *89*; relationship with
Chamberlain *89–95*; to Bacup as
'Miss Jones' *96–7*; invites
Chamberlain to the Argoed
98–102; visits Highbury *103–7*;
moves to York House *107*;
fantasies about Chamberlain
110–13; manages Katharine
Buildings *114–18*; returns to
Birmingham *118–20*; picnics
with Chamberlain *121–4*;
practises cultural imperialism on
tenants *124–8*; worries over Rosy
128–30; develops revulsion
against capitalism *130–3*; father's
stroke *133–5*; analysis of poverty
and letter published in *Pall Mall
Gazette 136–8*; Chamberlain
renews acquaintance with
Beatrice *139–47*; begins work for
Charles Booth *147*; final break
with Chamberlain *148–51*;
investigates Docks and
Sweatshops *152–62*;
Chamberlain remarries *163–5*;